THE

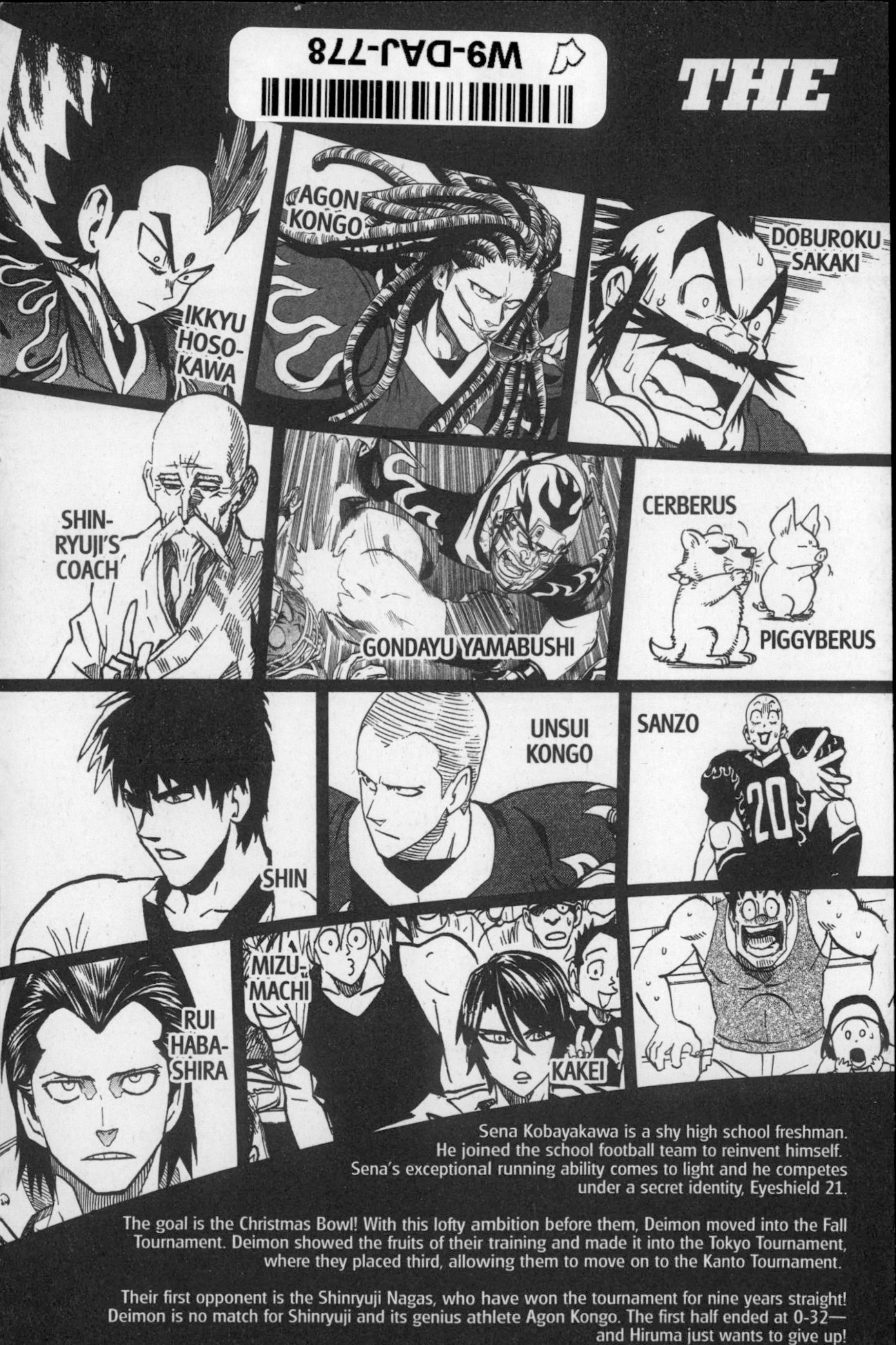
DOBUROKU SAKAKI
AGON KONGO
IKKYU HOSO-KAWA
CERBERUS
PIGGYBERUS
GONDAYU YAMABUSHI
SHIN-RYUJI'S COACH
SANZO
UNSUI KONGO
SHIN
KAKEI
MIZU-MACHI
RUI HABA-SHIRA

Sena Kobayakawa is a shy high school freshman. He joined the school football team to reinvent himself. Sena's exceptional running ability comes to light and he competes under a secret identity, Eyeshield 21.

The goal is the Christmas Bowl! With this lofty ambition before them, Deimon moved into the Fall Tournament. Deimon showed the fruits of their training and made it into the Tokyo Tournament, where they placed third, allowing them to move on to the Kanto Tournament.

Their first opponent is the Shinryuji Nagas, who have won the tournament for nine years straight! Deimon is no match for Shinryuji and its genius athlete Agon Kongo. The first half ended at 0-32—and Hiruma just wants to give up!

EYESHIELD 21

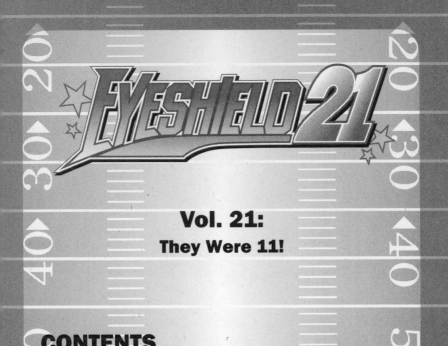

Vol. 21:
They Were 11!

CONTENTS

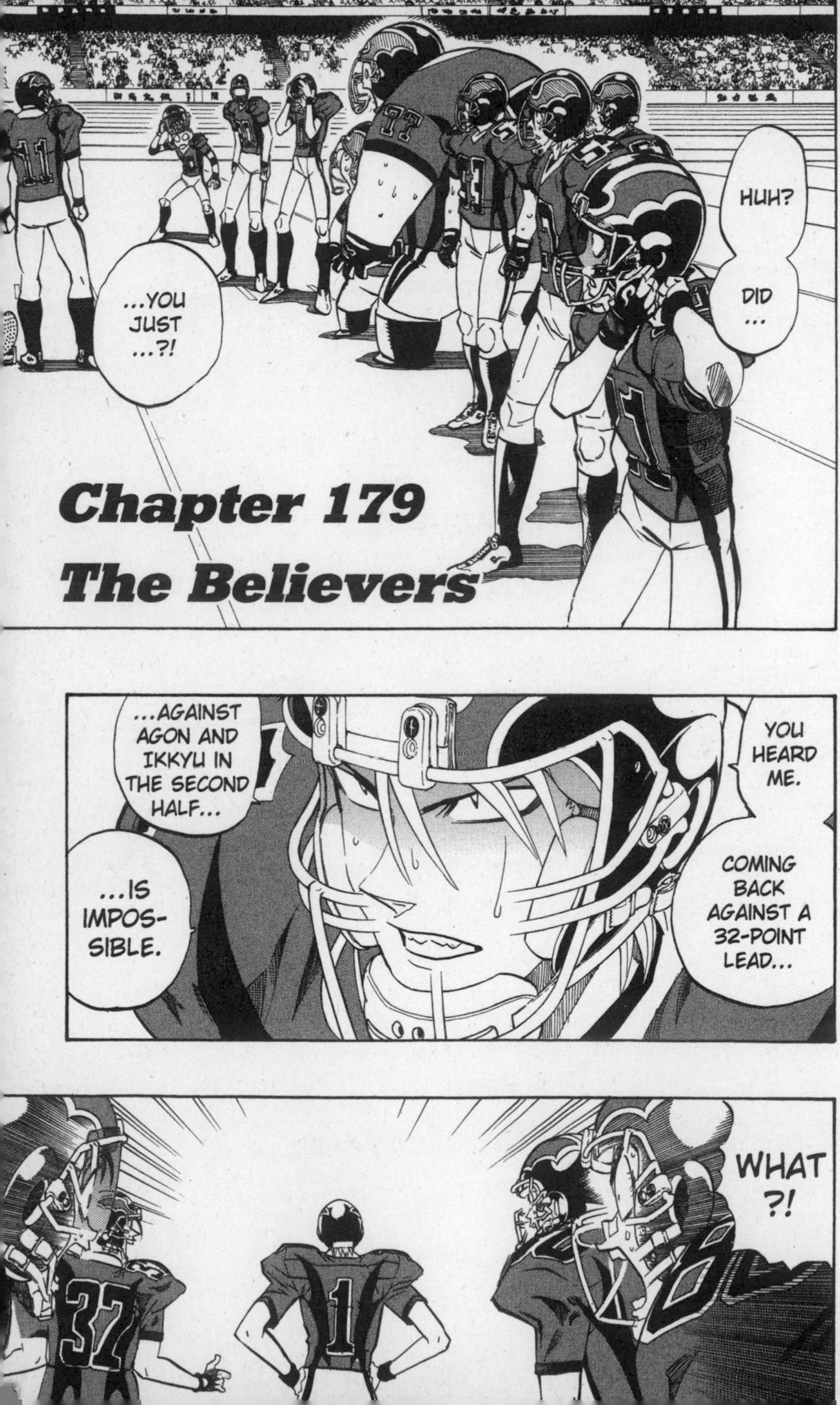
HUH? DID...
...YOU JUST ...?!
Chapter 179
The Believers
YOU HEARD ME.
COMING BACK AGAINST A 32-POINT LEAD...
...AGAINST AGON AND IKKYU IN THE SECOND HALF...
...IS IMPOS-SIBLE.
WHAT ?!

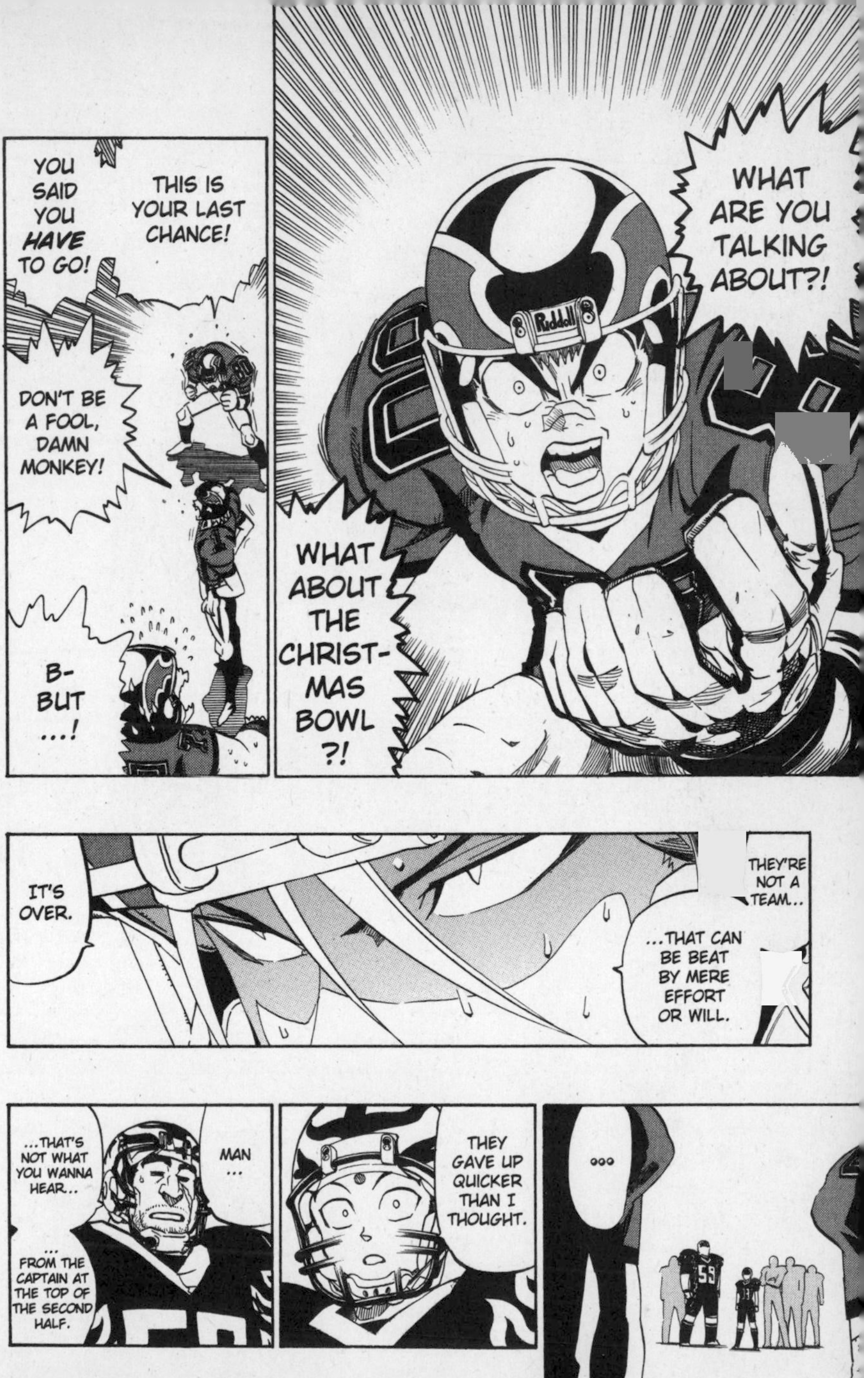
WHAT ARE YOU TALKING ABOUT?!
WHAT ABOUT THE CHRIST-MAS BOWL?!
THIS IS YOUR LAST CHANCE!
YOU SAID YOU *HAVE* TO GO!
DON'T BE A FOOL, DAMN MONKEY!
B-BUT ...!
THEY'RE NOT A TEAM...
...THAT CAN BE BEAT BY MERE EFFORT OR WILL.
IT'S OVER.
...
THEY GAVE UP QUICKER THAN I THOUGHT.
MAN ...
...THAT'S NOT WHAT YOU WANNA HEAR...
...FROM THE CAPTAIN AT THE TOP OF THE SECOND HALF.

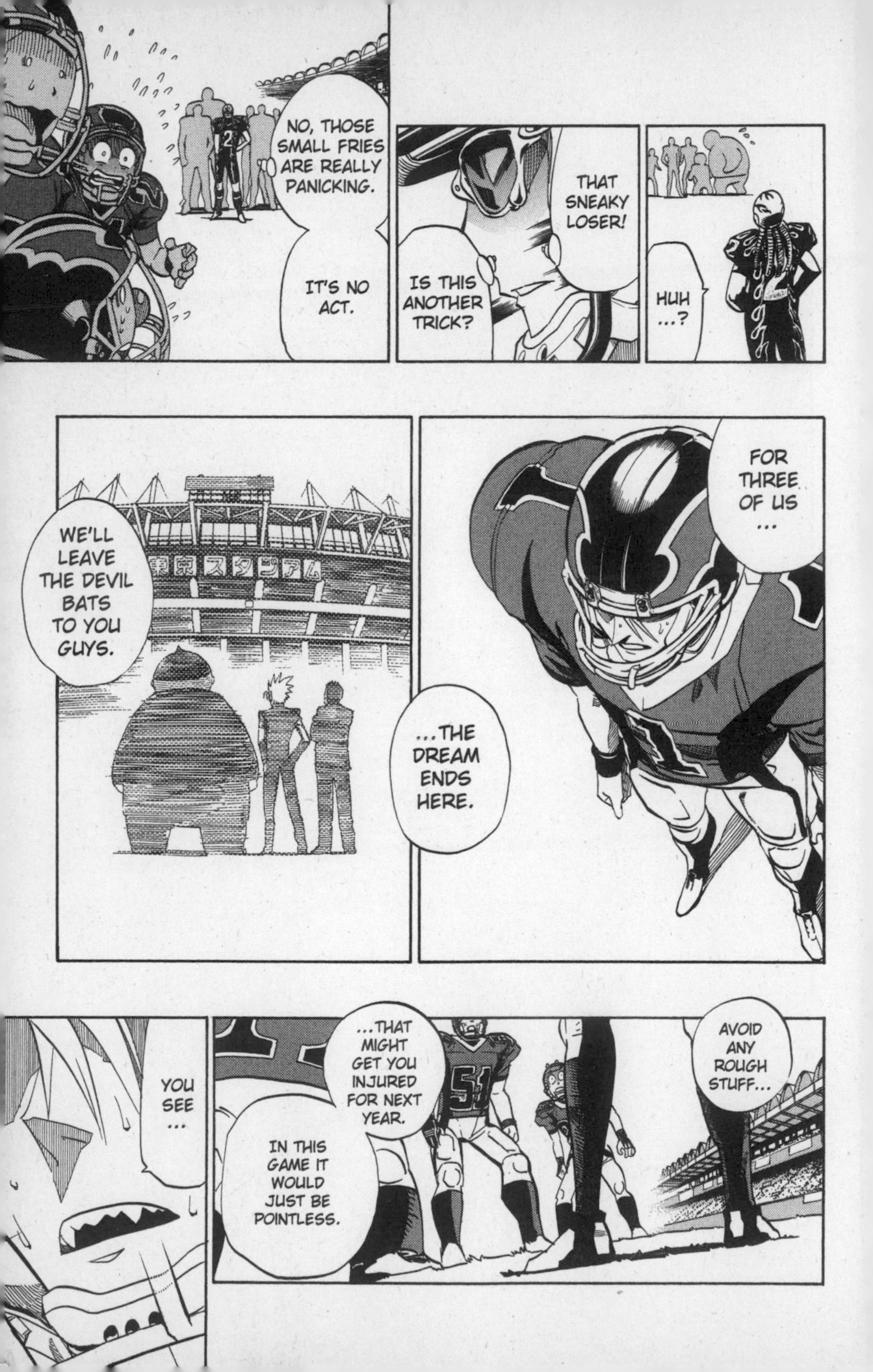
HUH ...?
THAT SNEAKY LOSER!
IS THIS ANOTHER TRICK?
NO, THOSE SMALL FRIES ARE REALLY PANICKING.
IT'S NO ACT.
FOR THREE OF US ...
...THE DREAM ENDS HERE.
WE'LL LEAVE THE DEVIL BATS TO YOU GUYS.
AVOID ANY ROUGH STUFF...
...THAT MIGHT GET YOU INJURED FOR NEXT YEAR.
IN THIS GAME IT WOULD JUST BE POINTLESS.
YOU SEE ...

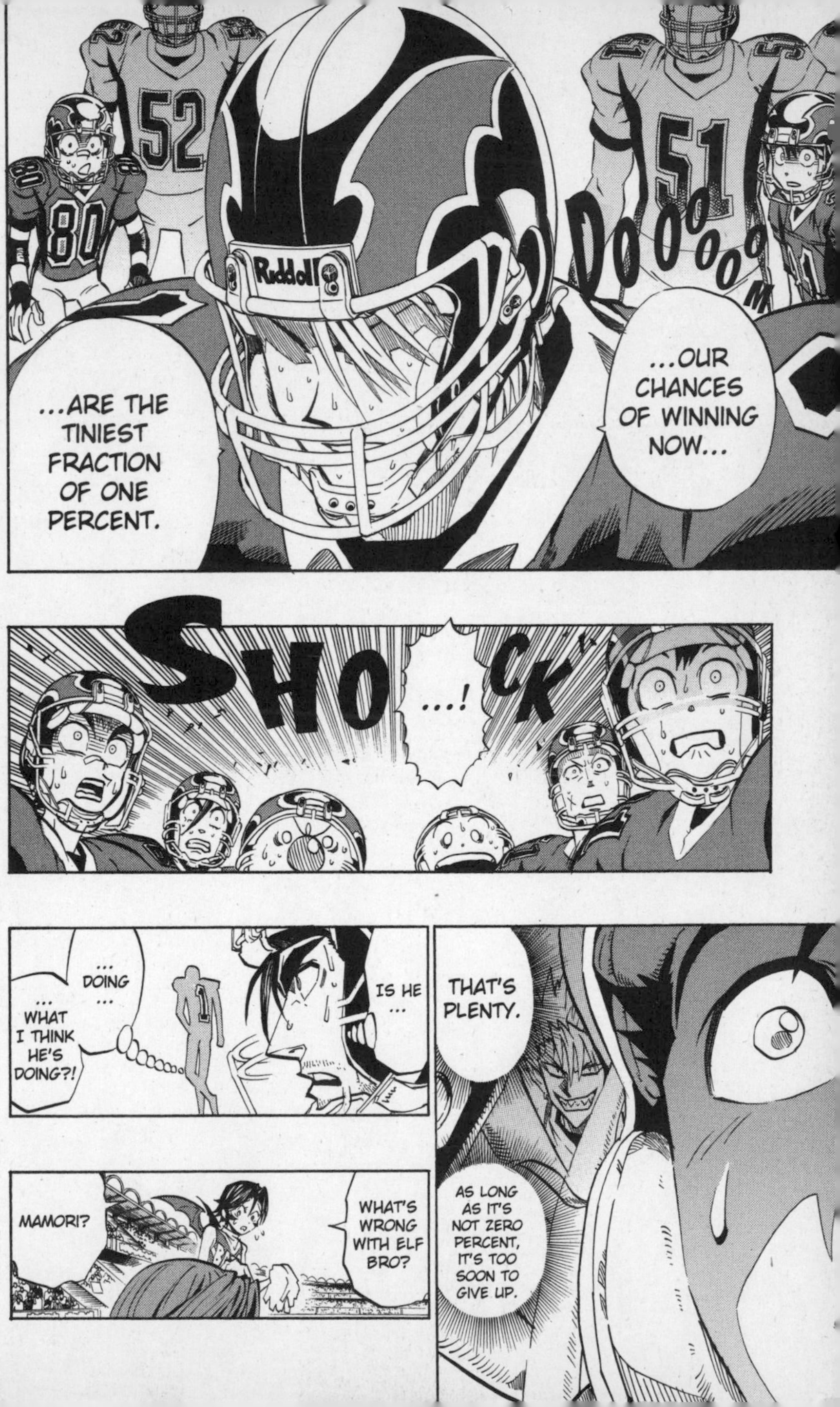
...OUR CHANCES OF WINNING NOW...
DOOOOOOM
...ARE THE TINIEST FRACTION OF ONE PERCENT.
SHOCK
...!
THAT'S PLENTY.
AS LONG AS IT'S NOT ZERO PERCENT, IT'S TOO SOON TO GIVE UP.
IS HE ...
... DOING ...
... WHAT I THINK HE'S DOING?!
WHAT'S WRONG WITH ELF BRO?
MAMORI?

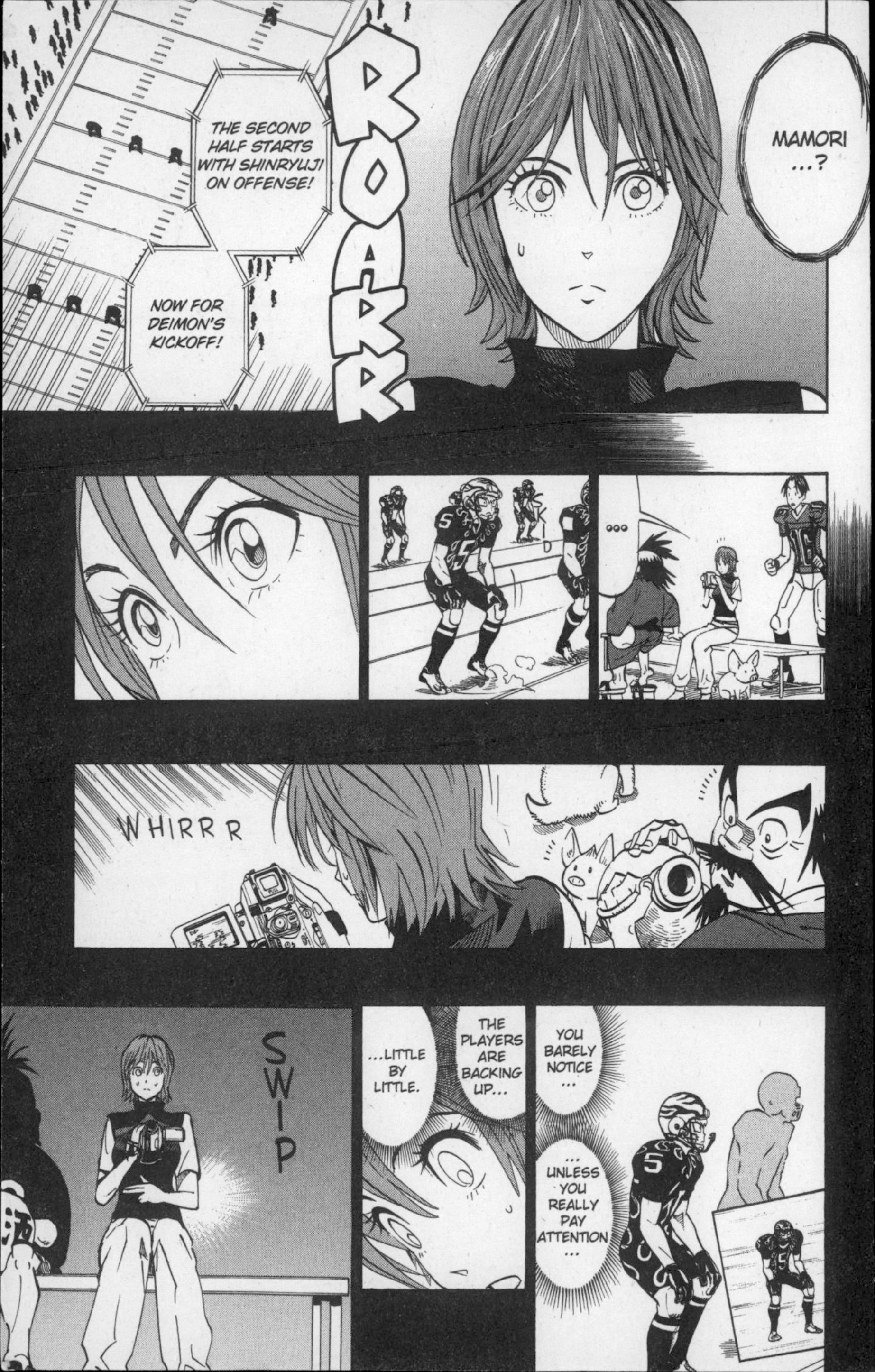
MAMORI ...?
ROARR
THE SECOND HALF STARTS WITH SHINRYUJI ON OFFENSE!
NOW FOR DEIMON'S KICKOFF!
...
WHIRRR
YOU BARELY NOTICE ...
... UNLESS YOU REALLY PAY ATTENTION ...
THE PLAYERS ARE BACKING UP...
...LITTLE BY LITTLE.
SWIP

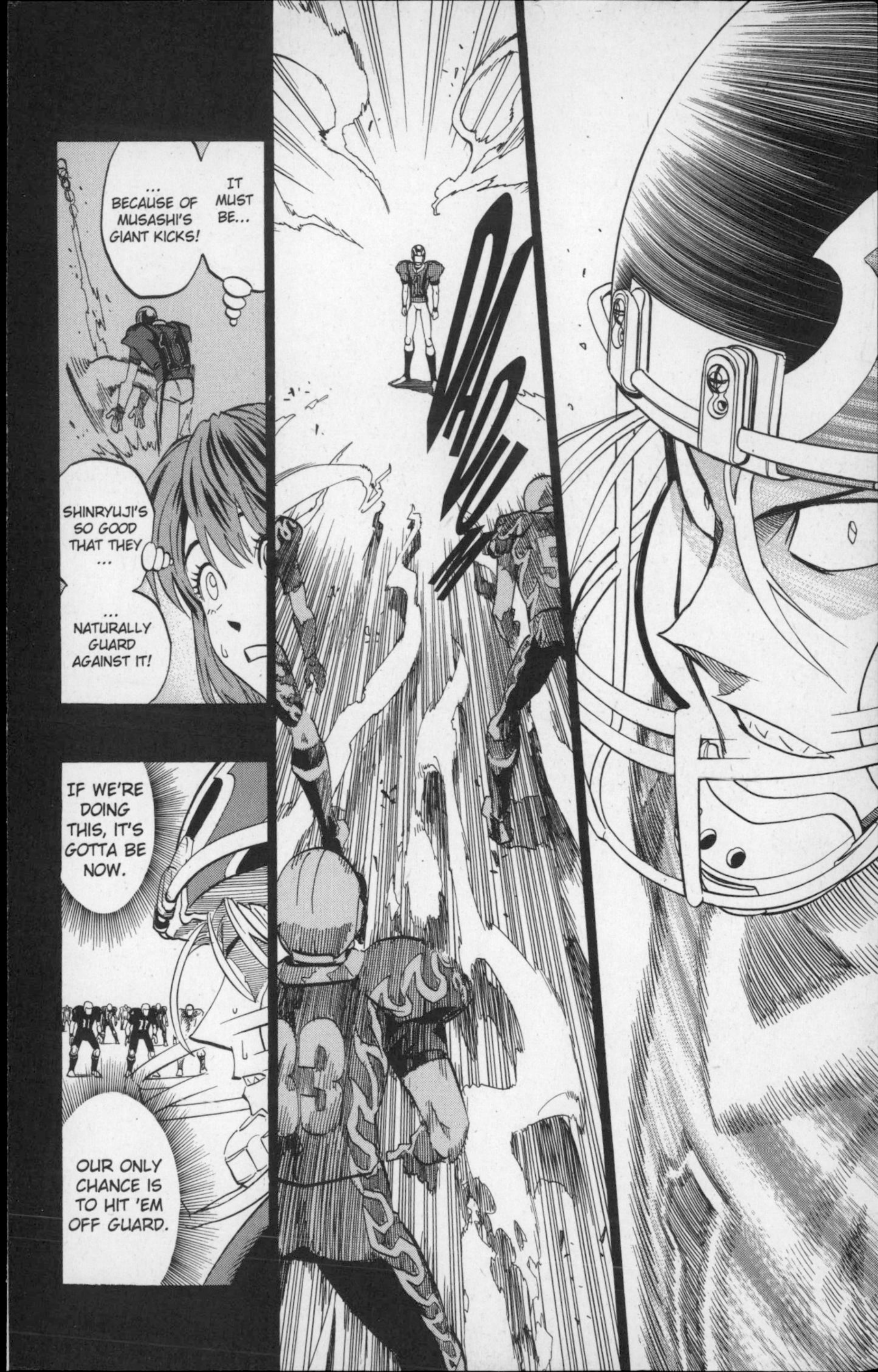
IT MUST BE...
... BECAUSE OF MUSASHI'S GIANT KICKS!
SHINRYUJI'S SO GOOD THAT THEY ...
... NATURALLY GUARD AGAINST IT!
IF WE'RE DOING THIS, IT'S GOTTA BE NOW.
OUR ONLY CHANCE IS TO HIT 'EM OFF GUARD.

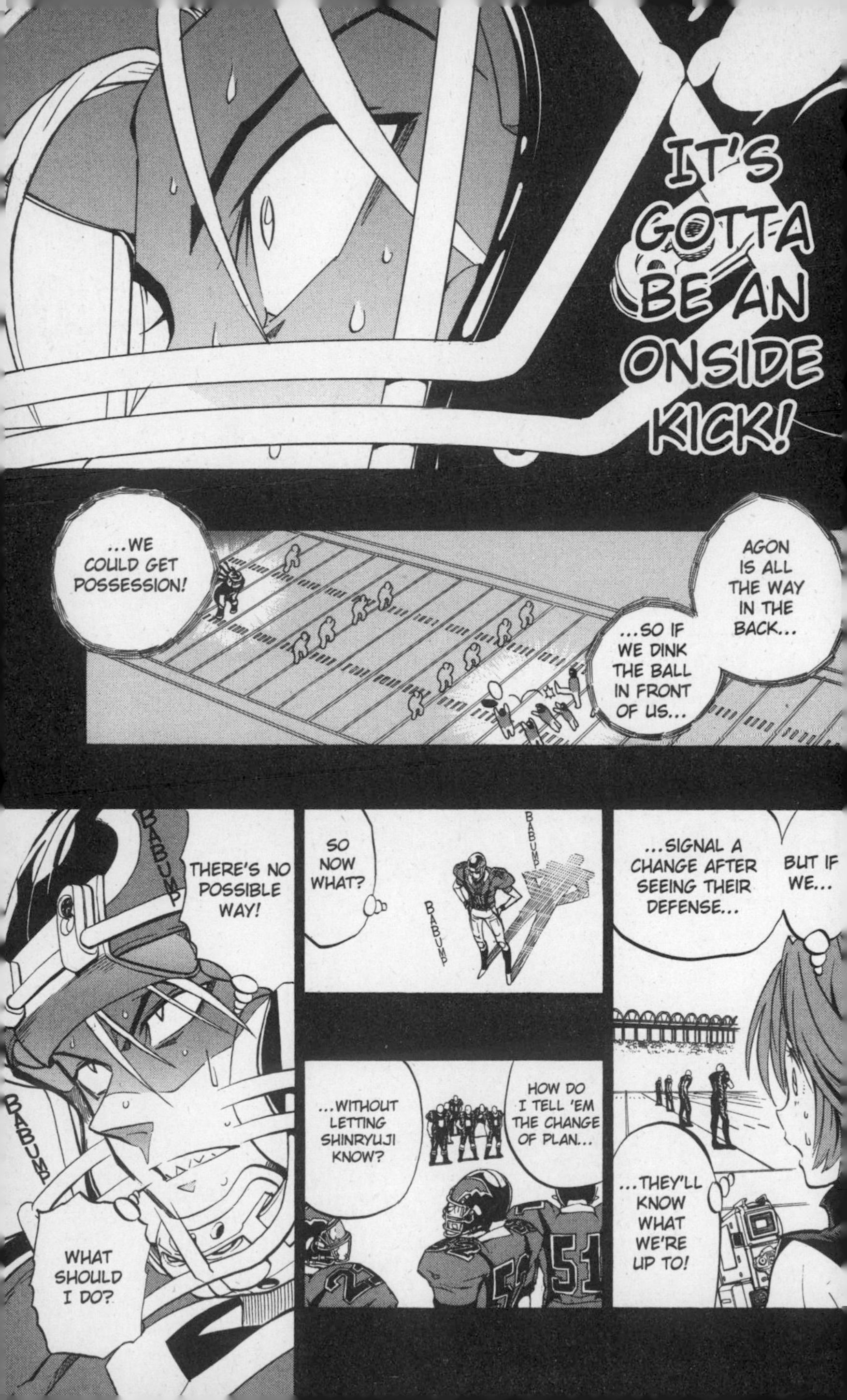
IT'S GOTTA BE AN ONSIDE KICK!
AGON IS ALL THE WAY IN THE BACK...
...SO IF WE DINK THE BALL IN FRONT OF US...
...WE COULD GET POSSESSION!
BUT IF WE...
...SIGNAL A CHANGE AFTER SEEING THEIR DEFENSE...
...THEY'LL KNOW WHAT WE'RE UP TO!
BABUMP
SO NOW WHAT?
BABUMP
HOW DO I TELL 'EM THE CHANGE OF PLAN...
...WITHOUT LETTING SHINRYUJI KNOW?
BABUMP
THERE'S NO POSSIBLE WAY!
BABUMP
WHAT SHOULD I DO?

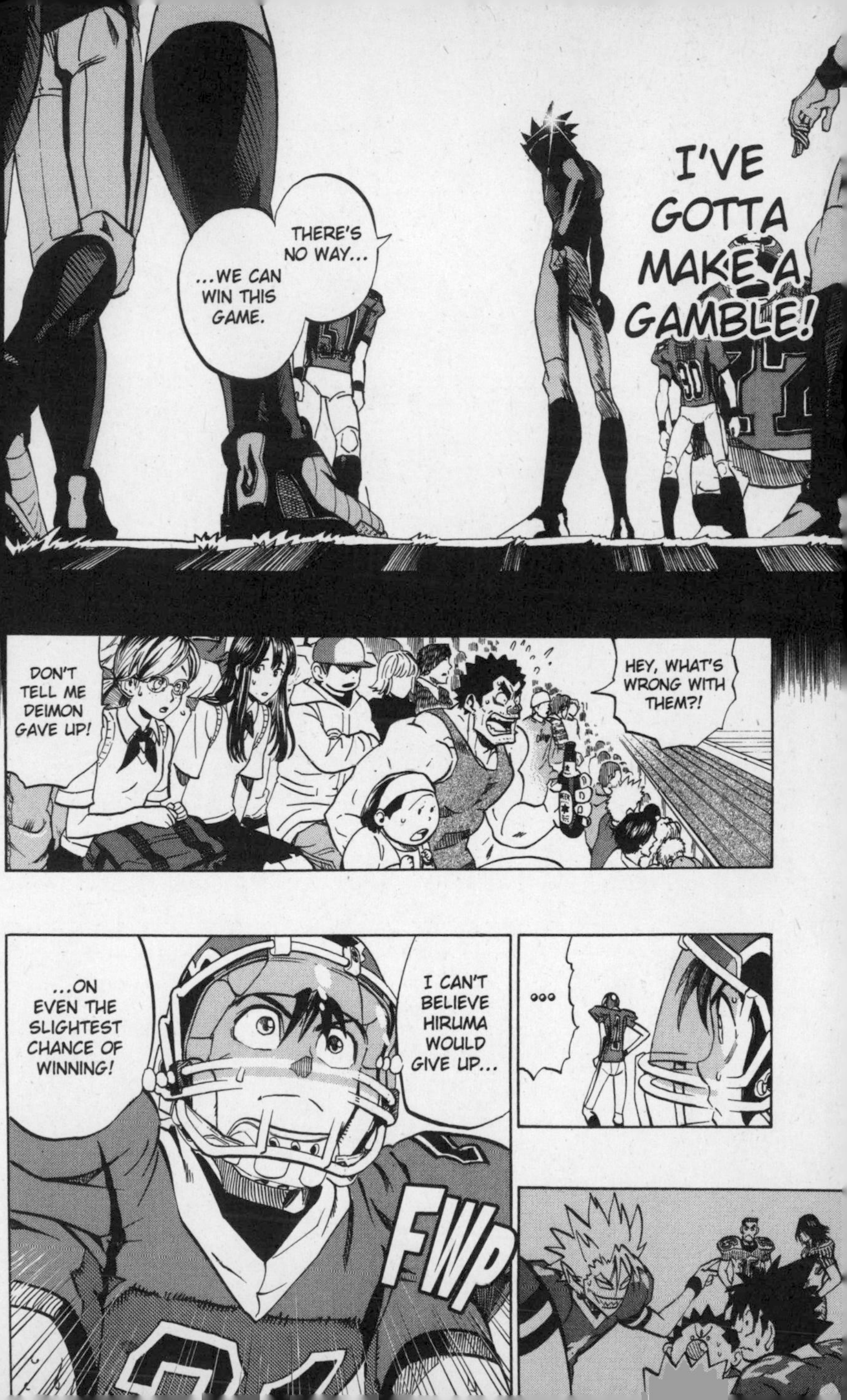
I'VE GOTTA MAKE A GAMBLE!
THERE'S NO WAY...
...WE CAN WIN THIS GAME.
HEY, WHAT'S WRONG WITH THEM?!
DON'T TELL ME DEIMON GAVE UP!
...
I CAN'T BELIEVE HIRUMA WOULD GIVE UP...
...ON EVEN THE SLIGHTEST CHANCE OF WINNING!
FWP

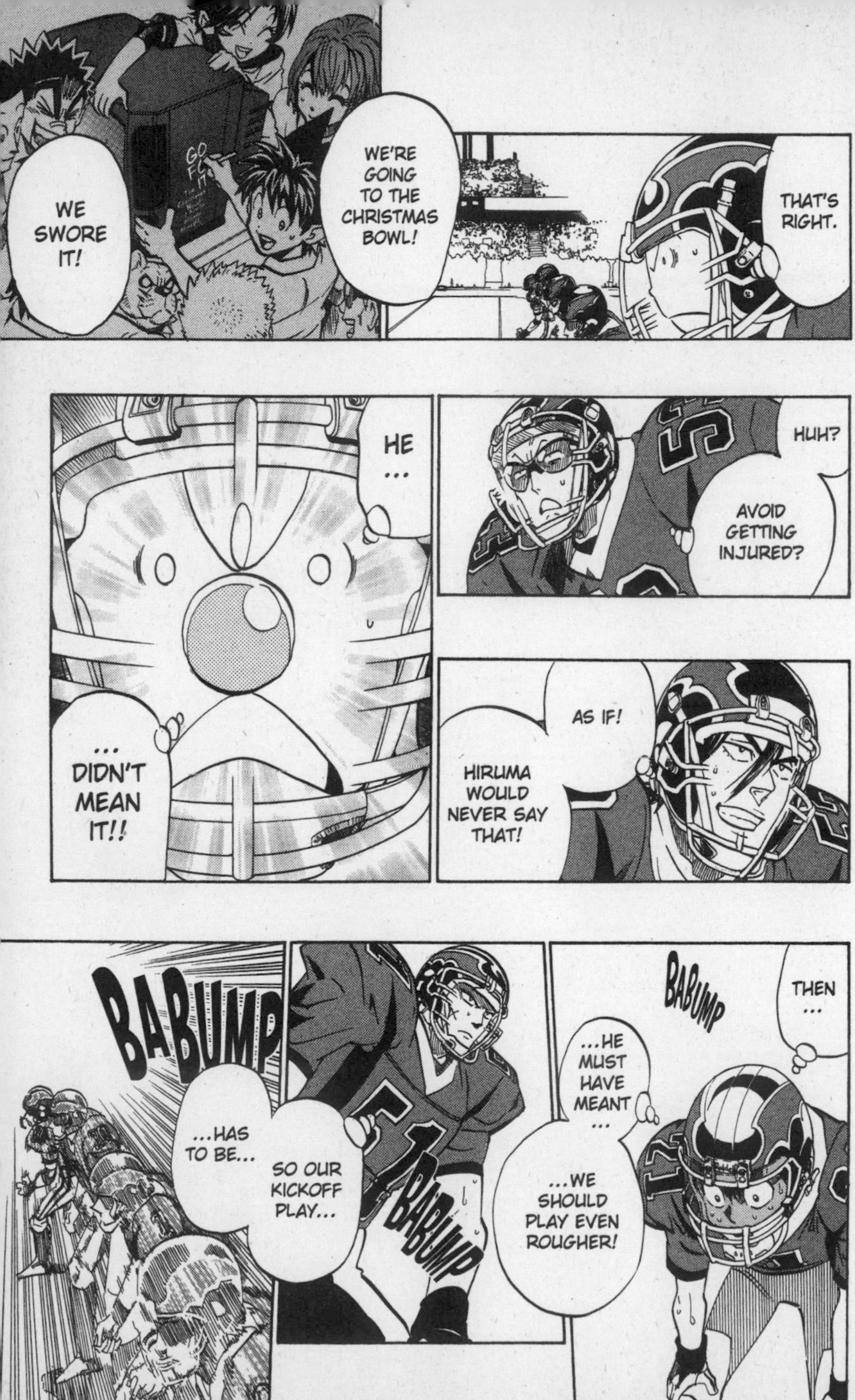
THAT'S RIGHT.
WE'RE GOING TO THE CHRISTMAS BOWL!
WE SWORE IT!
HUH?
AVOID GETTING INJURED?
AS IF!
HIRUMA WOULD NEVER SAY THAT!
HE ...
... DIDN'T MEAN IT!!
THEN ...
BABUMP
...HE MUST HAVE MEANT ...
...WE SHOULD PLAY EVEN ROUGHER!
BABUMP
SO OUR KICKOFF PLAY...
BABUMP
...HAS TO BE...

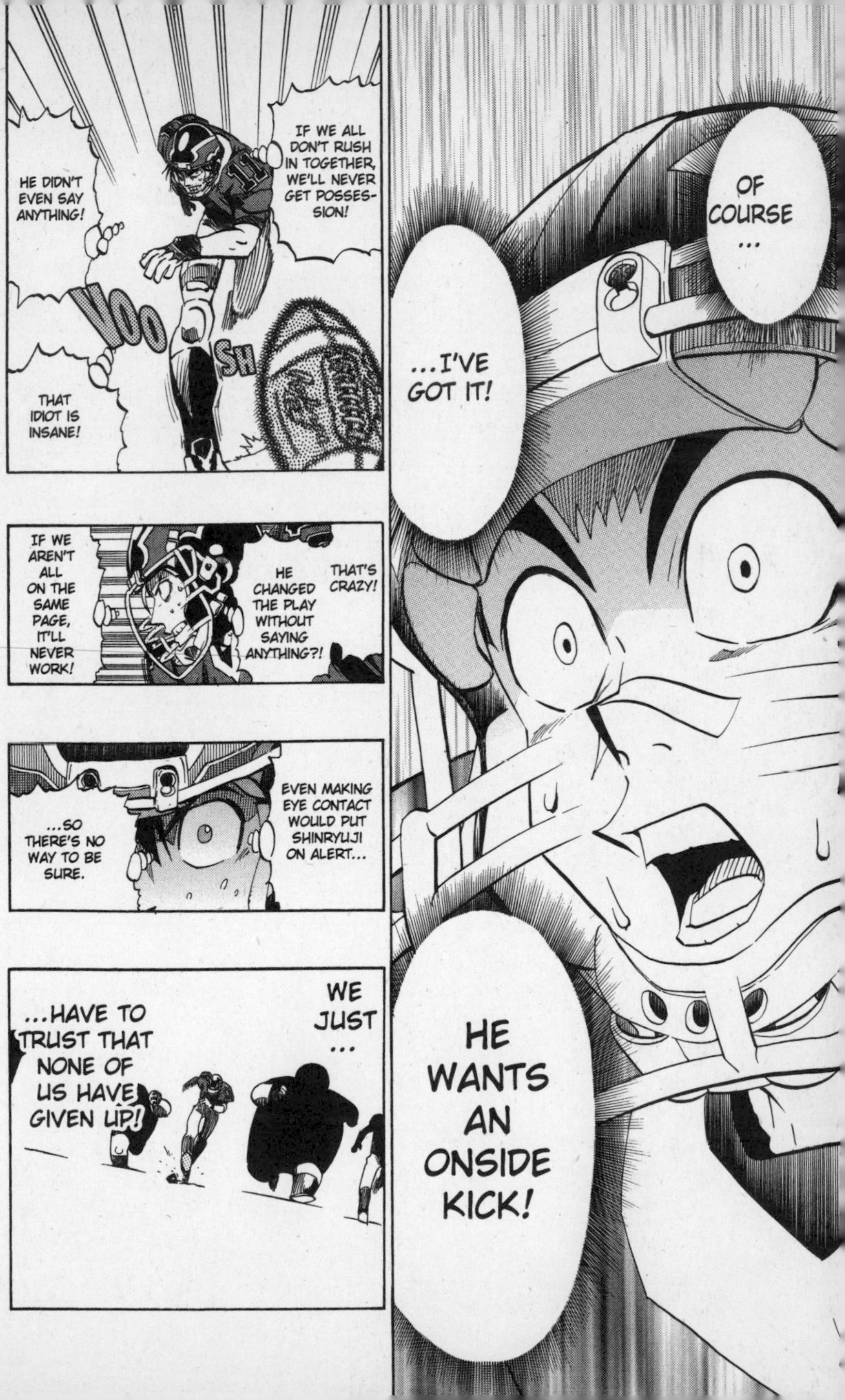
OF COURSE...
...I'VE GOT IT!
HE WANTS AN ONSIDE KICK!
IF WE ALL DON'T RUSH IN TOGETHER, WE'LL NEVER GET POSSESSION!
HE DIDN'T EVEN SAY ANYTHING!
VOOSH
THAT IDIOT IS INSANE!
THAT'S CRAZY!
HE CHANGED THE PLAY WITHOUT SAYING ANYTHING?!
IF WE AREN'T ALL ON THE SAME PAGE, IT'LL NEVER WORK!
EVEN MAKING EYE CONTACT WOULD PUT SHINRYUJI ON ALERT...
...SO THERE'S NO WAY TO BE SURE.
WE JUST...
...HAVE TO TRUST THAT NONE OF US HAVE GIVEN UP!

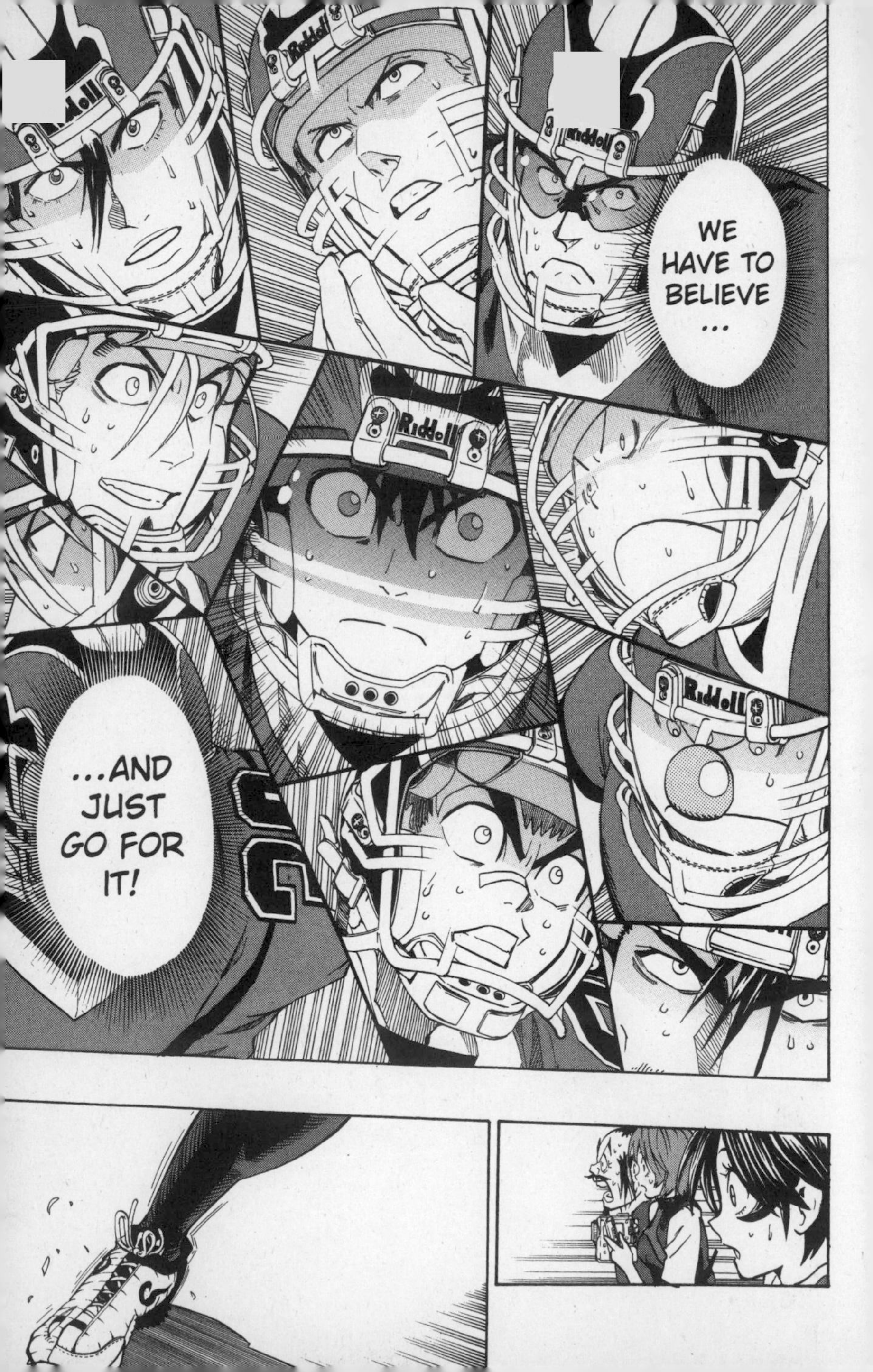
WE HAVE TO BELIEVE ...
...AND JUST GO FOR IT!

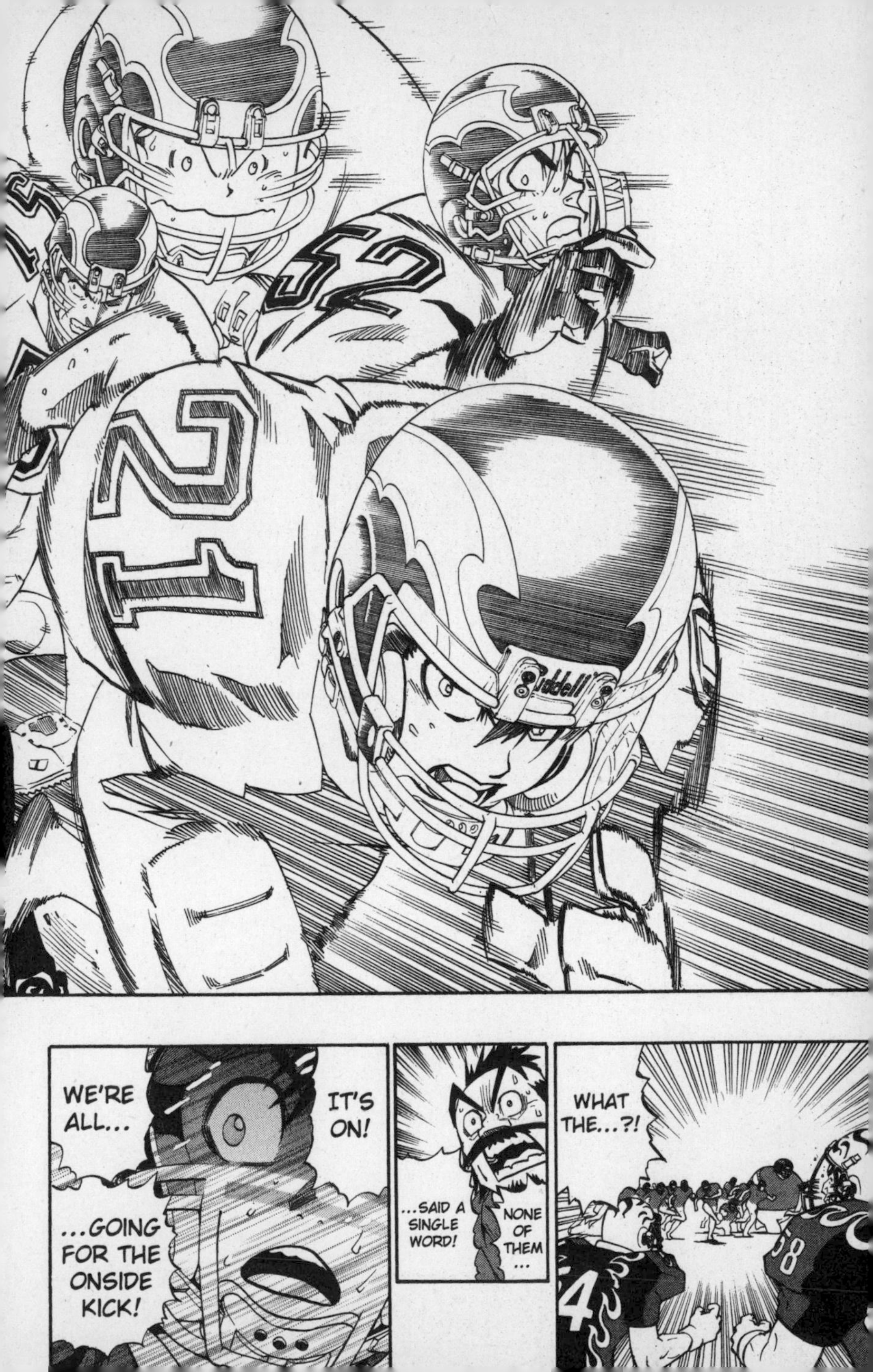
WHAT THE...?!
NONE OF THEM...
...SAID A SINGLE WORD!
IT'S ON!
WE'RE ALL...
...GOING FOR THE ONSIDE KICK!

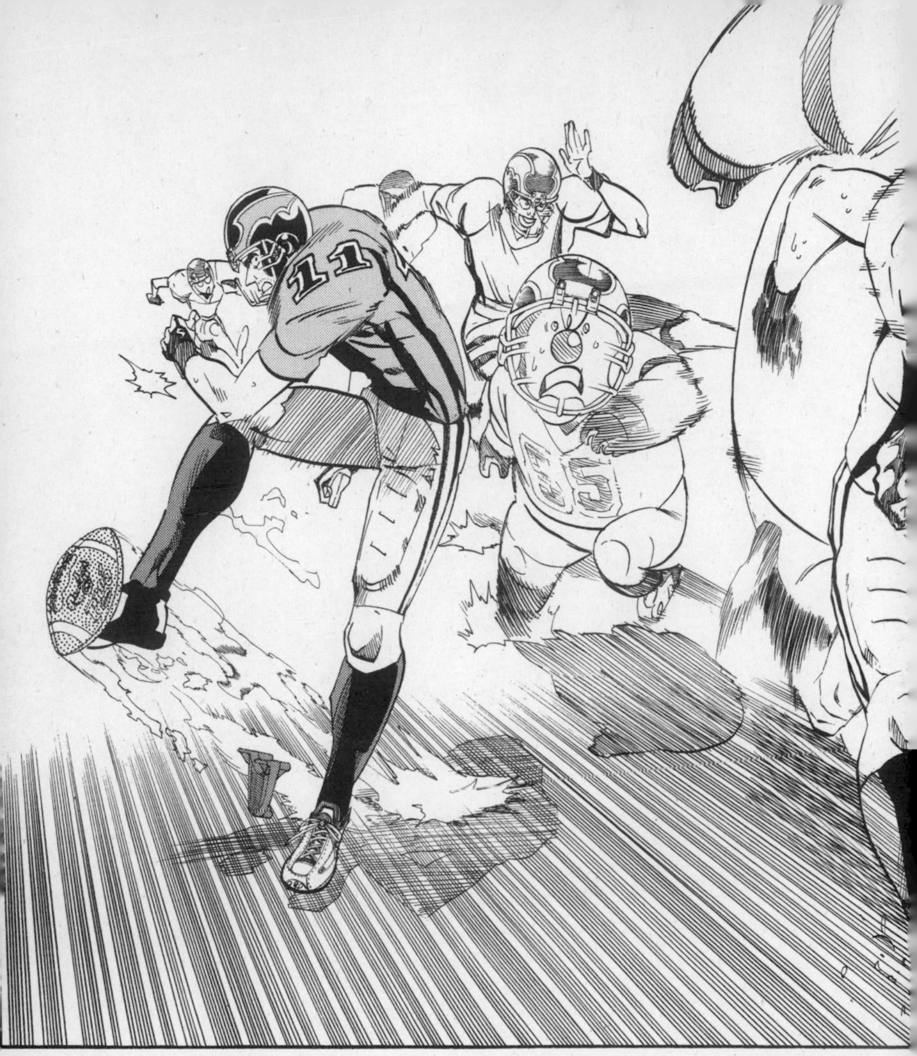

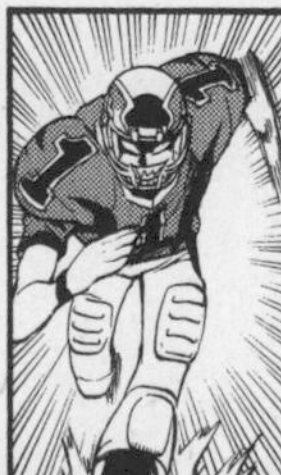

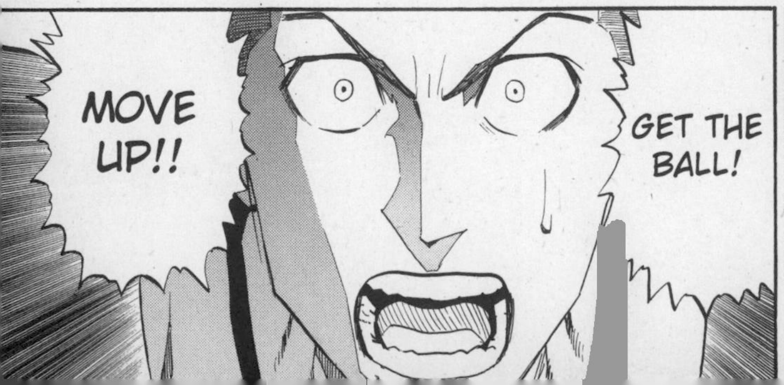
GET THE BALL!
MOVE UP!!

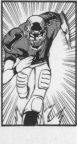

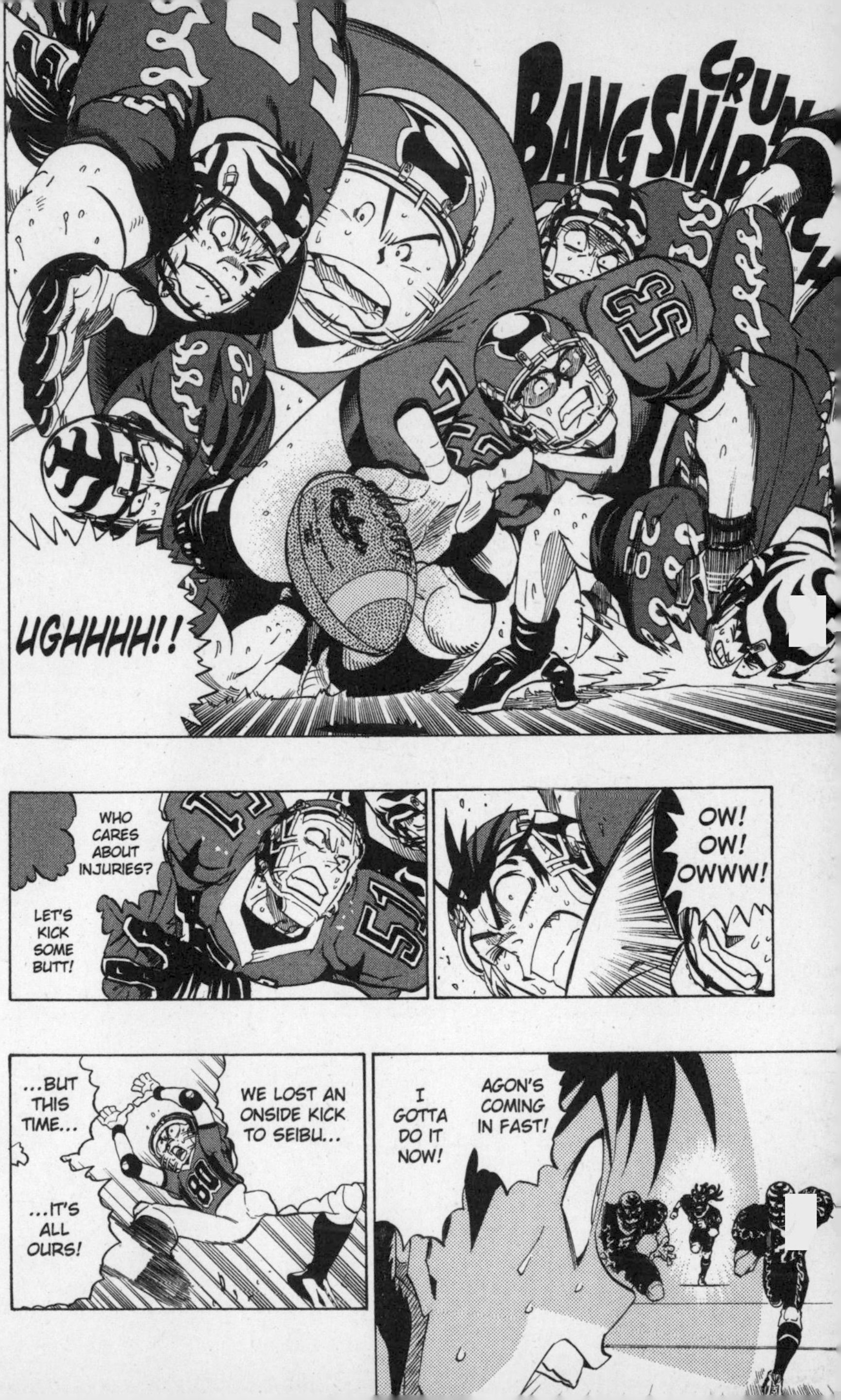
CRUN
BANG SNAP
UGHHHH!!
OW! OW! OWWW!
WHO CARES ABOUT INJURIES?
LET'S KICK SOME BUTT!
AGON'S COMING IN FAST!
I GOTTA DO IT NOW!
WE LOST AN ONSIDE KICK TO SEIBU...
...BUT THIS TIME...
...IT'S ALL OURS!

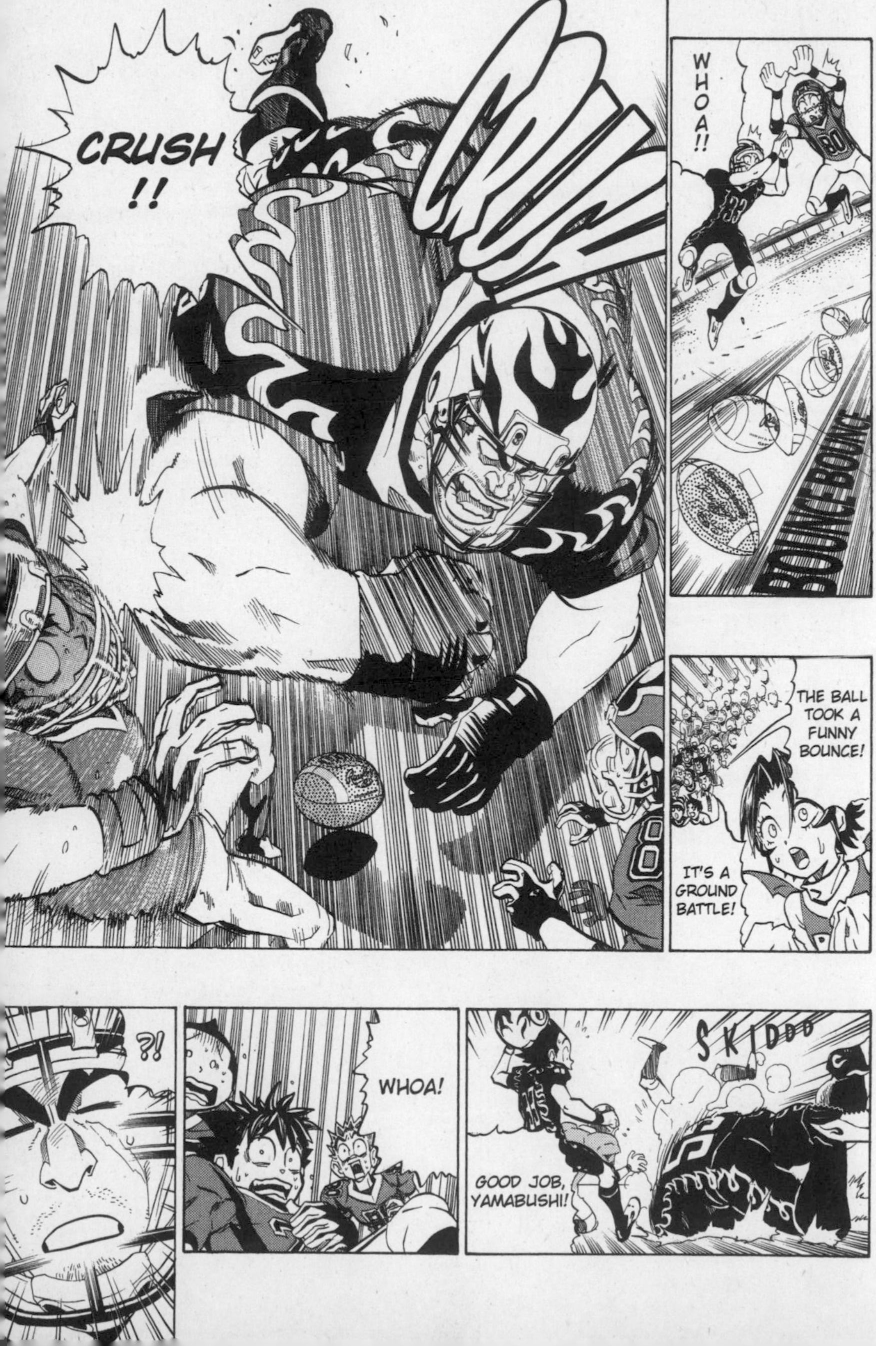
WHOA!!
BOUNCEBOUNCE
THE BALL TOOK A FUNNY BOUNCE!
IT'S A GROUND BATTLE!
CRUSH !!
SKIDDD
GOOD JOB, YAMABUSHI!
WHOA!
?!

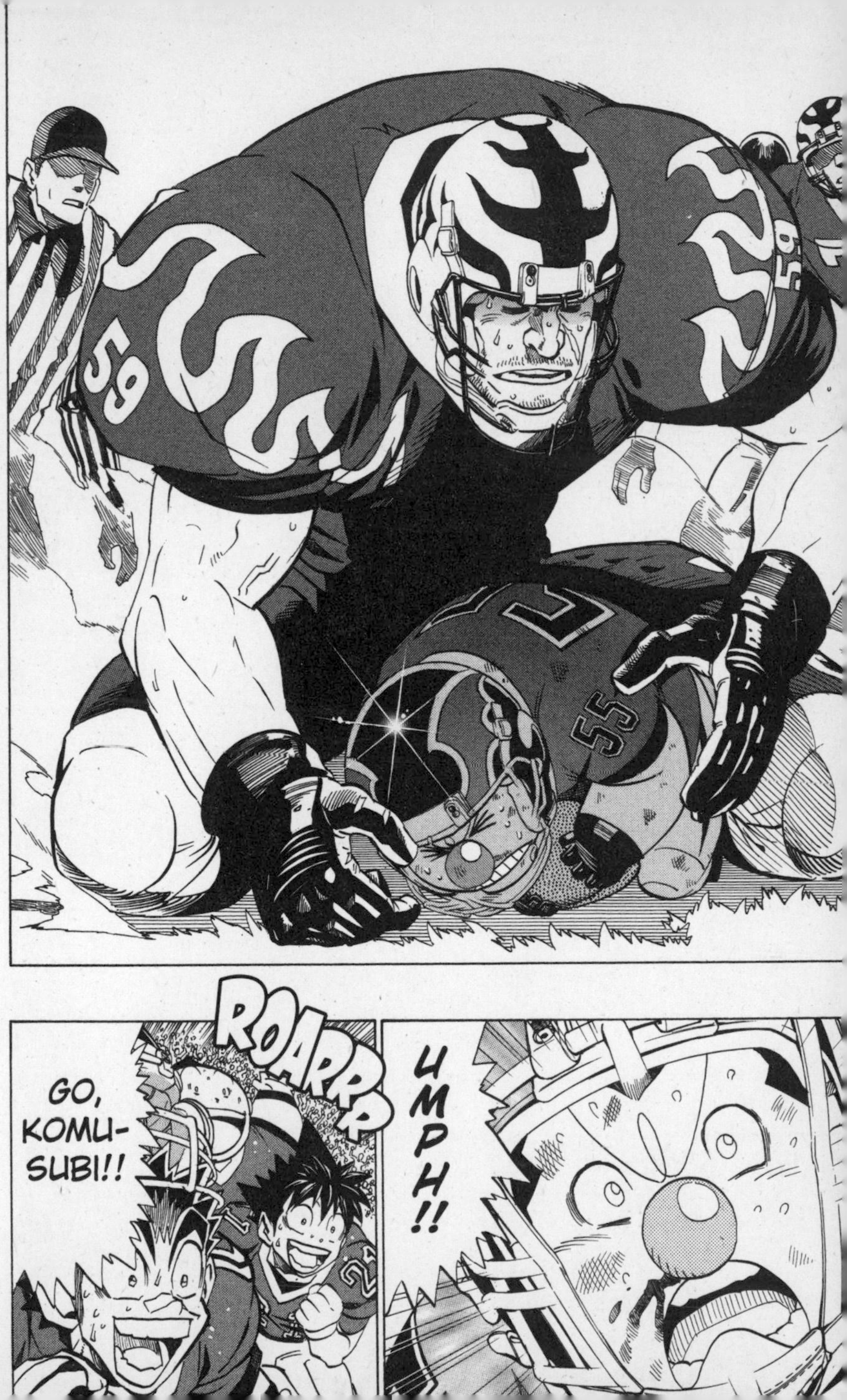
UMPH!!
ROARRR
GO, KOMUSUBI!!

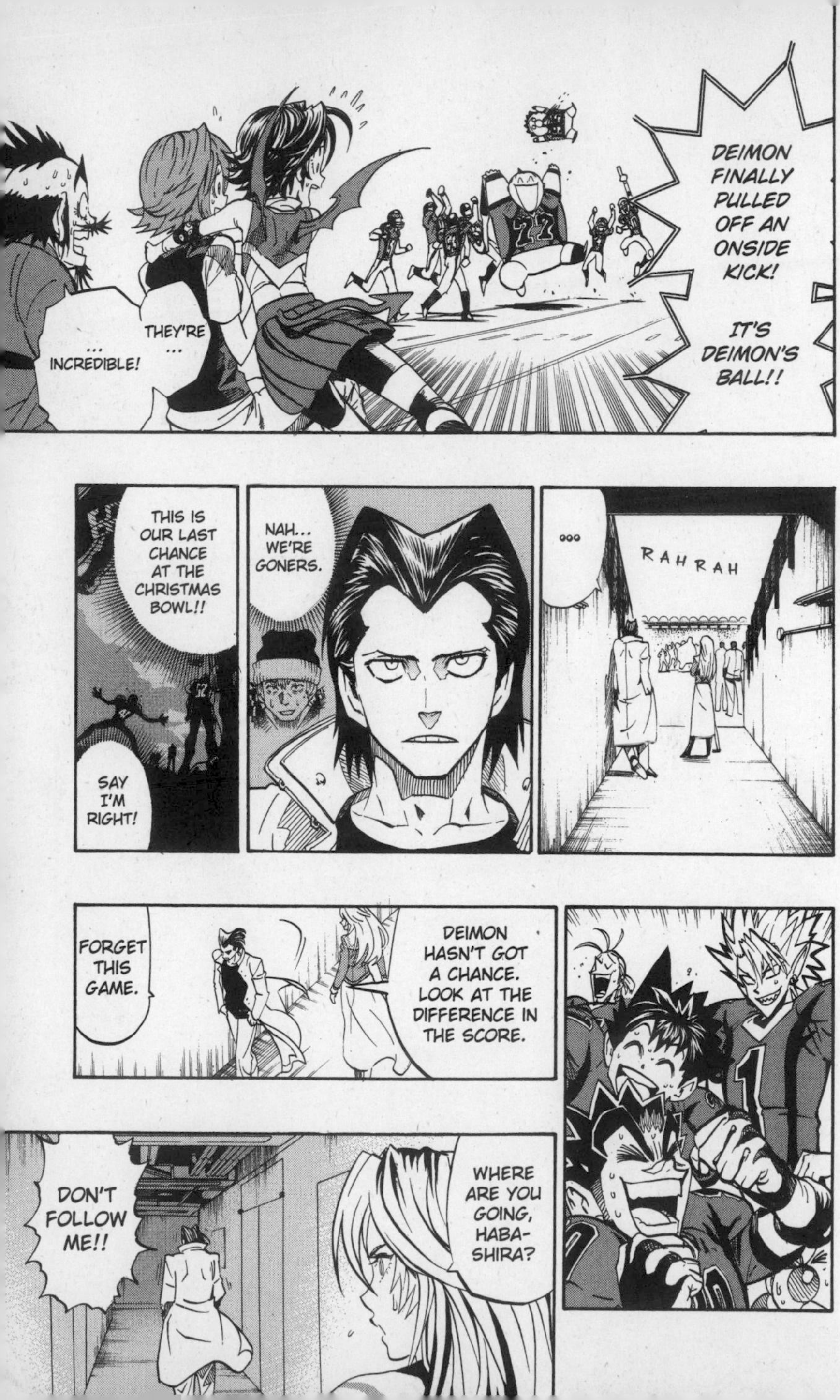
DEIMON FINALLY PULLED OFF AN ONSIDE KICK!
IT'S DEIMON'S BALL!!
THEY'RE ...
... INCREDIBLE!
...
RAHRAH
NAH... WE'RE GONERS.
THIS IS OUR LAST CHANCE AT THE CHRISTMAS BOWL!!
SAY I'M RIGHT!
DEIMON HASN'T GOT A CHANCE. LOOK AT THE DIFFERENCE IN THE SCORE.
FORGET THIS GAME.
WHERE ARE YOU GOING, HABA-SHIRA?
DON'T FOLLOW ME!!

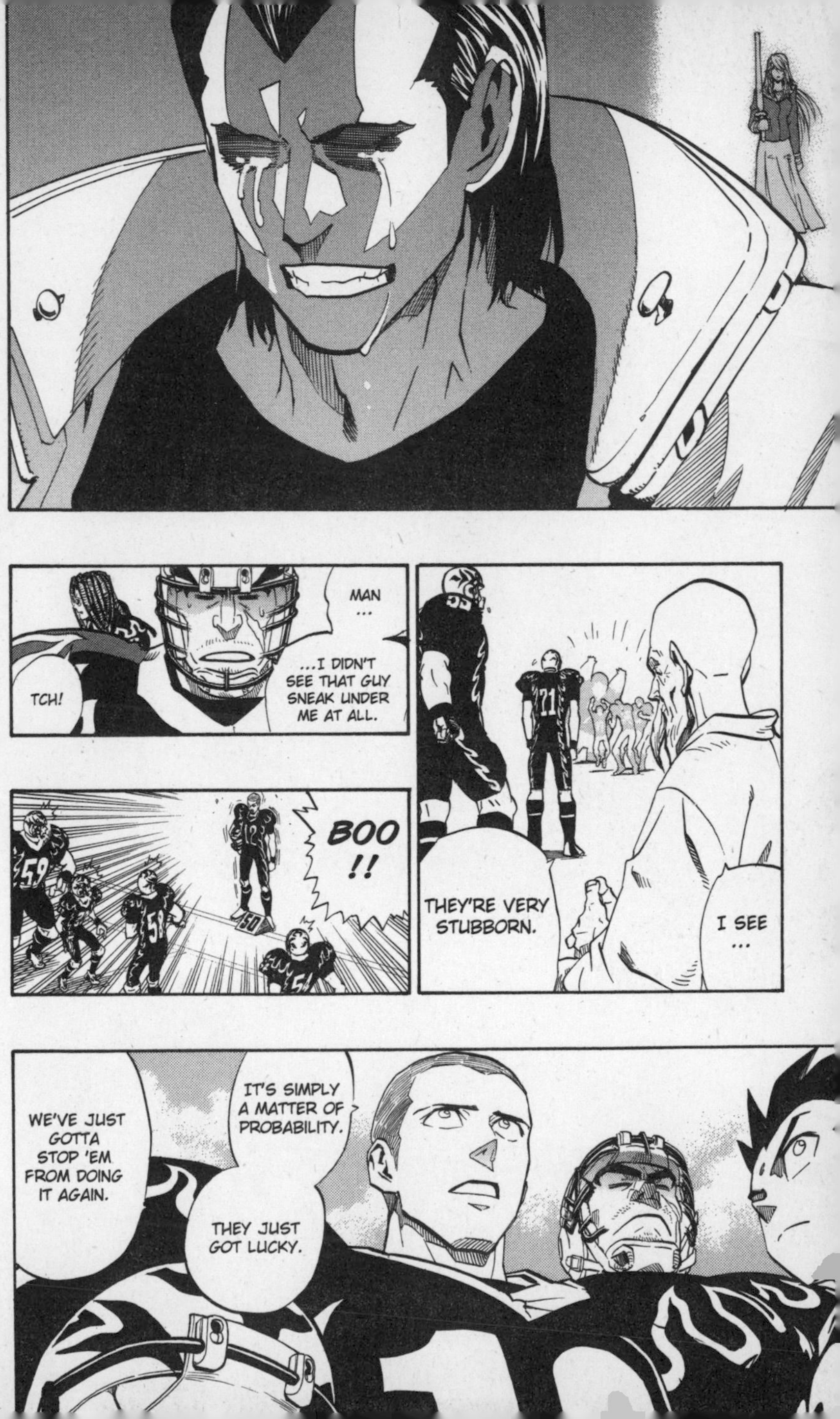
I SEE ...
THEY'RE VERY STUBBORN.
MAN ...
...I DIDN'T SEE THAT GUY SNEAK UNDER ME AT ALL.
TCH!
BOO !!
IT'S SIMPLY A MATTER OF PROBABILITY.
THEY JUST GOT LUCKY.
WE'VE JUST GOTTA STOP 'EM FROM DOING IT AGAIN.

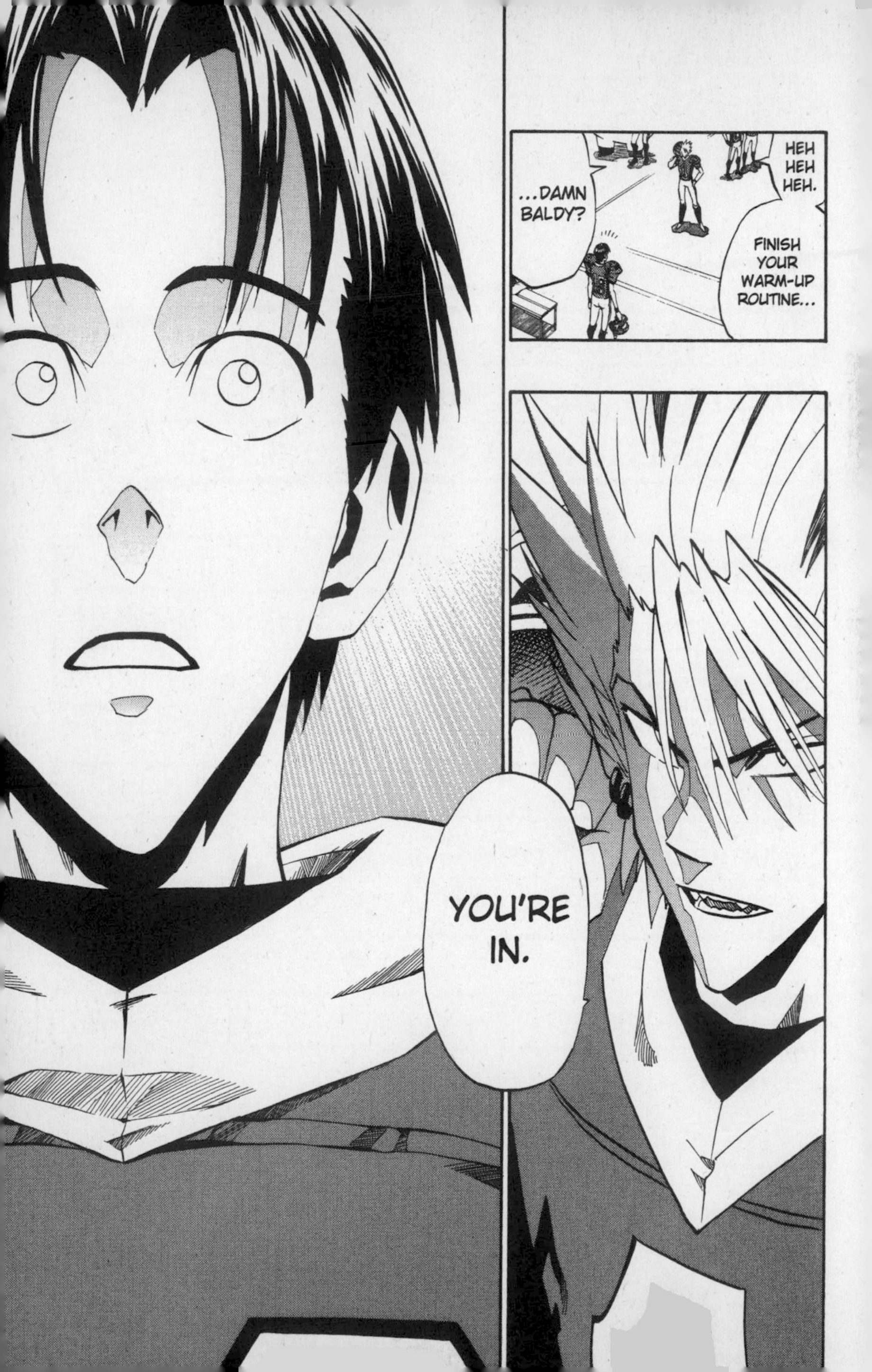
HEH HEH HEH.
FINISH YOUR WARM-UP ROUTINE...
...DAMN BALDY?
YOU'RE IN.

SHINRYUJI NAGAS

KANAGAWA DISTRICT TOURNAMENT RESULTS

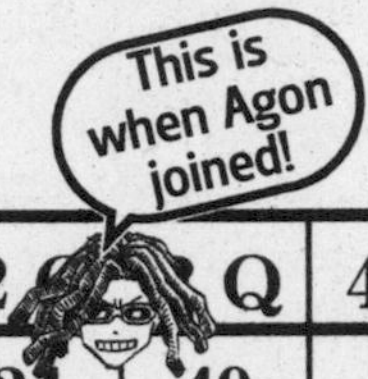
This is when Agon joined!

1st Round	1 Q	2 Q	3 Q	4 Q	Total
Shinryuji Nagas	20	24	40	42	126
Chukagai Ramens	0	0	0	0	0

2nd Round	1 Q	2 Q	3 Q	4 Q	Total
Sunayama All-Stars	0	0	0	0	0
Shinryuji Nagas	14	14	24	35	87

Semifinals	1 Q	2 Q	3 Q	4 Q	Total
Hakone Roten-Spa	0	0	0	0	0
Shinryuji Nagas	21	6	35	31	93

Finals	1 Q	2 Q	3 Q	[illegible]	Total
Shinryuji Nagas	7	14	13	27	61
Taiyo Sphinx	0	0	6	0	6

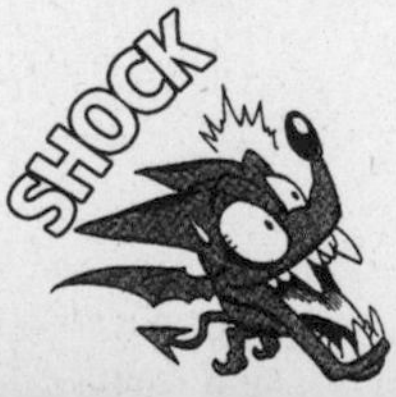
SHOCK

AMAZING!!

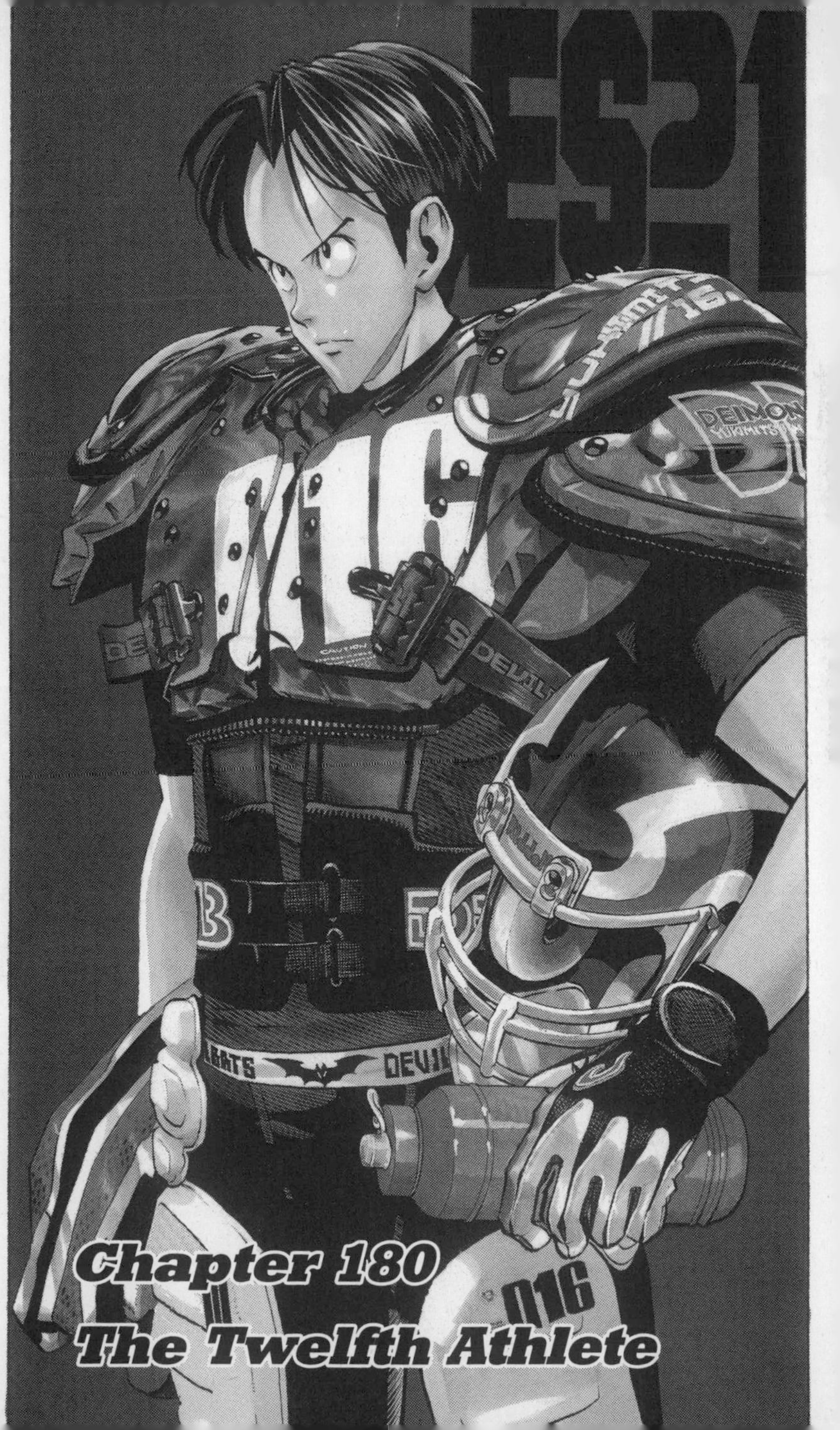
ES21
DEIMON
BATS DEVIL
016

Chapter 180
The Twelfth Athlete

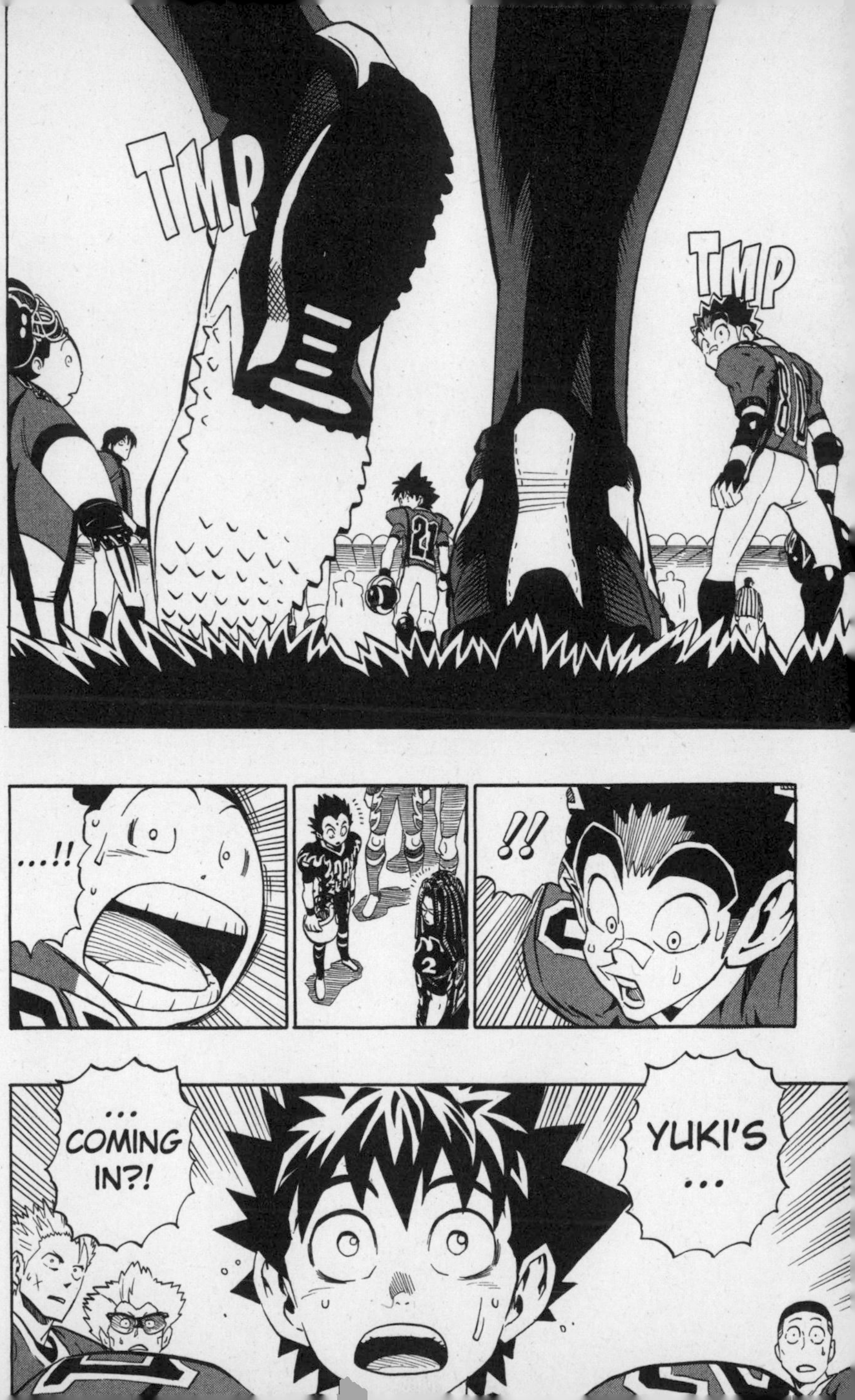
TMP
TMP
!!
...!!
YUKI'S ...
... COMING IN?!

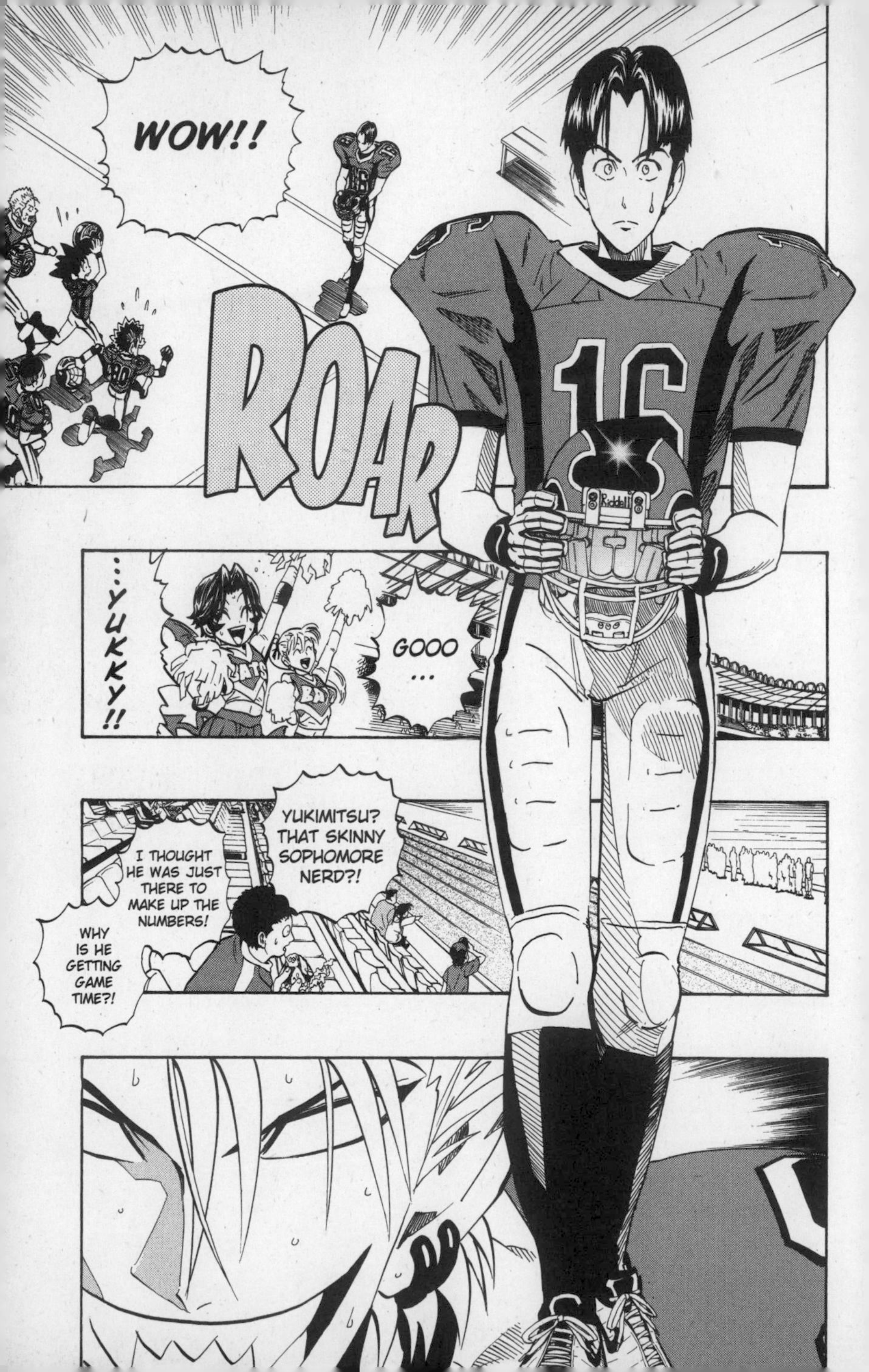
WOW!!
ROAR
GOOO ...
...YUKKY!!
YUKIMITSU? THAT SKINNY SOPHOMORE NERD?!
I THOUGHT HE WAS JUST THERE TO MAKE UP THE NUMBERS!
WHY IS HE GETTING GAME TIME?!

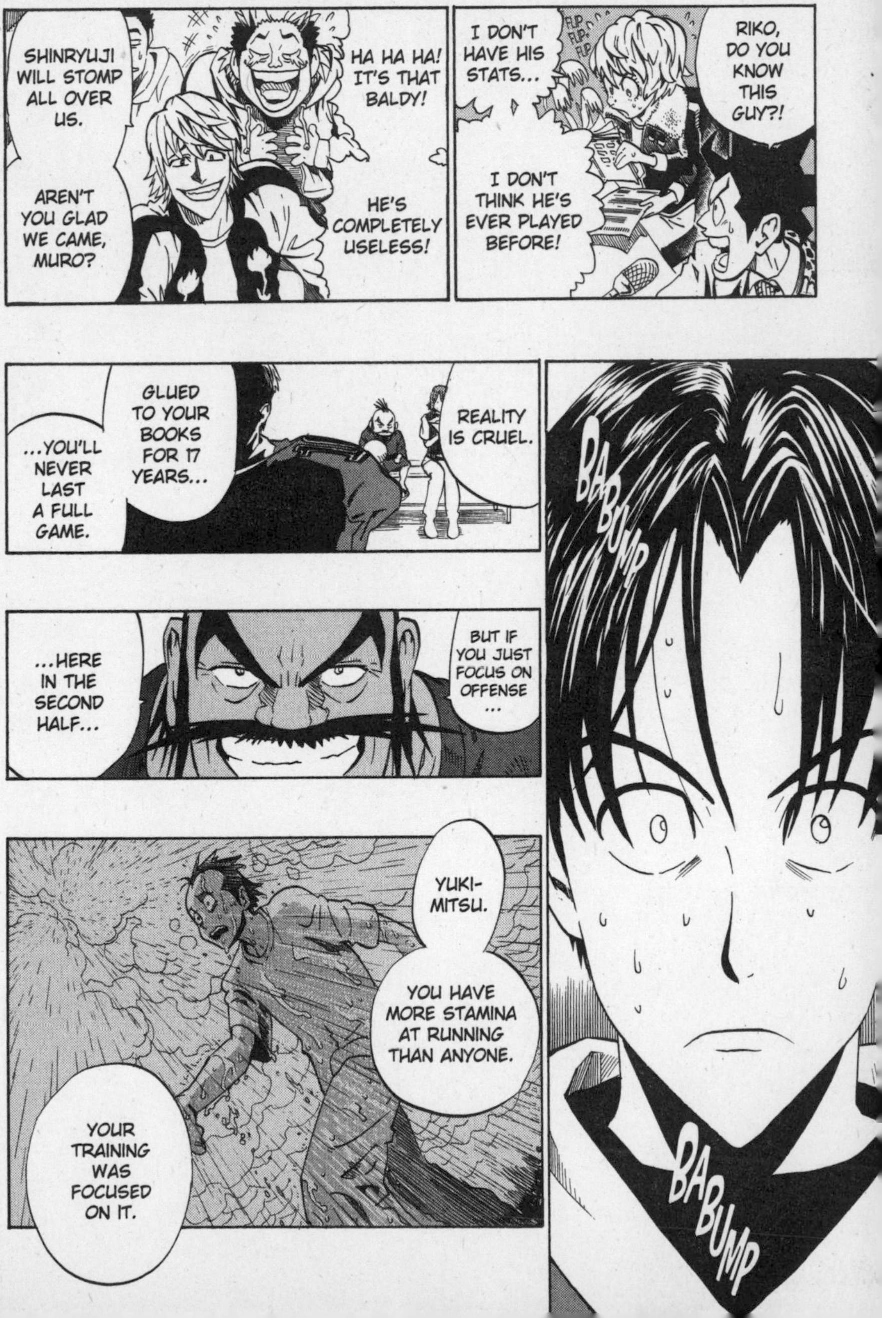
RIKO, DO YOU KNOW THIS GUY?!
FLIP FLIP FLIP
I DON'T HAVE HIS STATS...
I DON'T THINK HE'S EVER PLAYED BEFORE!
HA HA HA! IT'S THAT BALDY!
HE'S COMPLETELY USELESS!
SHINRYUJI WILL STOMP ALL OVER US.
AREN'T YOU GLAD WE CAME, MURO?
BABUMP
BABUMP
REALITY IS CRUEL.
GLUED TO YOUR BOOKS FOR 17 YEARS...
...YOU'LL NEVER LAST A FULL GAME.
BUT IF YOU JUST FOCUS ON OFFENSE ...
...HERE IN THE SECOND HALF...
YUKI-MITSU.
YOU HAVE MORE STAMINA AT RUNNING THAN ANYONE.
YOUR TRAINING WAS FOCUSED ON IT.

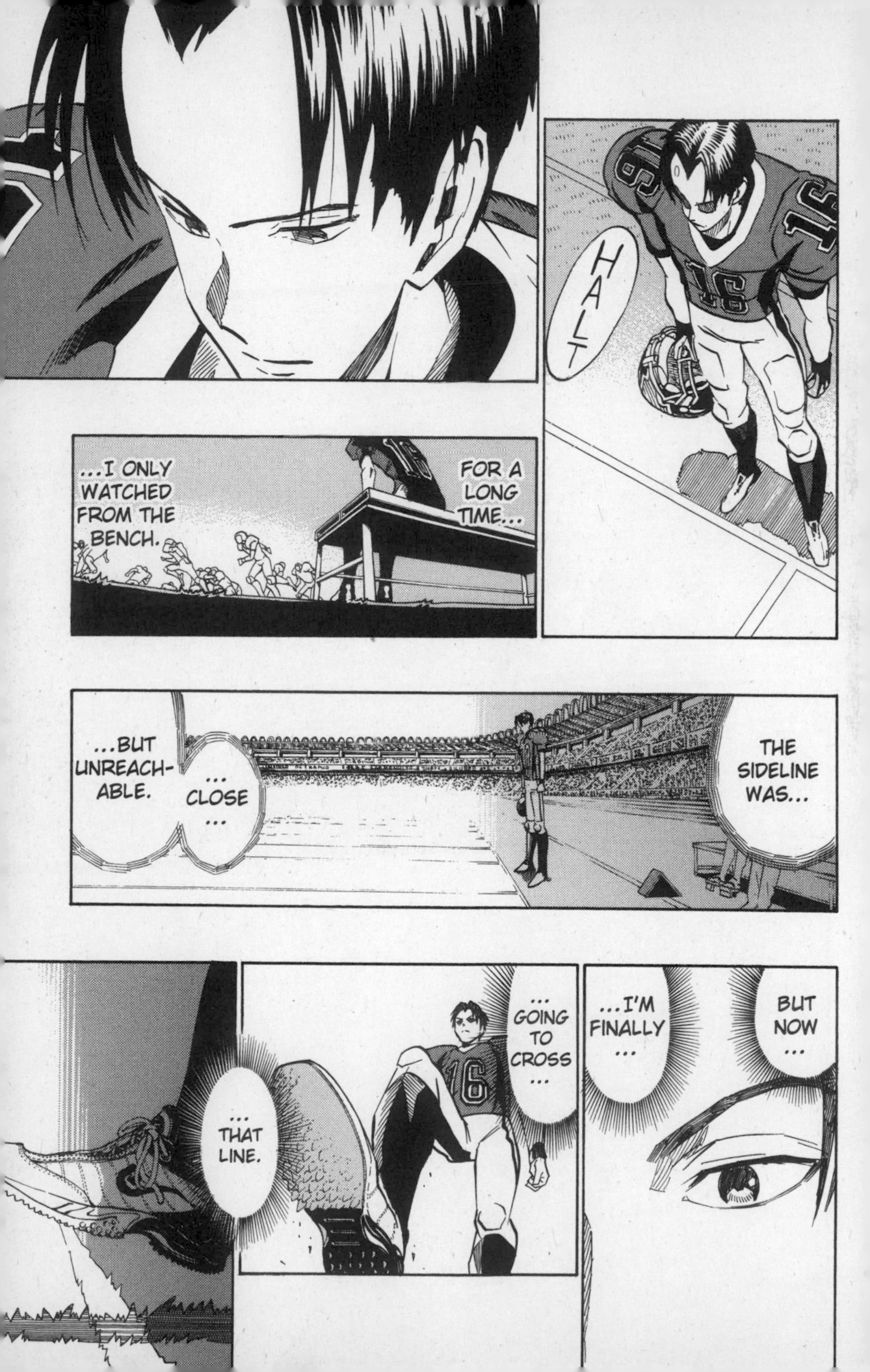
HALT
FOR A LONG TIME...
...I ONLY WATCHED FROM THE BENCH.
THE SIDELINE WAS...
...CLOSE...
...BUT UNREACHABLE.
BUT NOW...
...I'M FINALLY...
...GOING TO CROSS...
...THAT LINE.

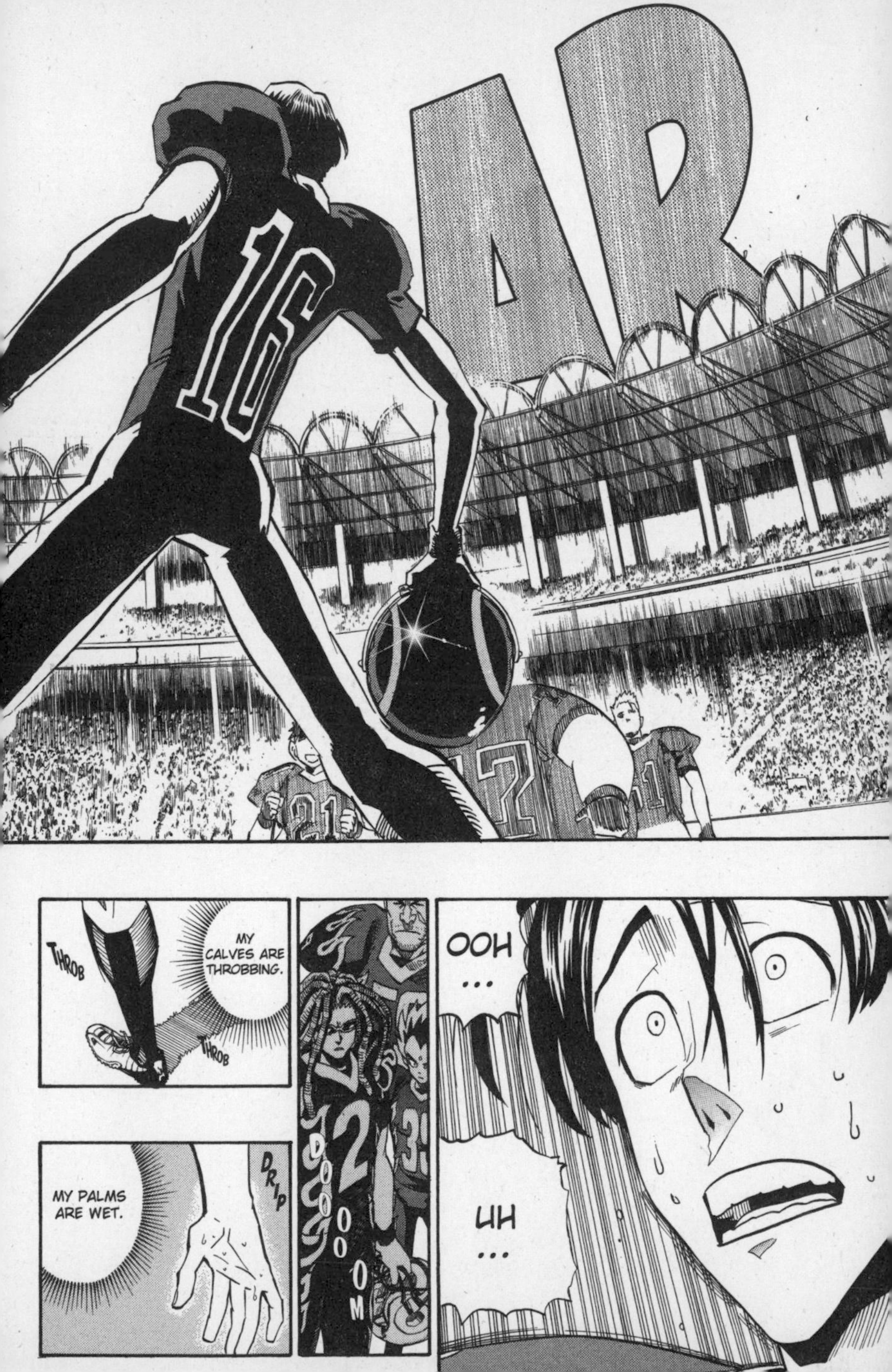
AR
OOH ...
UH ...
DOOOOOOOM
MY CALVES ARE THROBBING.
THROB
THROB
MY PALMS ARE WET.
DRIP

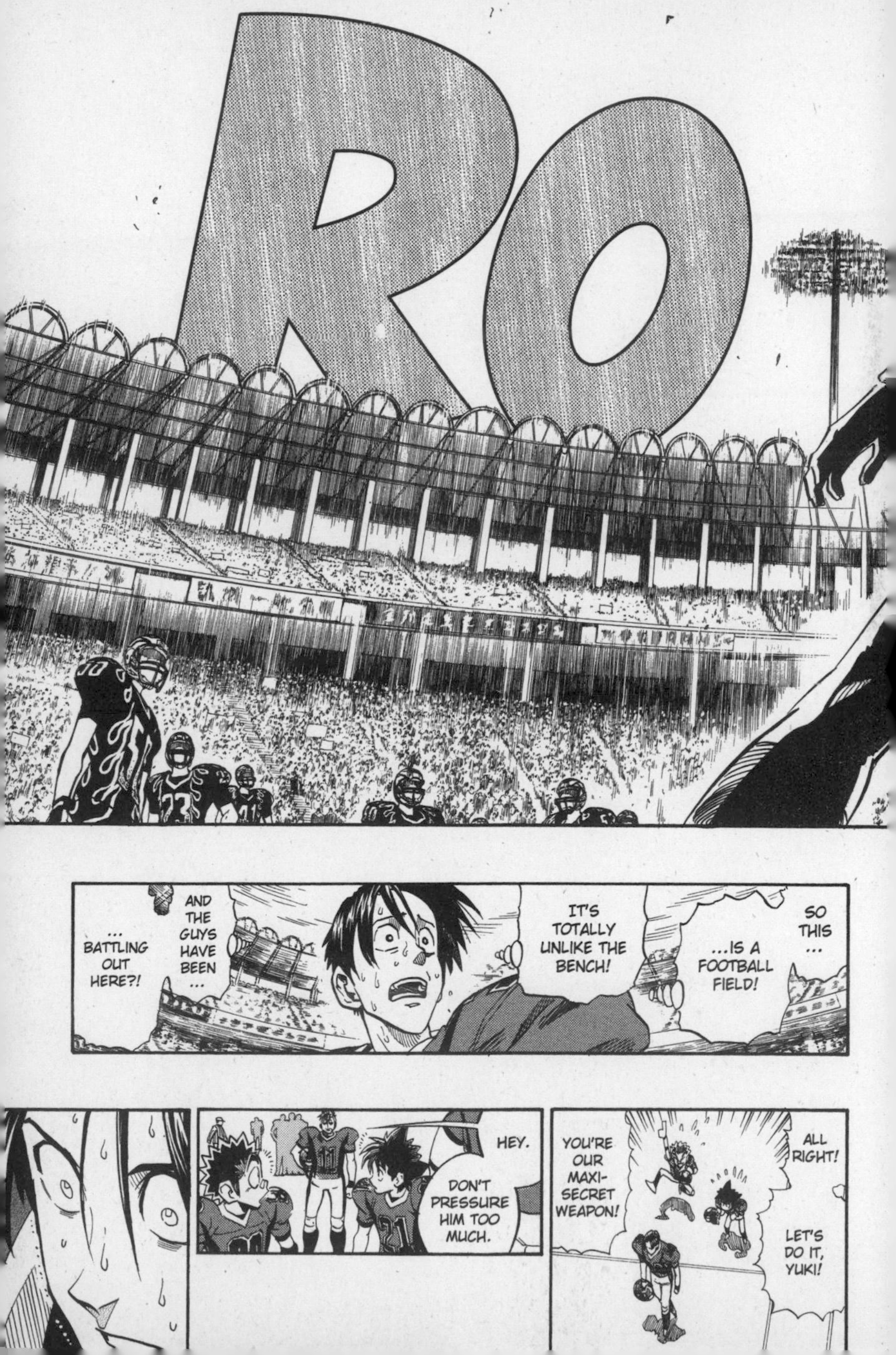
RO
SO THIS ...
...IS A FOOTBALL FIELD!
IT'S TOTALLY UNLIKE THE BENCH!
AND THE GUYS HAVE BEEN ...
... BATTLING OUT HERE?!
ALL RIGHT!
LET'S DO IT, YUKI!
YOU'RE OUR MAXI-SECRET WEAPON!
HEY.
DON'T PRESSURE HIM TOO MUCH.

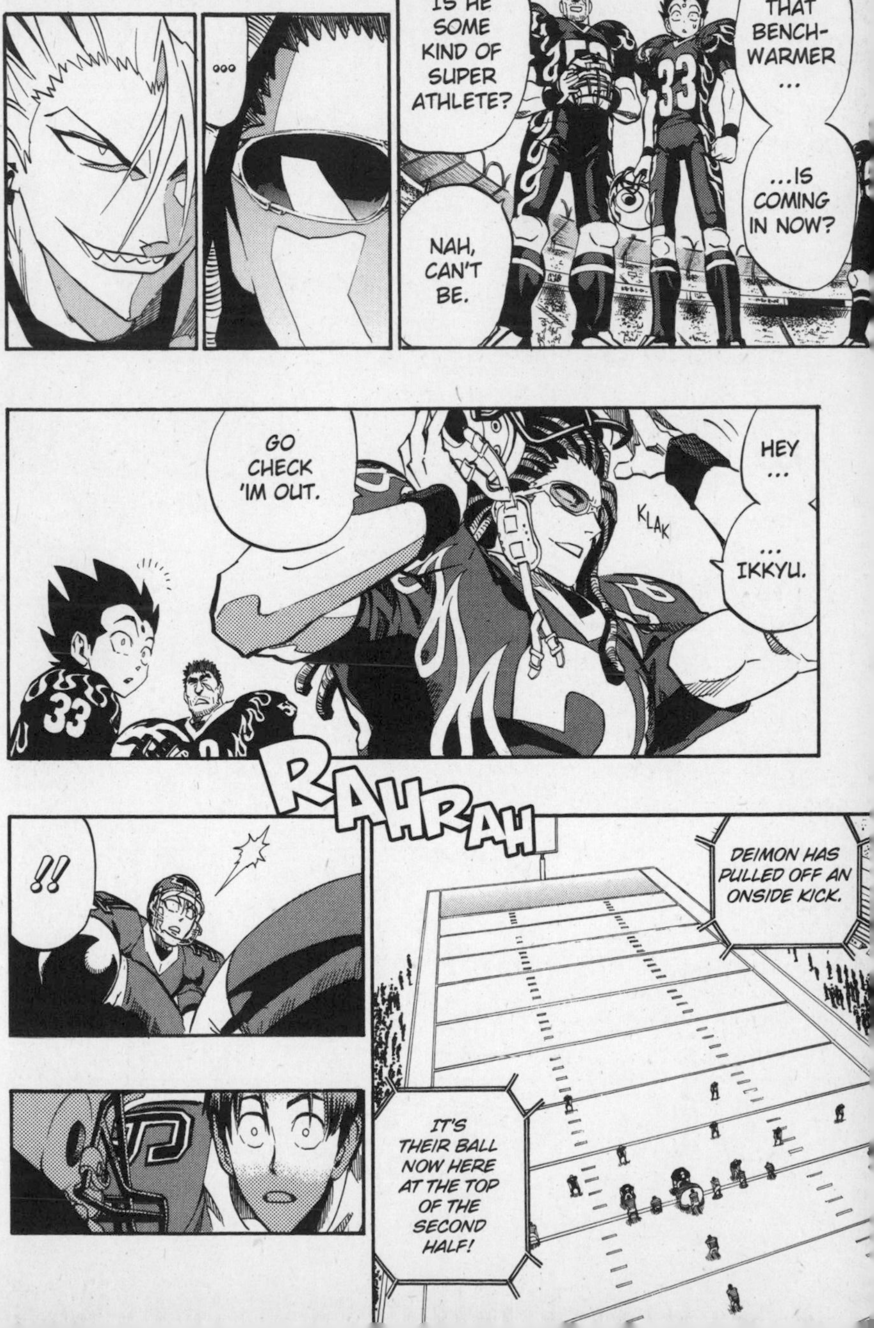
THAT BENCH-WARMER ...
...IS COMING IN NOW?
IS HE SOME KIND OF SUPER ATHLETE?
NAH, CAN'T BE.
...
HEY ...
... IKKYU.
KLAK
GO CHECK 'IM OUT.
RAHRAH
DEIMON HAS PULLED OFF AN ONSIDE KICK.
IT'S THEIR BALL NOW HERE AT THE TOP OF THE SECOND HALF!
!!

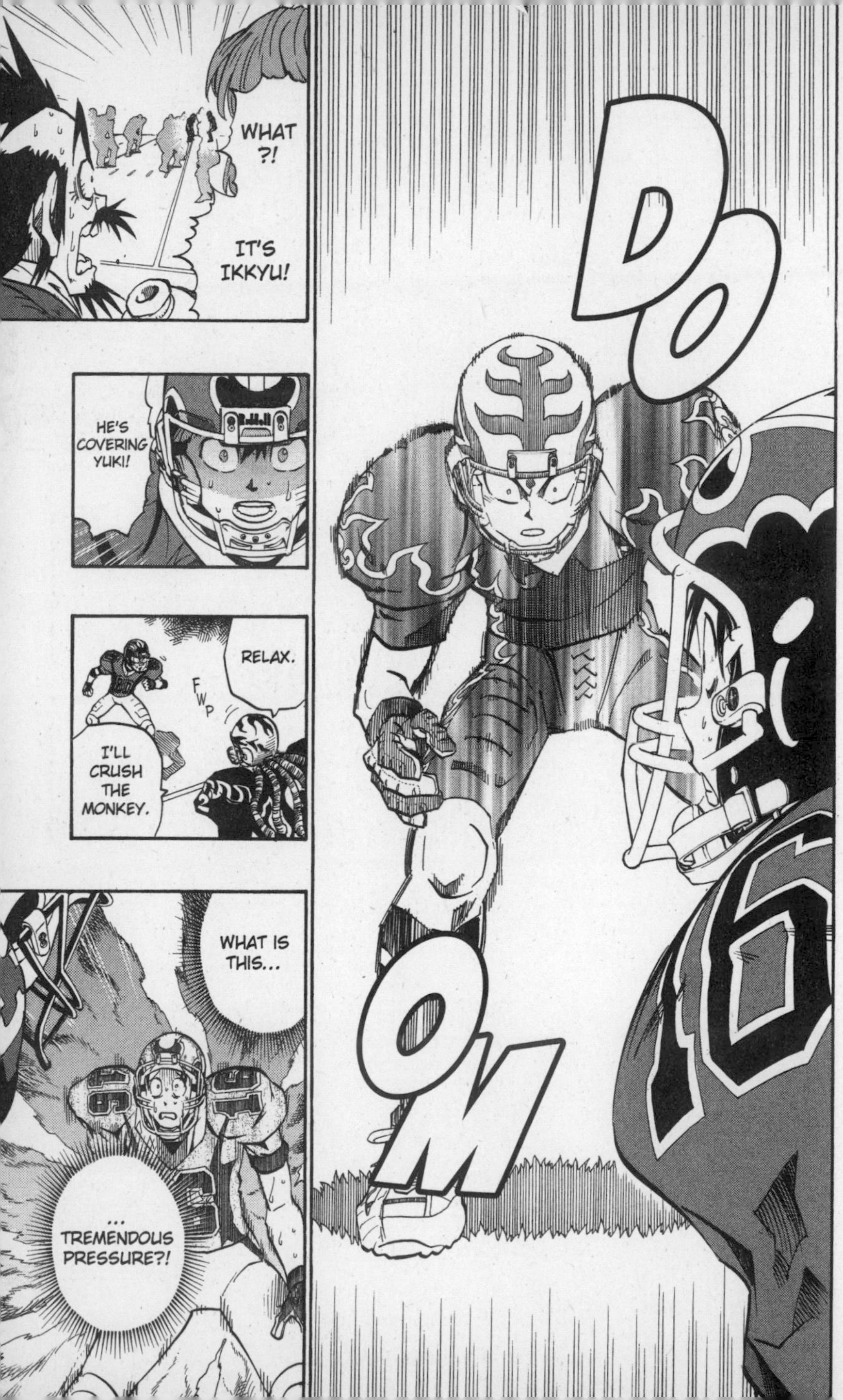
DOOM
WHAT ?!
IT'S IKKYU!
HE'S COVERING YUKI!
RELAX.
FWP
I'LL CRUSH THE MONKEY.
WHAT IS THIS...
... TREMENDOUS PRESSURE?!

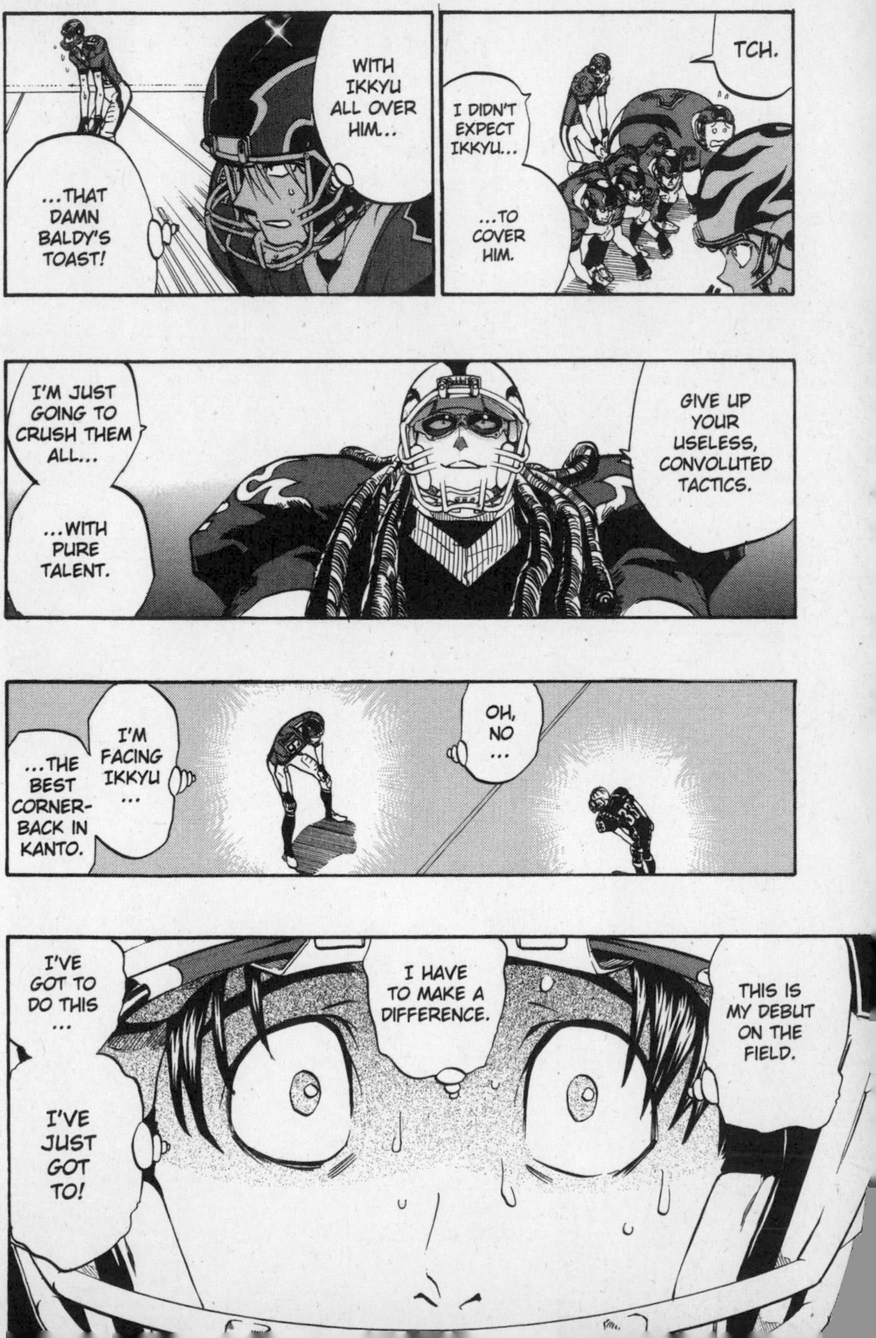
TCH.
I DIDN'T EXPECT IKKYU...
...TO COVER HIM.
WITH IKKYU ALL OVER HIM...
...THAT DAMN BALDY'S TOAST!
GIVE UP YOUR USELESS, CONVOLUTED TACTICS.
I'M JUST GOING TO CRUSH THEM ALL...
...WITH PURE TALENT.
OH, NO ...
I'M FACING IKKYU ...
...THE BEST CORNER-BACK IN KANTO.
THIS IS MY DEBUT ON THE FIELD.
I HAVE TO MAKE A DIFFERENCE.
I'VE GOT TO DO THIS ...
I'VE JUST GOT TO!

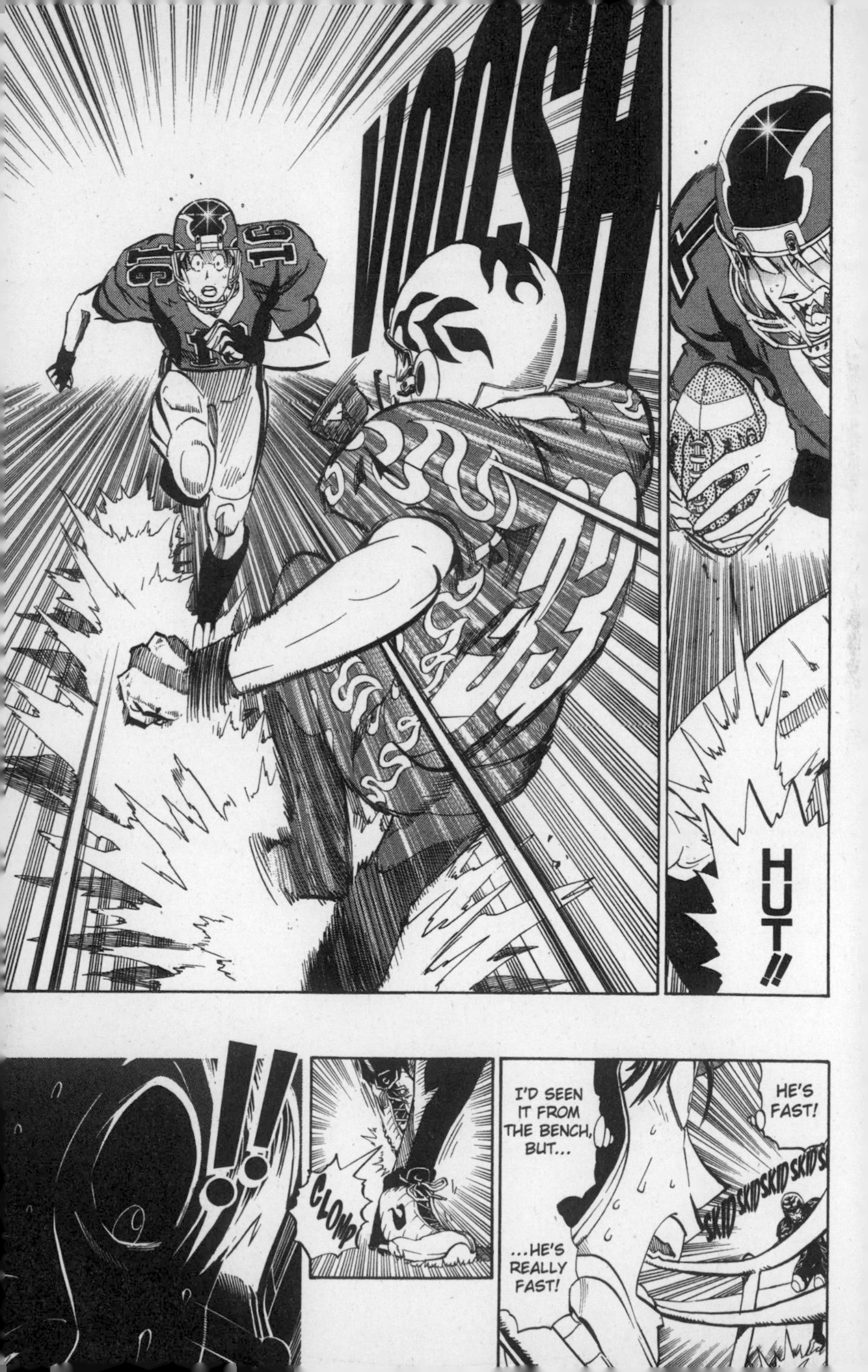
HUT!!
VOOSH
HE'S FAST!
I'D SEEN IT FROM THE BENCH, BUT...
...HE'S REALLY FAST!
SKID SKID SKID SKID
CLOMP
!!

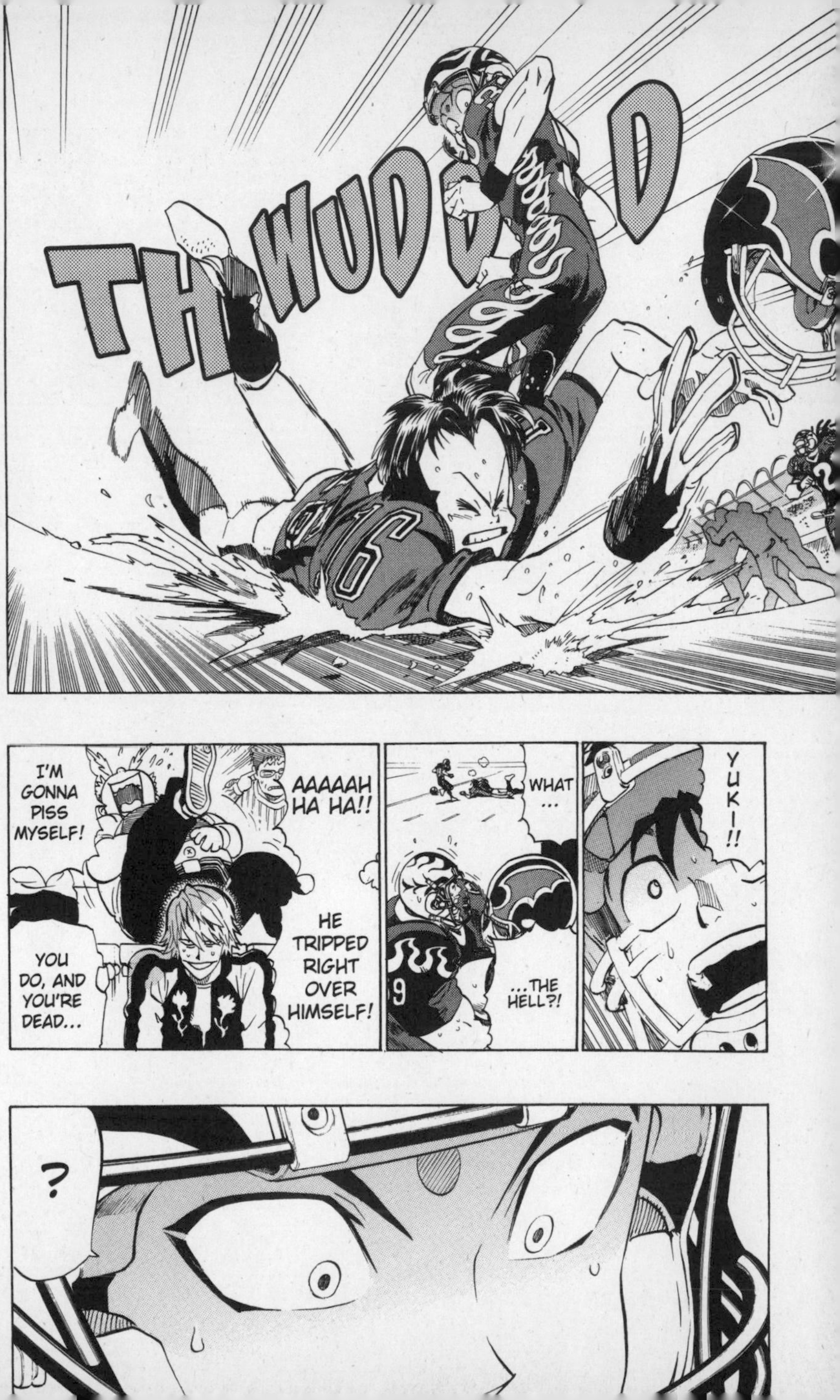
THWUD D
YUKI!!
WHAT...
...THE HELL?!
AAAAAH HA HA!!
I'M GONNA PISS MYSELF!
HE TRIPPED RIGHT OVER HIMSELF!
YOU DO, AND YOU'RE DEAD...
?

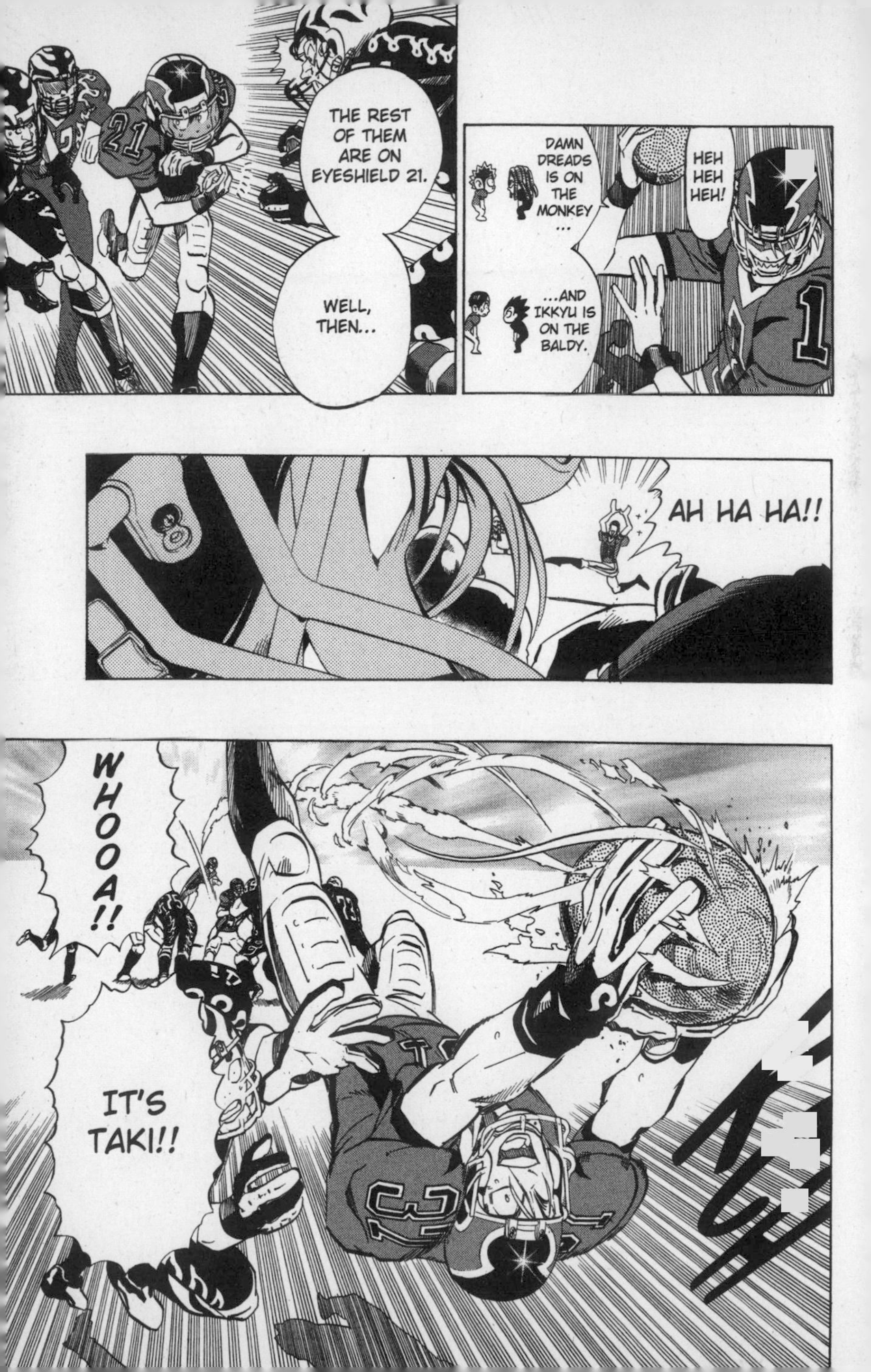
HEH HEH HEH!
DAMN DREADS IS ON THE MONKEY...
...AND IKKYU IS ON THE BALDY.
THE REST OF THEM ARE ON EYESHIELD 21.
WELL, THEN...
AH HA HA!!
WHOOOA!!
IT'S TAKI!!

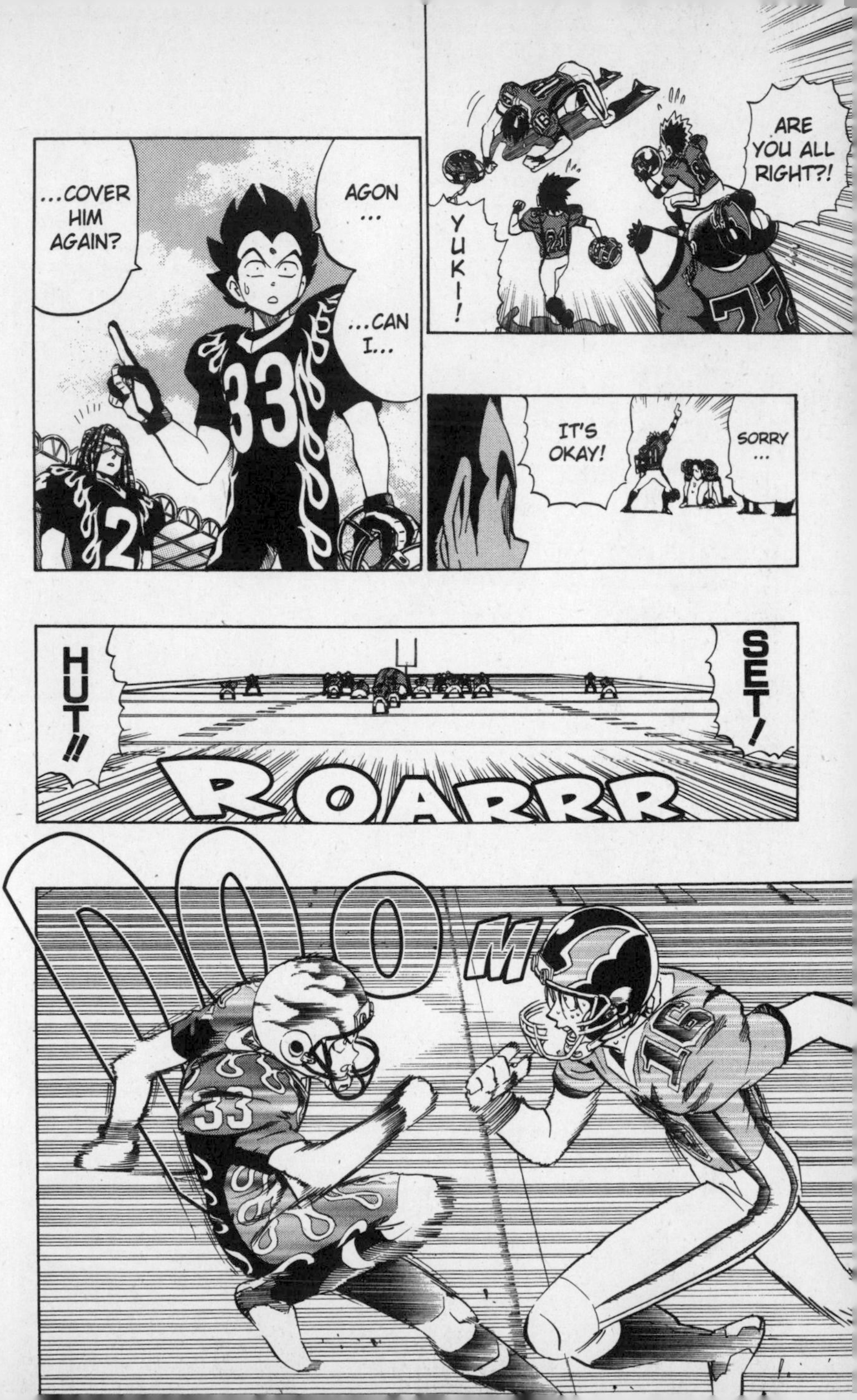
ARE YOU ALL RIGHT?!
YUKI!!
SORRY...
IT'S OKAY!
AGON...
...CAN I...
...COVER HIM AGAIN?
SET!
HUT!!
ROARRR
DOOOM

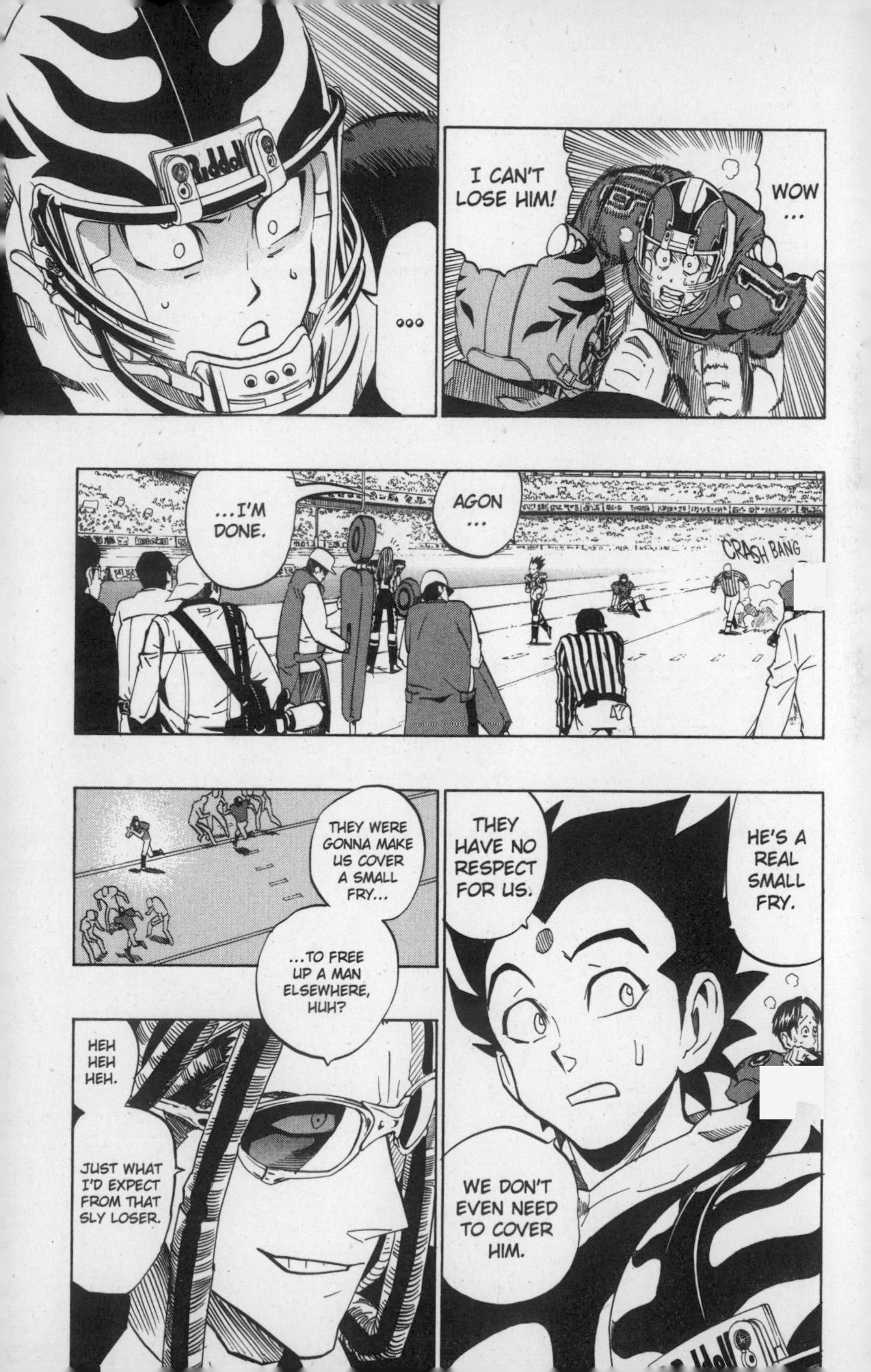
WOW ...
I CAN'T LOSE HIM!
CRASH BANG
AGON ...
...I'M DONE.
HE'S A REAL SMALL FRY.
THEY HAVE NO RESPECT FOR US.
WE DON'T EVEN NEED TO COVER HIM.
THEY WERE GONNA MAKE US COVER A SMALL FRY...
...TO FREE UP A MAN ELSEWHERE, HUH?
HEH HEH HEH.
JUST WHAT I'D EXPECT FROM THAT SLY LOSER.

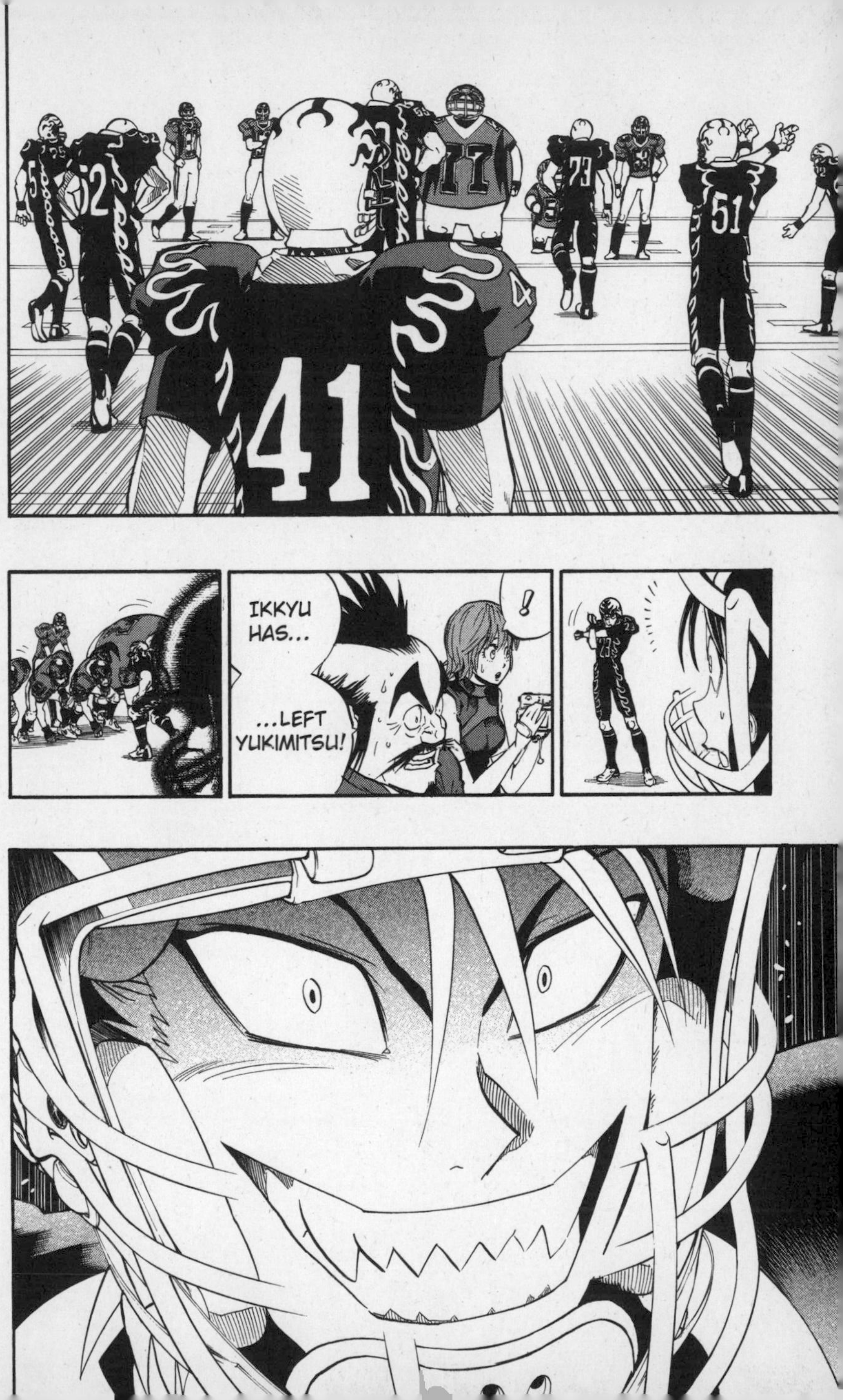
!
IKKYU HAS...
...LEFT YUKIMITSU!

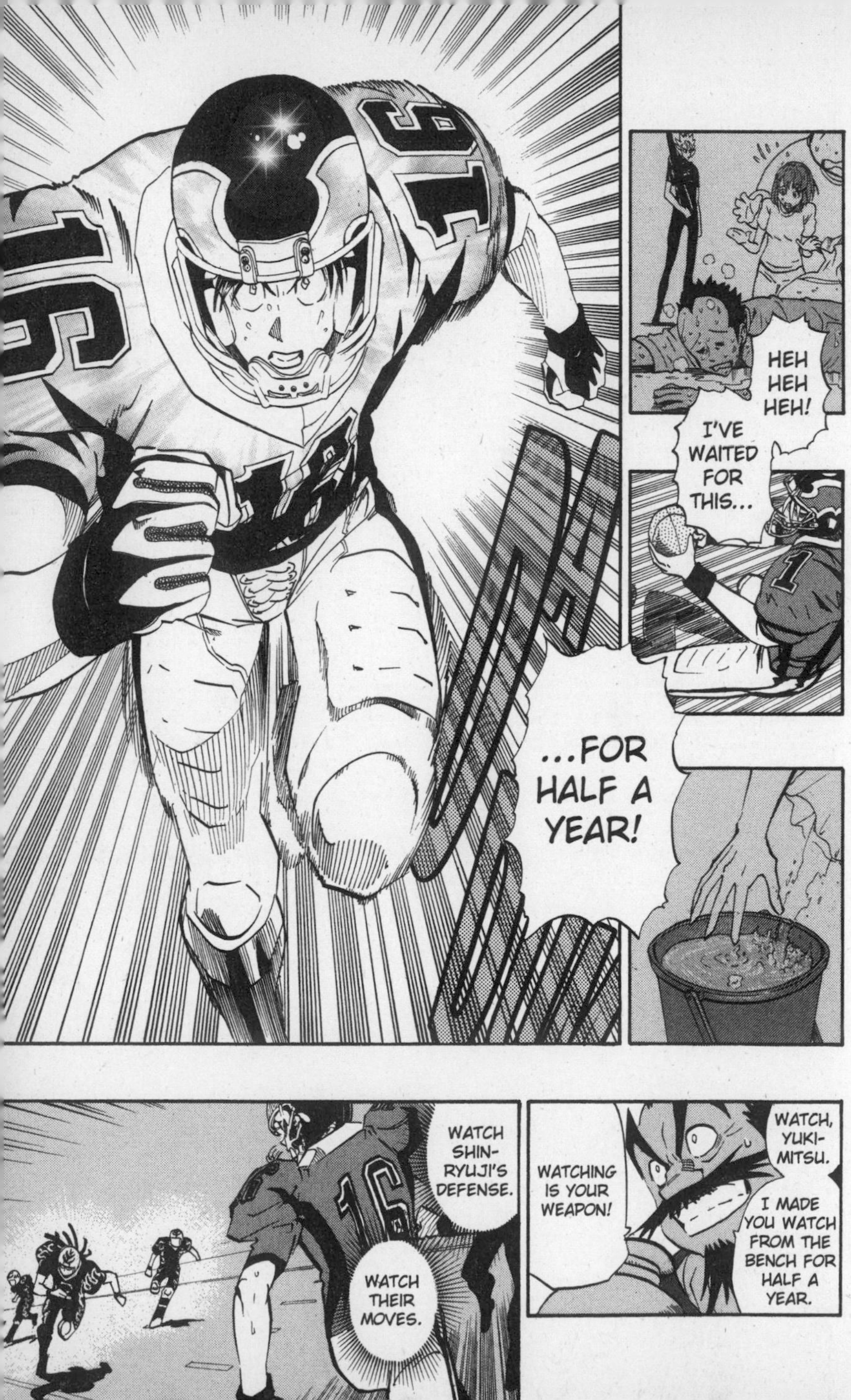
HEH HEH HEH!
I'VE WAITED FOR THIS...
...FOR HALF A YEAR!
WATCH, YUKI-MITSU.
I MADE YOU WATCH FROM THE BENCH FOR HALF A YEAR.
WATCHING IS YOUR WEAPON!
WATCH SHIN-RYUJI'S DEFENSE.
WATCH THEIR MOVES.

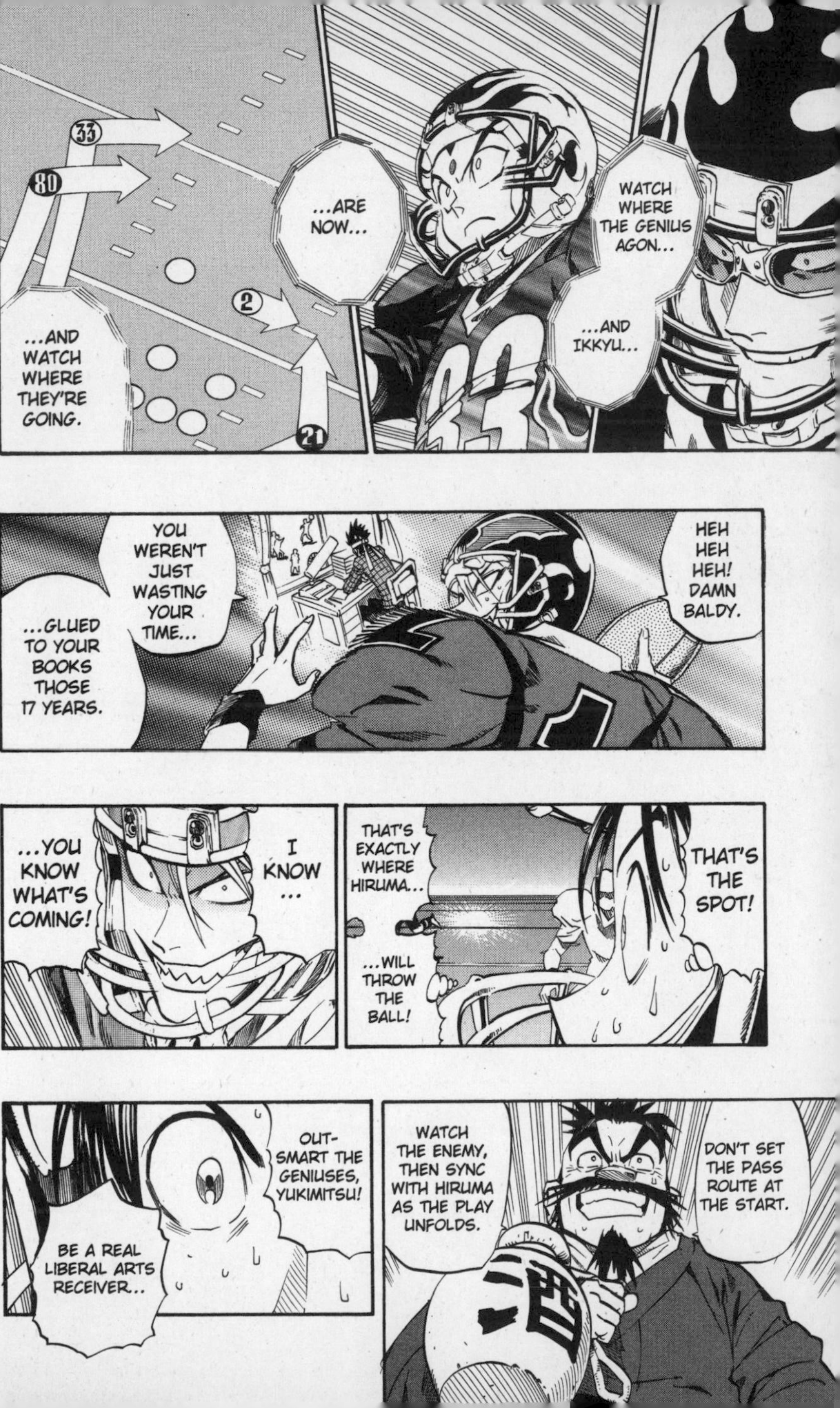
WATCH WHERE THE GENIUS AGON...
...AND IKKYU...
...ARE NOW...
33
80
2
21
...AND WATCH WHERE THEY'RE GOING.
HEH HEH HEH! DAMN BALDY.
YOU WEREN'T JUST WASTING YOUR TIME...
...GLUED TO YOUR BOOKS THOSE 17 YEARS.
THAT'S THE SPOT!
THAT'S EXACTLY WHERE HIRUMA...
...WILL THROW THE BALL!
I KNOW...
...YOU KNOW WHAT'S COMING!
DON'T SET THE PASS ROUTE AT THE START.
WATCH THE ENEMY, THEN SYNC WITH HIRUMA AS THE PLAY UNFOLDS.
OUT-SMART THE GENIUSES, YUKIMITSU!
BE A REAL LIBERAL ARTS RECEIVER...

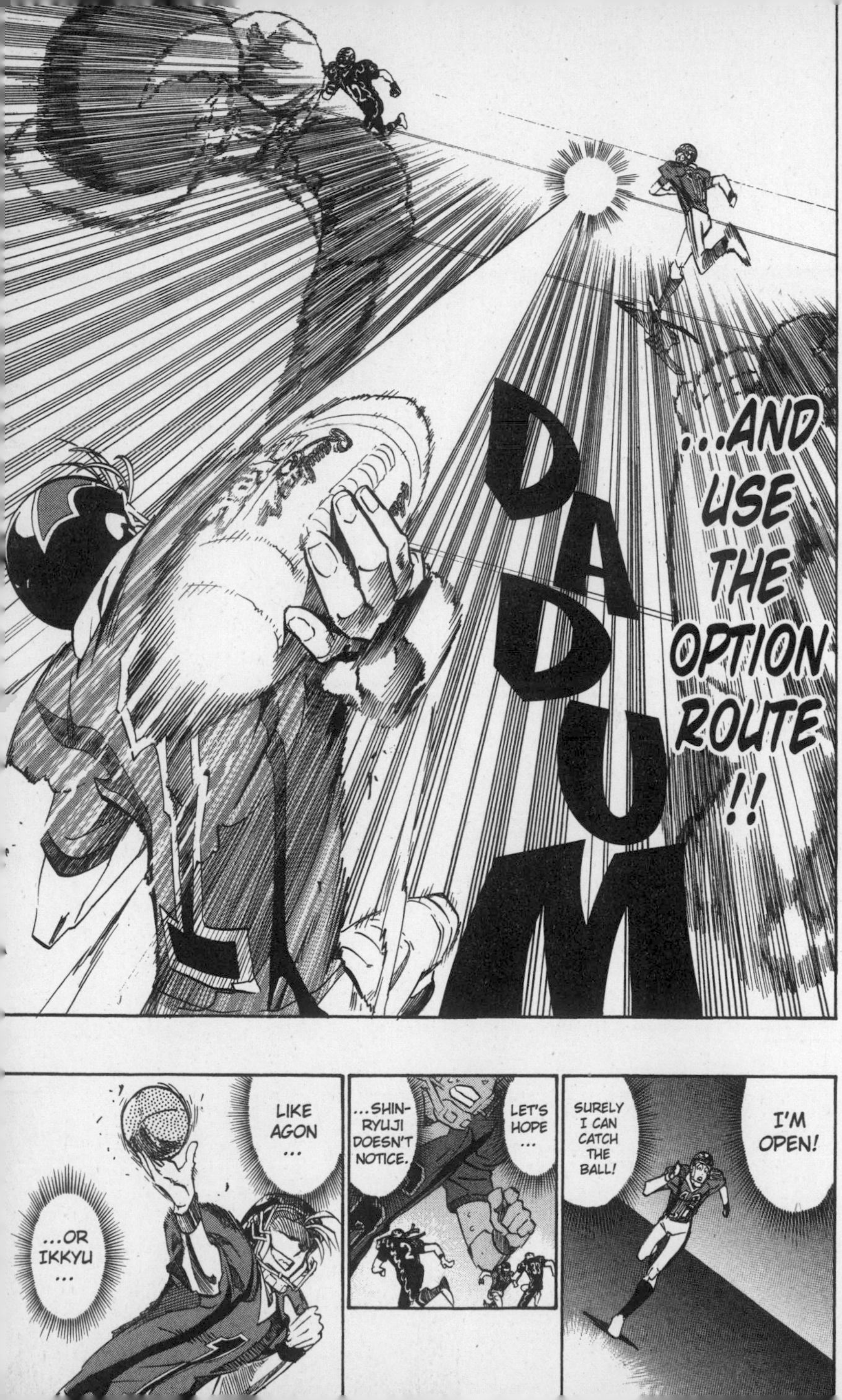
...AND USE THE OPTION ROUTE!!
DADUM
I'M OPEN!
SURELY I CAN CATCH THE BALL!
LET'S HOPE ...
...SHIN-RYUJI DOESN'T NOTICE.
LIKE AGON ...
...OR IKKYU ...

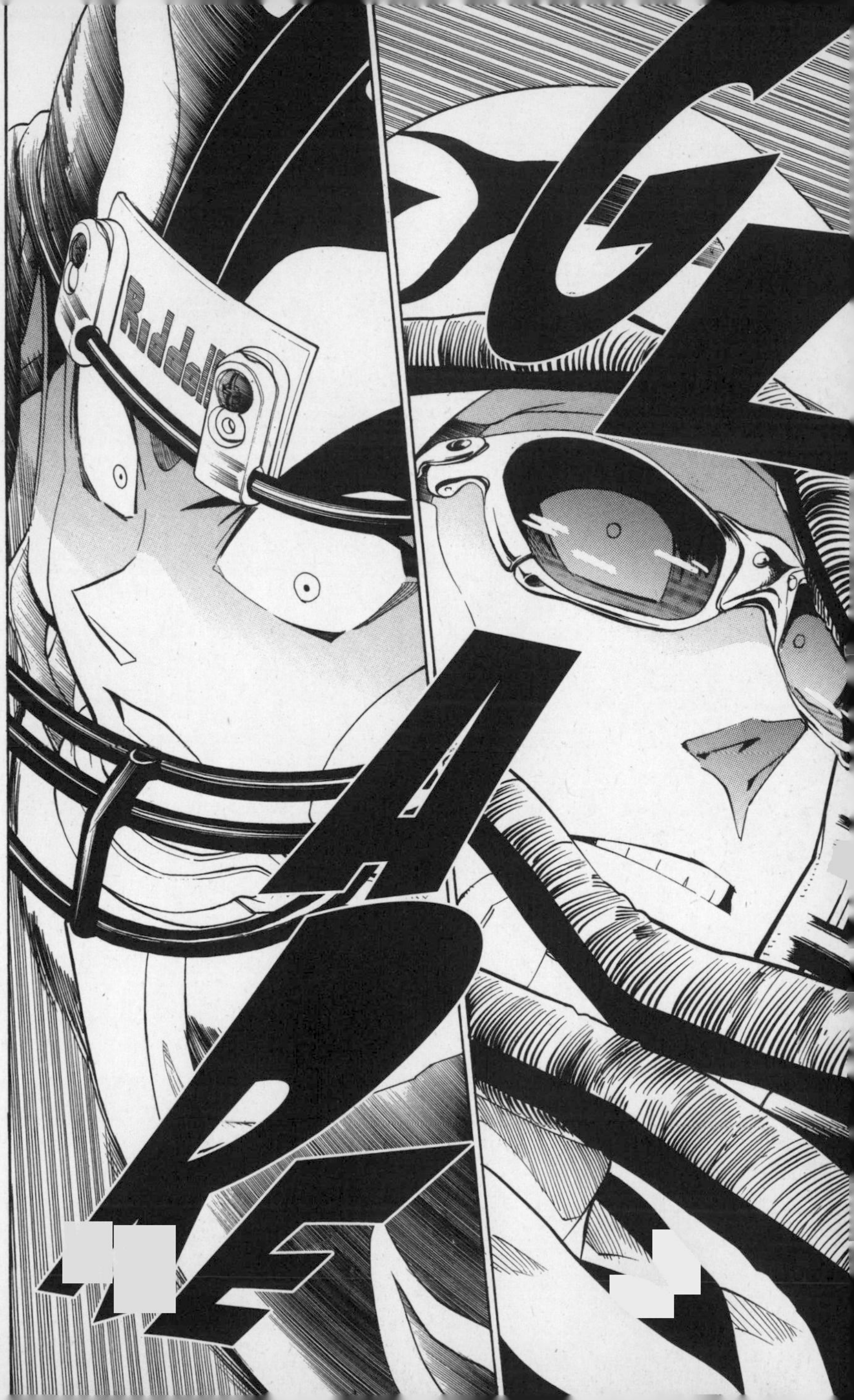

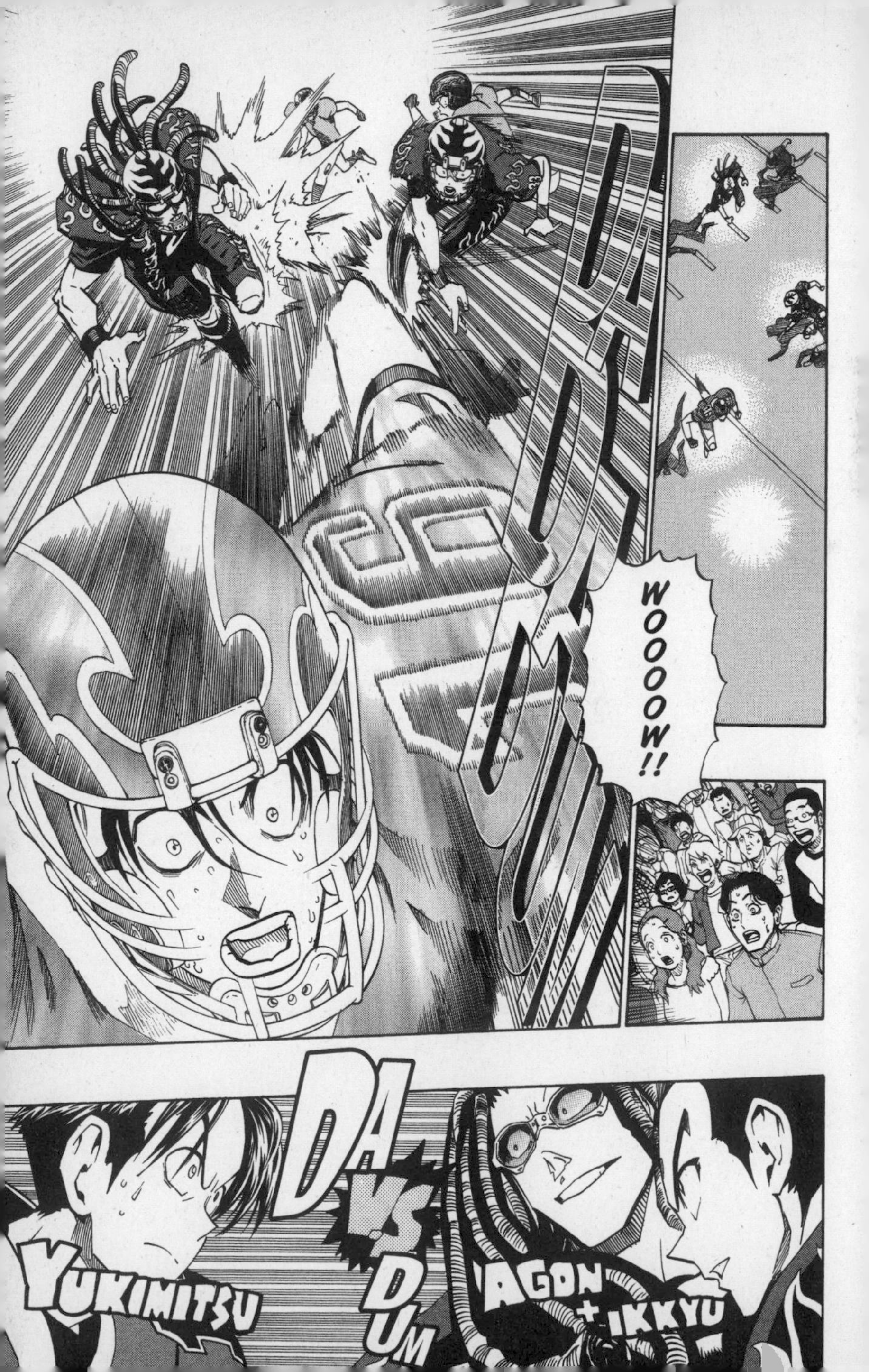
DADUM
WOOOOOW!!
DA VS. DUM
YUKIMITSU
AGON + IKKYU

Investigation File #070

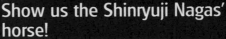

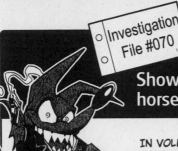

Show us the Shinryuji Nagas' horse!

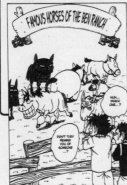

IN VOLUME 9, BEN'S RANCH HAD HORSES THAT LOOKED LIKE PLAYERS FROM EACH OF THE TEAMS. WHAT WOULD THE HORSES LOOK LIKE FOR THE SHINRYUJI NAGAS IF THEY WERE ON THE WEST COAST OF THE US?

FAMOUS HORSES OF THE BEN RANCH
HUH... WHICH ONE...?
DON'T THEY REMIND YOU OF SOMEONE ...?

Caller

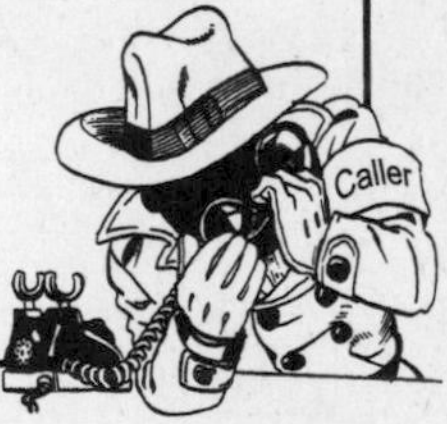

T. M., Akita Prefecture

NEIGH

SHOCK

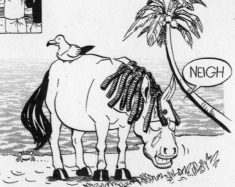

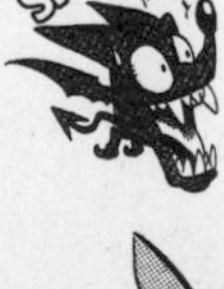

IT LOOKS LIKE SEVERAL PLAYERS MIXED TOGETHER!

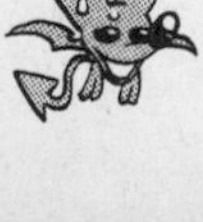

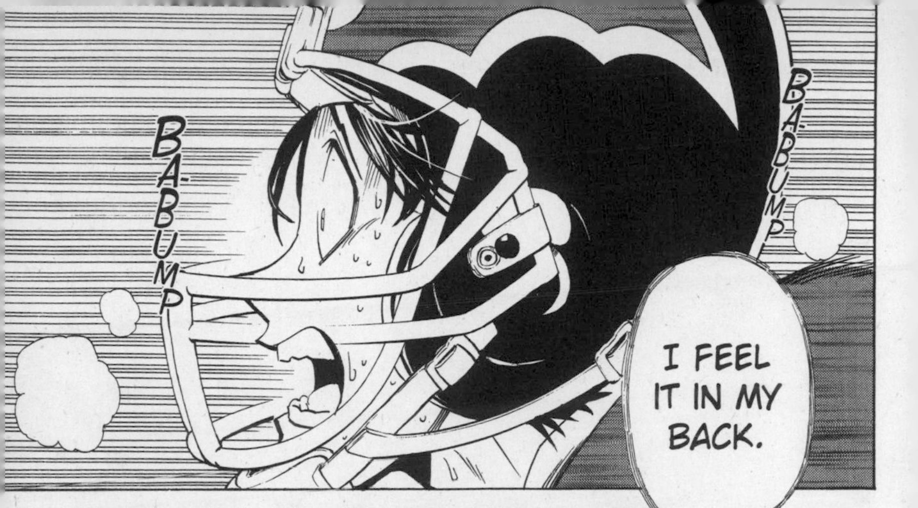
BA-BABUMP
I FEEL IT IN MY BACK.
BA-BABUMP

Chapter 181 The Power of Mediocrity

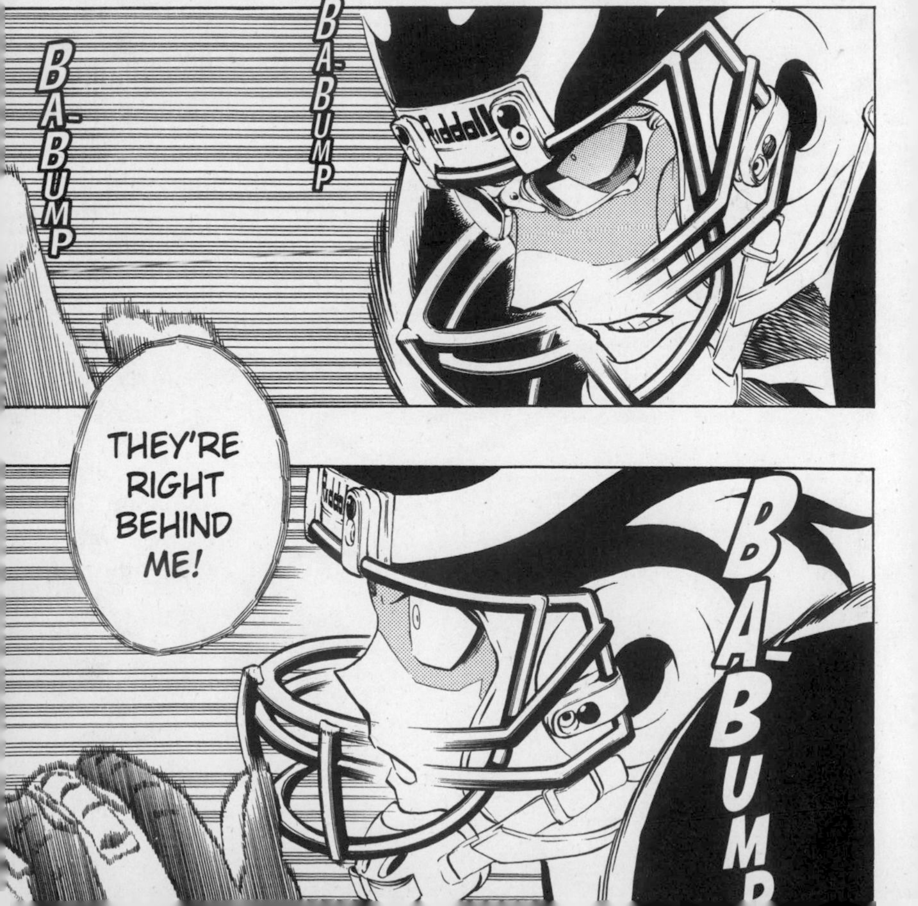
BA-BABUMP
BA-BABUMP
BA-BABUMP
THEY'RE RIGHT BEHIND ME!

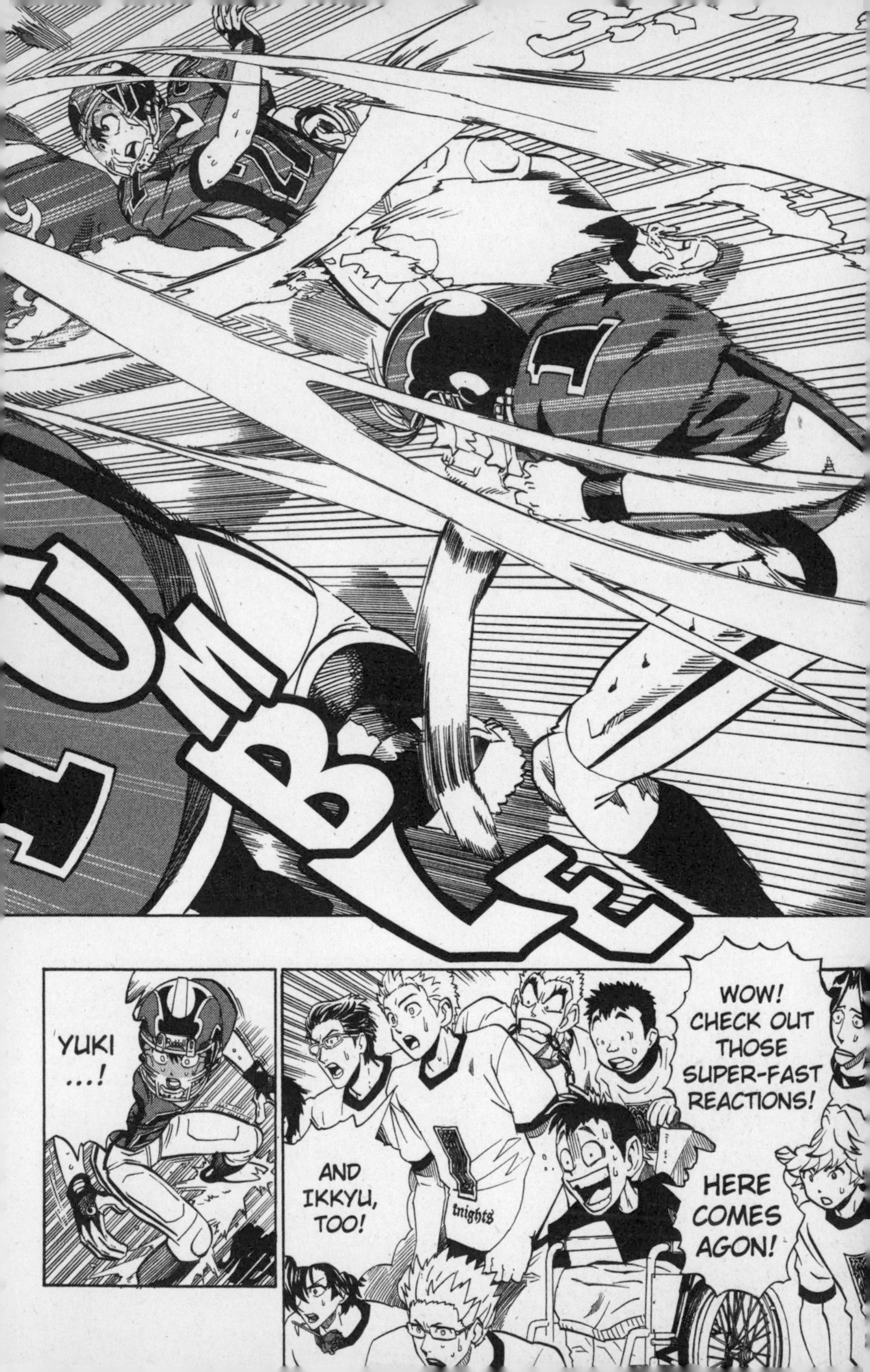
UMBLE
WOW! CHECK OUT THOSE SUPER-FAST REACTIONS!
HERE COMES AGON!
AND IKKYU, TOO!
YUKI ...!

Chapter 181 The Power of Mediocrity

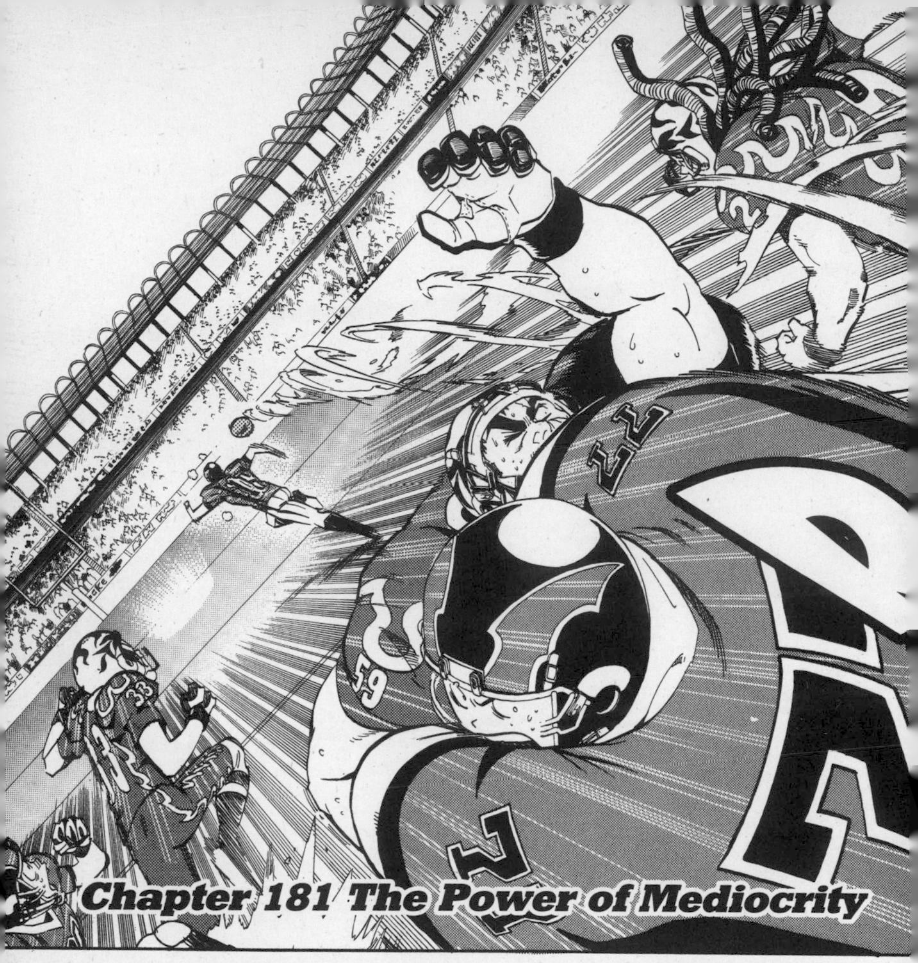

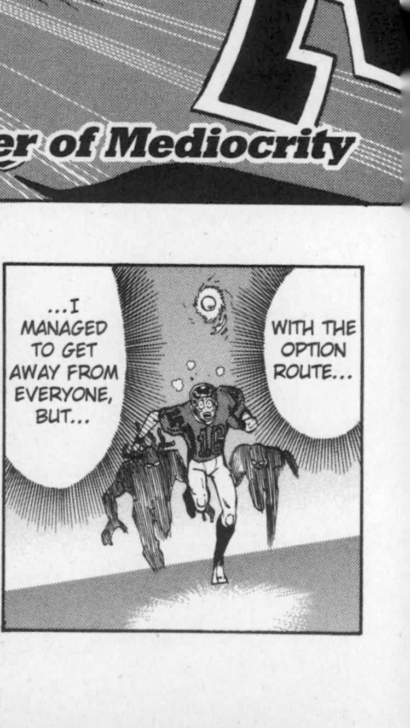
WITH THE OPTION ROUTE...
...I MANAGED TO GET AWAY FROM EVERYONE, BUT...

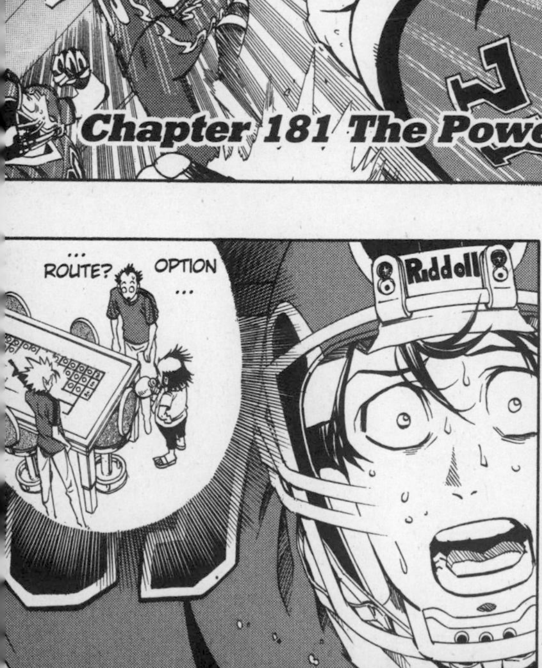
OPTION ...
... ROUTE?
Riddoll

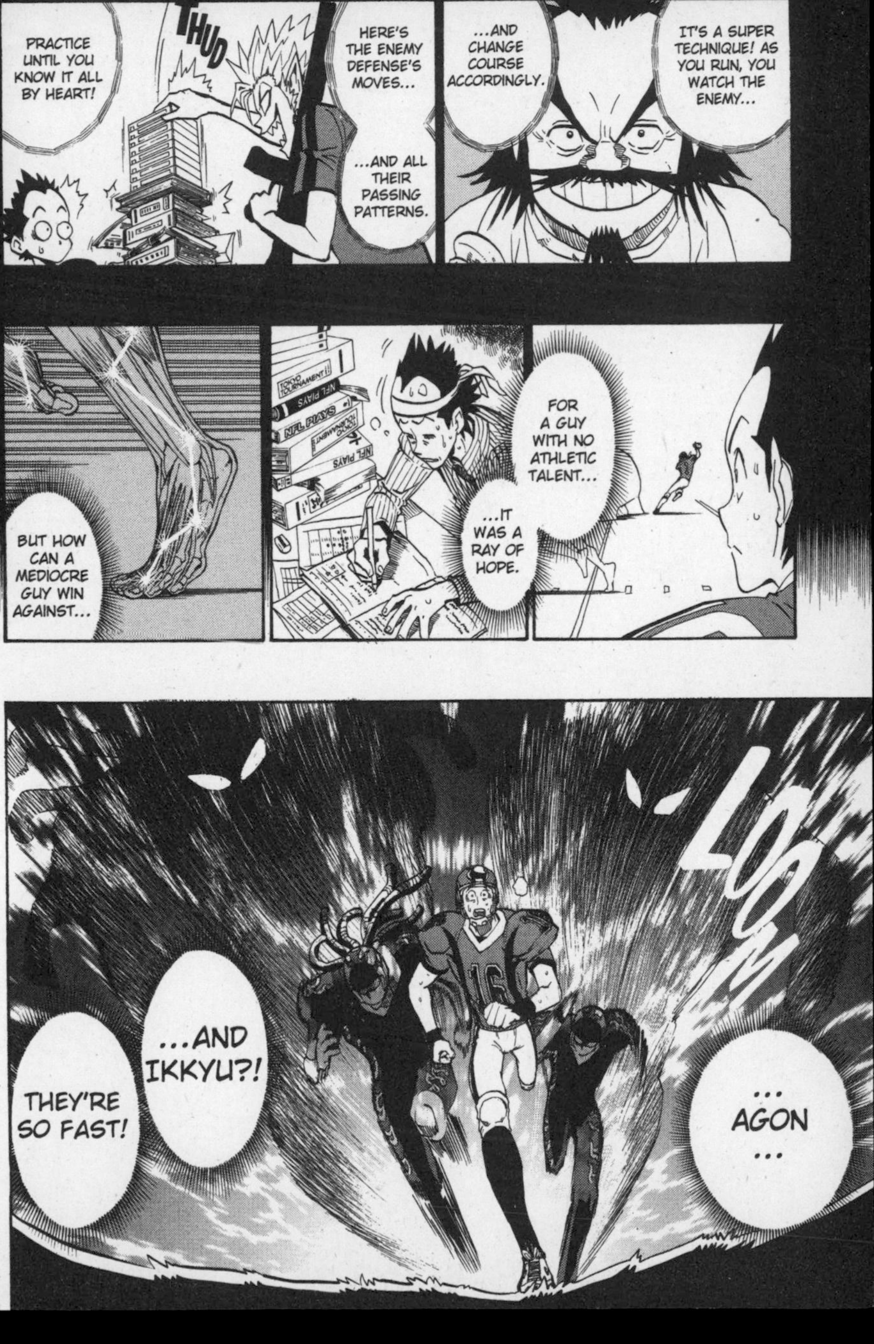
IT'S A SUPER TECHNIQUE! AS YOU RUN, YOU WATCH THE ENEMY...
...AND CHANGE COURSE ACCORDINGLY.
HERE'S THE ENEMY DEFENSE'S MOVES...
...AND ALL THEIR PASSING PATTERNS.
THUD
PRACTICE UNTIL YOU KNOW IT ALL BY HEART!
FOR A GUY WITH NO ATHLETIC TALENT...
...IT WAS A RAY OF HOPE.
BUT HOW CAN A MEDIOCRE GUY WIN AGAINST...
LOOM
...AGON...
...AND IKKYU?!
THEY'RE SO FAST!

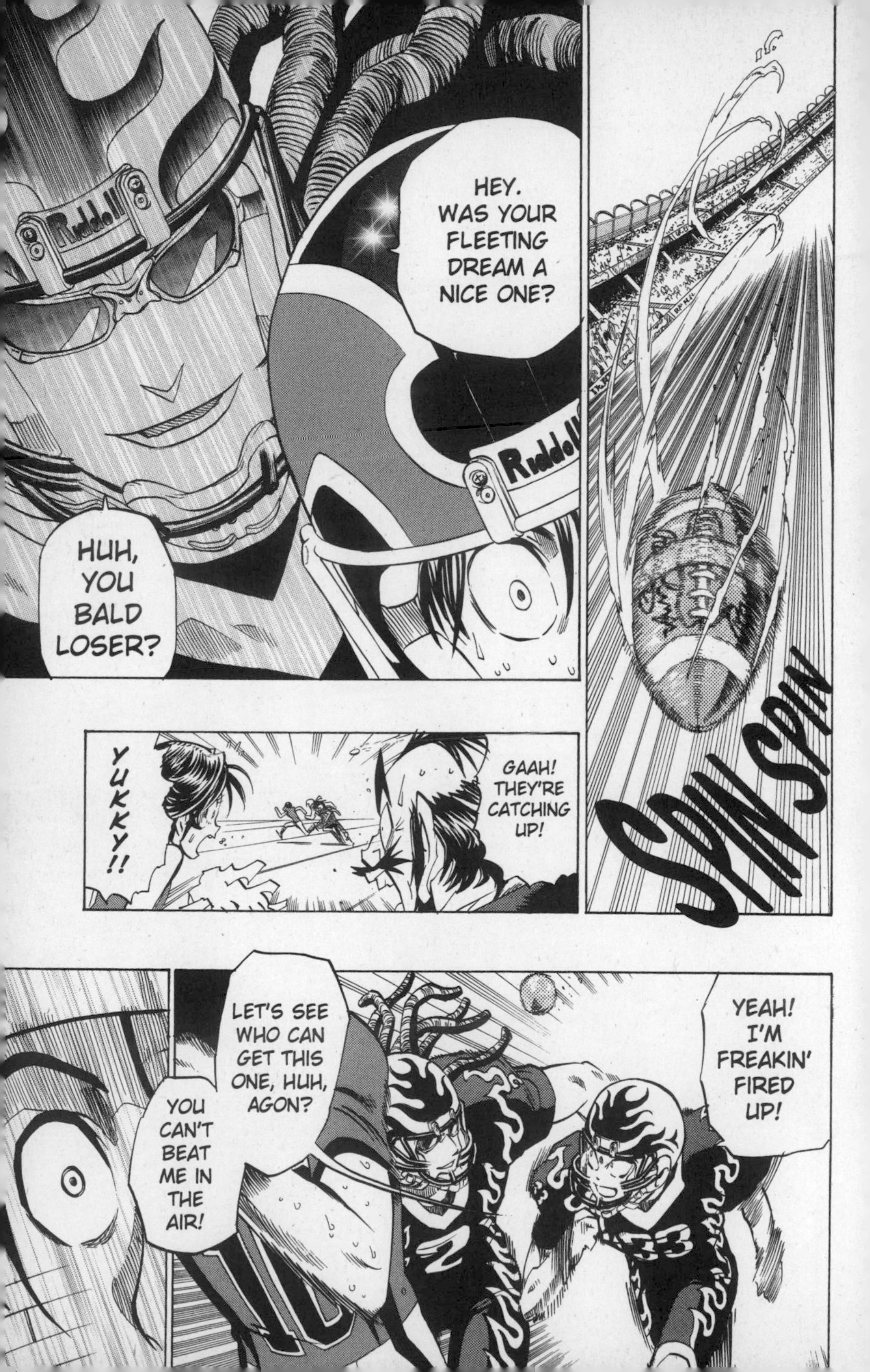
SPIN SPIN
HEY. WAS YOUR FLEETING DREAM A NICE ONE?
HUH, YOU BALD LOSER?
GAAH! THEY'RE CATCHING UP!
YUKKY!!
YEAH! I'M FREAKIN' FIRED UP!
LET'S SEE WHO CAN GET THIS ONE, HUH, AGON?
YOU CAN'T BEAT ME IN THE AIR!

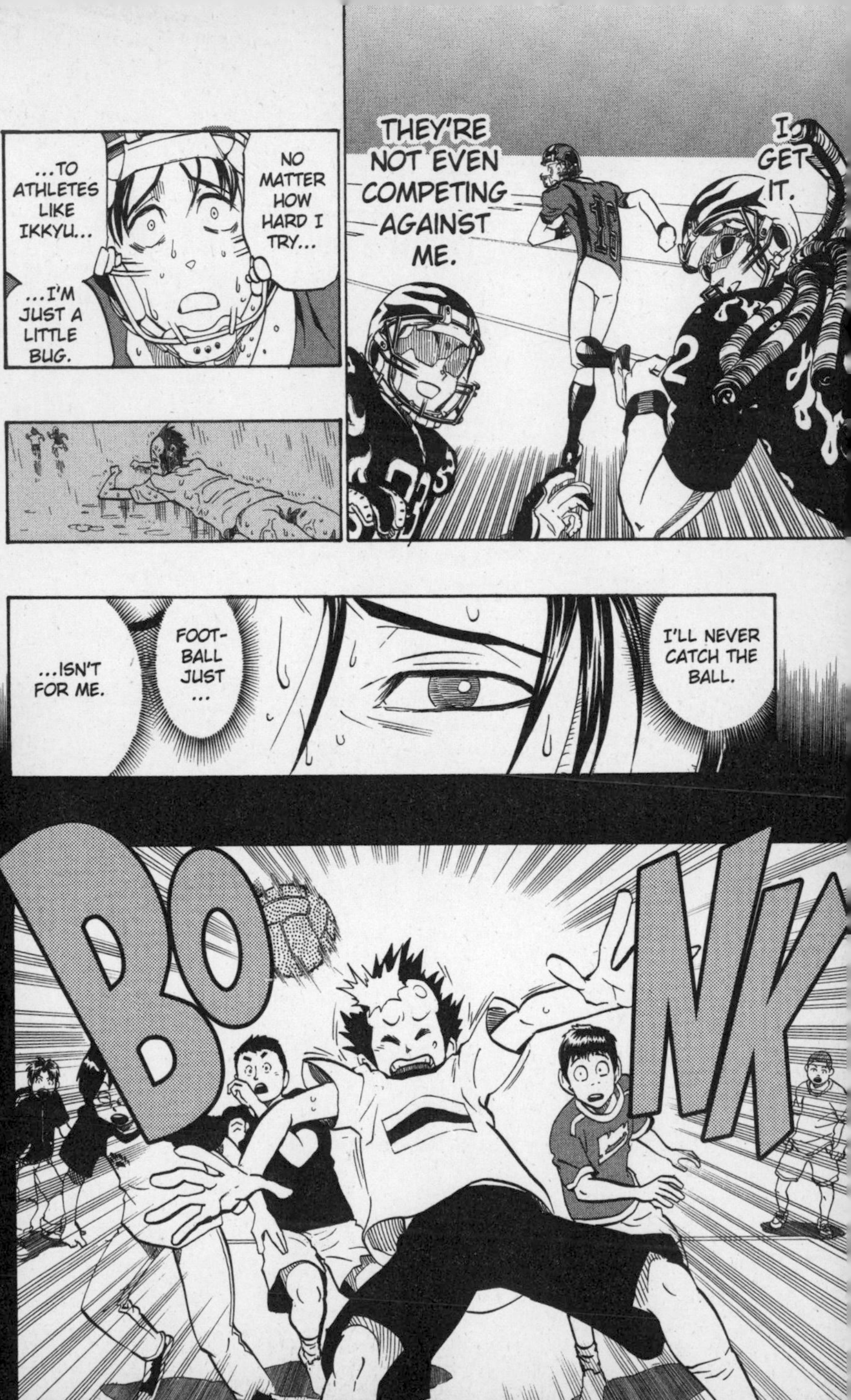
I GET IT.
THEY'RE NOT EVEN COMPETING AGAINST ME.
NO MATTER HOW HARD I TRY...
...TO ATHLETES LIKE IKKYU...
...I'M JUST A LITTLE BUG.
I'LL NEVER CATCH THE BALL.
FOOT-BALL JUST ...
...ISN'T FOR ME.
BONK

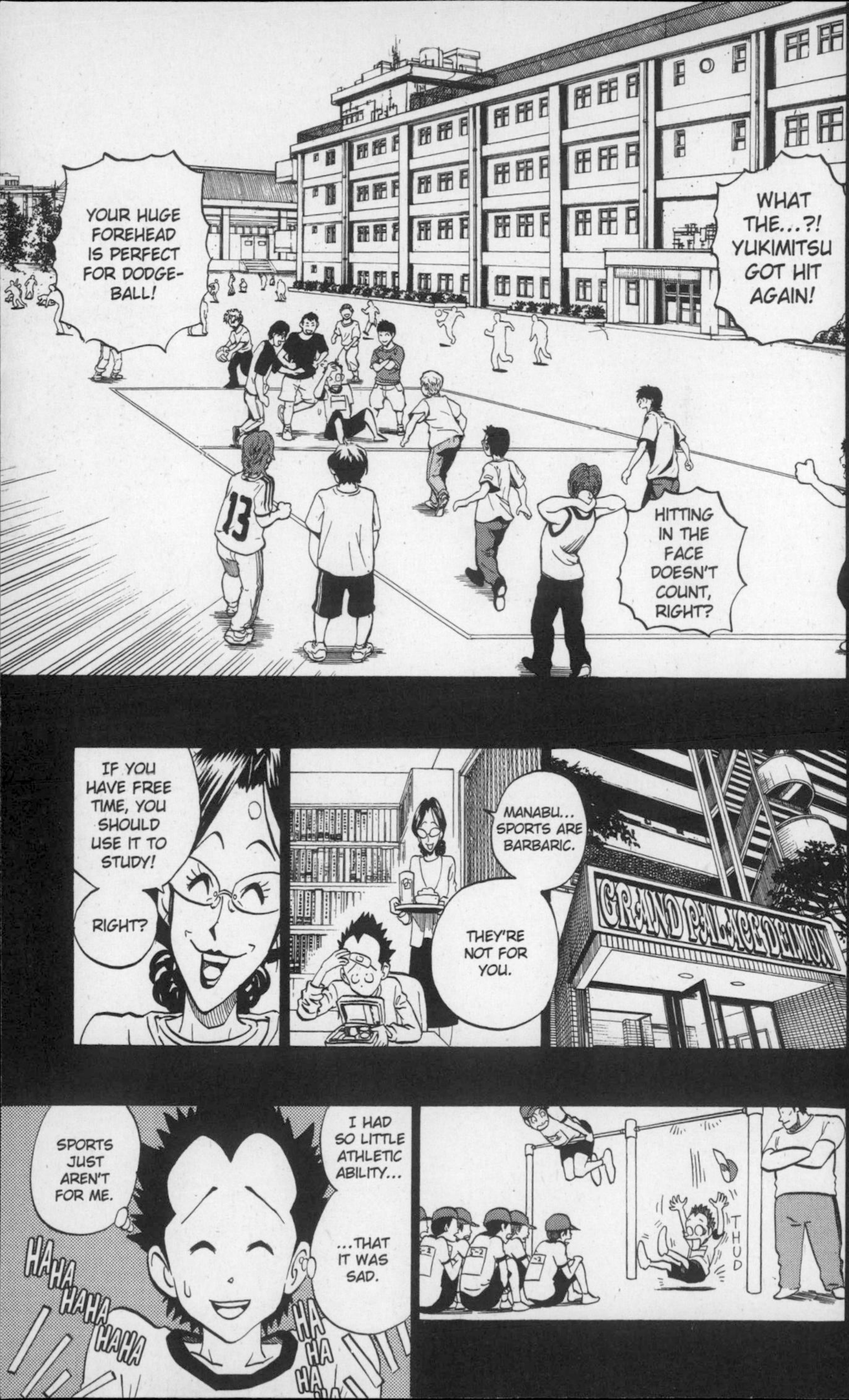
WHAT THE...?! YUKIMITSU GOT HIT AGAIN!
YOUR HUGE FOREHEAD IS PERFECT FOR DODGE-BALL!
HITTING IN THE FACE DOESN'T COUNT, RIGHT?
GRAND PALACE DEIMON
MANABU... SPORTS ARE BARBARIC.
THEY'RE NOT FOR YOU.
IF YOU HAVE FREE TIME, YOU SHOULD USE IT TO STUDY!
RIGHT?
THUD
I HAD SO LITTLE ATHLETIC ABILITY...
...THAT IT WAS SAD.
SPORTS JUST AREN'T FOR ME.
HAHA HAHA HAHA
HA HA HA HA

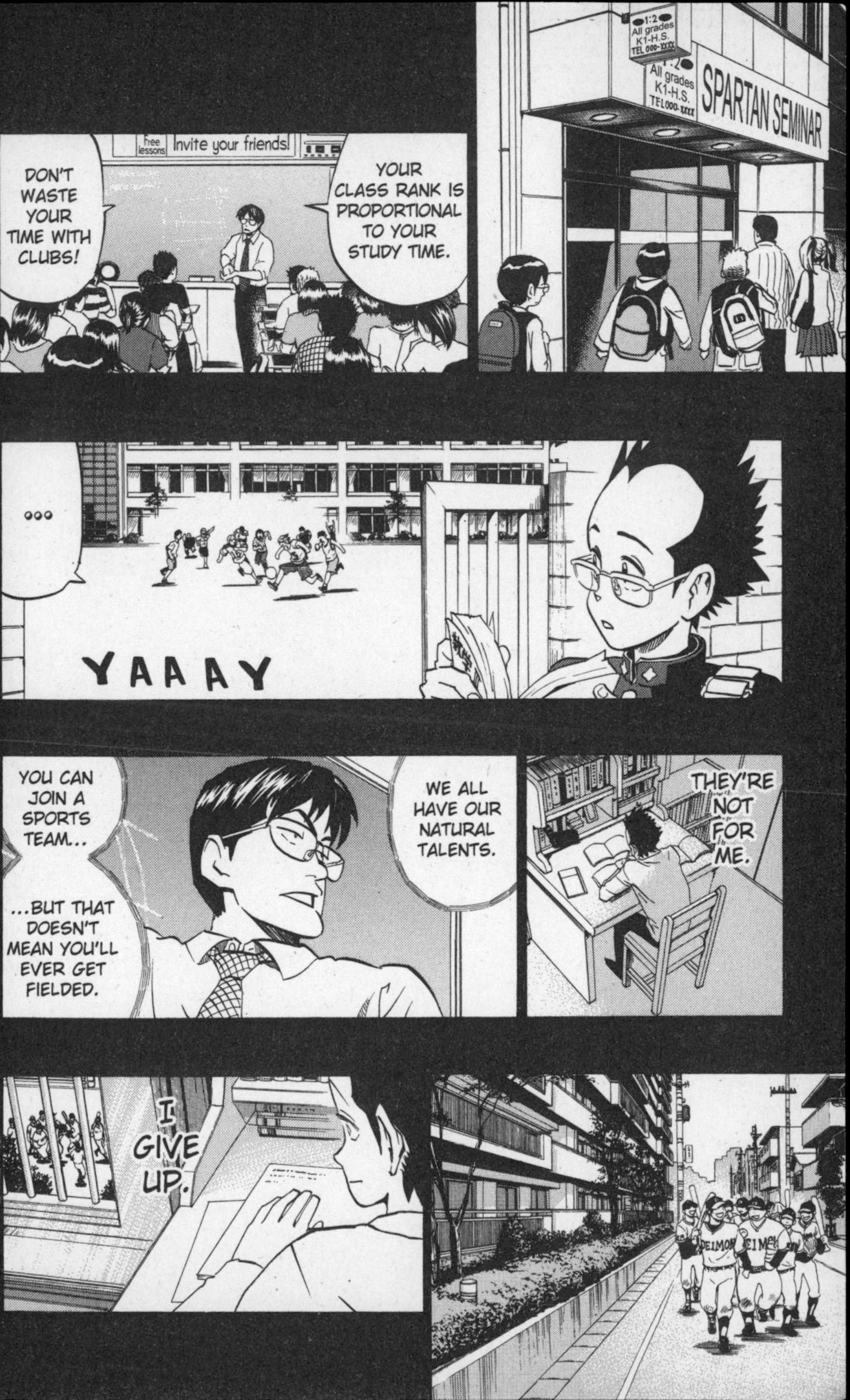

1:2
All grades
K1-H.S.
TEL 000-XXXX
1:2
All grades
K1-H.S.
TEL 000-XXXX
SPARTAN SEMINAR
Free lessons
Invite your friends!
YOUR CLASS RANK IS PROPORTIONAL TO YOUR STUDY TIME.
DON'T WASTE YOUR TIME WITH CLUBS!
...
YAAAY
THEY'RE NOT FOR ME.
WE ALL HAVE OUR NATURAL TALENTS.
YOU CAN JOIN A SPORTS TEAM...
...BUT THAT DOESN'T MEAN YOU'LL EVER GET FIELDED.
DEIMON
I GIVE UP.

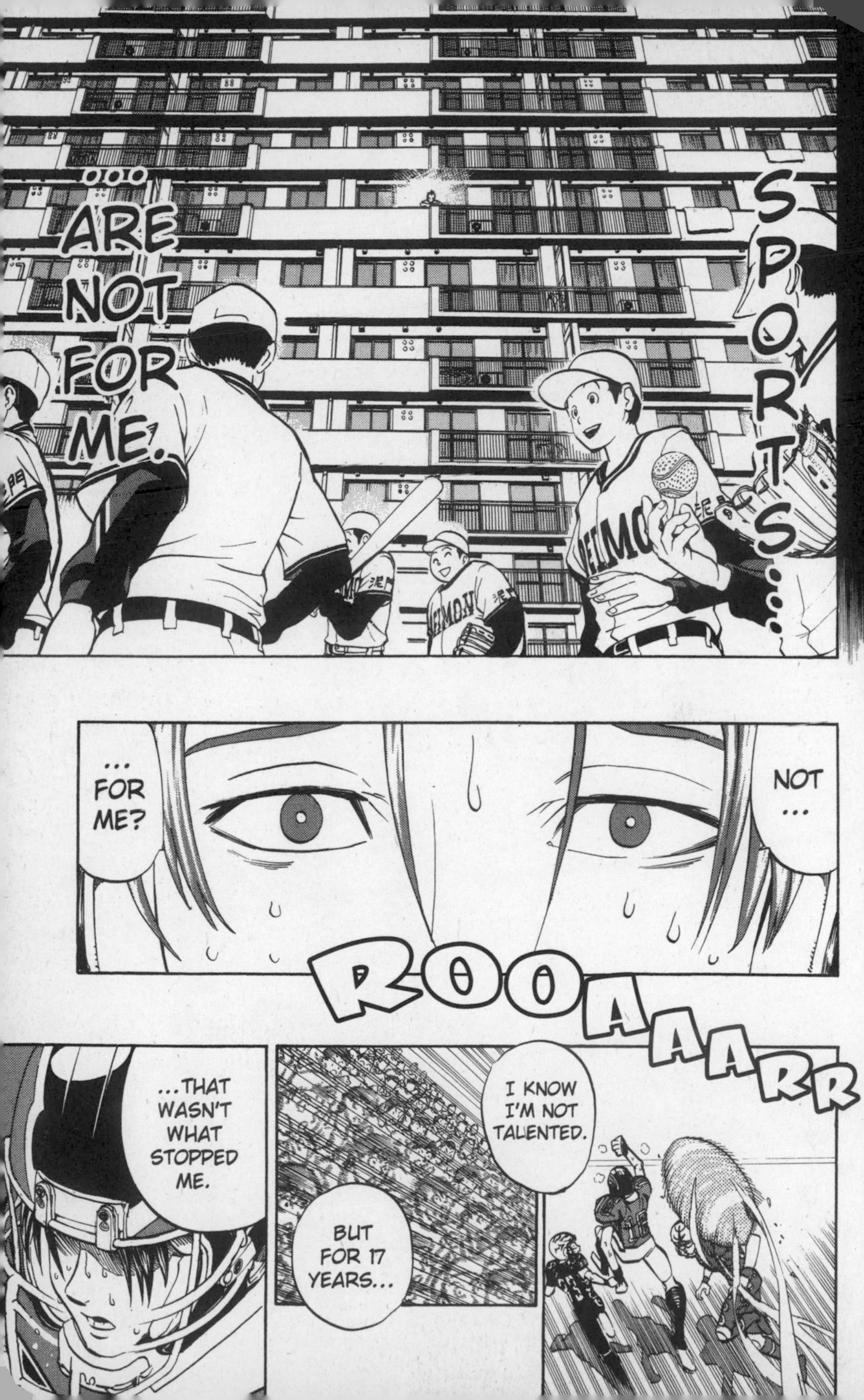
SPORTS...
...ARE NOT FOR ME.
NOT...
...FOR ME?
ROOOAAAARR
I KNOW I'M NOT TALENTED.
BUT FOR 17 YEARS...
...THAT WASN'T WHAT STOPPED ME.

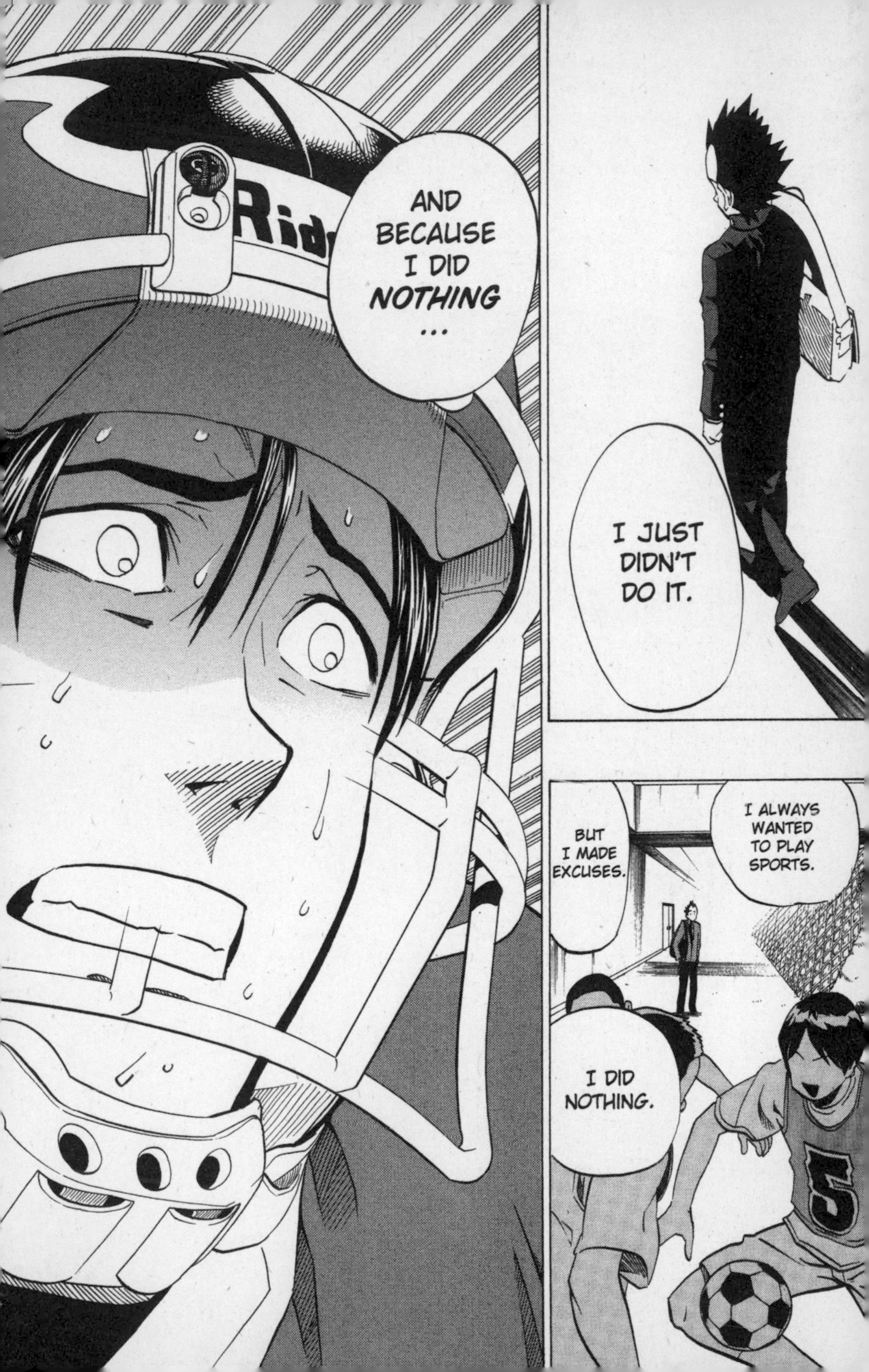
I JUST DIDN'T DO IT.
I ALWAYS WANTED TO PLAY SPORTS.
BUT I MADE EXCUSES.
I DID NOTHING.
AND BECAUSE I DID *NOTHING* ...

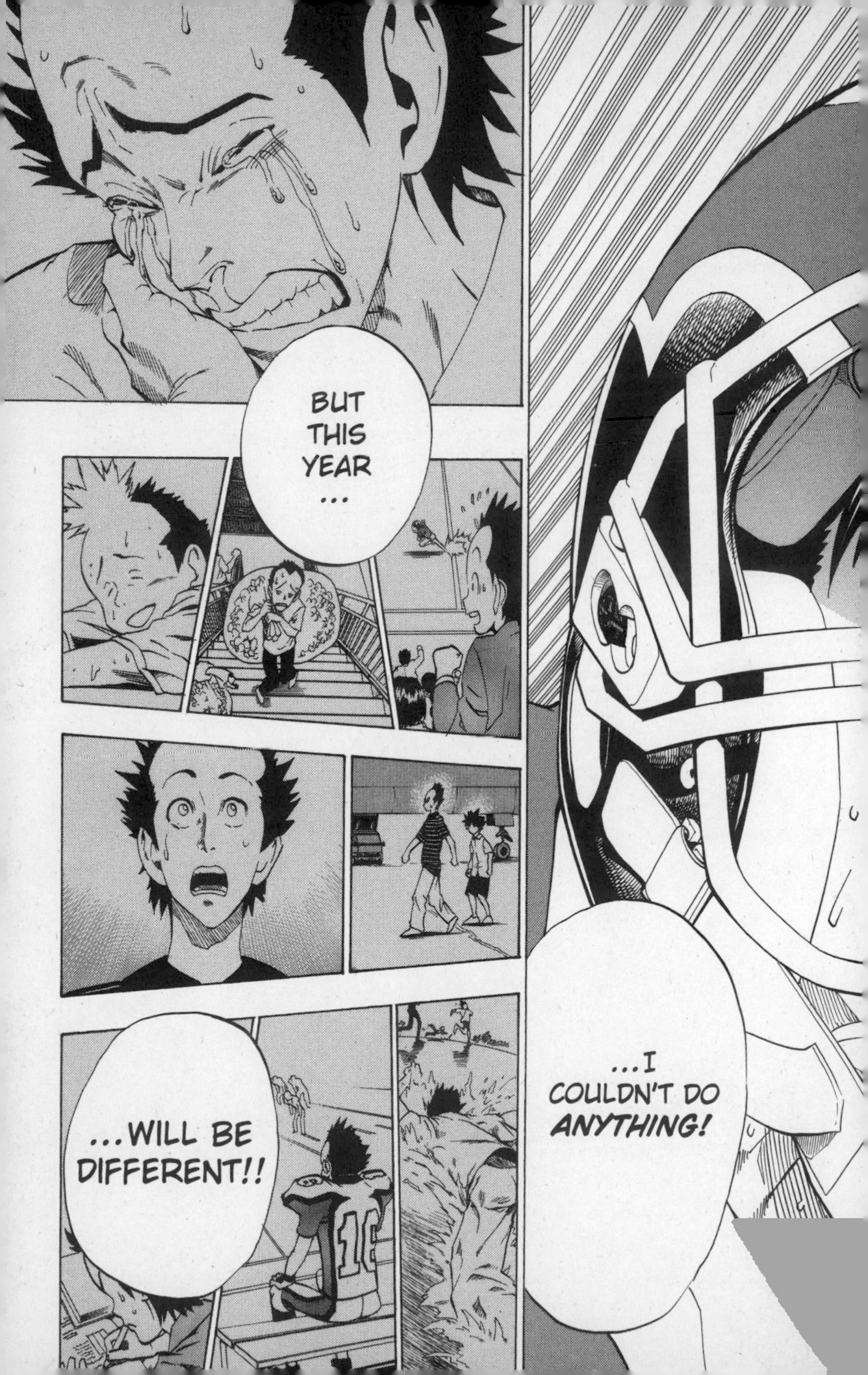
...I COULDN'T DO *ANYTHING!*
BUT THIS YEAR...
...WILL BE DIFFERENT!!

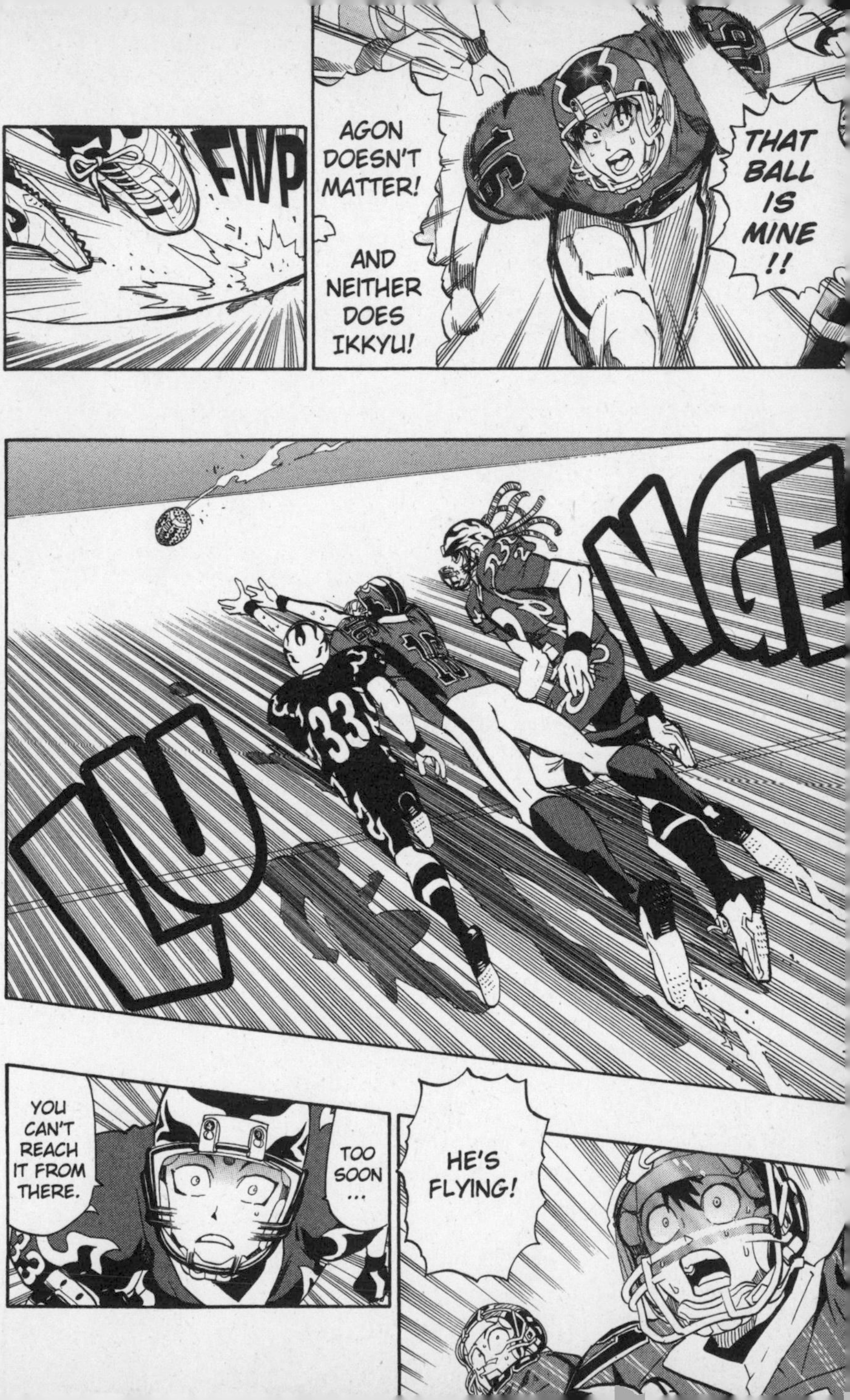
THAT BALL IS MINE!!
AGON DOESN'T MATTER!
AND NEITHER DOES IKKYU!
FWP
LUNGE
HE'S FLYING!
TOO SOON...
YOU CAN'T REACH IT FROM THERE.

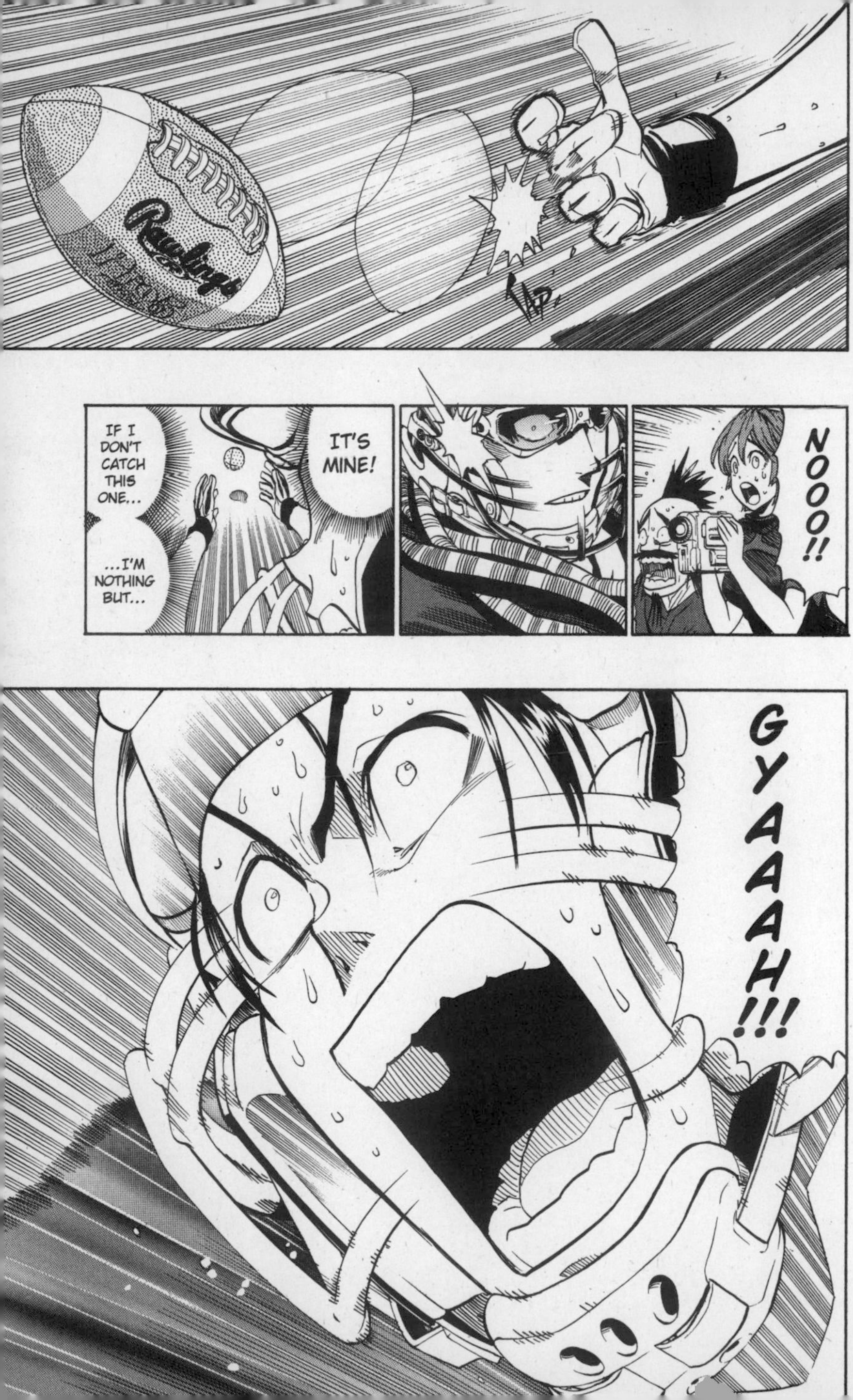
NOOOO!!
IT'S MINE!
IF I DON'T CATCH THIS ONE...
...I'M NOTHING BUT...
GYAAAAH!!!

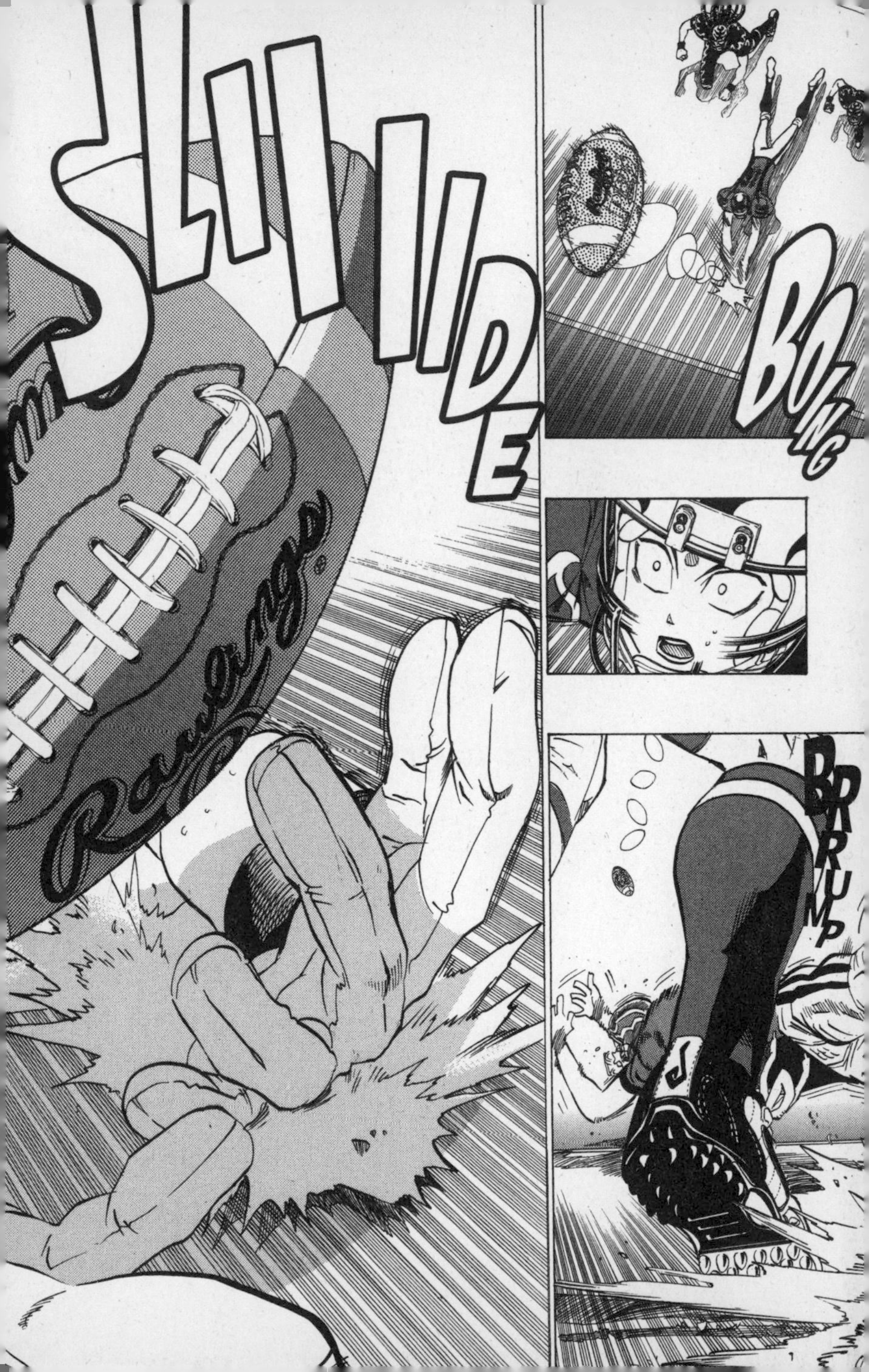
BOING
BRRUMP
SLIIIIDE
Rawlings

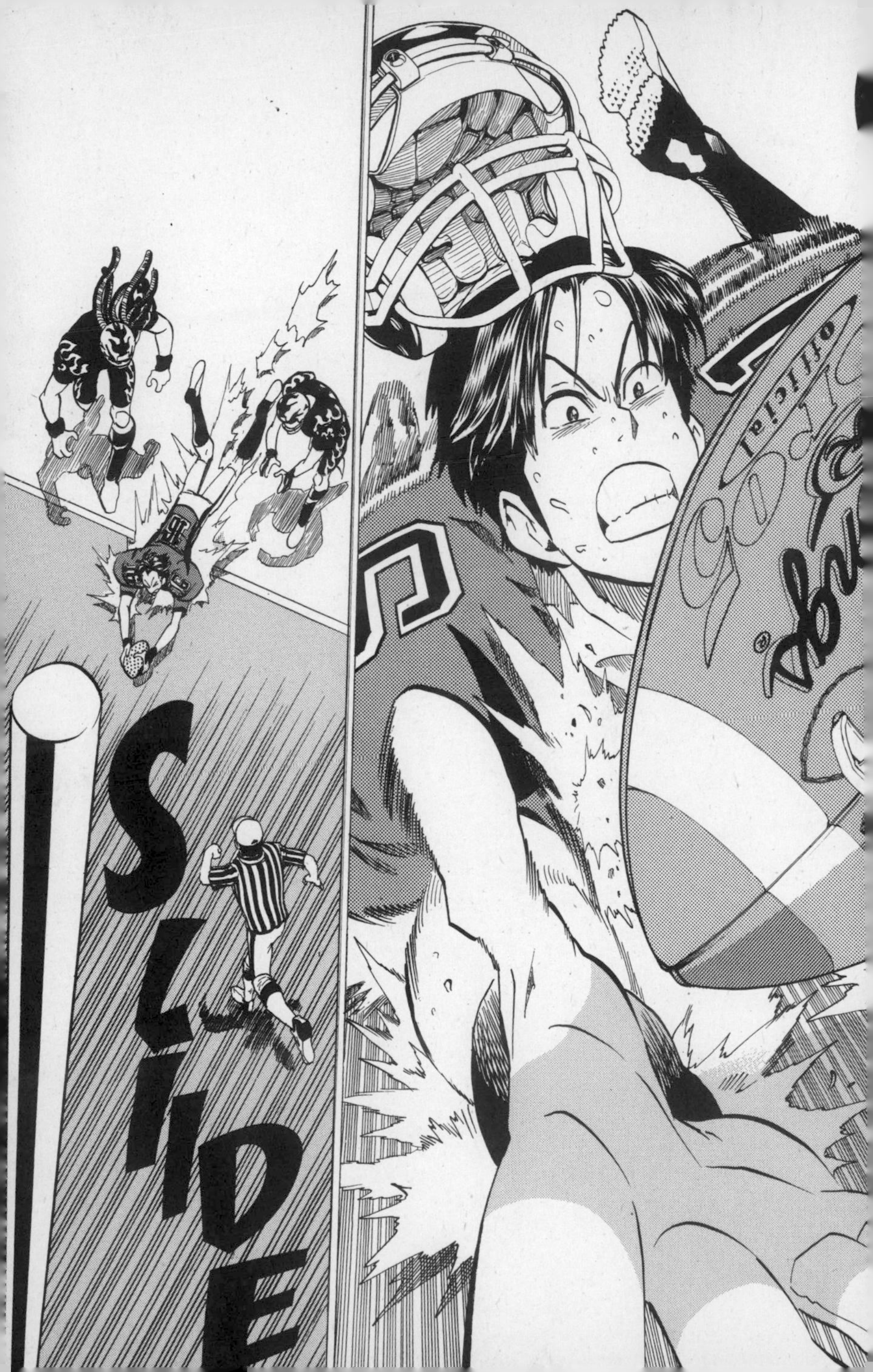
official
SLIDE

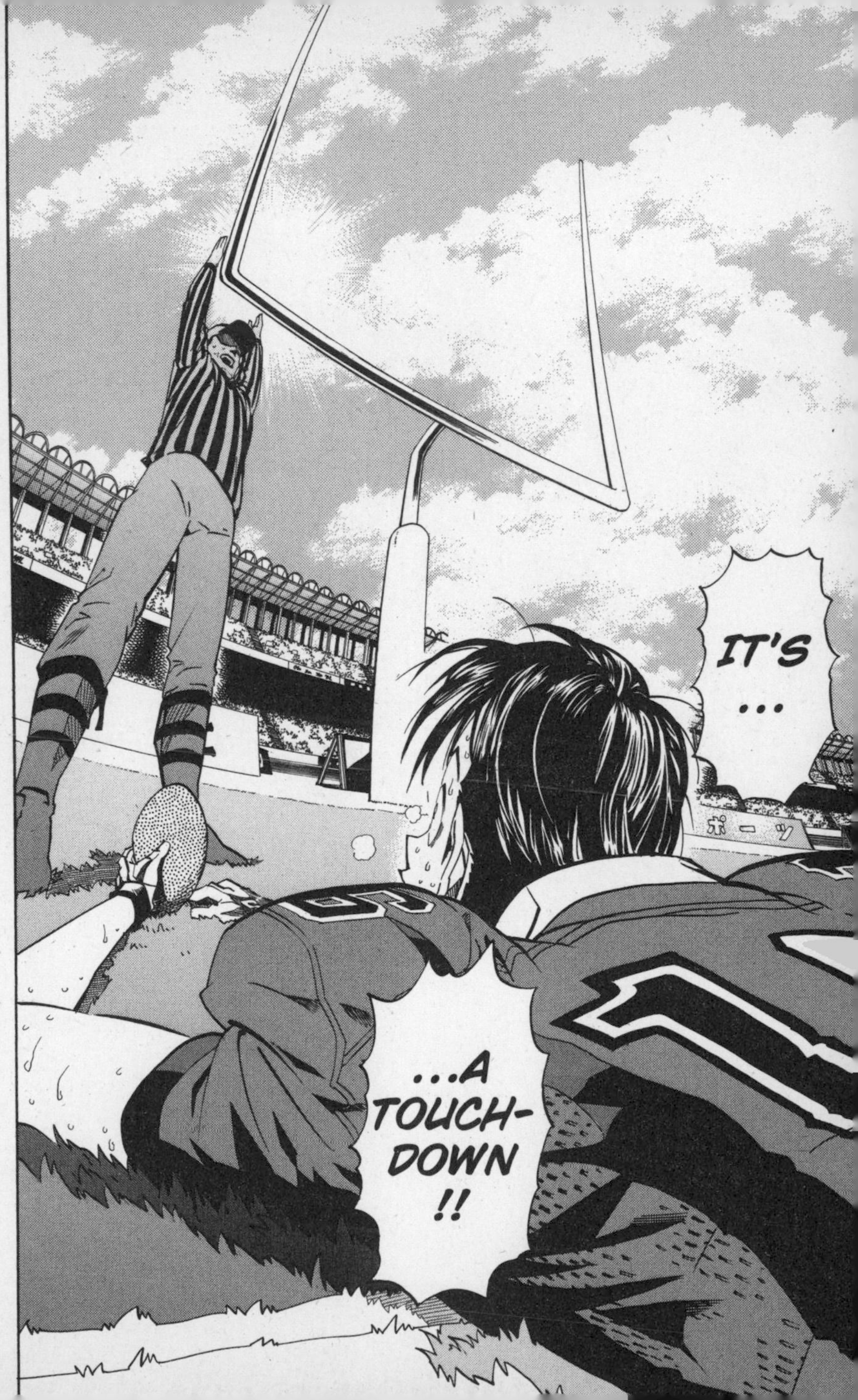
IT'S ...
...A TOUCH-DOWN!!
ポーツ

DEVIL BATS 0 0 0 32 [3]

PB BS 16 16 0

DEVIL BATS 6

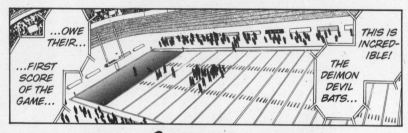

THIS IS INCREDIBLE!

...OWE THEIR...

THE DEIMON DEVIL BATS...

...FIRST SCORE OF THE GAME...

YAAAy

YEAAH!!

...TO THE SECRET WARRIOR...

...MANABU YUKI-MITSU!!

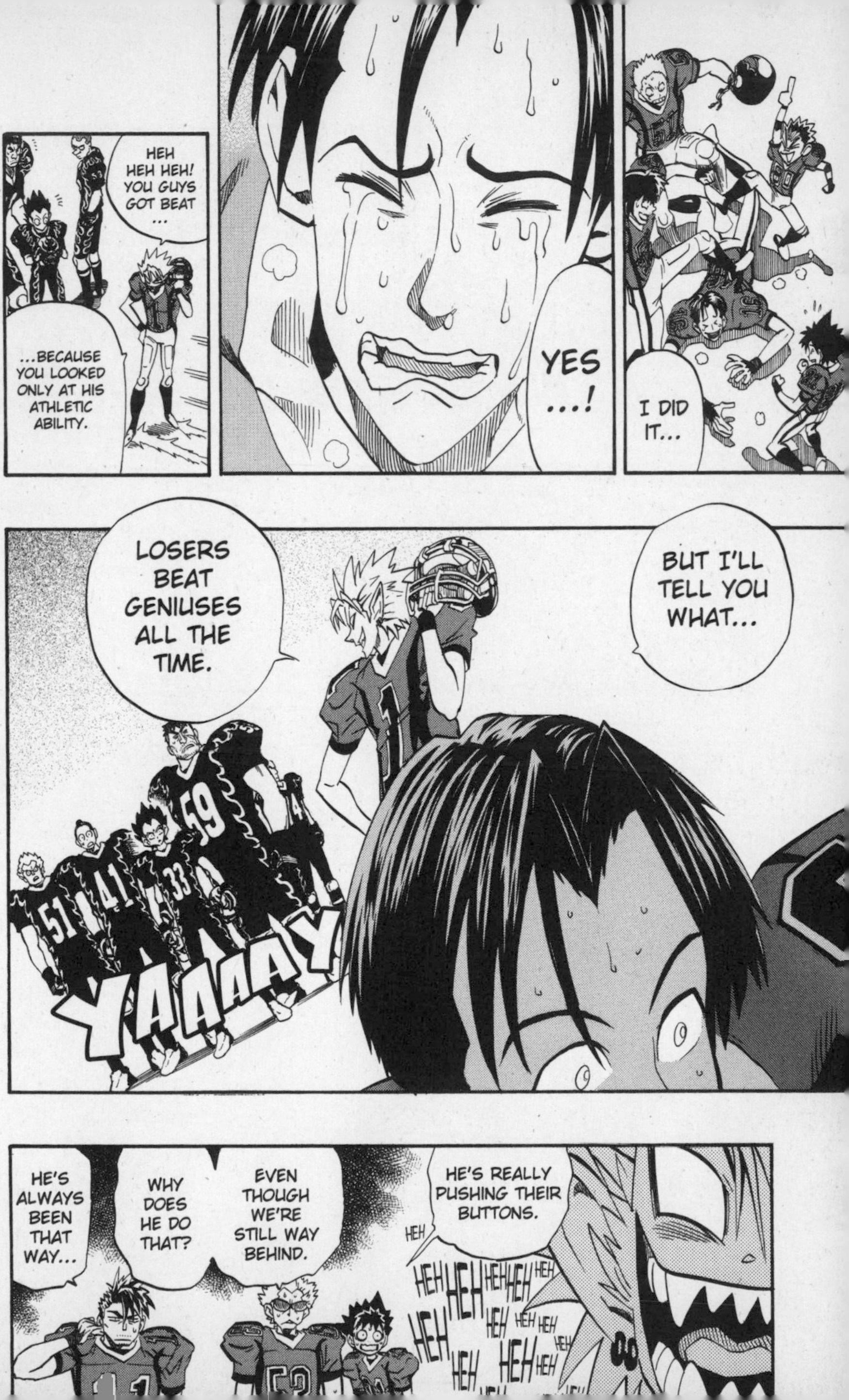
I DID IT...
YES ...!
HEH HEH HEH! YOU GUYS GOT BEAT ...
...BECAUSE YOU LOOKED ONLY AT HIS ATHLETIC ABILITY.
BUT I'LL TELL YOU WHAT...
LOSERS BEAT GENIUSES ALL THE TIME.
YAAAAY
HEH HEH HEH HEH HEH HEH
HE'S REALLY PUSHING THEIR BUTTONS.
EVEN THOUGH WE'RE STILL WAY BEHIND.
WHY DOES HE DO THAT?
HE'S ALWAYS BEEN THAT WAY...

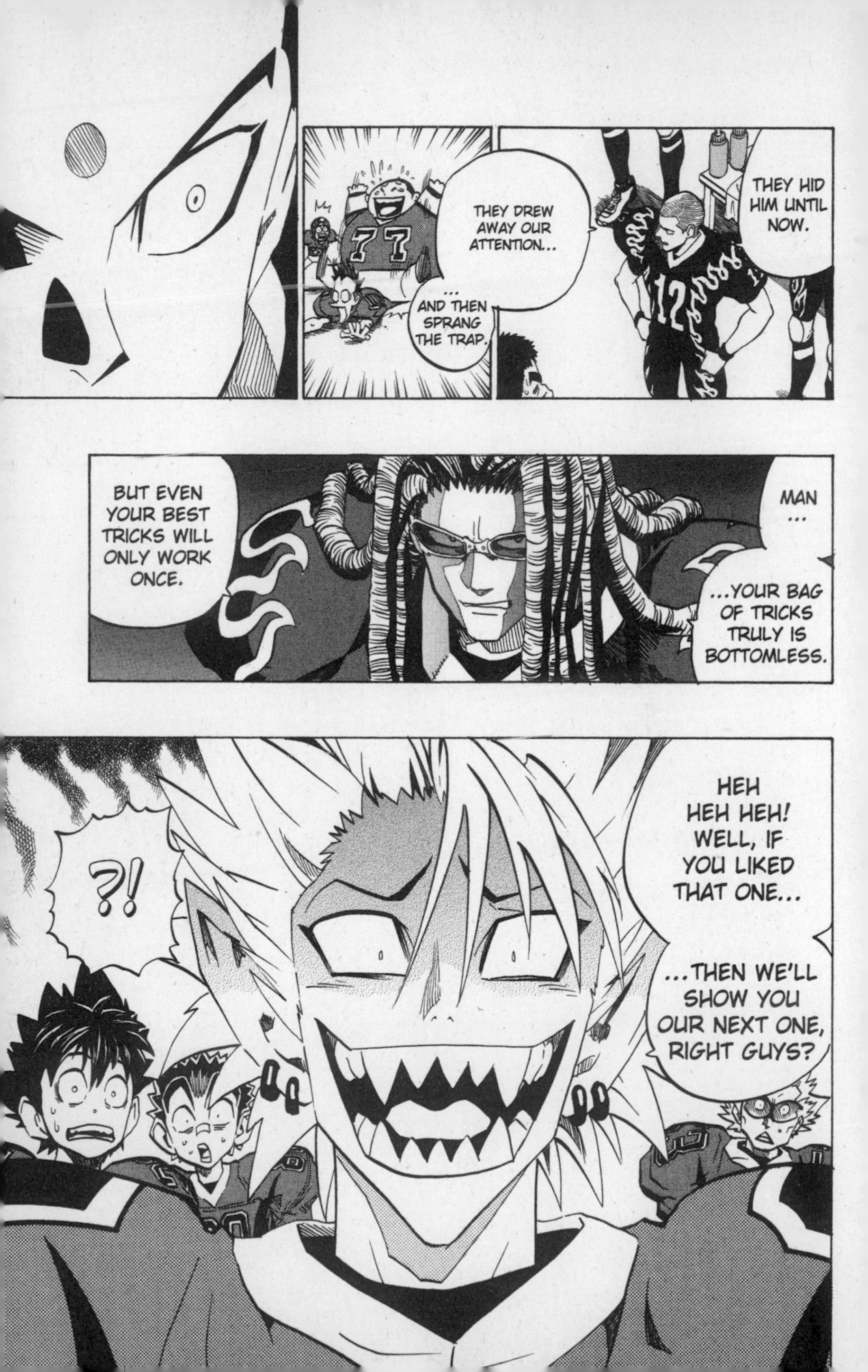
THEY HID HIM UNTIL NOW.
THEY DREW AWAY OUR ATTENTION...
...AND THEN SPRANG THE TRAP.
MAN...
...YOUR BAG OF TRICKS TRULY IS BOTTOMLESS.
BUT EVEN YOUR BEST TRICKS WILL ONLY WORK ONCE.
HEH HEH HEH! WELL, IF YOU LIKED THAT ONE...
...THEN WE'LL SHOW YOU OUR NEXT ONE, RIGHT GUYS?
?!

Eyeshield 21 Survey Corner

Devil Bat 021

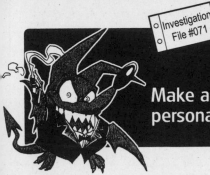

Investigation File #071

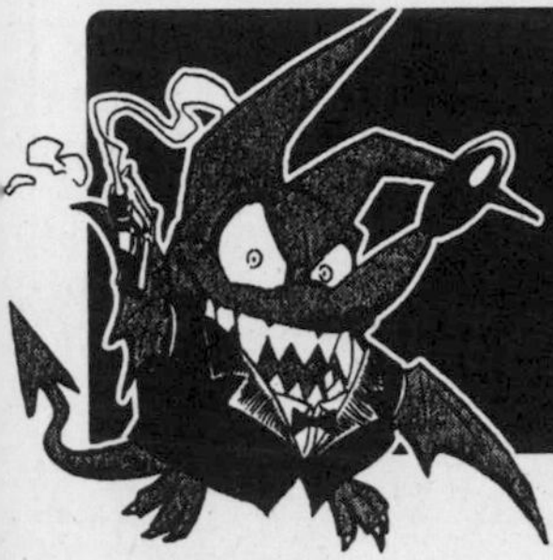

Make an Eyeshield 21 personality test!

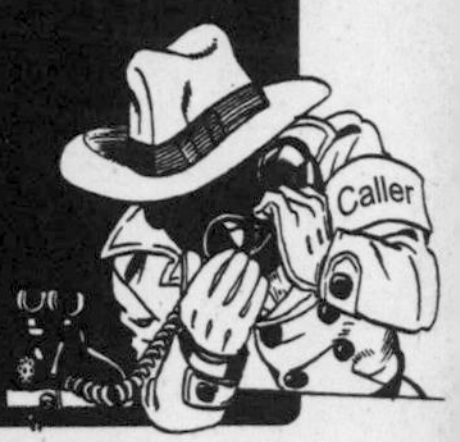
Caller

H. T., Ibaraki Prefecture

**You're an adventurer.
As you hack through the jungle,
a tiger suddenly leaps out!
You manage to use your backpack as a shield and escape, but the backpack got a hole in it and you lost all your valuables!
There's only one item left when you look inside.
What is it?**

① Survival knife
② Map to the city
③ Food
④ Souvenir photographs
⑤ Nothing

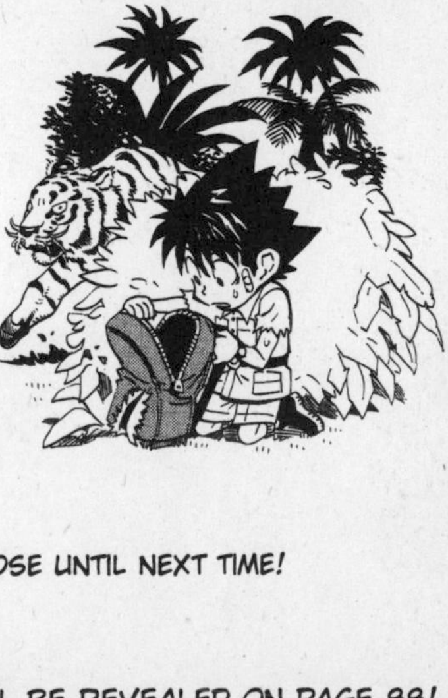

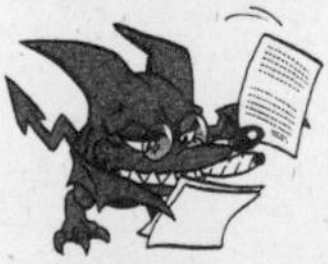

REMEMBER WHAT YOU CHOSE UNTIL NEXT TIME!

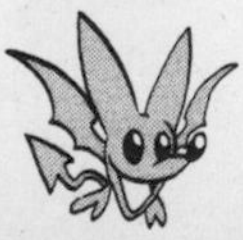

YOUR PERSONALITY WILL BE REVEALED ON PAGE 88!

Chapter 182
Hiruma vs. the Kongos

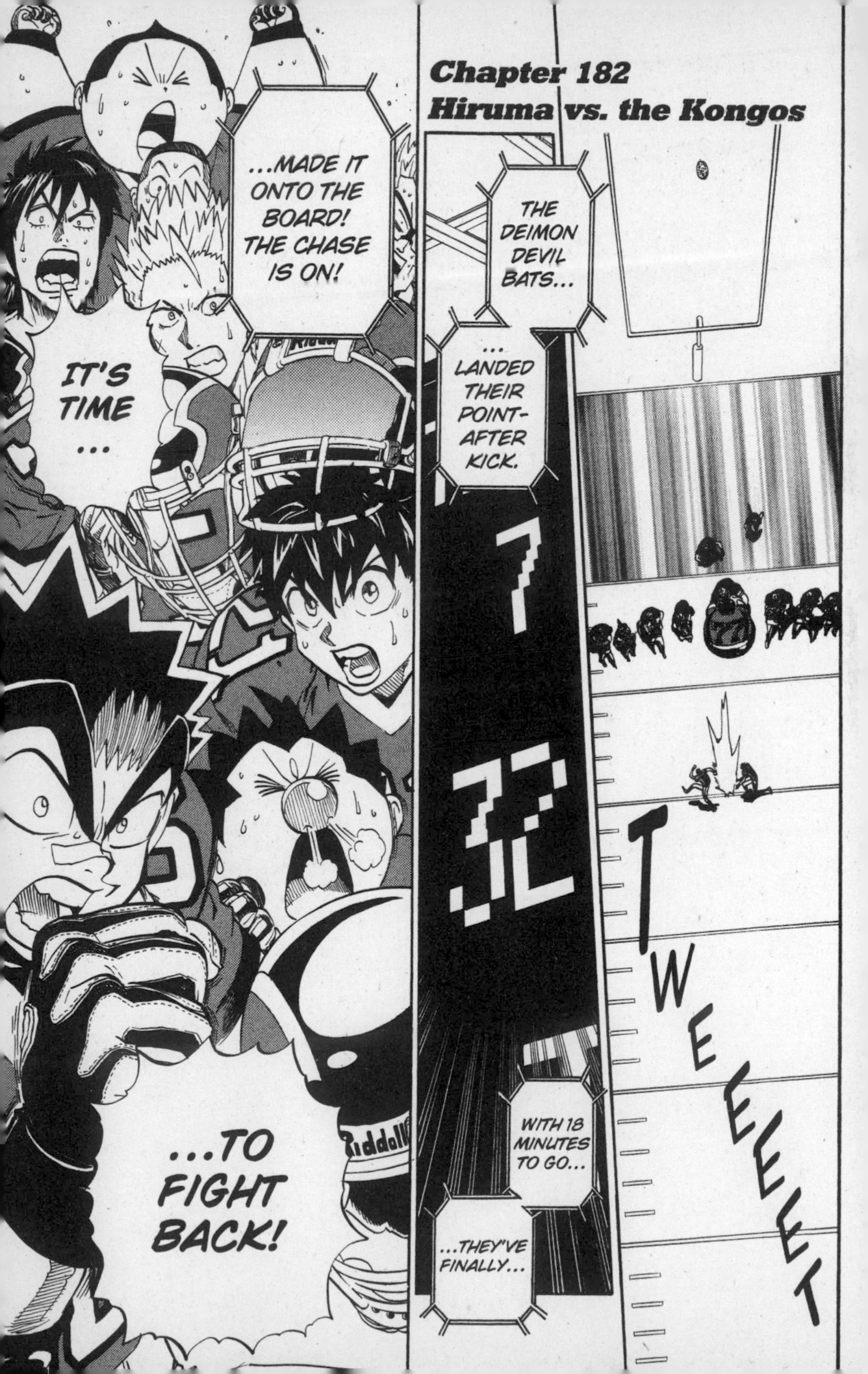
THE DEIMON DEVIL BATS...
...LANDED THEIR POINT-AFTER KICK.
7
TWEEEET
WITH 18 MINUTES TO GO...
...THEY'VE FINALLY...
...MADE IT ONTO THE BOARD! THE CHASE IS ON!
IT'S TIME...
...TO FIGHT BACK!

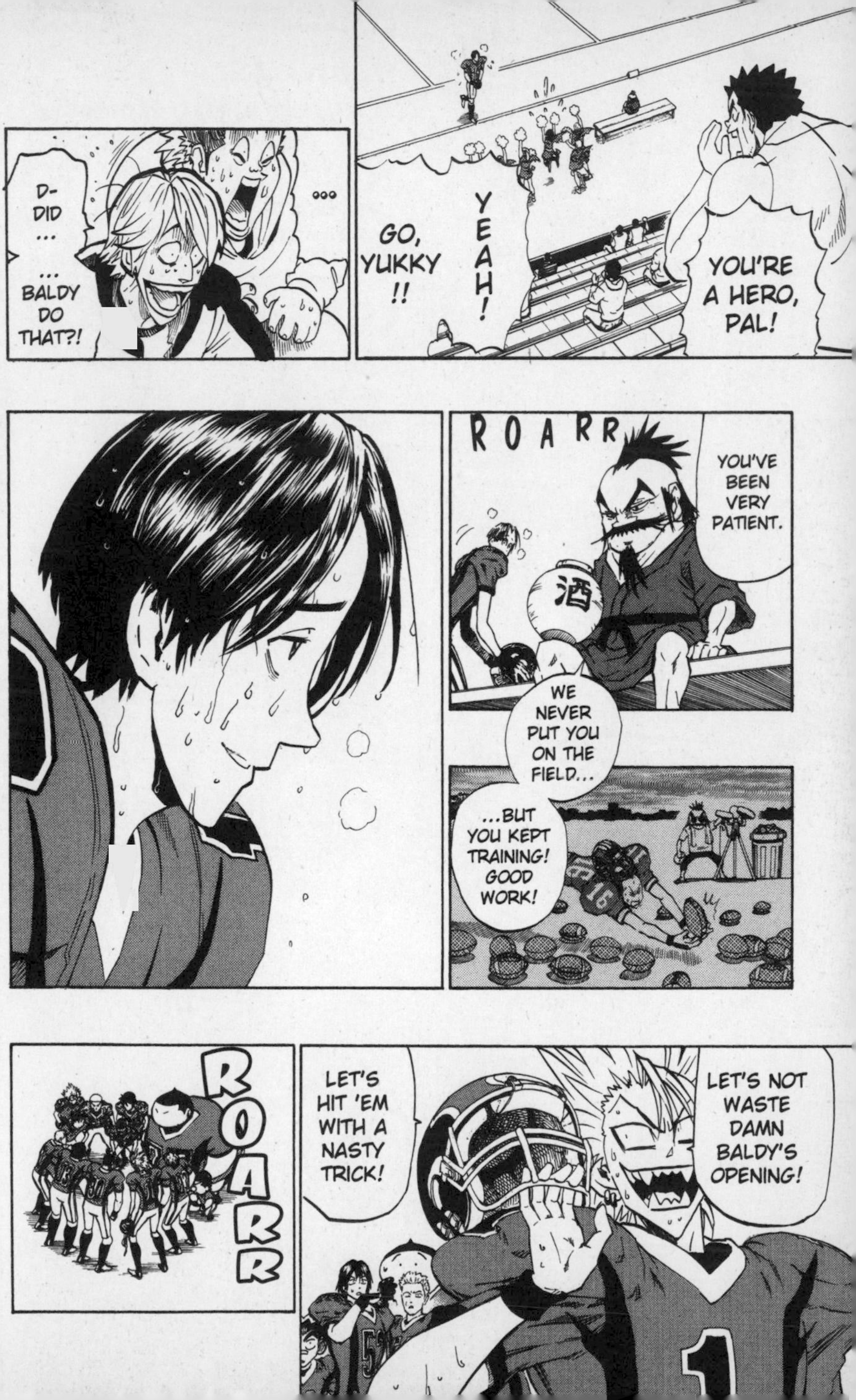
YOU'RE A HERO, PAL!
YEAH!
GO, YUKKY!!
...
D-DID ... ... BALDY DO THAT?!
ROARR
YOU'VE BEEN VERY PATIENT.
酒
WE NEVER PUT YOU ON THE FIELD...
...BUT YOU KEPT TRAINING! GOOD WORK!
LET'S NOT WASTE DAMN BALDY'S OPENING!
LET'S HIT 'EM WITH A NASTY TRICK!
ROARR

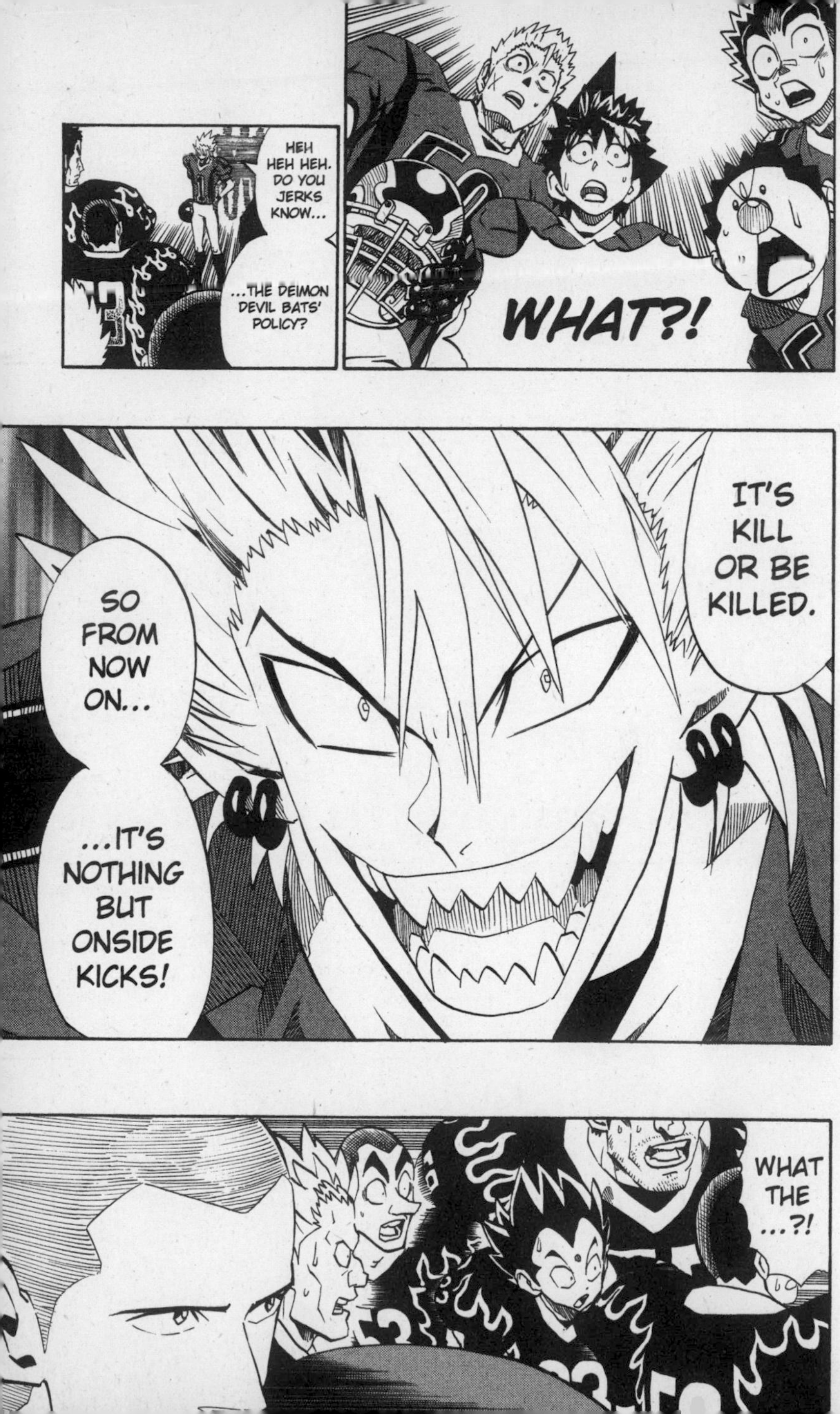
WHAT?!
HEH HEH HEH. DO YOU JERKS KNOW...
...THE DEIMON DEVIL BATS' POLICY?
IT'S KILL OR BE KILLED.
SO FROM NOW ON...
...IT'S NOTHING BUT ONSIDE KICKS!
WHAT THE ...?!

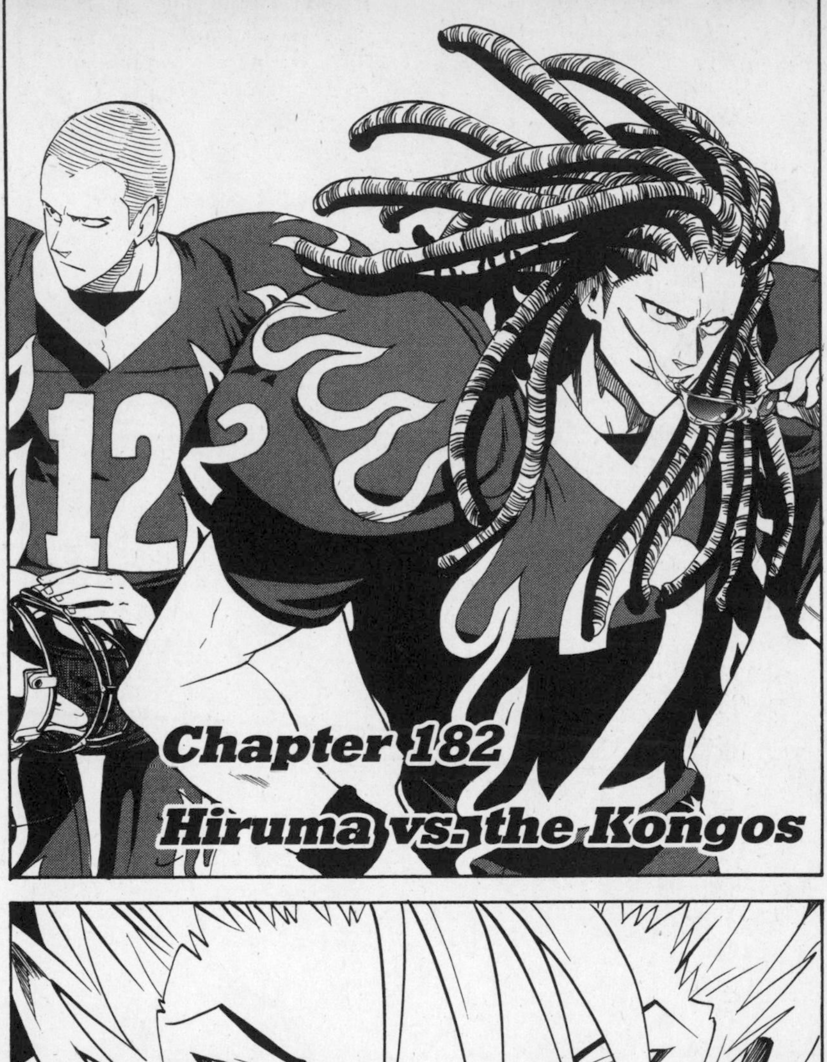
Chapter 182
Hiruma vs. the Kongos

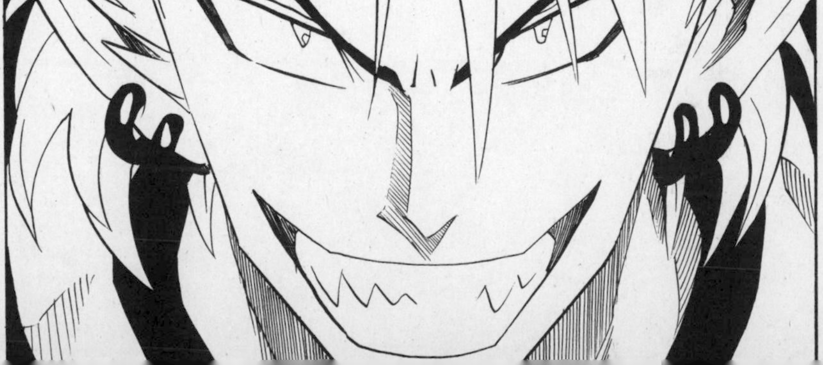

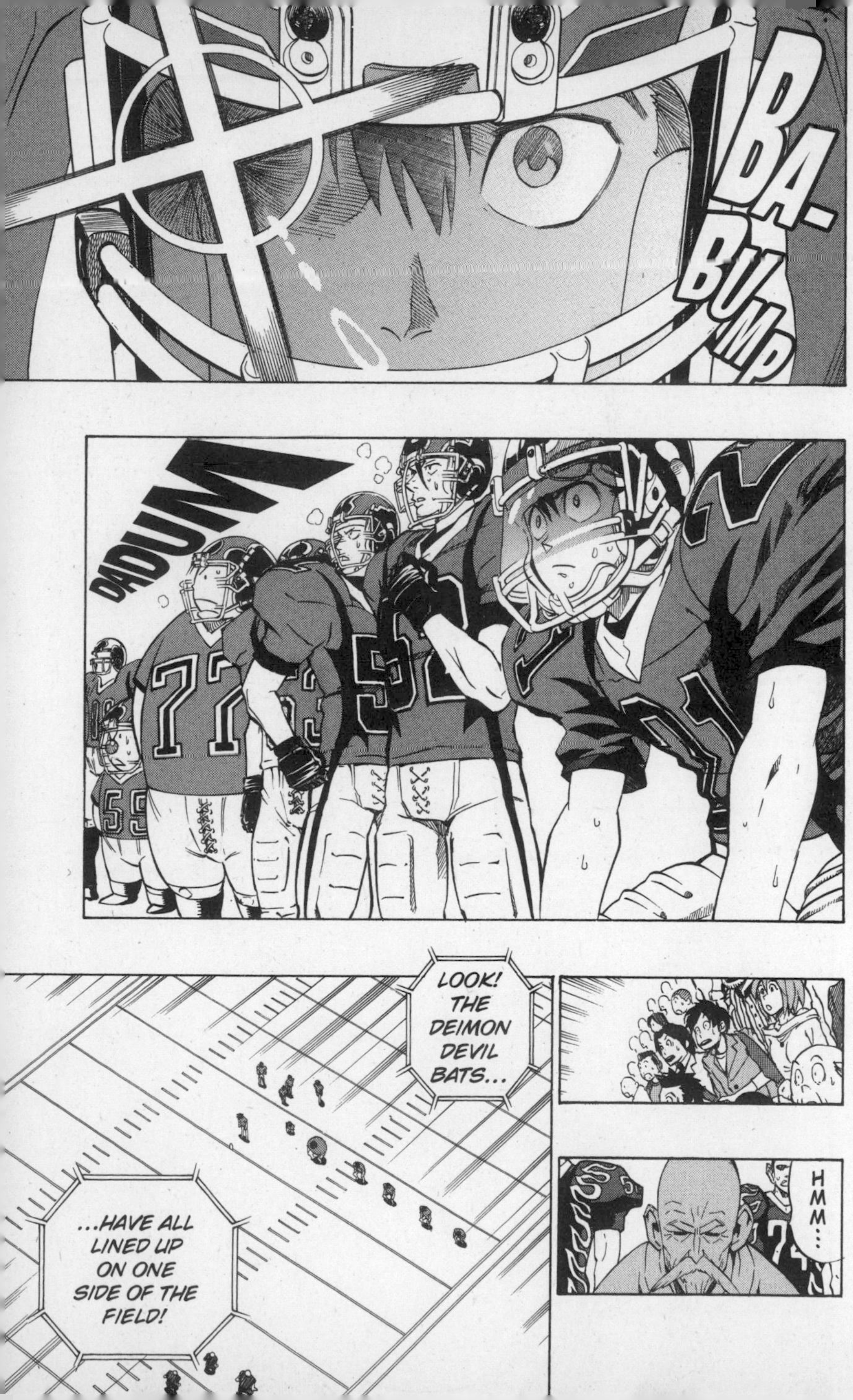
BA-BA-BUMP
DADUM
HMM...
LOOK! THE DEIMON DEVIL BATS...
...HAVE ALL LINED UP ON ONE SIDE OF THE FIELD!

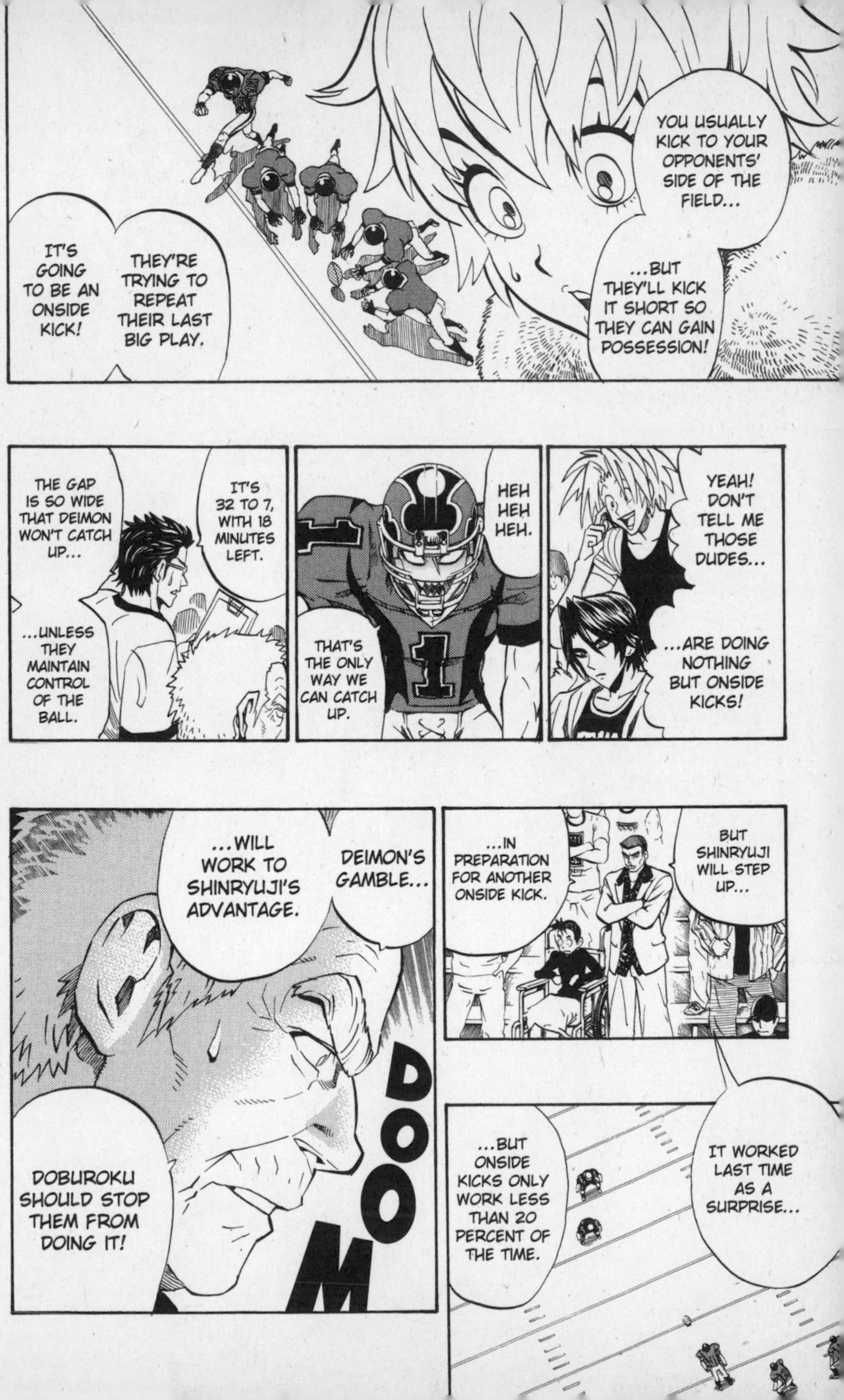
YOU USUALLY KICK TO YOUR OPPONENTS' SIDE OF THE FIELD...
...BUT THEY'LL KICK IT SHORT SO THEY CAN GAIN POSSESSION!
THEY'RE TRYING TO REPEAT THEIR LAST BIG PLAY.
IT'S GOING TO BE AN ONSIDE KICK!
YEAH! DON'T TELL ME THOSE DUDES...
...ARE DOING NOTHING BUT ONSIDE KICKS!
HEH HEH HEH.
THAT'S THE ONLY WAY WE CAN CATCH UP.
IT'S 32 TO 7, WITH 18 MINUTES LEFT.
THE GAP IS SO WIDE THAT DEIMON WON'T CATCH UP...
...UNLESS THEY MAINTAIN CONTROL OF THE BALL.
BUT SHINRYUJI WILL STEP UP...
...IN PREPARATION FOR ANOTHER ONSIDE KICK.
IT WORKED LAST TIME AS A SURPRISE...
...BUT ONSIDE KICKS ONLY WORK LESS THAN 20 PERCENT OF THE TIME.
DEIMON'S GAMBLE...
...WILL WORK TO SHINRYUJI'S ADVANTAGE.
DOBUROKU SHOULD STOP THEM FROM DOING IT!
DOOM

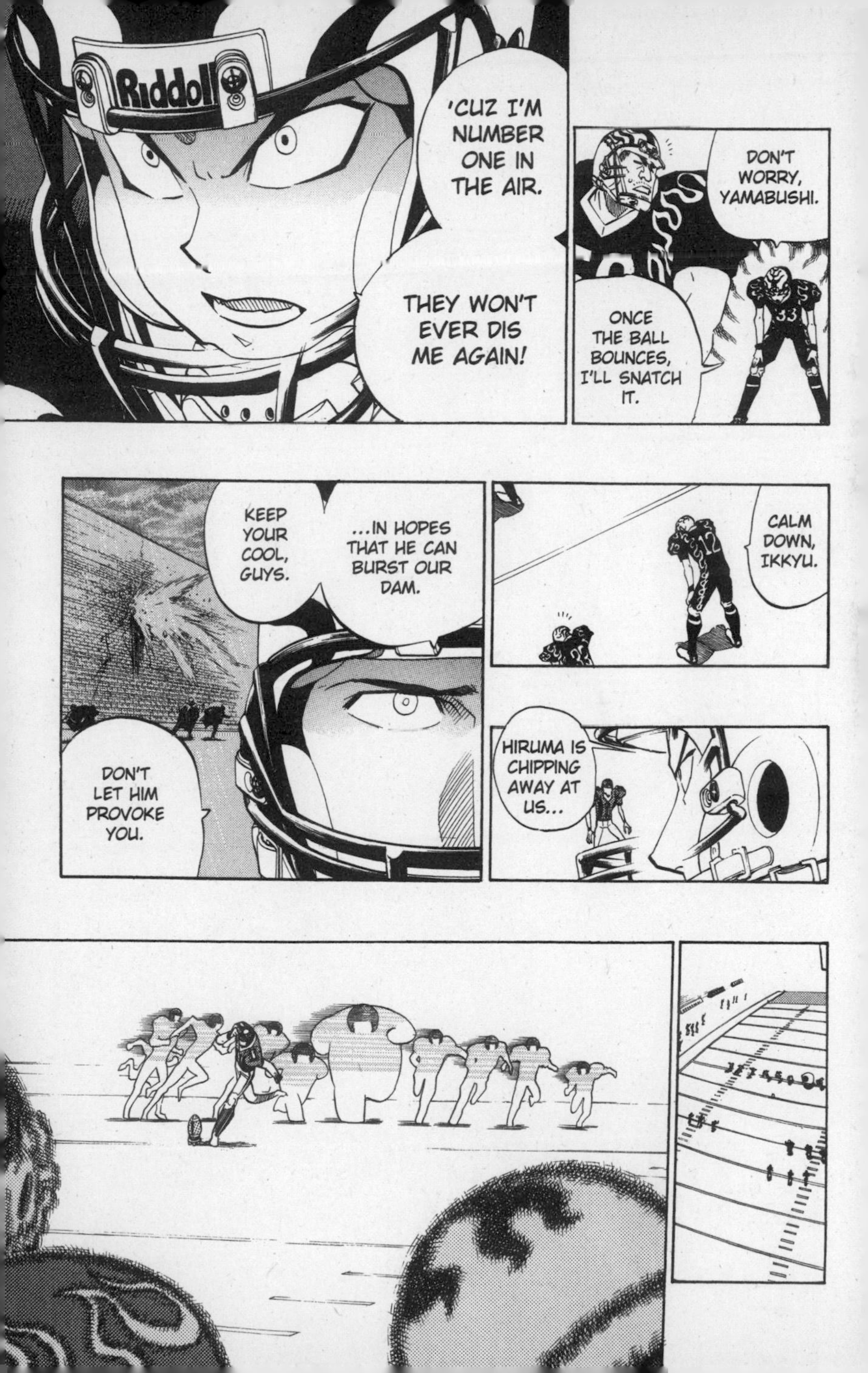
DON'T WORRY, YAMABUSHI.
ONCE THE BALL BOUNCES, I'LL SNATCH IT.
Riddoll
'CUZ I'M NUMBER ONE IN THE AIR.
THEY WON'T EVER DIS ME AGAIN!
CALM DOWN, IKKYU.
HIRUMA IS CHIPPING AWAY AT US...
...IN HOPES THAT HE CAN BURST OUR DAM.
KEEP YOUR COOL, GUYS.
DON'T LET HIM PROVOKE YOU.

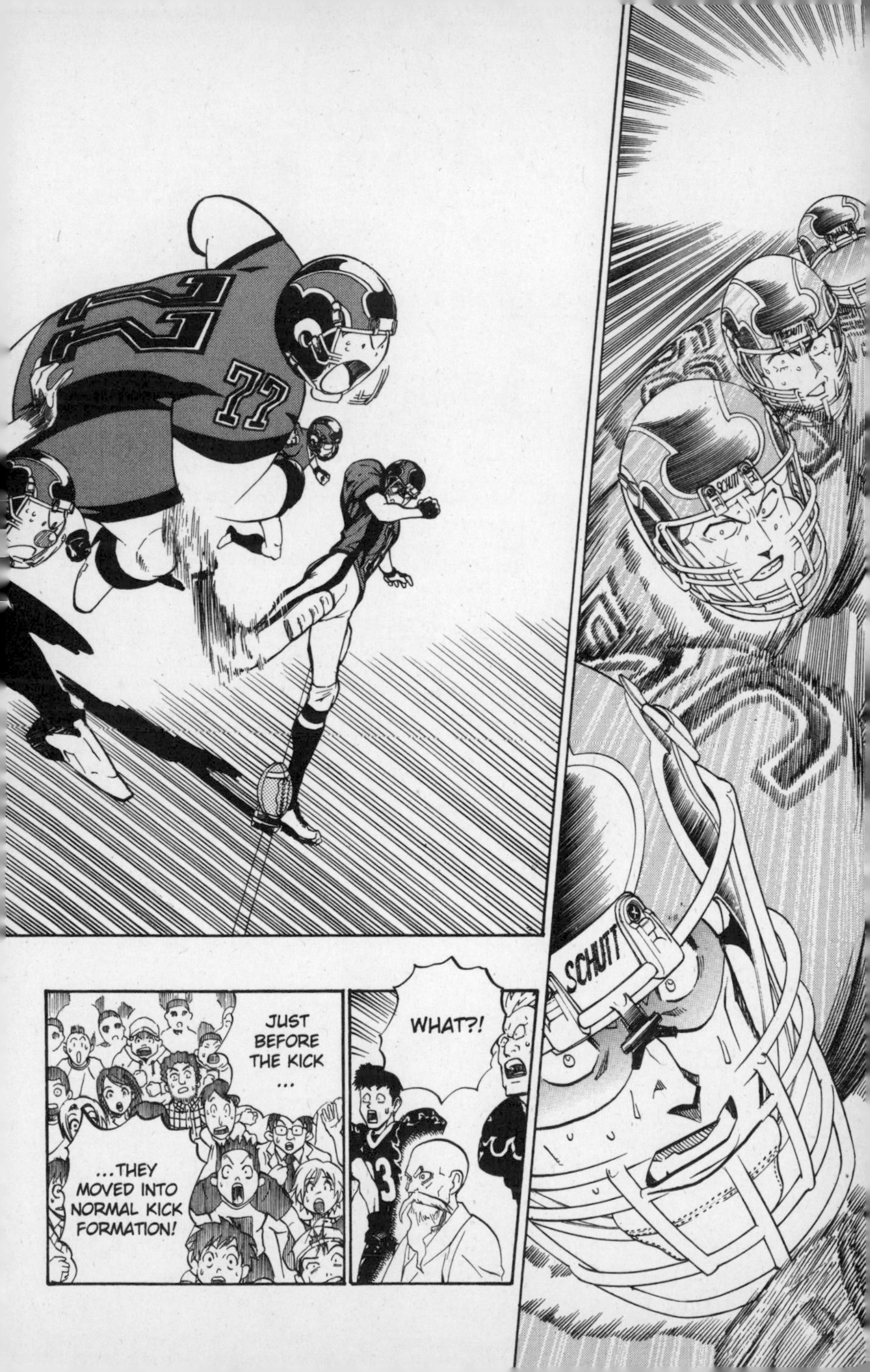
SCHUTT
WHAT?!
JUST BEFORE THE KICK ...
...THEY MOVED INTO NORMAL KICK FORMATION!

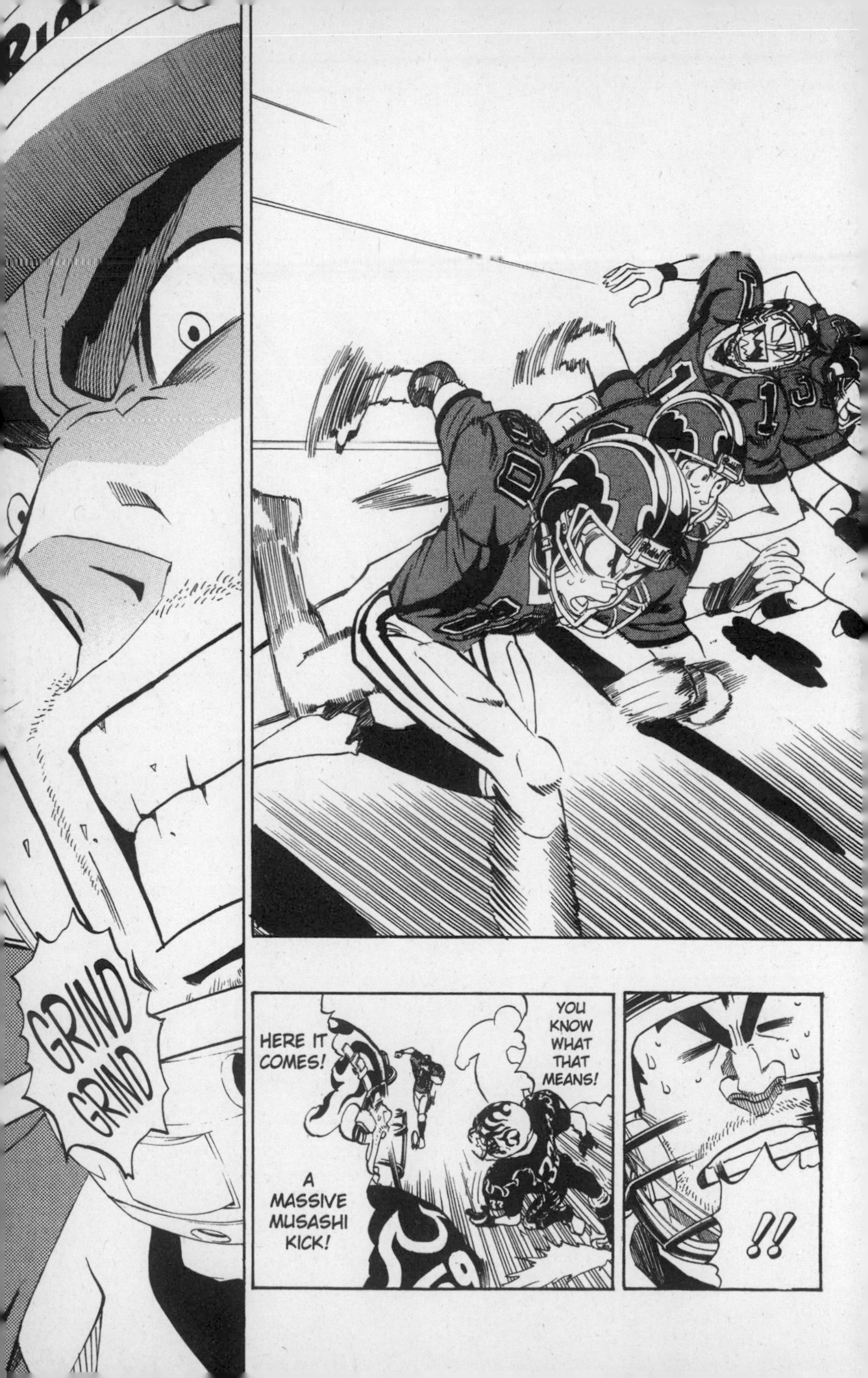
!!
YOU KNOW WHAT THAT MEANS!
HERE IT COMES!
A MASSIVE MUSASHI KICK!
GRIND GRIND

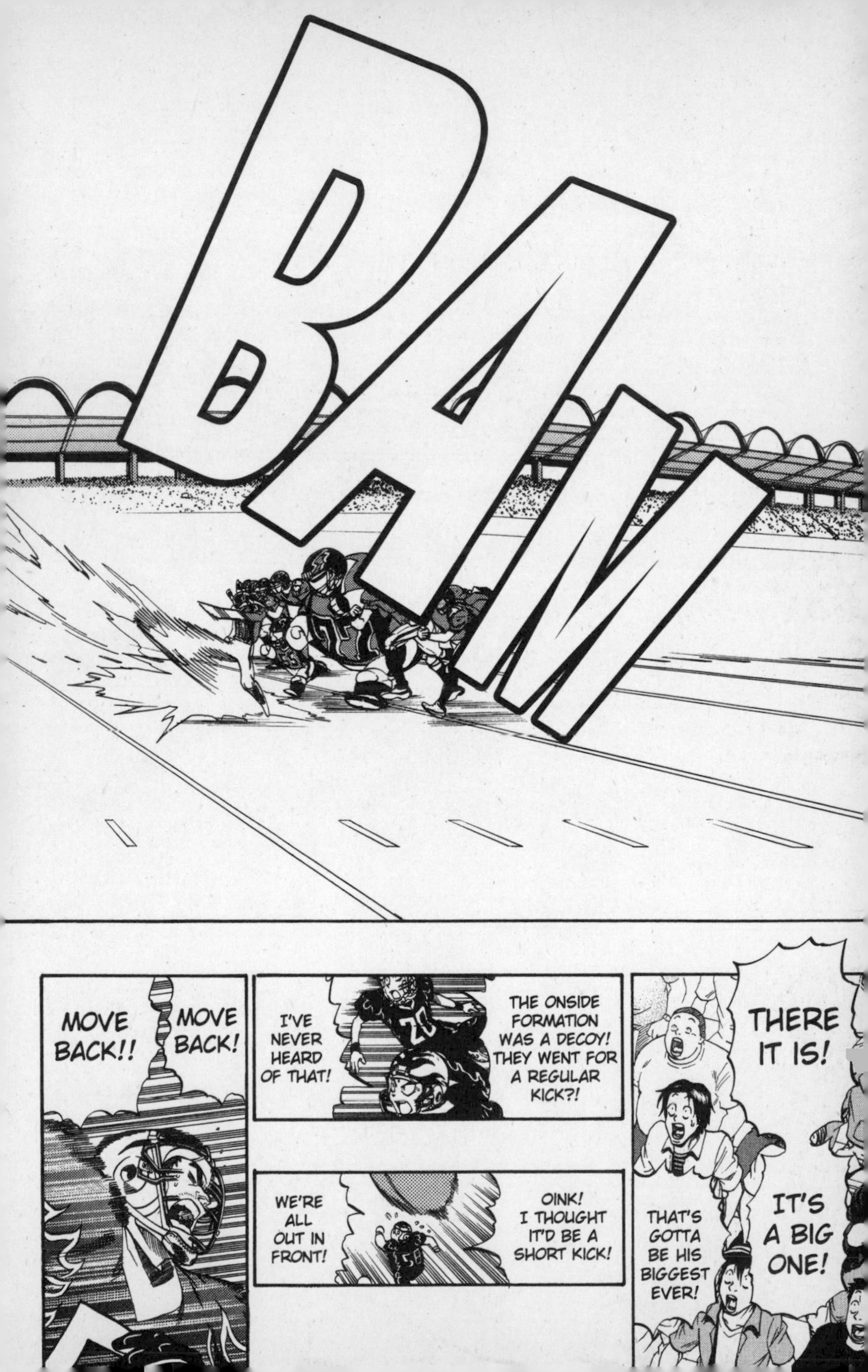
BAM
THERE IT IS!
IT'S A BIG ONE!
THAT'S GOTTA BE HIS BIGGEST EVER!
THE ONSIDE FORMATION WAS A DECOY! THEY WENT FOR A REGULAR KICK?!
I'VE NEVER HEARD OF THAT!
OINK! I THOUGHT IT'D BE A SHORT KICK!
WE'RE ALL OUT IN FRONT!
MOVE BACK!
MOVE BACK!!

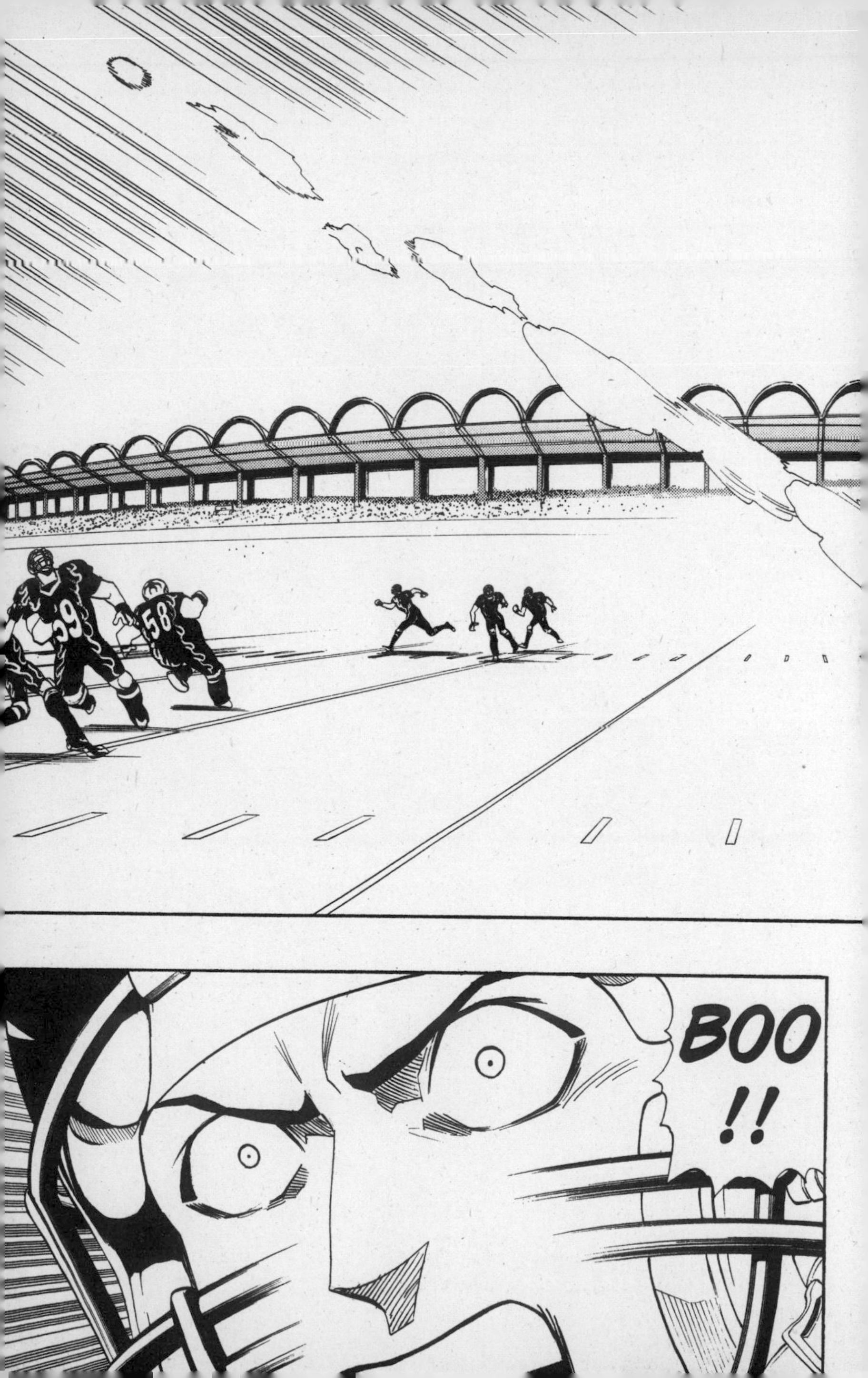
BOO
!!

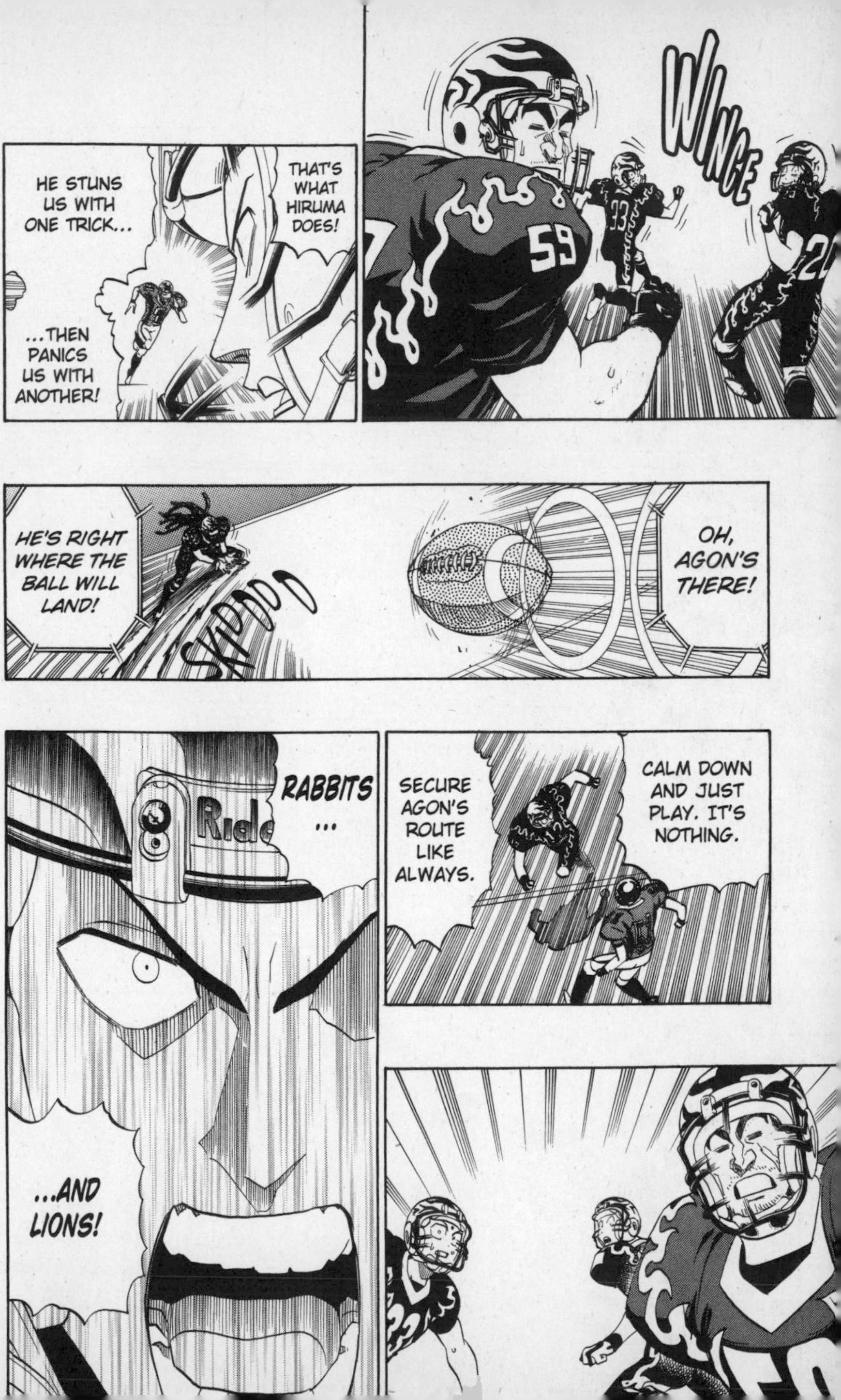
WINCE
THAT'S WHAT HIRUMA DOES!
HE STUNS US WITH ONE TRICK...
...THEN PANICS US WITH ANOTHER!
OH, AGON'S THERE!
HE'S RIGHT WHERE THE BALL WILL LAND!
CALM DOWN AND JUST PLAY. IT'S NOTHING.
SECURE AGON'S ROUTE LIKE ALWAYS.
RABBITS...
...AND LIONS!

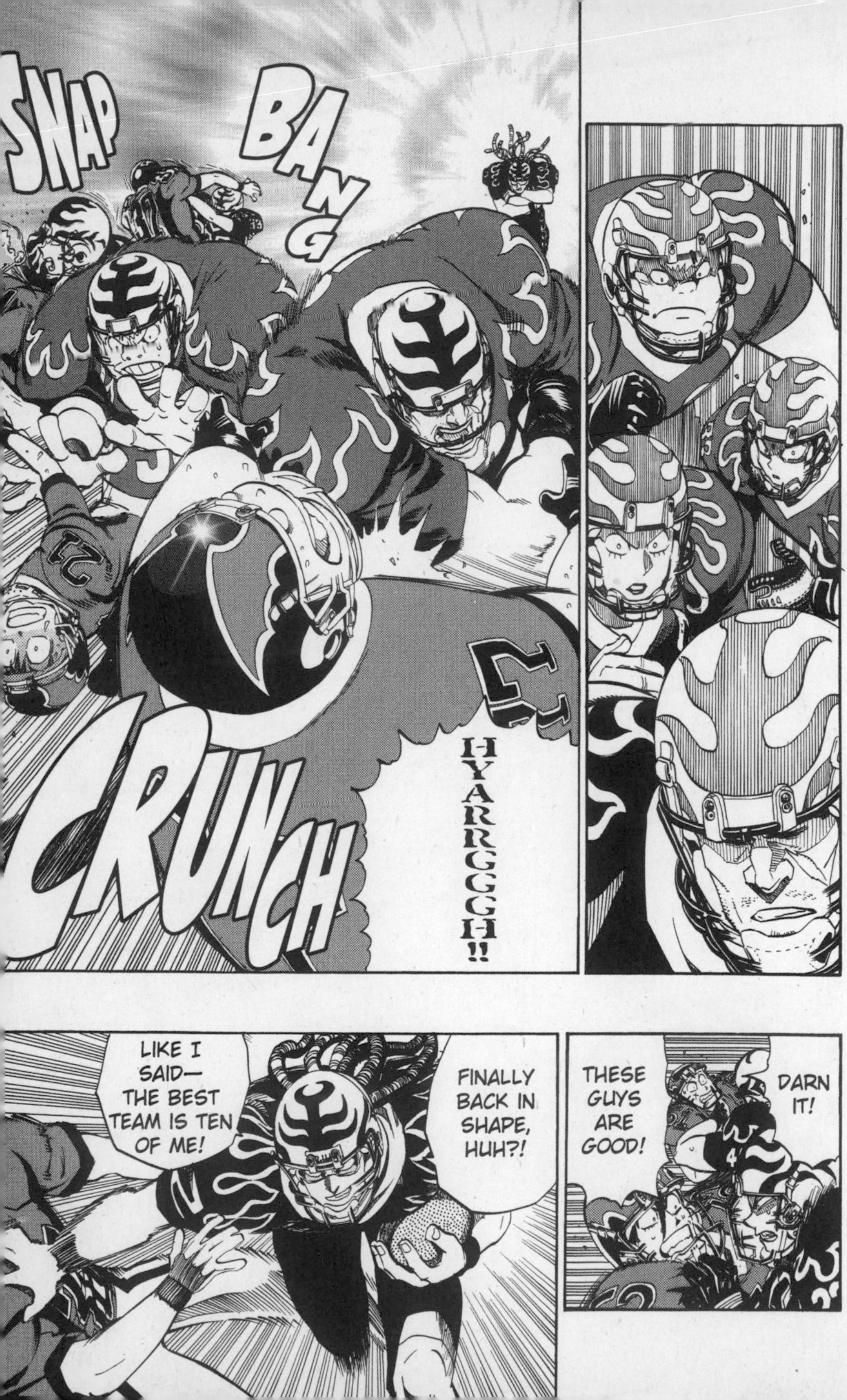
BANG
SNAP
HYARRGGGH!!
CRUNCH
DARN IT!
THESE GUYS ARE GOOD!
FINALLY BACK IN SHAPE, HUH?!
LIKE I SAID— THE BEST TEAM IS TEN OF ME!

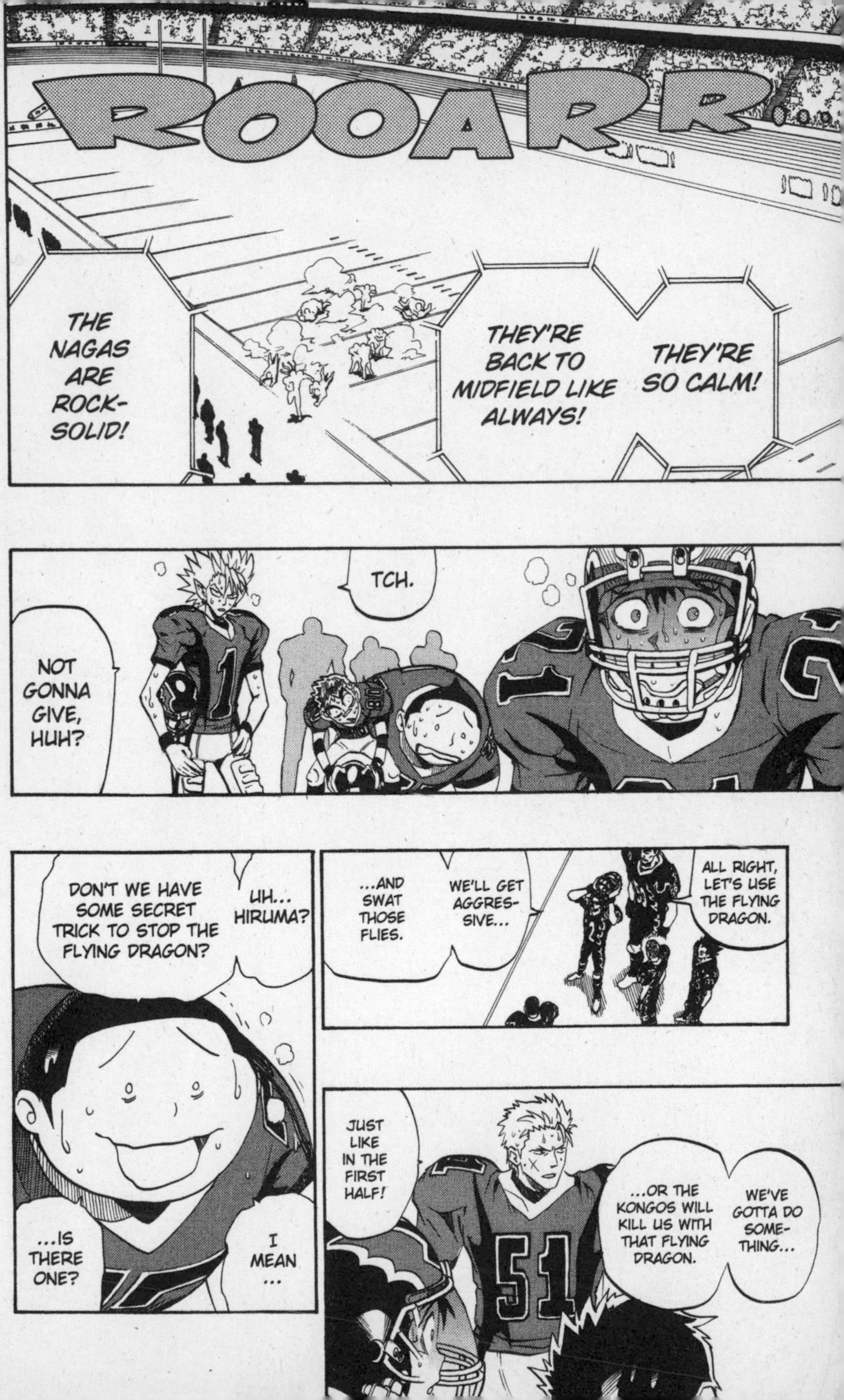
ROOARR...
THEY'RE SO CALM!
THEY'RE BACK TO MIDFIELD LIKE ALWAYS!
THE NAGAS ARE ROCK-SOLID!
TCH.
NOT GONNA GIVE, HUH?
ALL RIGHT, LET'S USE THE FLYING DRAGON.
WE'LL GET AGGRES-SIVE...
...AND SWAT THOSE FLIES.
WE'VE GOTTA DO SOME-THING...
...OR THE KONGOS WILL KILL US WITH THAT FLYING DRAGON.
JUST LIKE IN THE FIRST HALF!
UH... HIRUMA?
DON'T WE HAVE SOME SECRET TRICK TO STOP THE FLYING DRAGON?
I MEAN...
...IS THERE ONE?

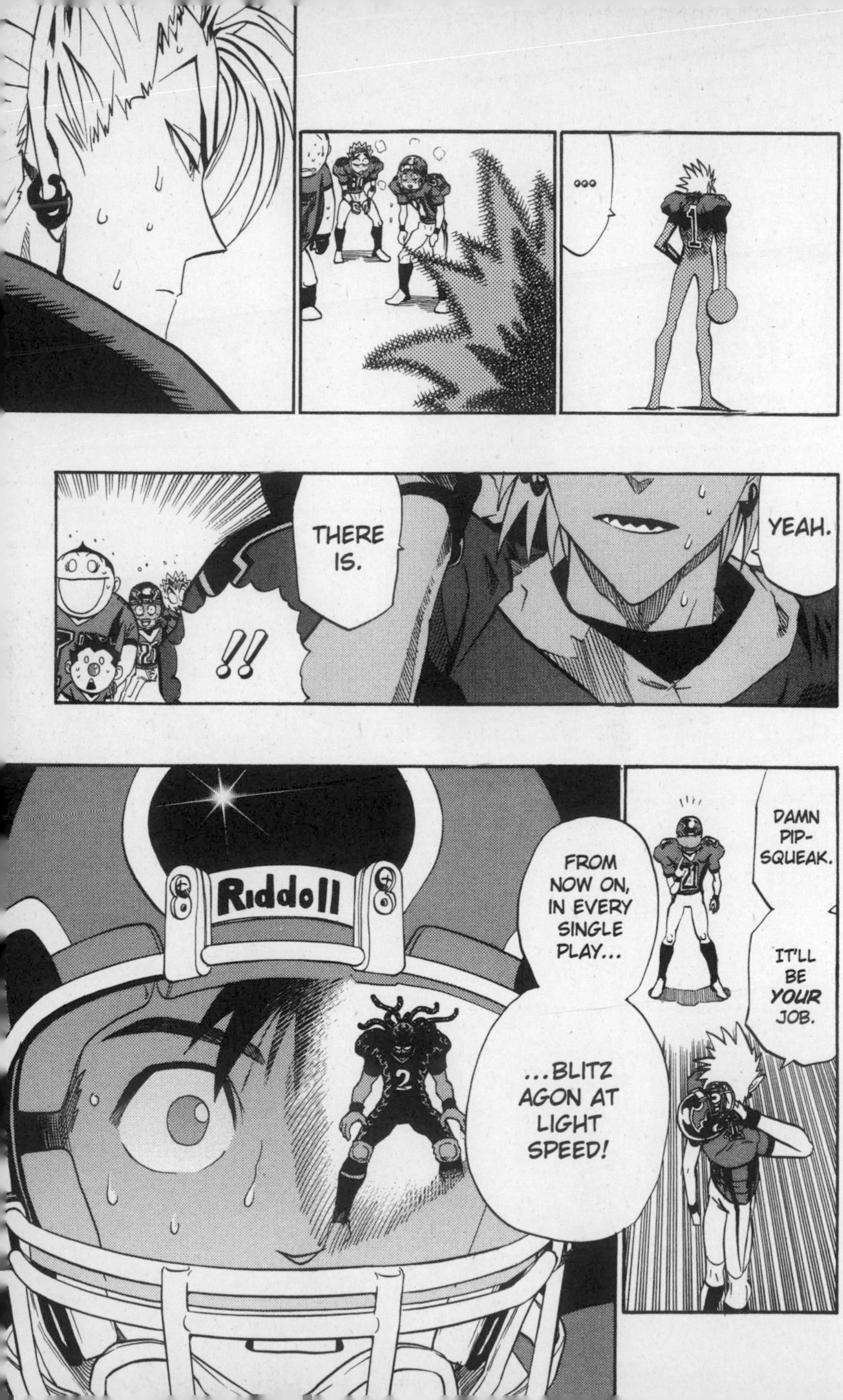
...
YEAH.
THERE IS.
!!
DAMN PIP-SQUEAK.
IT'LL BE *YOUR* JOB.
Riddoll
FROM NOW ON, IN EVERY SINGLE PLAY...
...BLITZ AGON AT LIGHT SPEED!

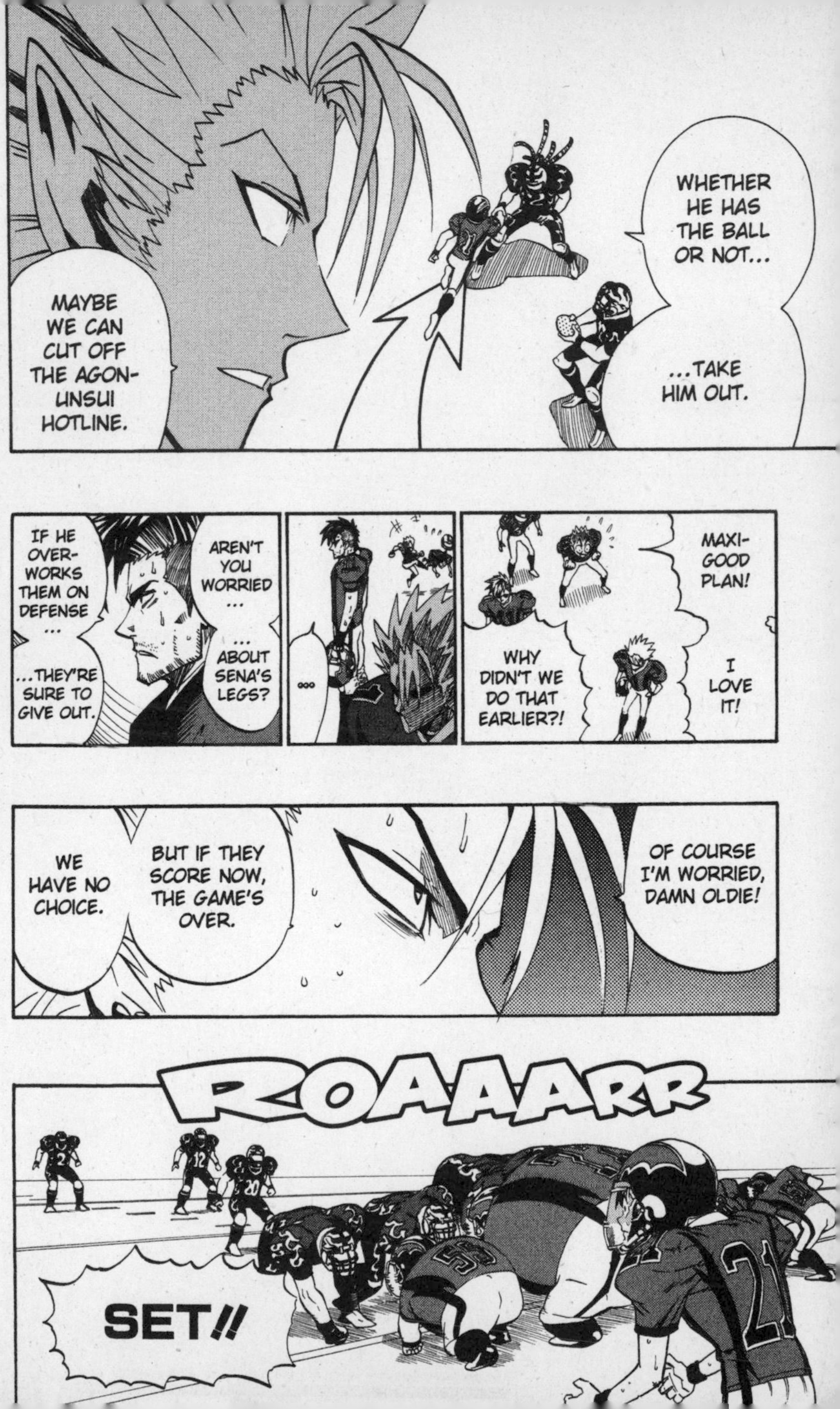
WHETHER HE HAS THE BALL OR NOT...
...TAKE HIM OUT.
MAYBE WE CAN CUT OFF THE AGON-UNSUI HOTLINE.
MAXI-GOOD PLAN!
I LOVE IT!
WHY DIDN'T WE DO THAT EARLIER?!
...
AREN'T YOU WORRIED ...
... ABOUT SENA'S LEGS?
IF HE OVER-WORKS THEM ON DEFENSE ...
...THEY'RE SURE TO GIVE OUT.
OF COURSE I'M WORRIED, DAMN OLDIE!
BUT IF THEY SCORE NOW, THE GAME'S OVER.
WE HAVE NO CHOICE.
ROAAARR
SET!!

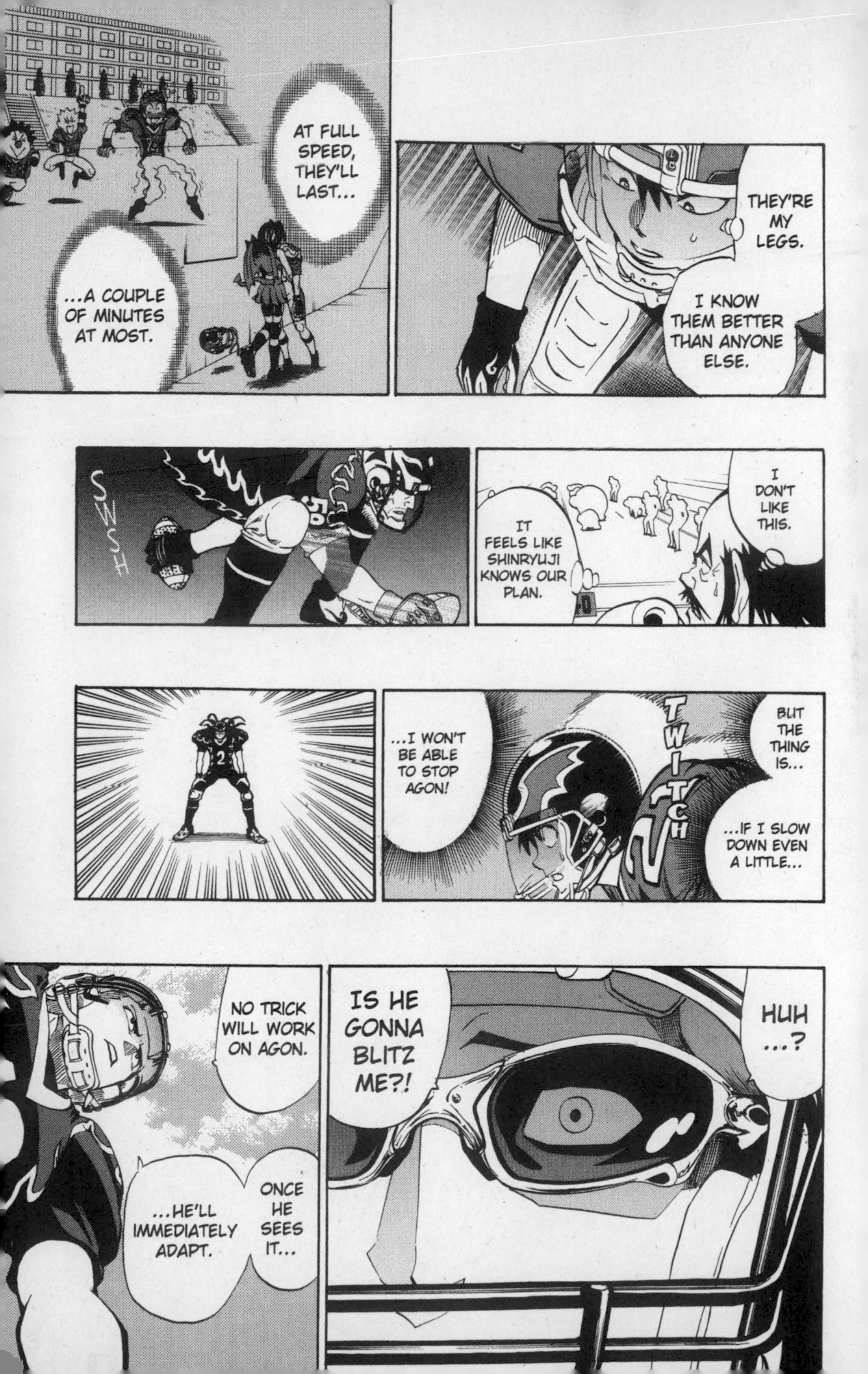
THEY'RE MY LEGS.
I KNOW THEM BETTER THAN ANYONE ELSE.
AT FULL SPEED, THEY'LL LAST...
...A COUPLE OF MINUTES AT MOST.
I DON'T LIKE THIS.
IT FEELS LIKE SHINRYUJI KNOWS OUR PLAN.
SWSH
BUT THE THING IS...
...IF I SLOW DOWN EVEN A LITTLE...
TWITCH
...I WON'T BE ABLE TO STOP AGON!
HUH ...?
IS HE GONNA BLITZ ME?!
NO TRICK WILL WORK ON AGON.
ONCE HE SEES IT...
...HE'LL IMMEDIATELY ADAPT.

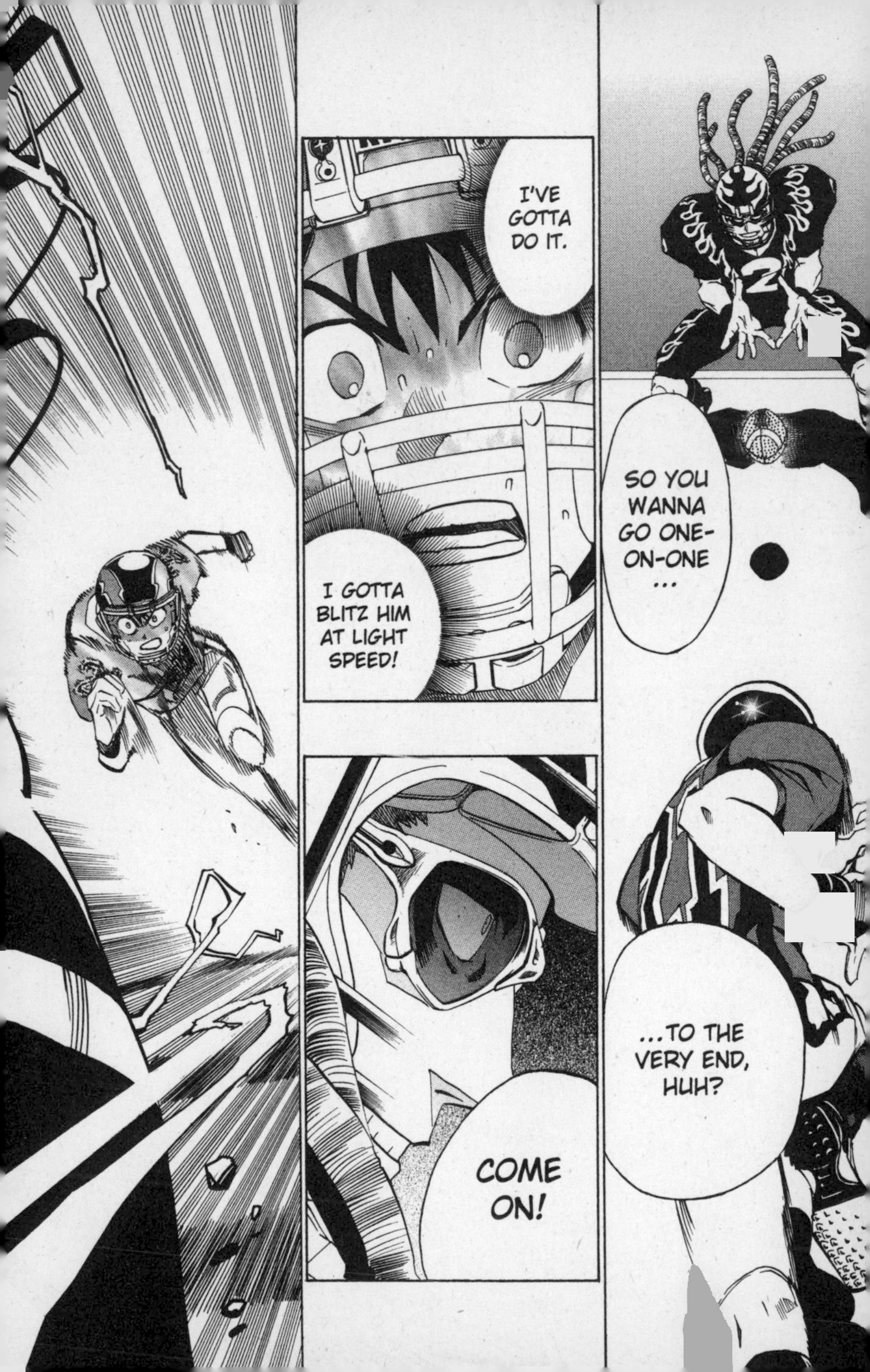
SO YOU WANNA GO ONE-ON-ONE ...
...TO THE VERY END, HUH?
I'VE GOTTA DO IT.
I GOTTA BLITZ HIM AT LIGHT SPEED!
COME ON!

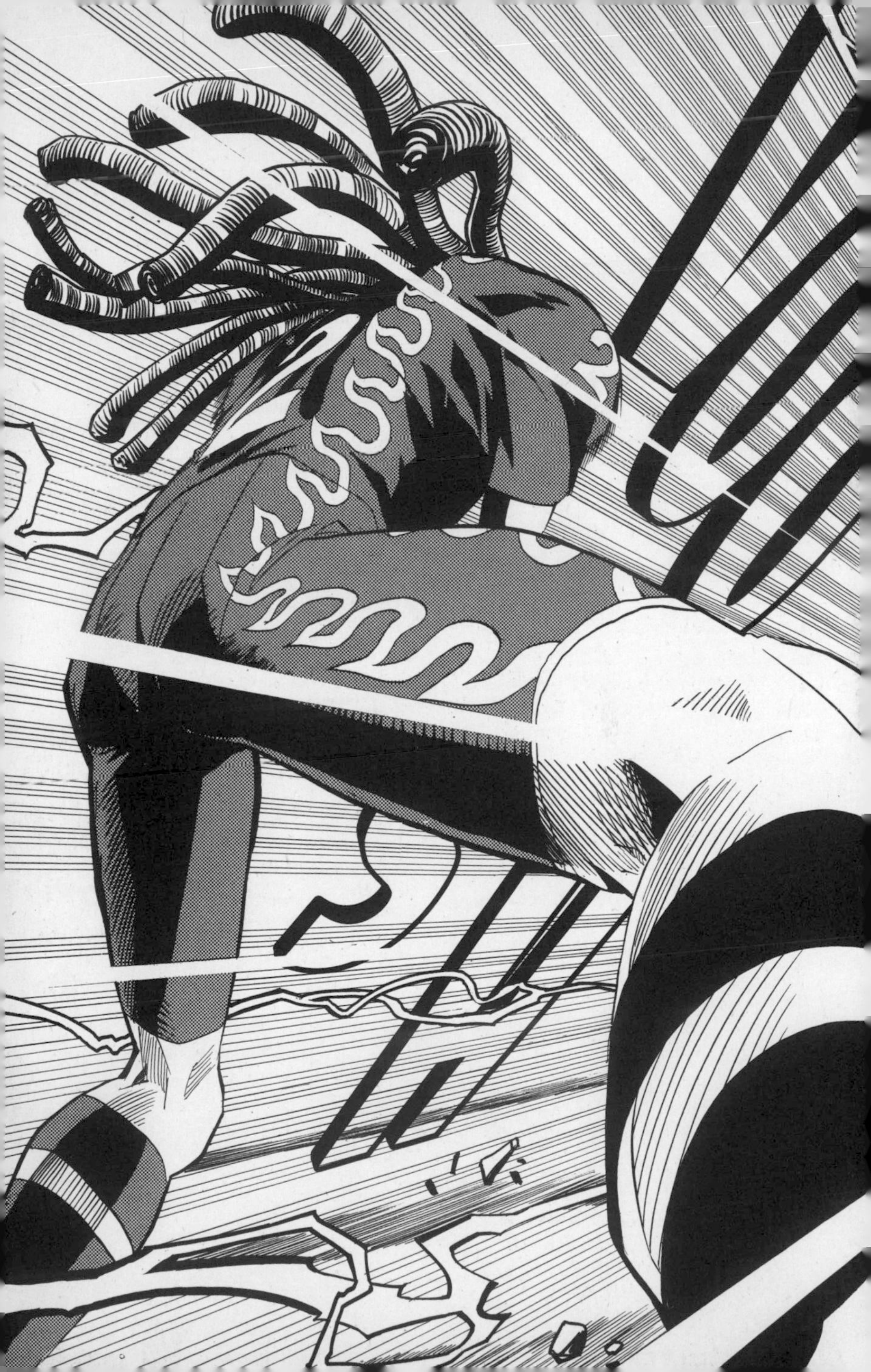

Personality Test Results

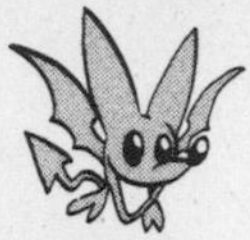

WHAT DID YOU CHOOSE IN THE PERSONALITY TEST ON PAGE 68?
THE ANSWER WILL TELL YOU WHO WOULD BE THE **BEST PARTNER** FOR YOU!

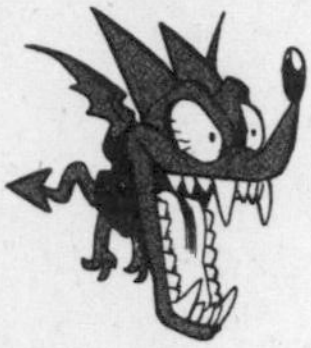

IF YOU STUDY OR WORK WITH THIS PERSON, EVERYTHING WILL GO GREAT!

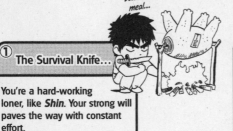

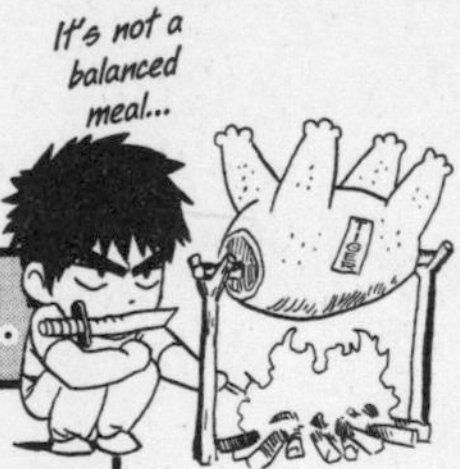
It's not a balanced meal...

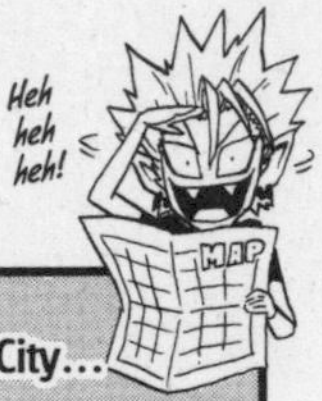
Heh heh heh!
MAP

① The Survival Knife...

You're a hard-working loner, like ***Shin***. Your strong will paves the way with constant effort.

② Map to the City...

You rely on strategy and tactics, just like ***Hiruma***. Your best weapon is information! If you pair up with Hiruma, together you'll be invincible!

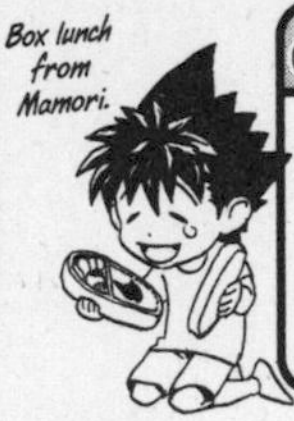
Box lunch from Mamori.

③ Food...

You're an average joe, like ***Sena***. With no special weapons or power, you need strength of heart to survive. Sena is the perfect partner for you!

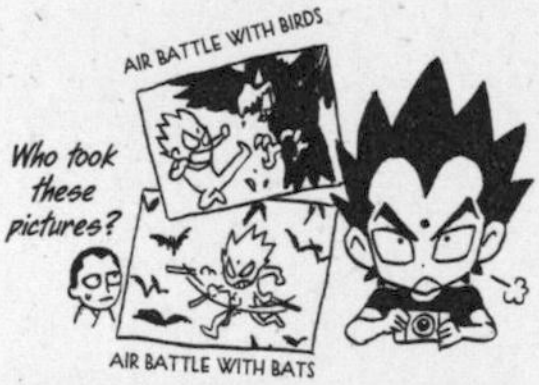
AIR BATTLE WITH BIRDS
Who took these pictures?
AIR BATTLE WITH BATS

④ Souvenir Photos...

Like ***Ikkyu***, you are very proud. You would hate to lose these pictures of yourself. Ikkyu is proud of his skills in the air, so he'd understand.

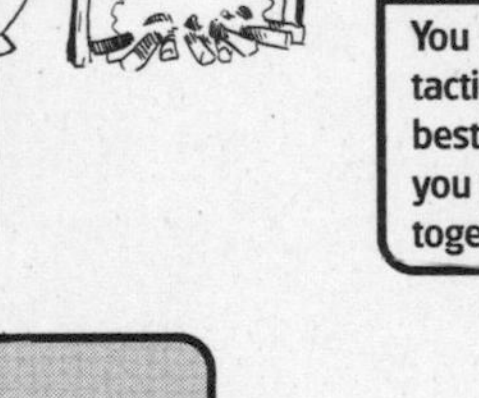

⑤ Nothing...

Like ***Agon***, you trust only your own talent. Luck isn't necessary for you and Agon, so you guys move forward on the basis of only your natural abilities!

Chapter 183
Instinct

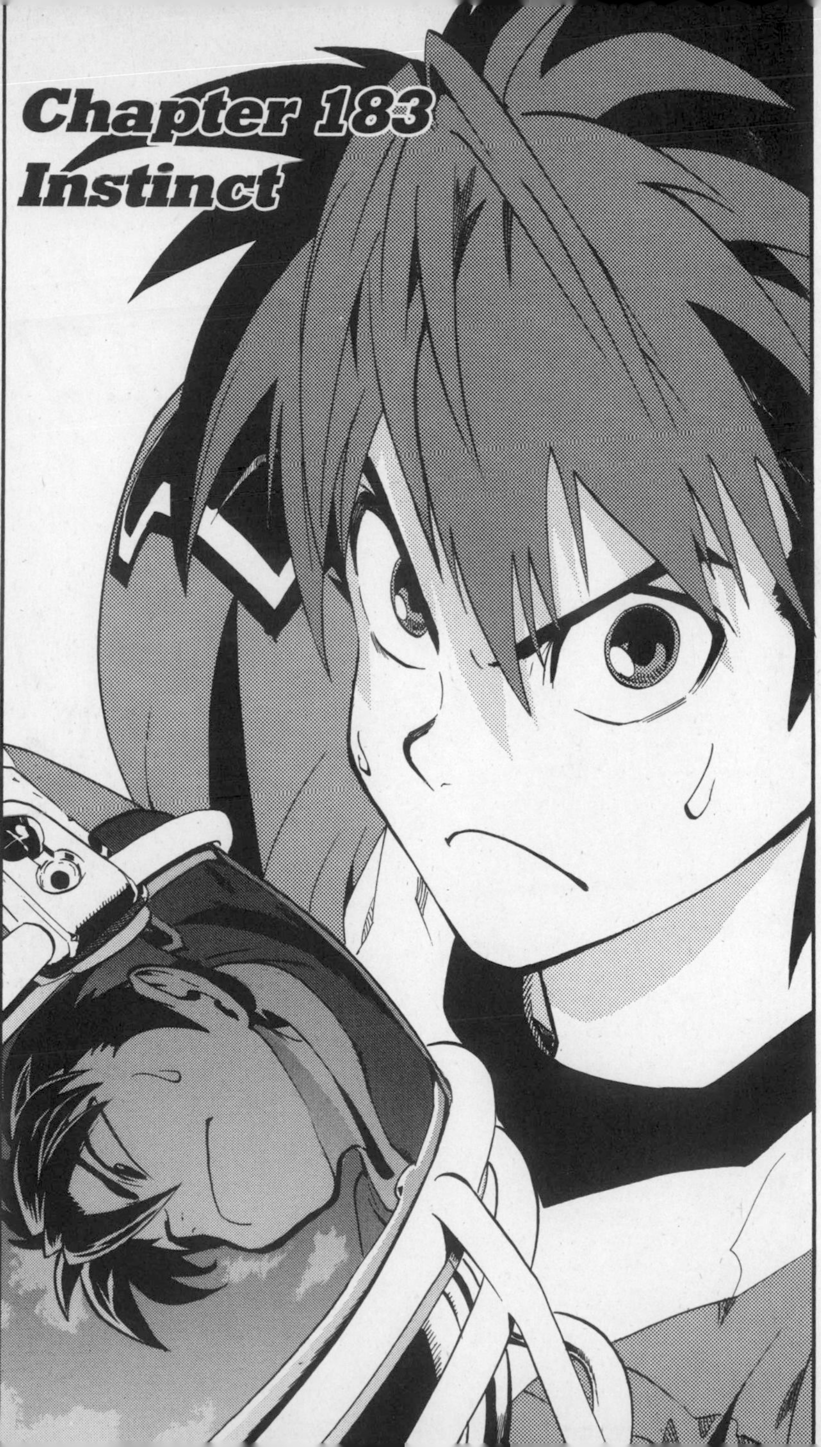

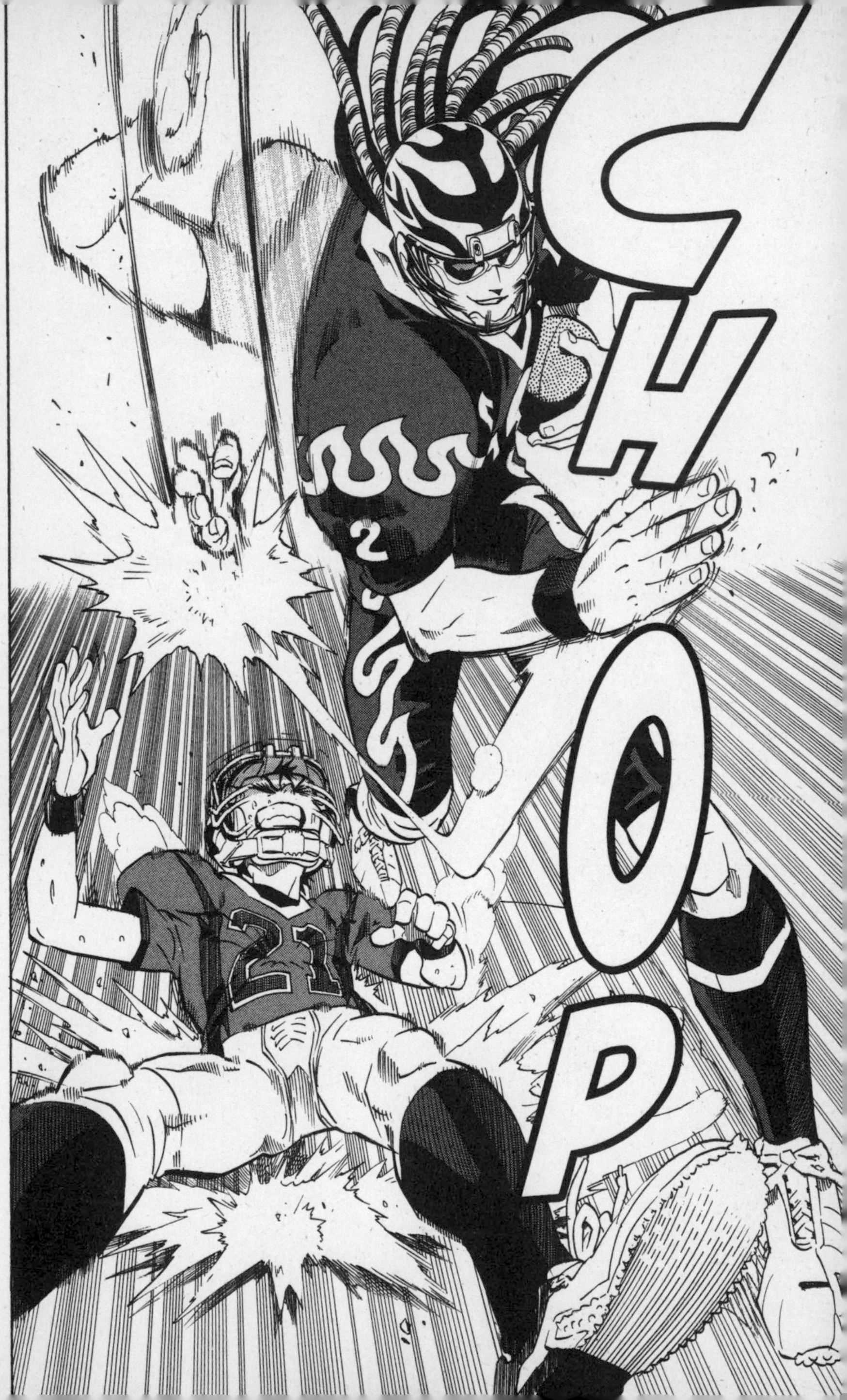
CHOP

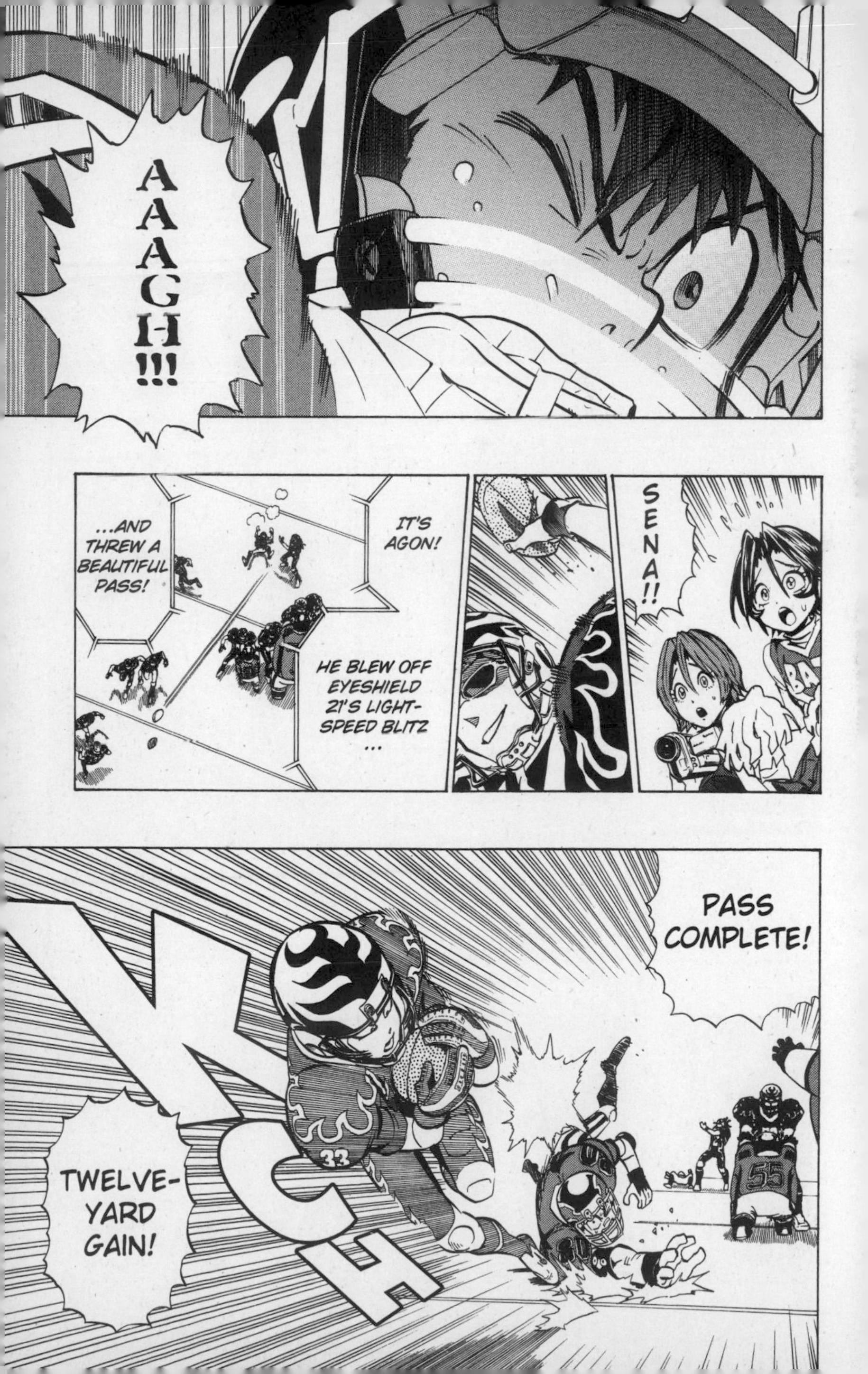
AAAGH!!!
SENA!!
IT'S AGON!
HE BLEW OFF EYESHIELD 21'S LIGHT-SPEED BLITZ ...
...AND THREW A BEAUTIFUL PASS!
PASS COMPLETE!
TWELVE-YARD GAIN!

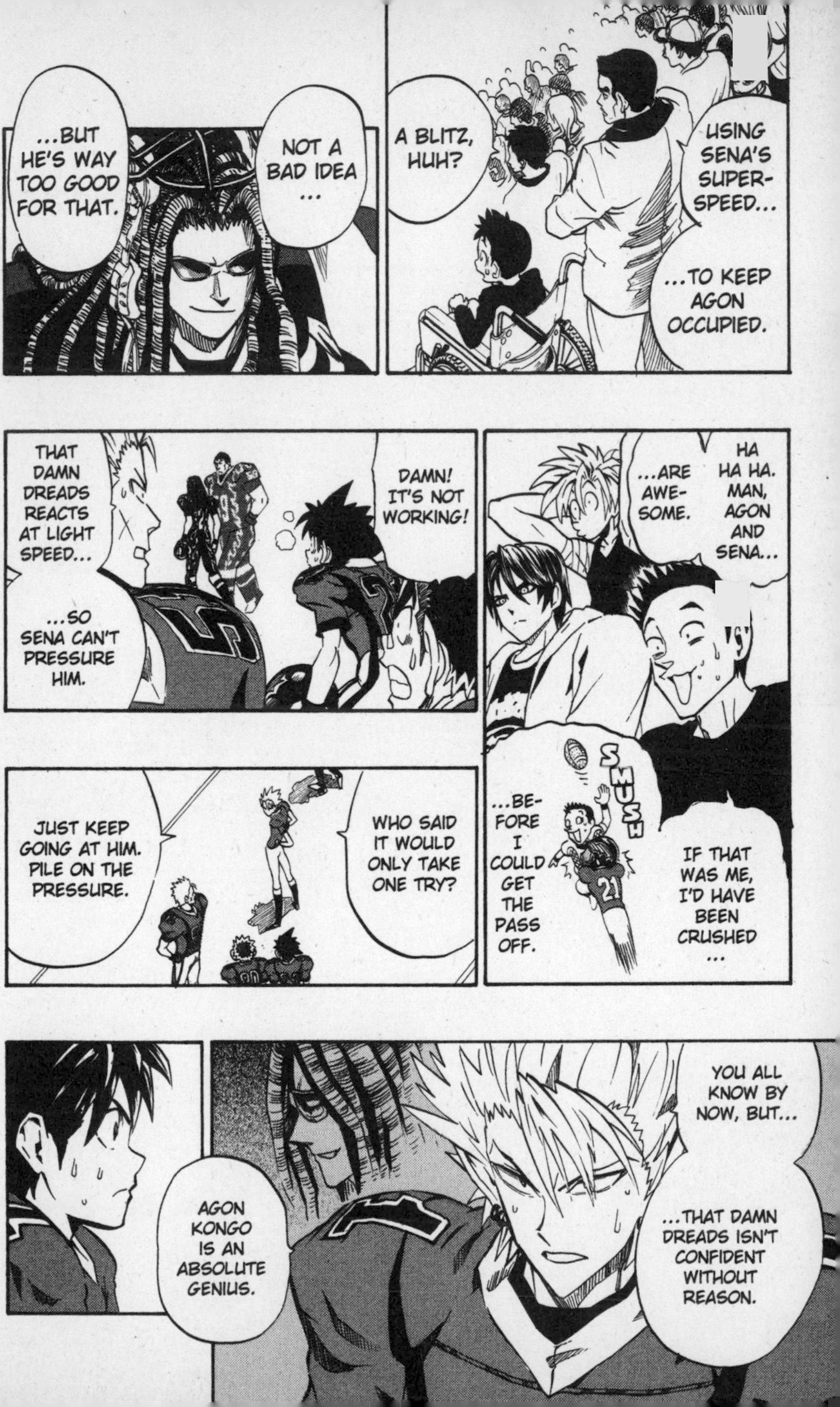
USING SENA'S SUPER-SPEED...
...TO KEEP AGON OCCUPIED.
A BLITZ, HUH?
NOT A BAD IDEA ...
...BUT HE'S WAY TOO GOOD FOR THAT.
HA HA HA. MAN, AGON AND SENA...
...ARE AWE-SOME.
IF THAT WAS ME, I'D HAVE BEEN CRUSHED ...
SMUSH
...BE-FORE I COULD GET THE PASS OFF.
DAMN! IT'S NOT WORKING!
THAT DAMN DREADS REACTS AT LIGHT SPEED...
...SO SENA CAN'T PRESSURE HIM.
WHO SAID IT WOULD ONLY TAKE ONE TRY?
JUST KEEP GOING AT HIM. PILE ON THE PRESSURE.
YOU ALL KNOW BY NOW, BUT...
...THAT DAMN DREADS ISN'T CONFIDENT WITHOUT REASON.
AGON KONGO IS AN ABSOLUTE GENIUS.

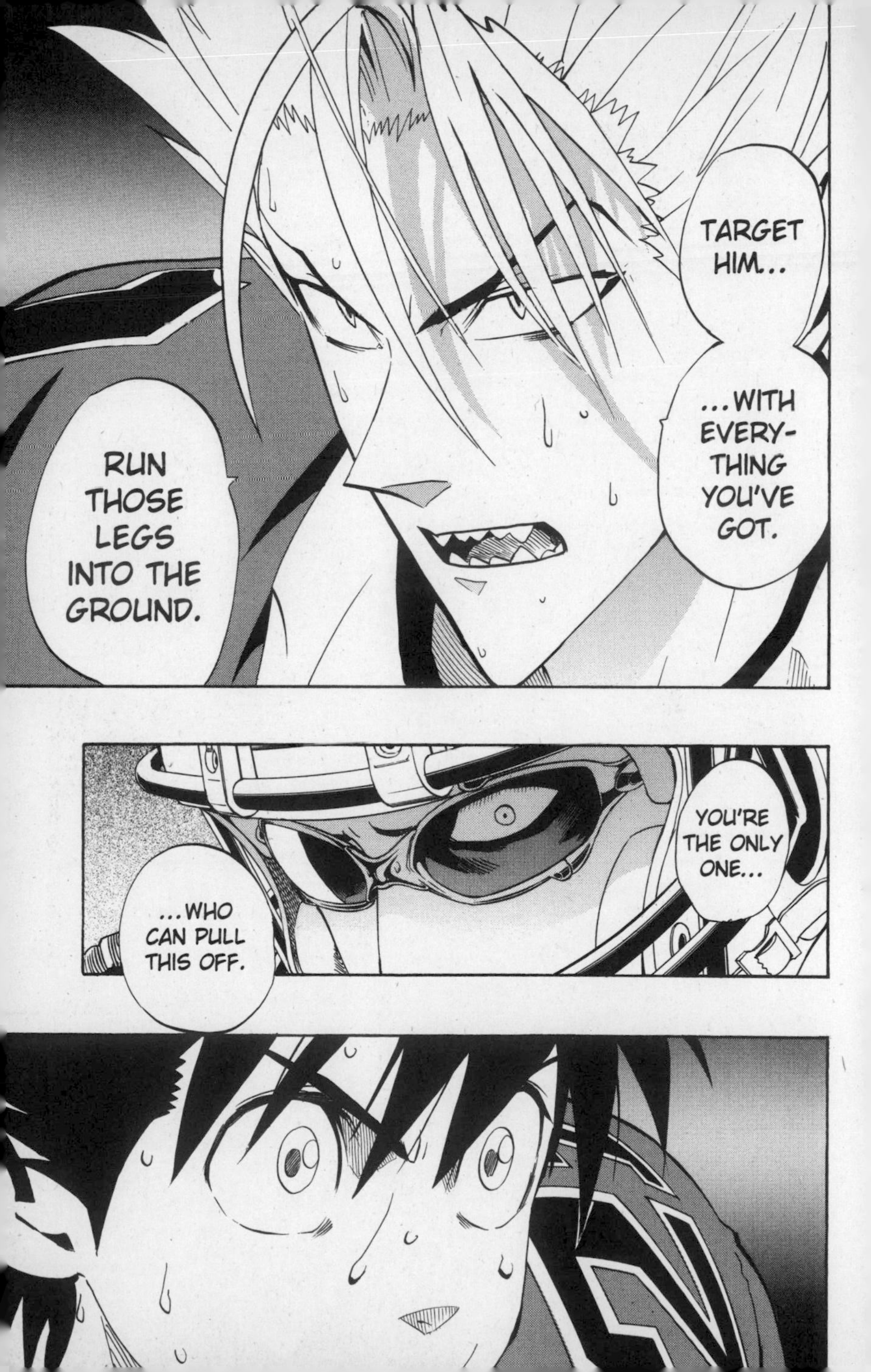
TARGET HIM...
...WITH EVERY-THING YOU'VE GOT.
RUN THOSE LEGS INTO THE GROUND.
YOU'RE THE ONLY ONE...
...WHO CAN PULL THIS OFF.

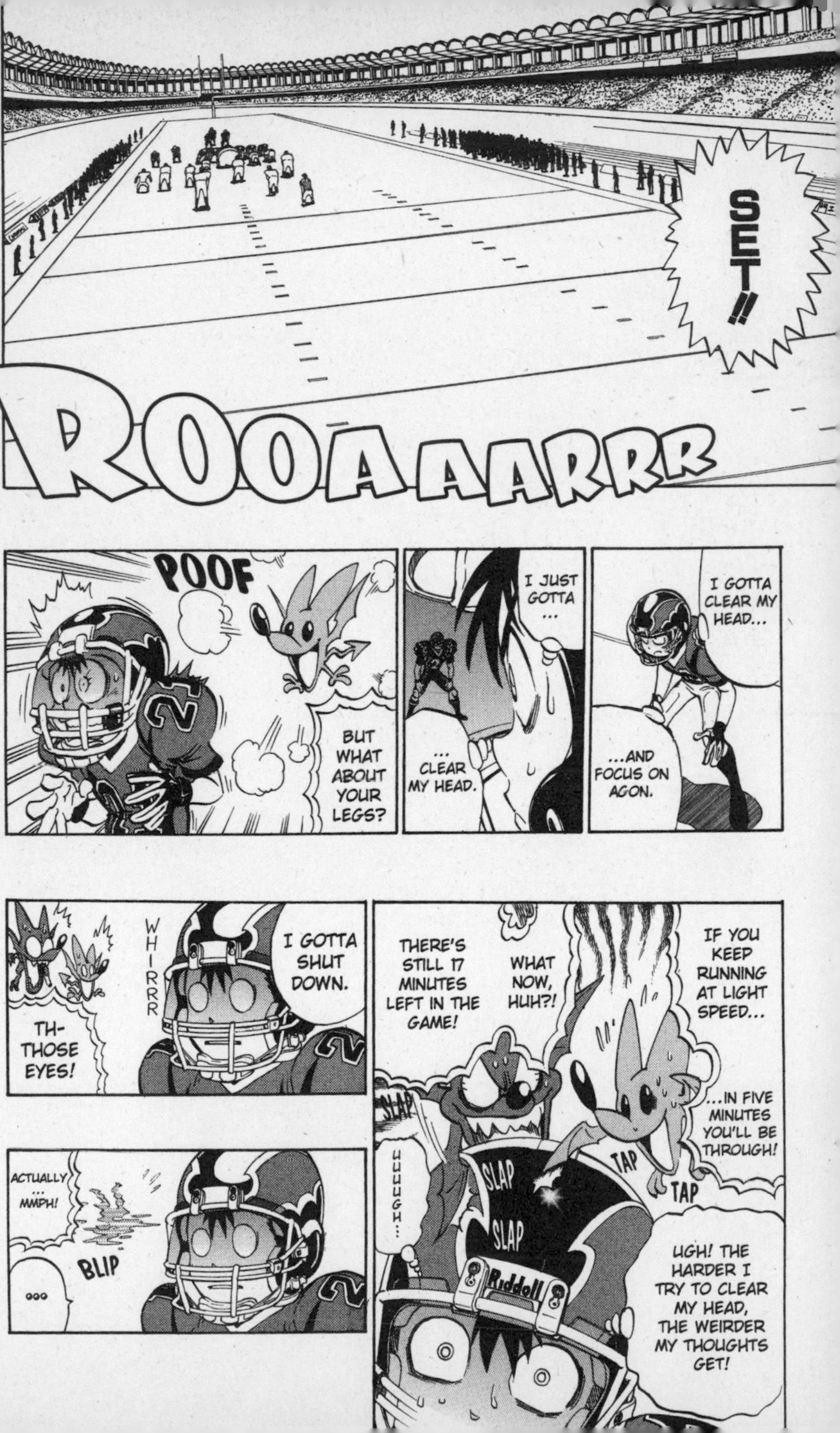
SET!!
ROOOAAARRR
I GOTTA CLEAR MY HEAD...
...AND FOCUS ON AGON.
I JUST GOTTA ...
... CLEAR MY HEAD.
POOF
BUT WHAT ABOUT YOUR LEGS?
IF YOU KEEP RUNNING AT LIGHT SPEED...
WHAT NOW, HUH?!
THERE'S STILL 17 MINUTES LEFT IN THE GAME!
...IN FIVE MINUTES YOU'LL BE THROUGH!
SLAP
TAP
TAP
SLAP
SLAP
HUUUGH...
Riddell
UGH! THE HARDER I TRY TO CLEAR MY HEAD, THE WEIRDER MY THOUGHTS GET!
I GOTTA SHUT DOWN.
WHIRRR
TH-THOSE EYES!
ACTUALLY ... MMPH!
BLIP
...

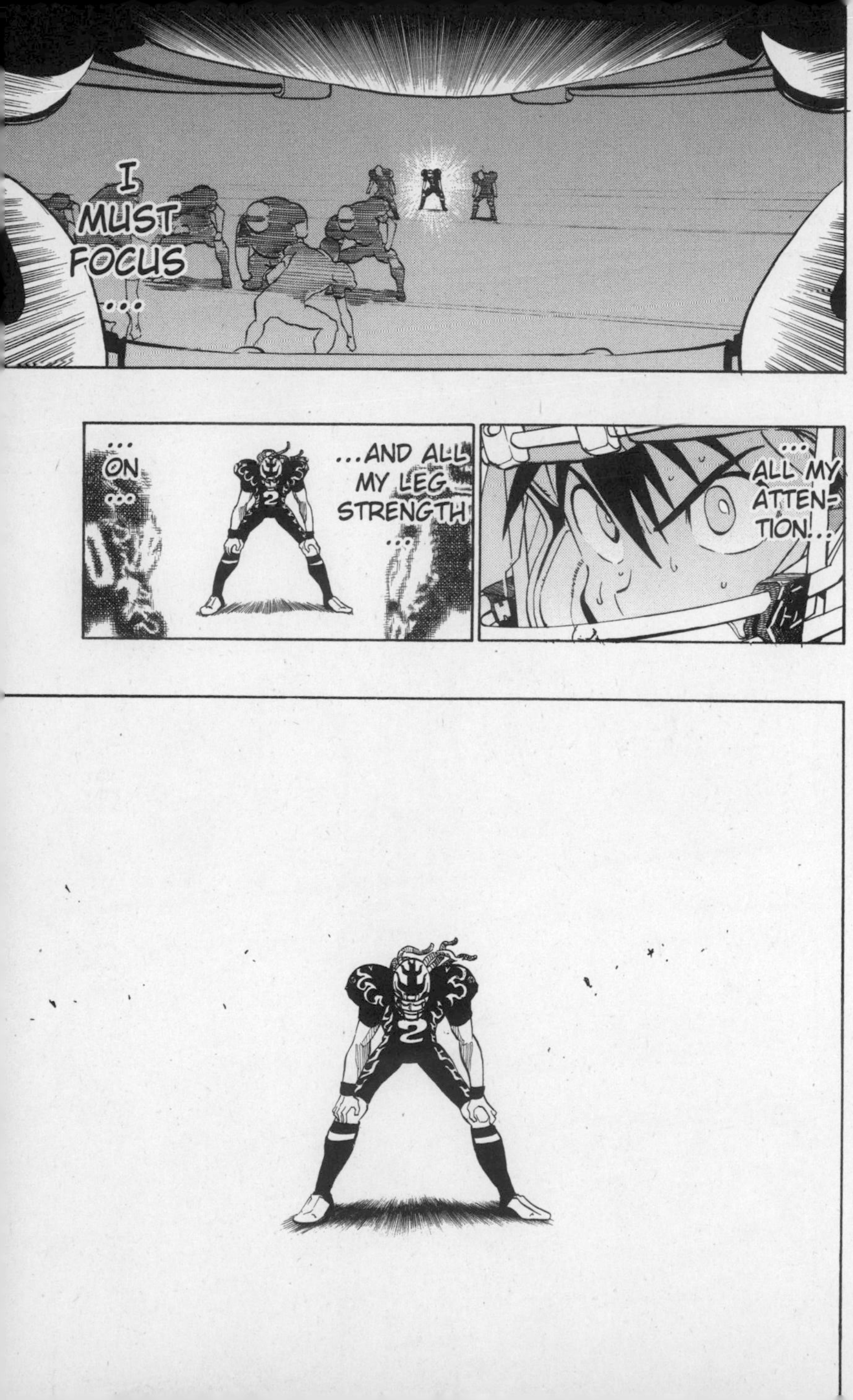
I MUST FOCUS ...
... ALL MY ATTEN-TION!...
...AND ALL MY LEG STRENGTH ...
... ON ...

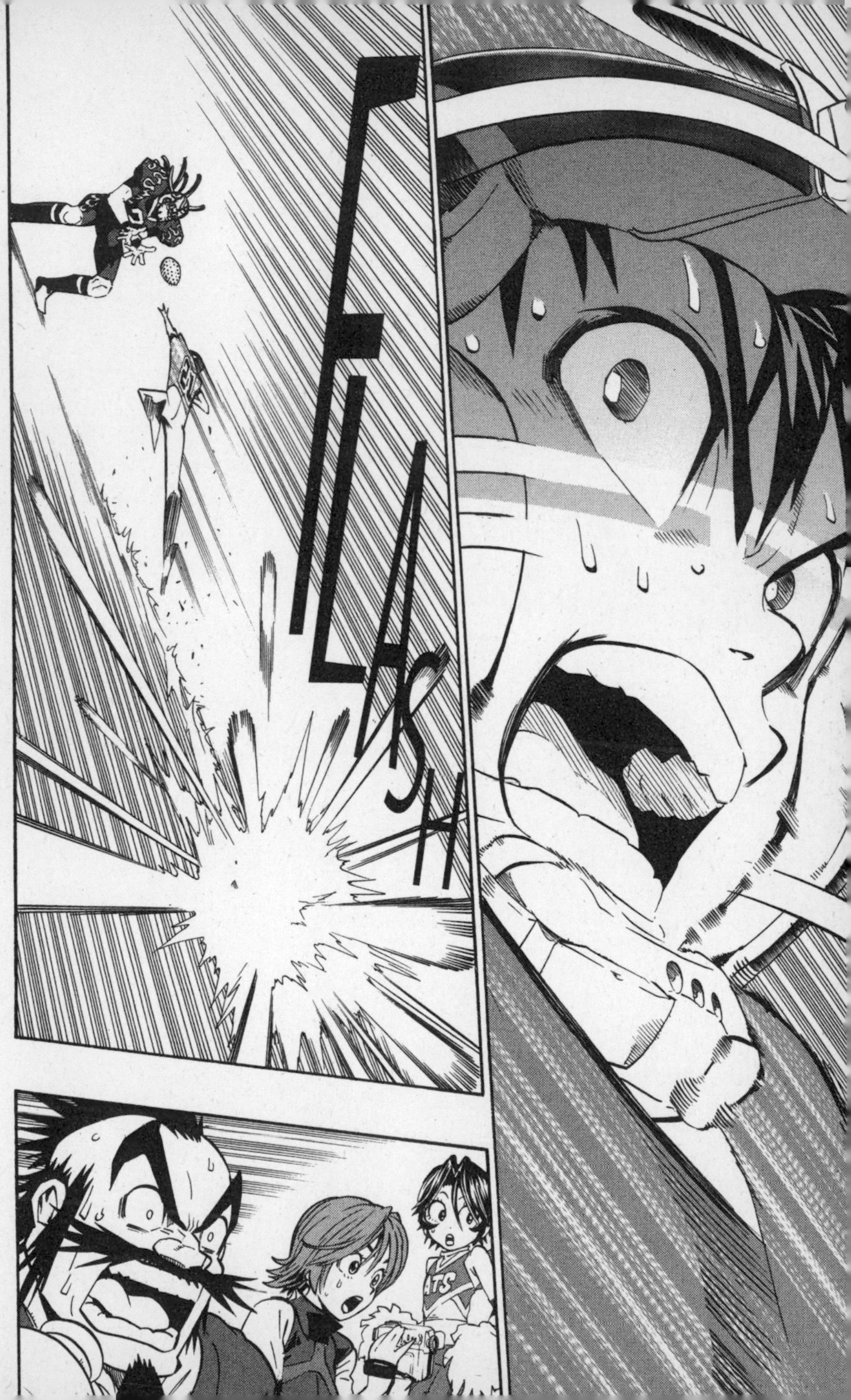
FLASH

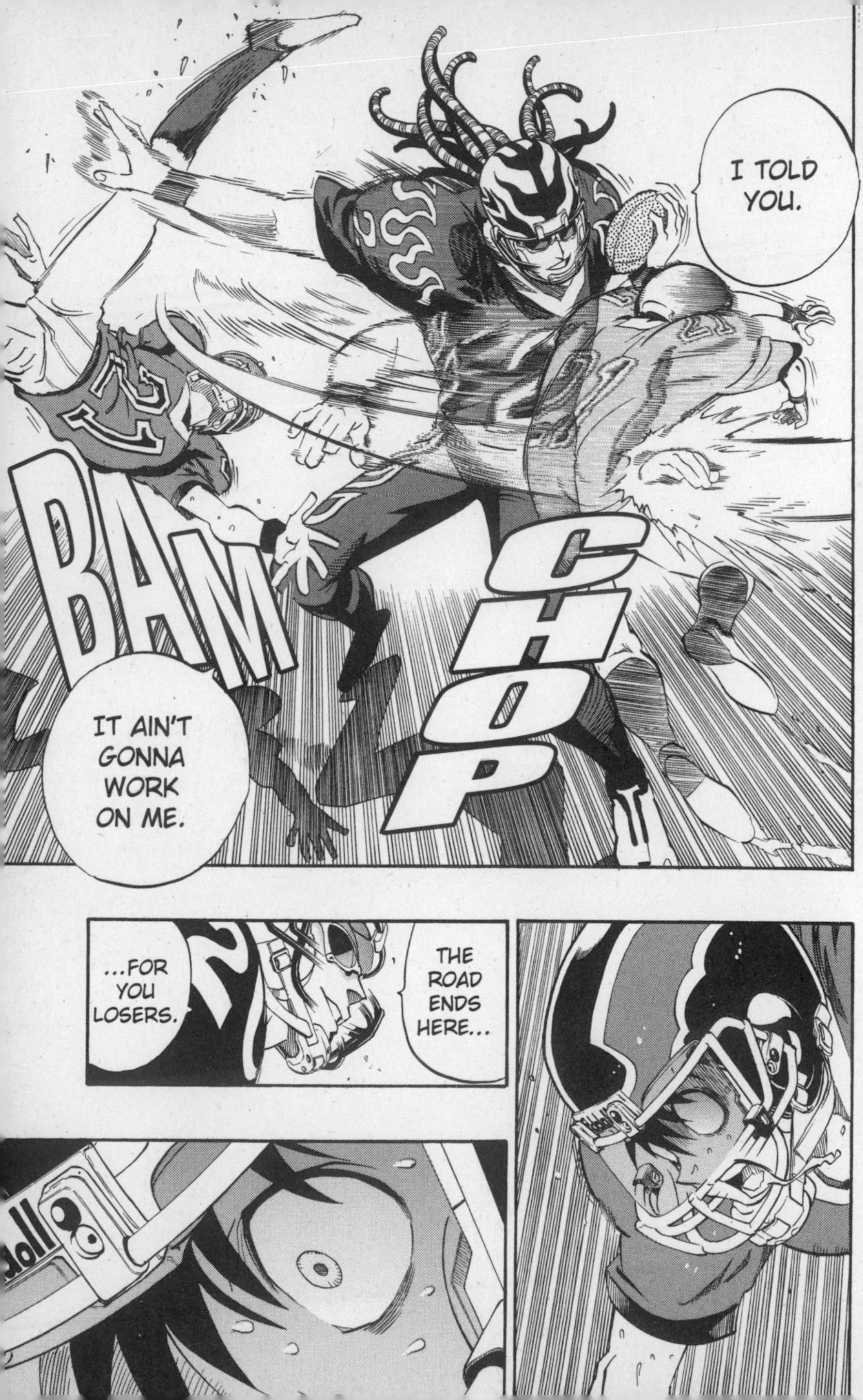
I TOLD YOU.
CHOP
BAM
IT AIN'T GONNA WORK ON ME.
THE ROAD ENDS HERE...
...FOR YOU LOSERS.

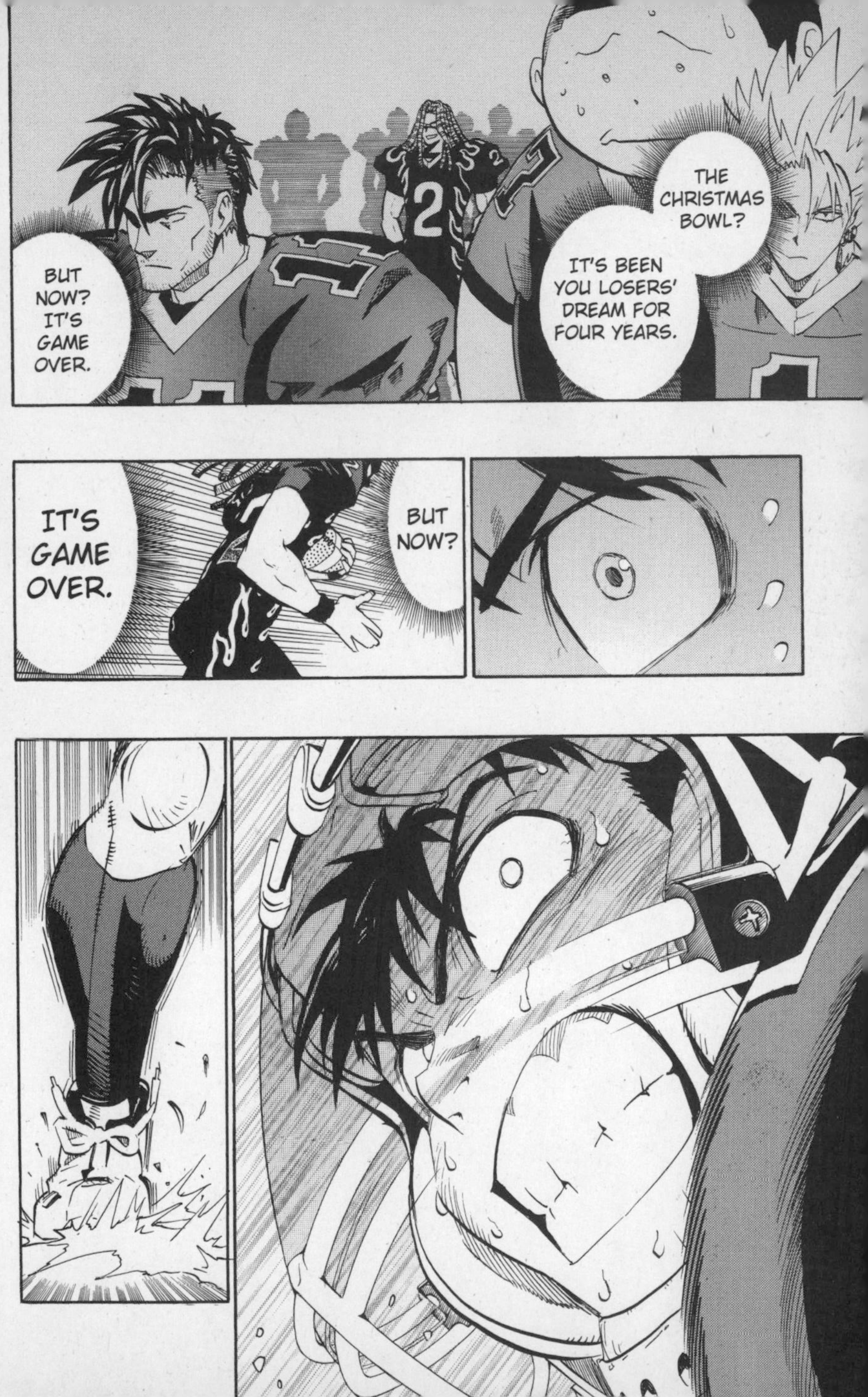
THE CHRISTMAS BOWL?
IT'S BEEN YOU LOSERS' DREAM FOR FOUR YEARS.
BUT NOW? IT'S GAME OVER.
BUT NOW?
IT'S GAME OVER.

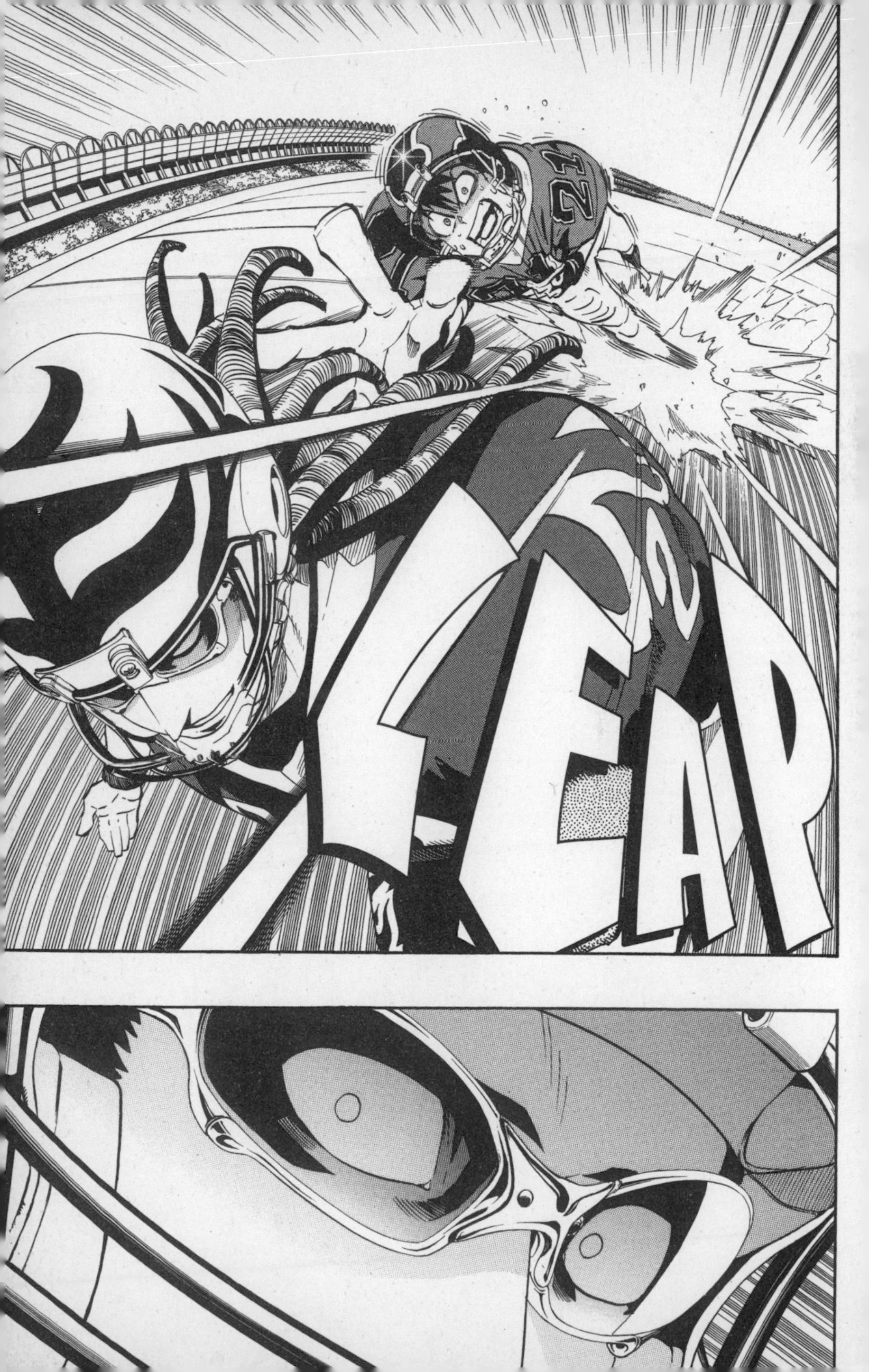
LEAP

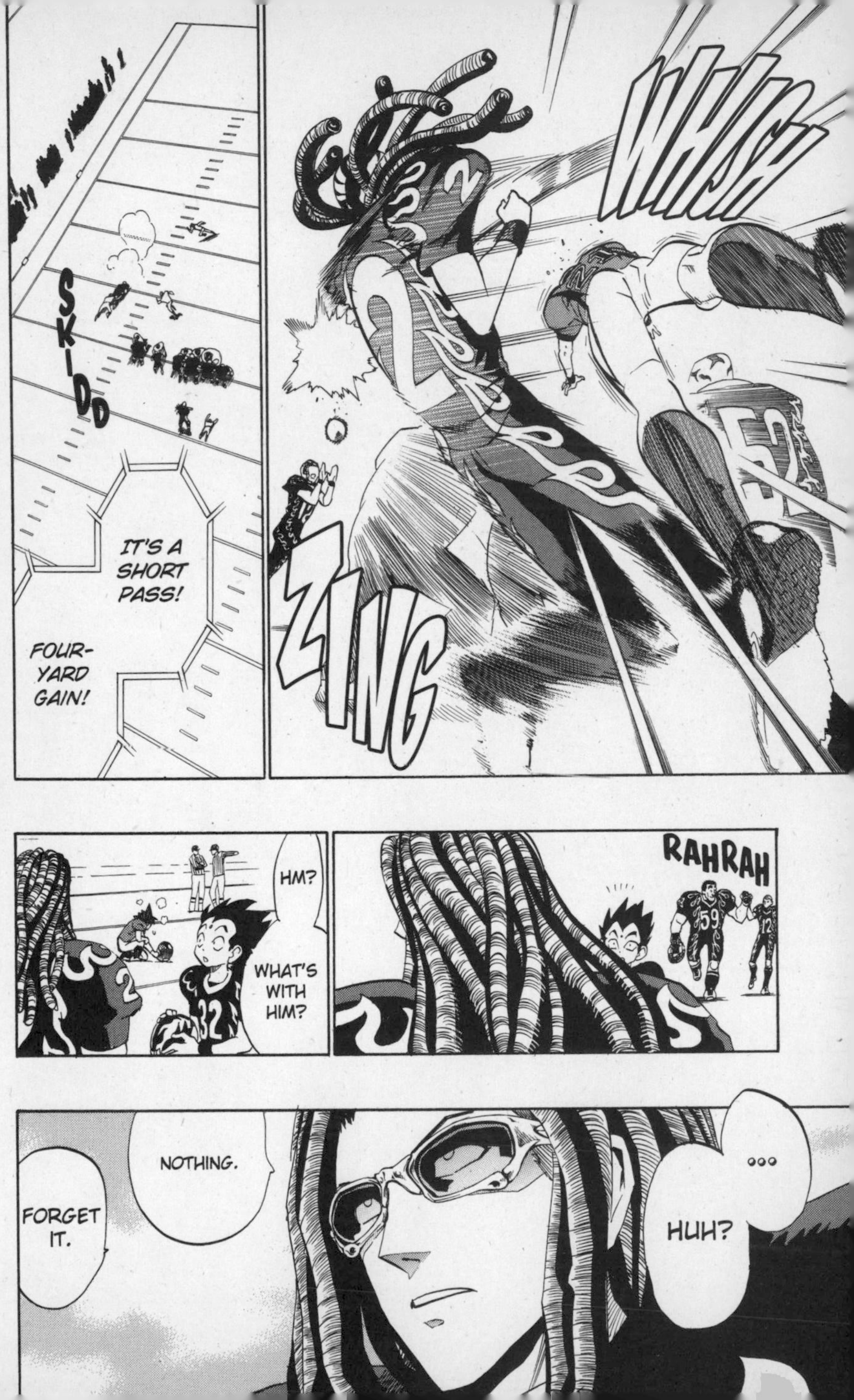
WHISH
ZING
SKIDD
IT'S A SHORT PASS!
FOUR-YARD GAIN!
RAHRAH
HM?
WHAT'S WITH HIM?
...
HUH?
NOTHING.
FORGET IT.

READ THIS WAY

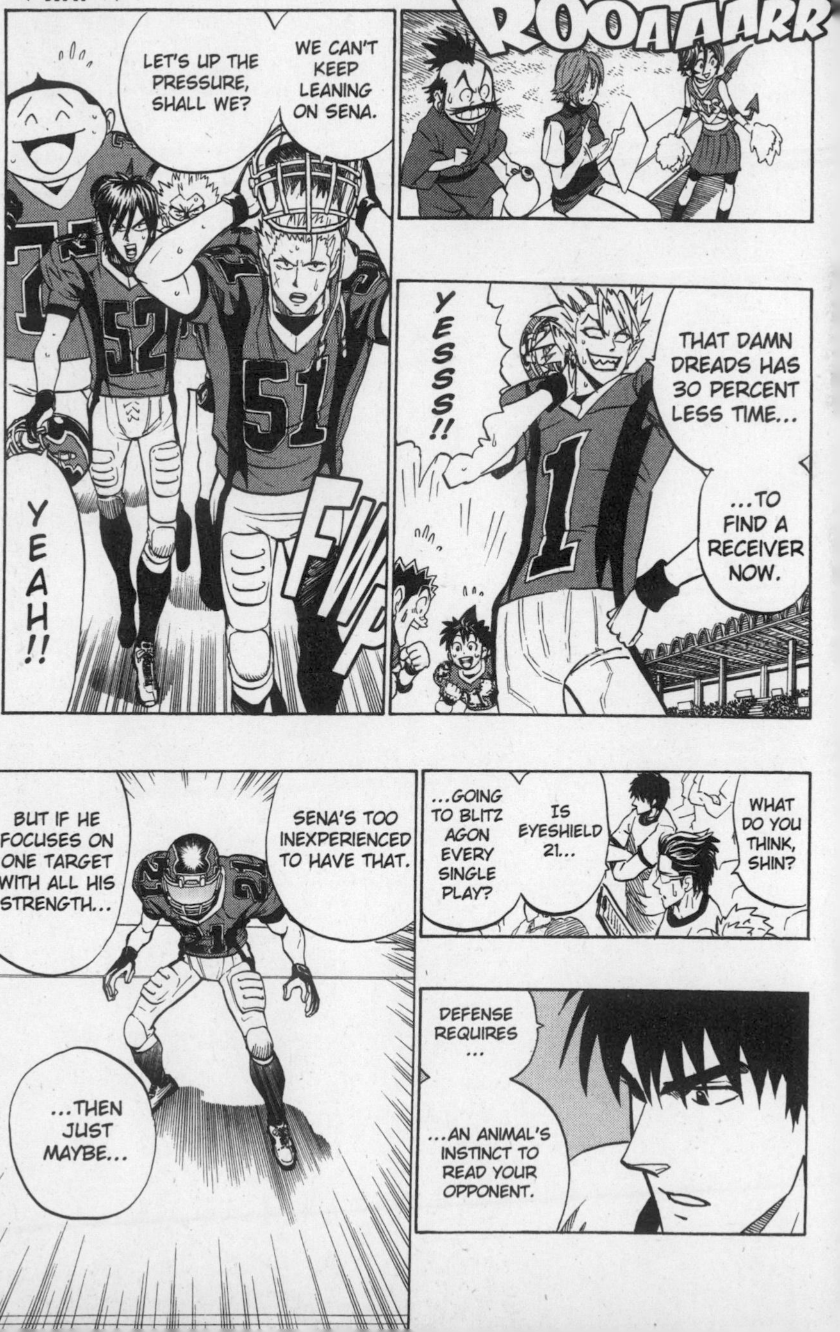
ROOOAAARR
YESSS!!
THAT DAMN DREADS HAS 30 PERCENT LESS TIME...
...TO FIND A RECEIVER NOW.
WE CAN'T KEEP LEANING ON SENA.
LET'S UP THE PRESSURE, SHALL WE?
YEAH!!
FWIP
WHAT DO YOU THINK, SHIN?
IS EYESHIELD 21...
...GOING TO BLITZ AGON EVERY SINGLE PLAY?
DEFENSE REQUIRES...
...AN ANIMAL'S INSTINCT TO READ YOUR OPPONENT.
SENA'S TOO INEXPERIENCED TO HAVE THAT.
BUT IF HE FOCUSES ON ONE TARGET WITH ALL HIS STRENGTH...
...THEN JUST MAYBE...

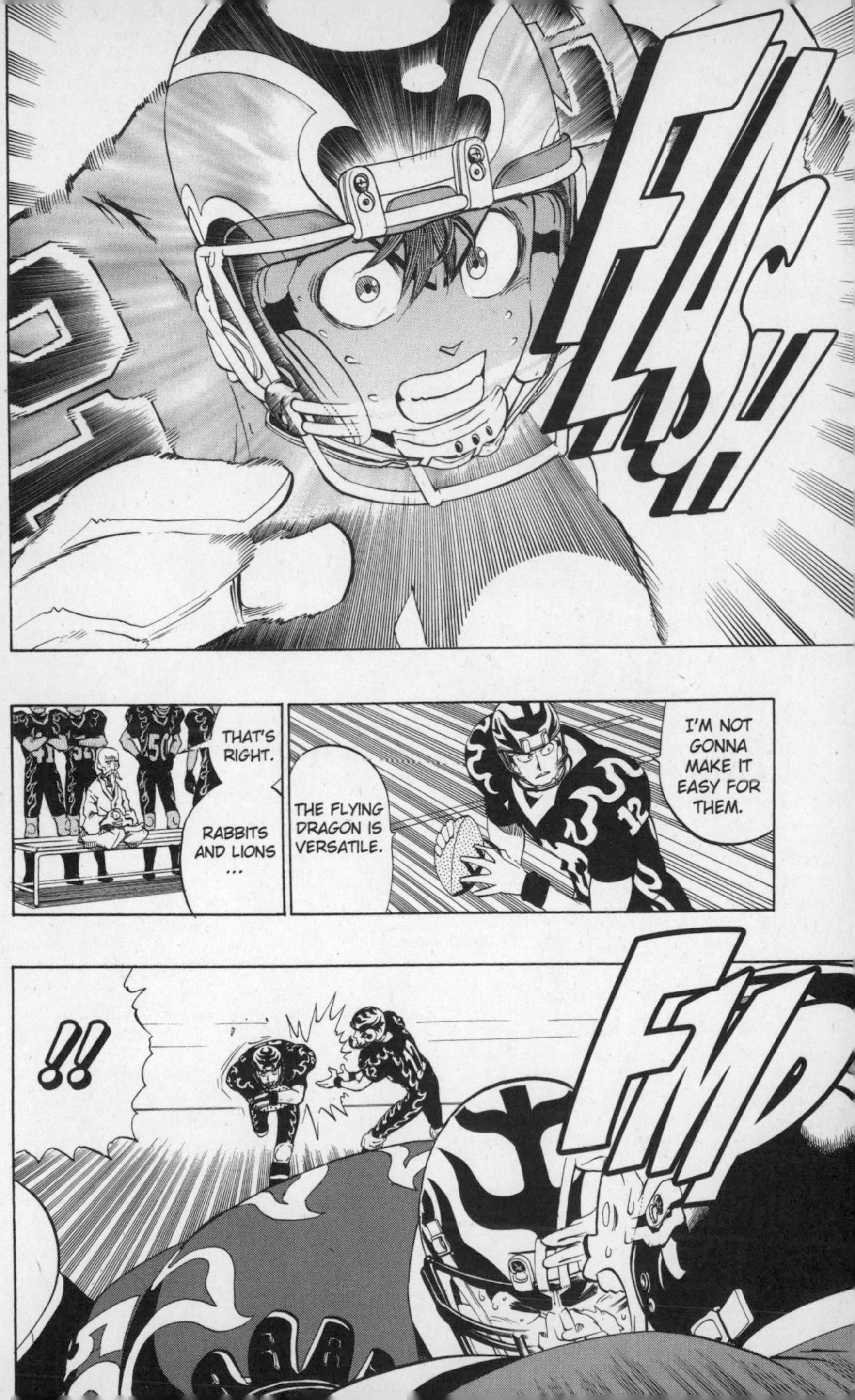
I'M NOT GONNA MAKE IT EASY FOR THEM.
THE FLYING DRAGON IS VERSATILE.
THAT'S RIGHT.
RABBITS AND LIONS ...
!!

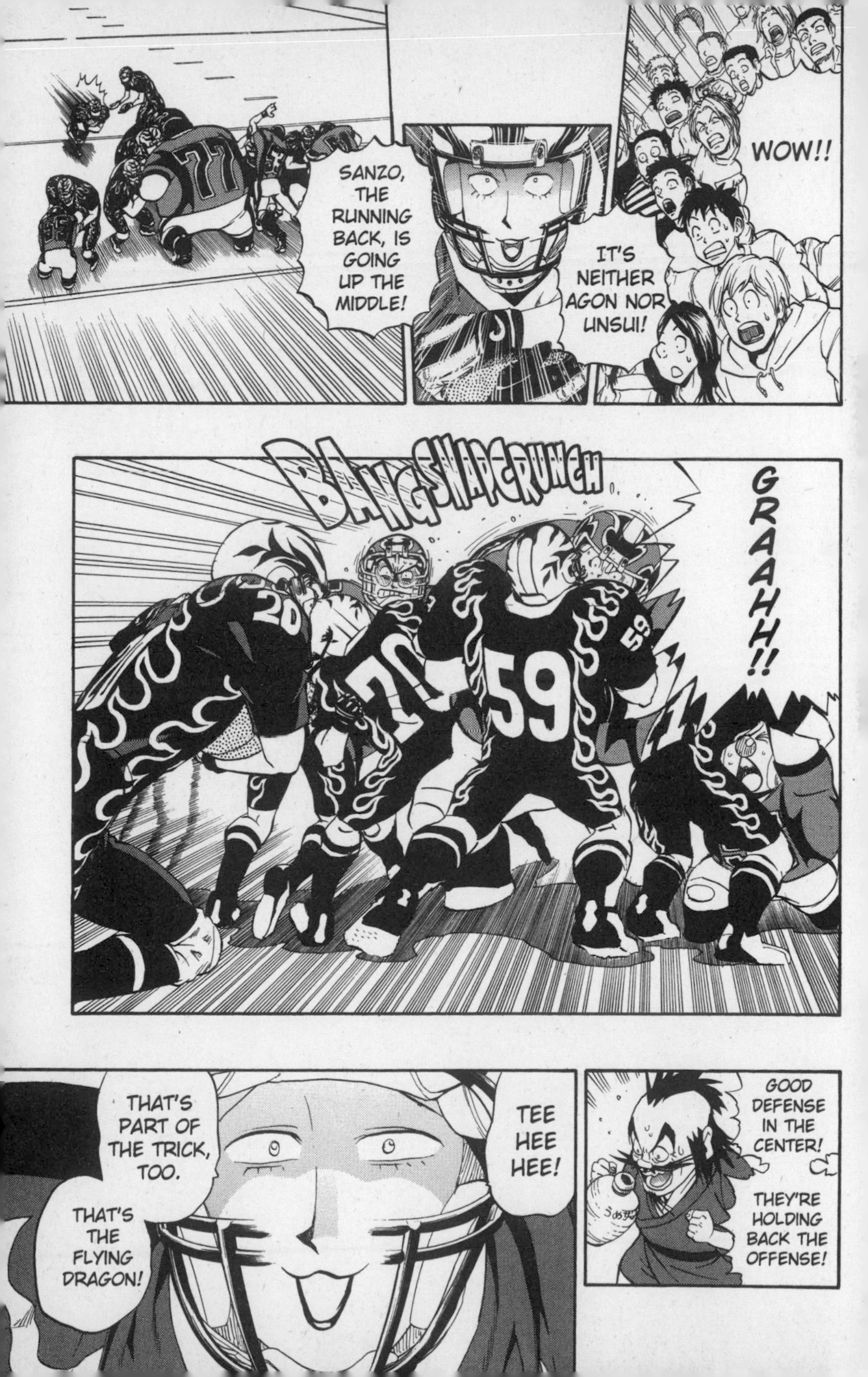
WOW!!
IT'S NEITHER AGON NOR UNSUI!
SANZO, THE RUNNING BACK, IS GOING UP THE MIDDLE!
GRAAHH!!
BANGSNAPCRUNCH
GOOD DEFENSE IN THE CENTER!
THEY'RE HOLDING BACK THE OFFENSE!
TEE HEE HEE!
THAT'S PART OF THE TRICK, TOO.
THAT'S THE FLYING DRAGON!

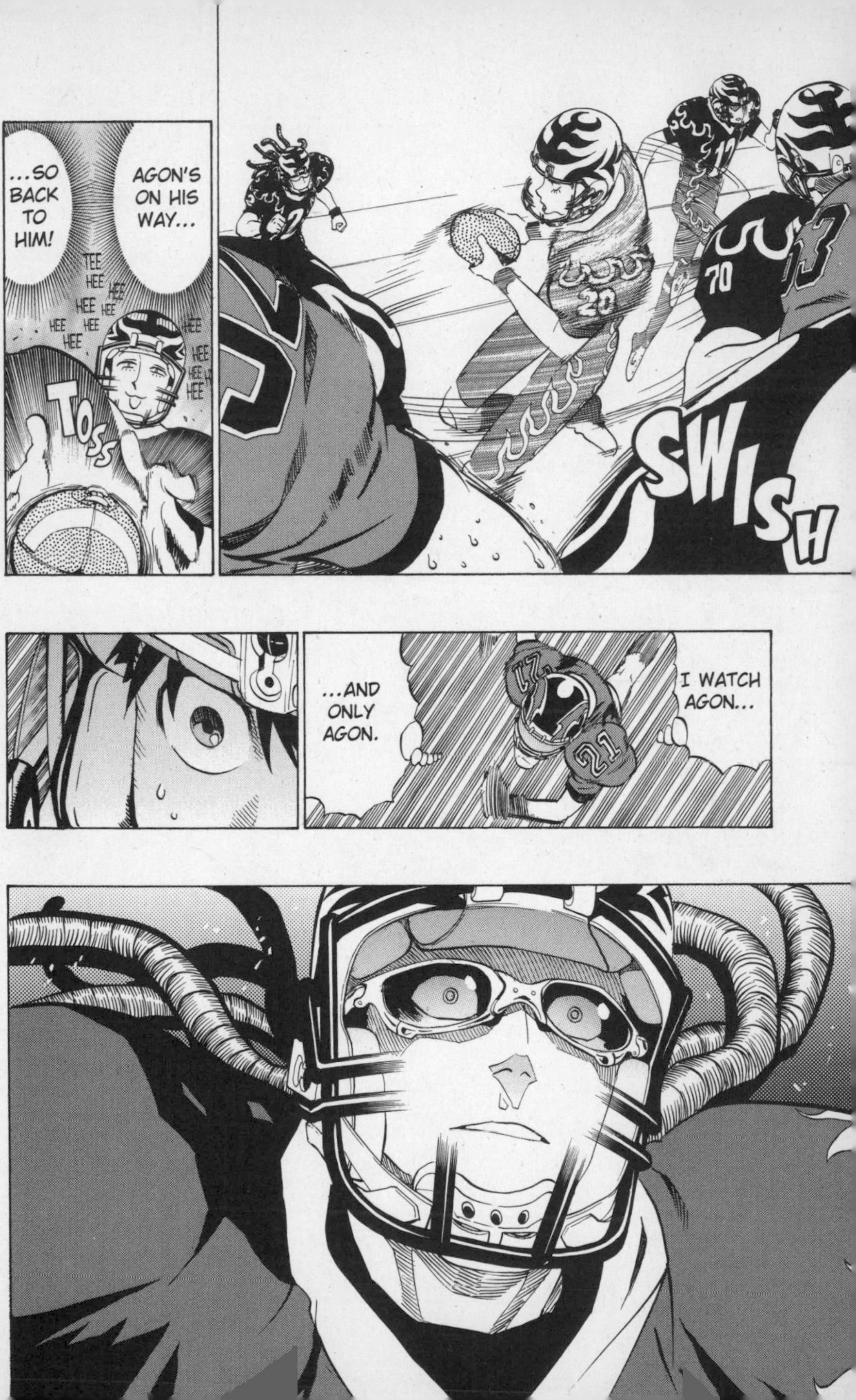
SWISH
AGON'S ON HIS WAY...
...SO BACK TO HIM!
TEE HEE HEE HEE HEE HEE HEE HEE HEE HEE HEE HEE
TOSS
I WATCH AGON...
...AND ONLY AGON.

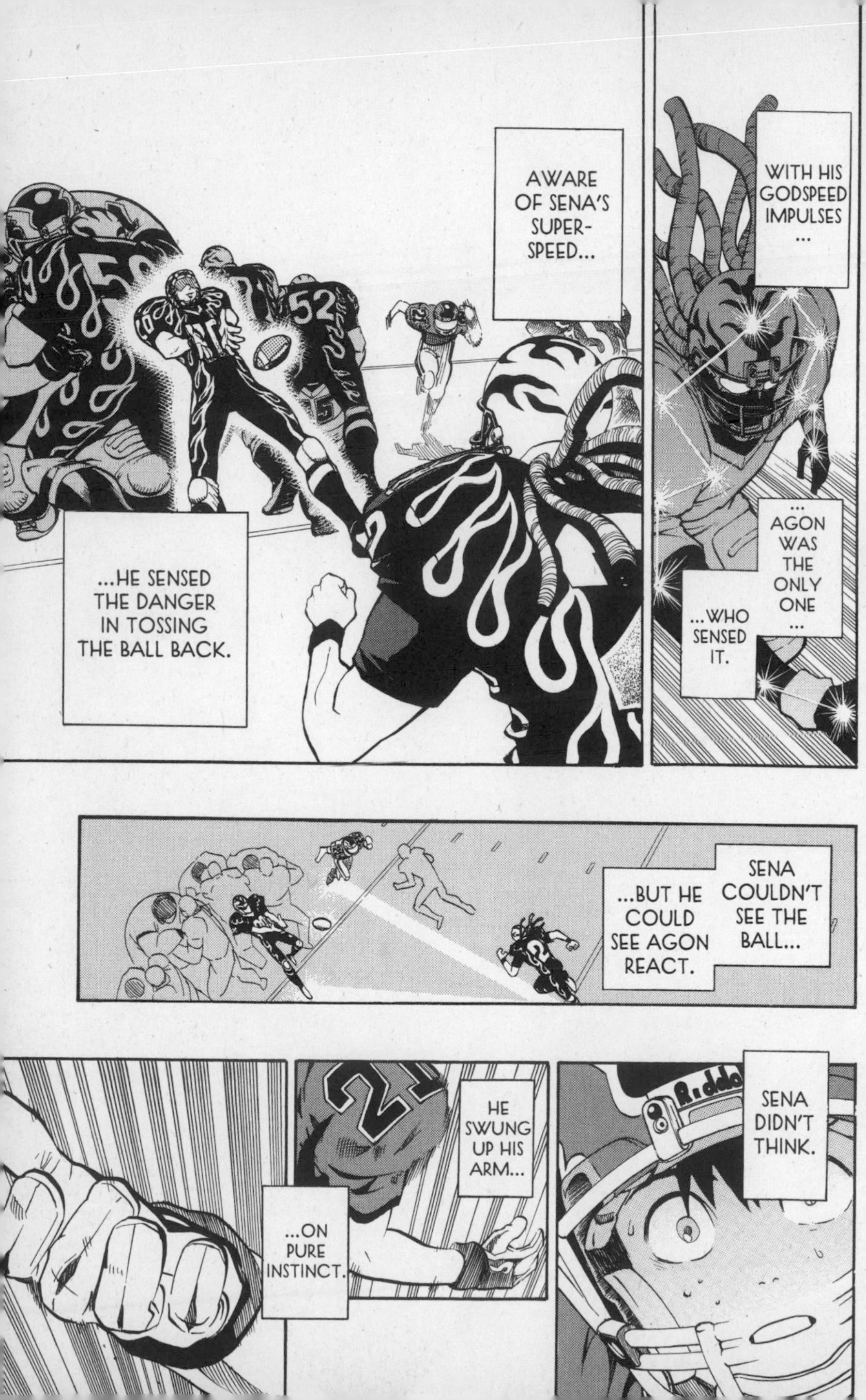
WITH HIS GODSPEED IMPULSES ...
... AGON WAS THE ONLY ONE ...
...WHO SENSED IT.
AWARE OF SENA'S SUPER-SPEED...
...HE SENSED THE DANGER IN TOSSING THE BALL BACK.
SENA COULDN'T SEE THE BALL...
...BUT HE COULD SEE AGON REACT.
SENA DIDN'T THINK.
HE SWUNG UP HIS ARM...
...ON PURE INSTINCT.

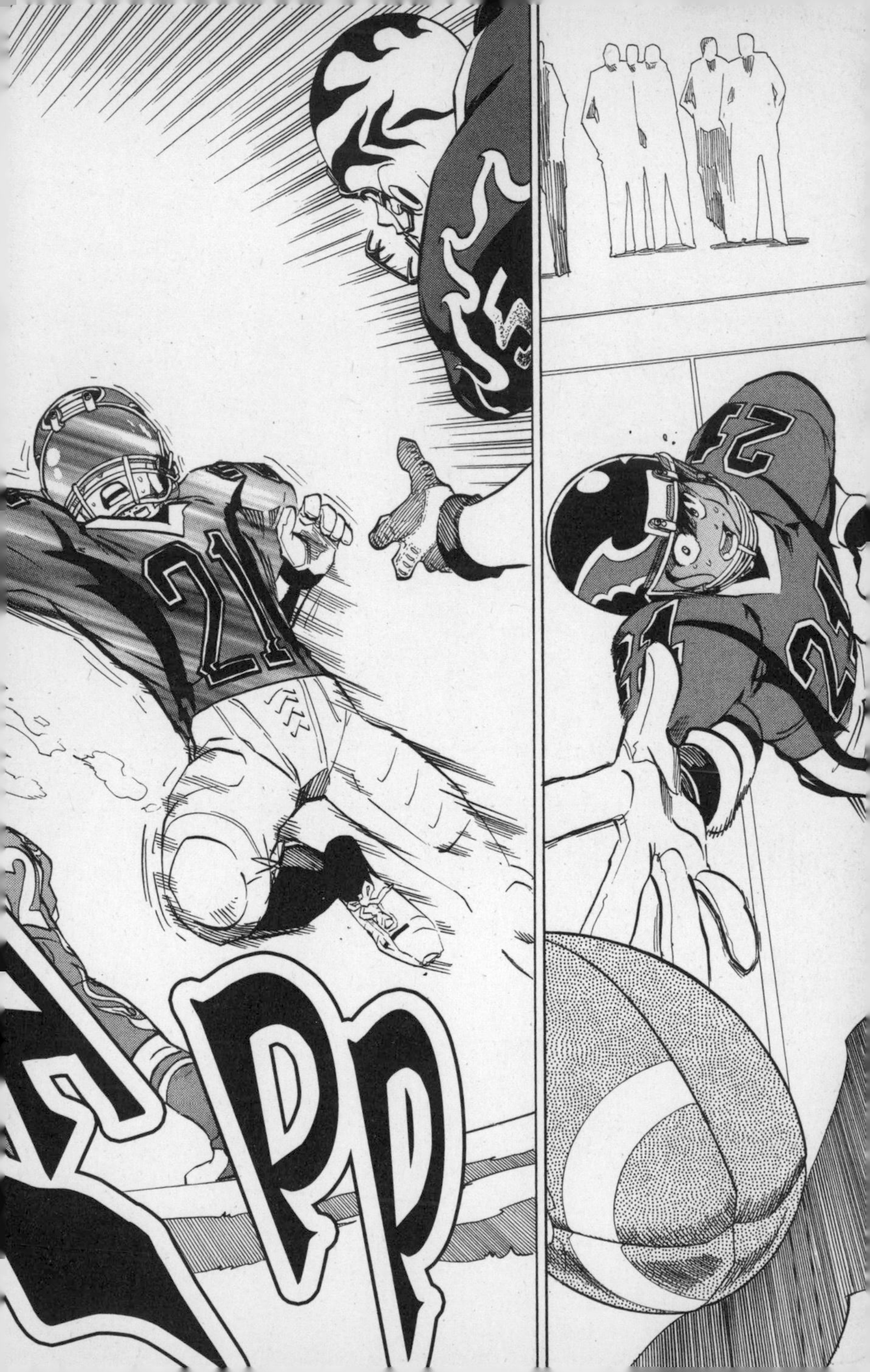
PP

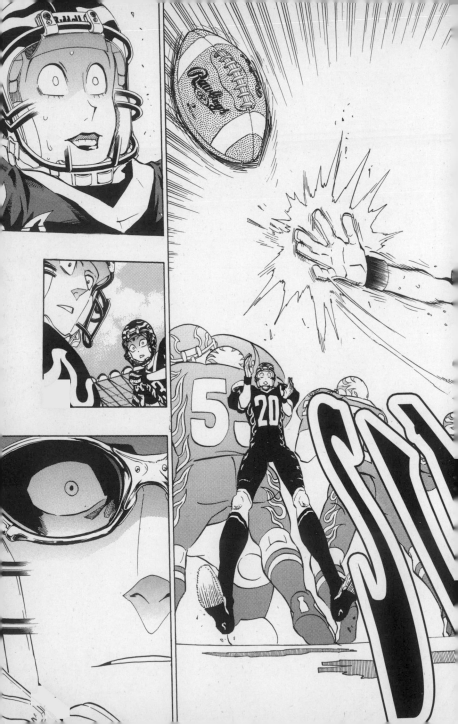

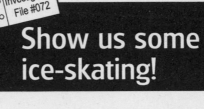

Investigation File #072

Show us some ice-skating!

SUZUNA IS GOOD AT INLINE SKATING, BUT WHAT ABOUT ICE-SKATING?

Sakura Sorakiyomi, Aichi Prefecture

TRACKS: GO DEIMON DEVIL BATS!

WHOAAAAAAAAAAAA!!

Chapter 184 They Were 11!

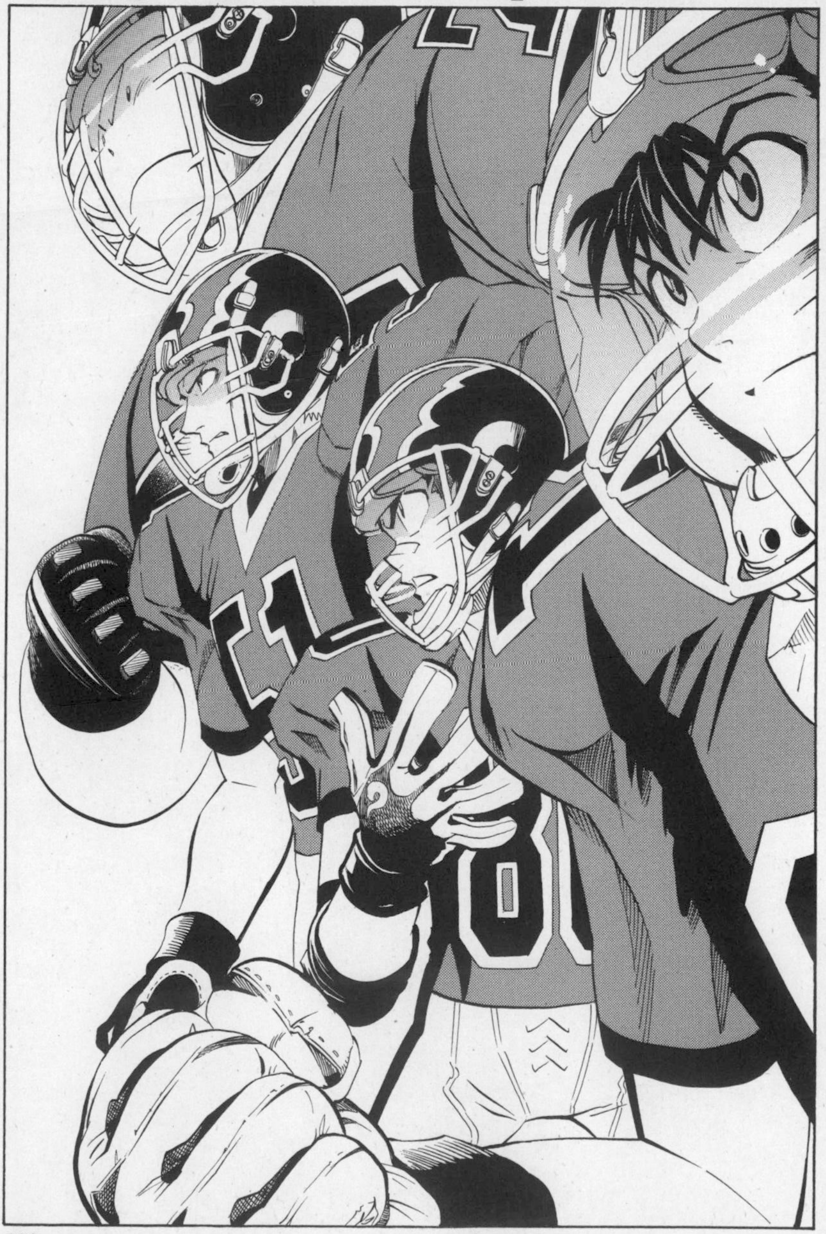

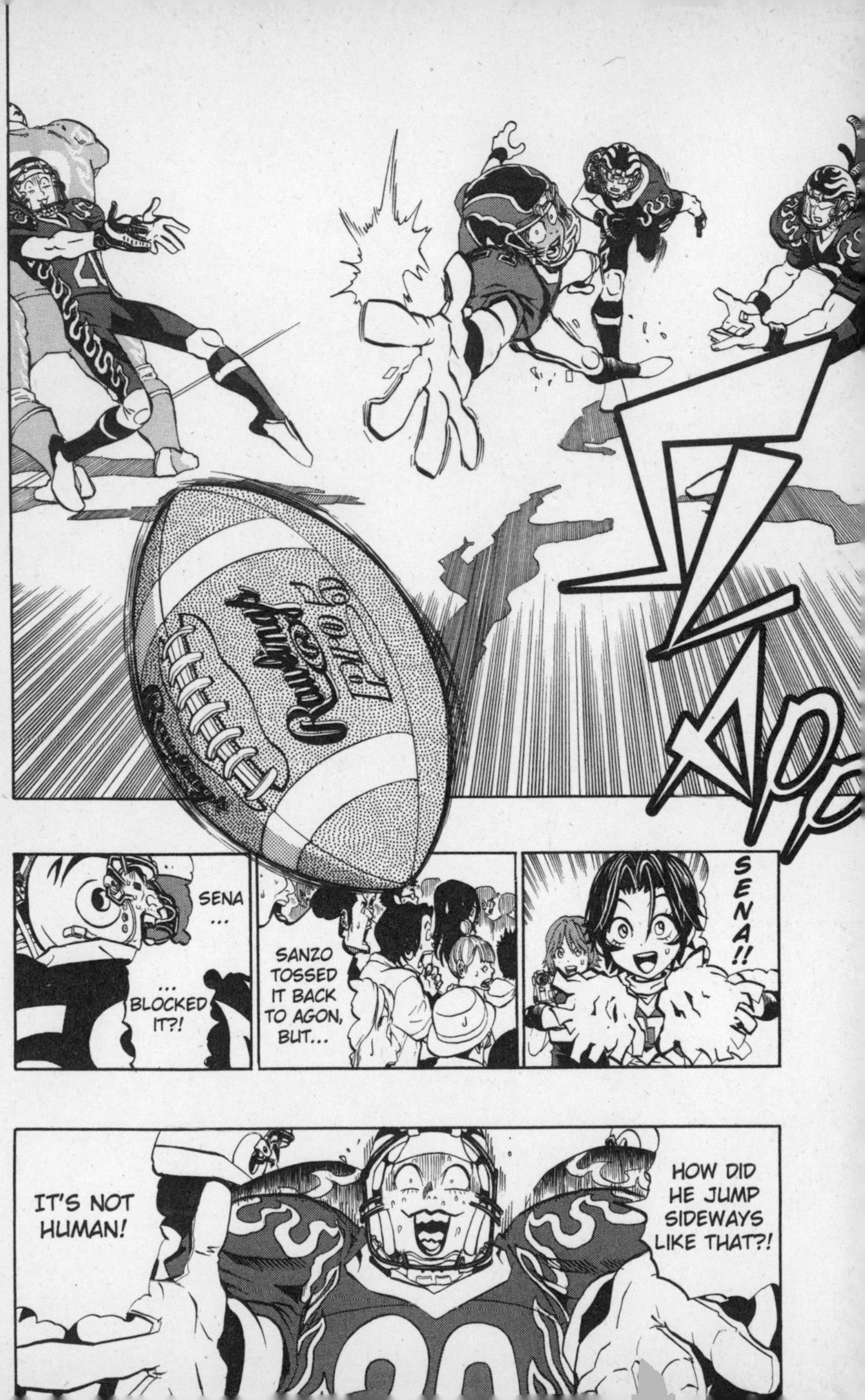
SENA!!
SANZO TOSSED IT BACK TO AGON, BUT...
SENA ...
... BLOCKED IT?!
HOW DID HE JUMP SIDEWAYS LIKE THAT?!
IT'S NOT HUMAN!

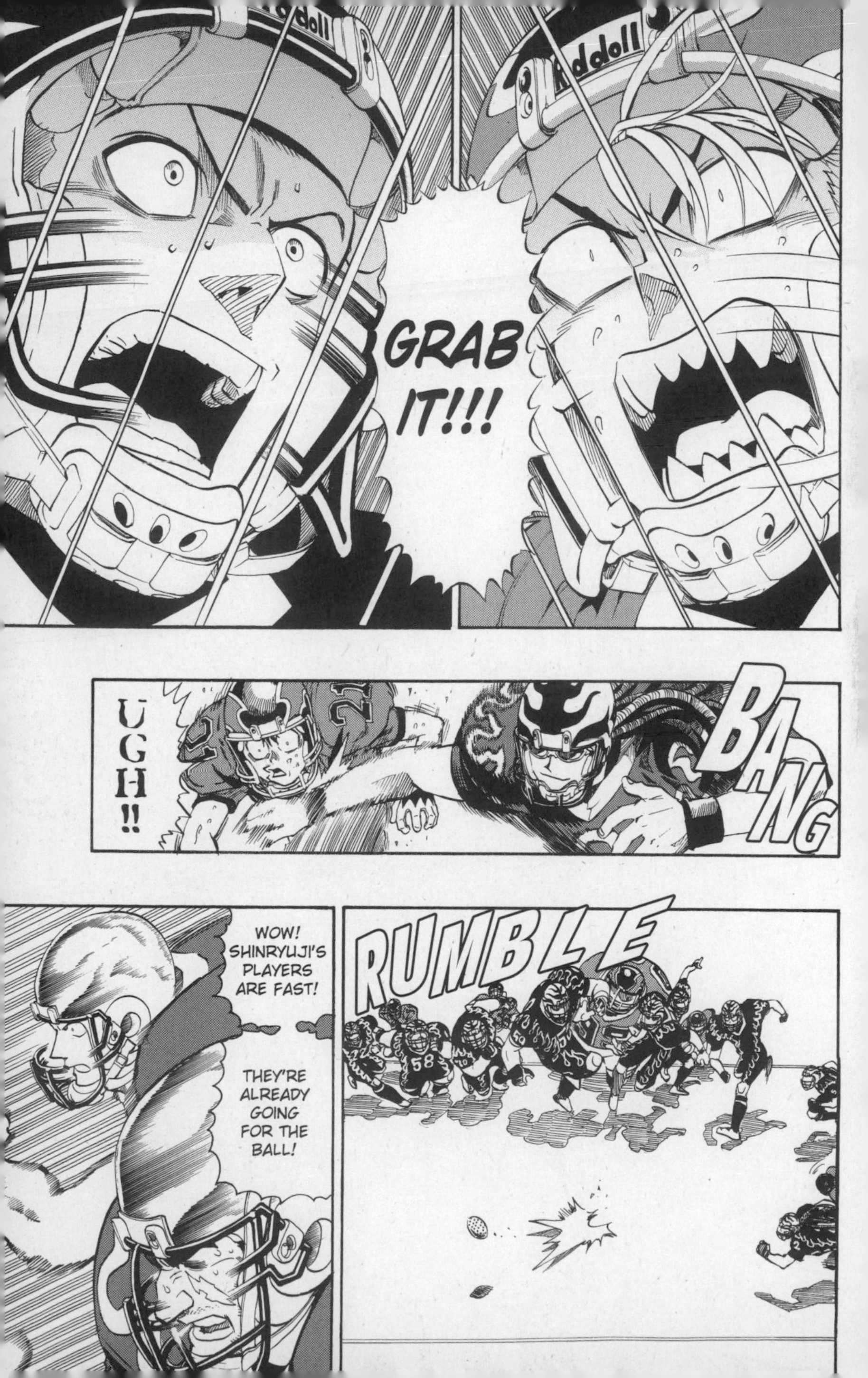
GRAB IT!!!
BANG
UGH!!
RUMBLE
WOW! SHINRYUJI'S PLAYERS ARE FAST!
THEY'RE ALREADY GOING FOR THE BALL!

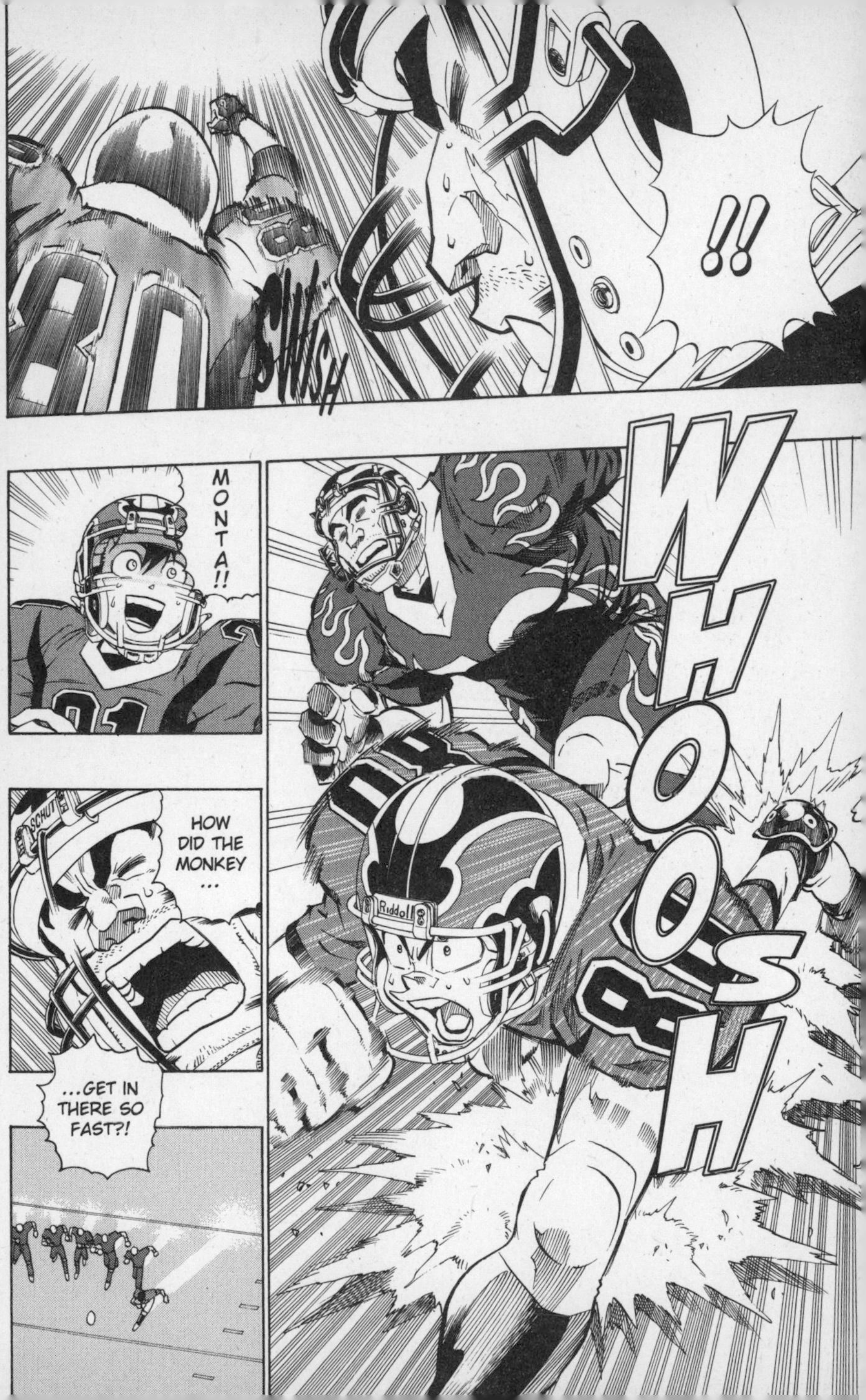
!!
SWISH
WHOOSH
MONTA!!
HOW DID THE MONKEY ...
...GET IN THERE SO FAST?!

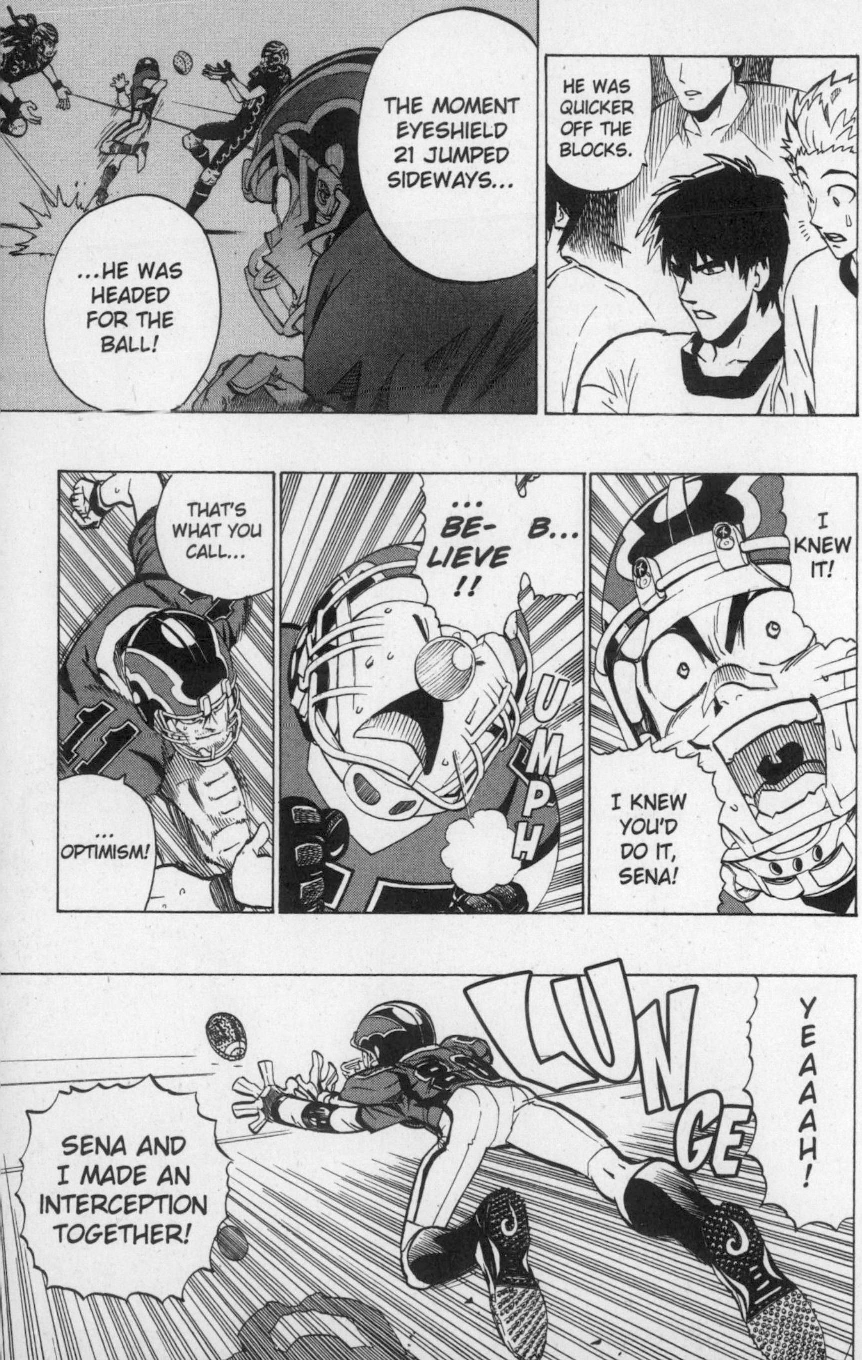
HE WAS QUICKER OFF THE BLOCKS.
THE MOMENT EYESHIELD 21 JUMPED SIDEWAYS...
...HE WAS HEADED FOR THE BALL!
I KNEW IT!
I KNEW YOU'D DO IT, SENA!
B...
...BE-LIEVE!!
UMPH
THAT'S WHAT YOU CALL...
...OPTIMISM!
YEAAAAH!
LUNGE
SENA AND I MADE AN INTERCEPTION TOGETHER!

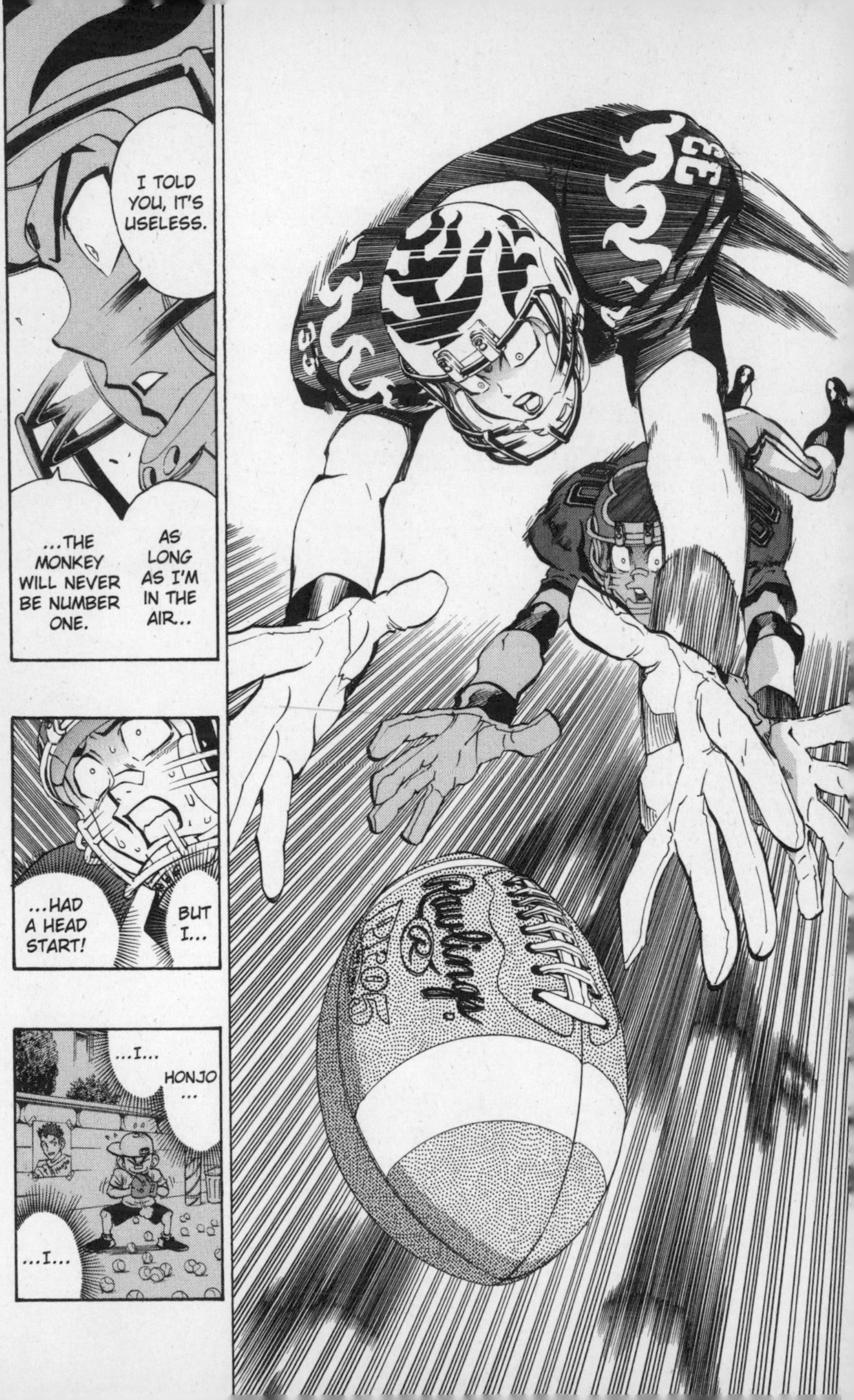
I TOLD YOU, IT'S USELESS.
AS LONG AS I'M IN THE AIR...
...THE MONKEY WILL NEVER BE NUMBER ONE.
BUT I...
...HAD A HEAD START!
...I...
HONJO ...
...I...

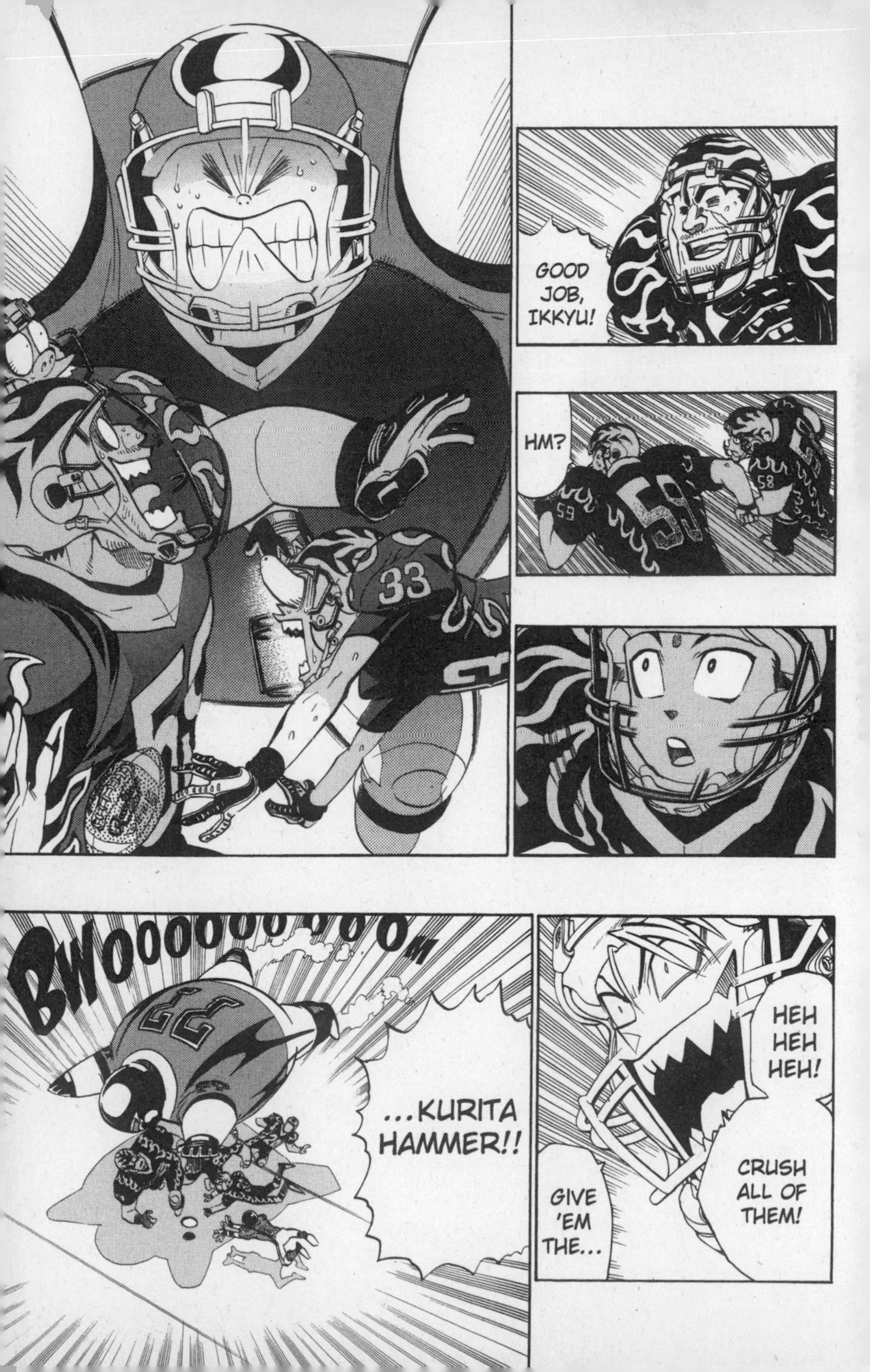
GOOD JOB, IKKYU!
HM?
HEH HEH HEH!
CRUSH ALL OF THEM!
GIVE 'EM THE...
...KURITA HAMMER!!
BWOOOOOOOOOOOM

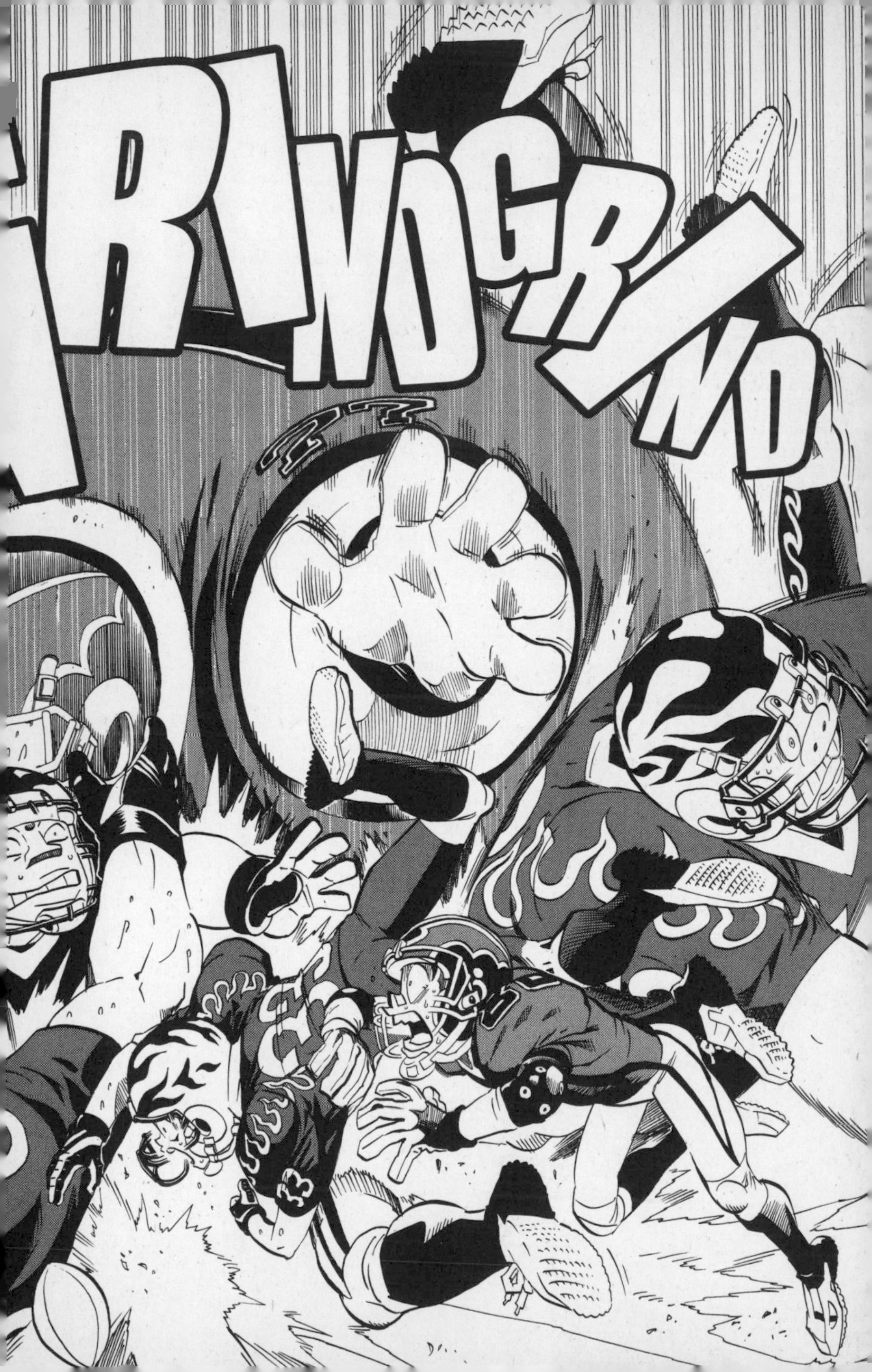
GRIND GRIND

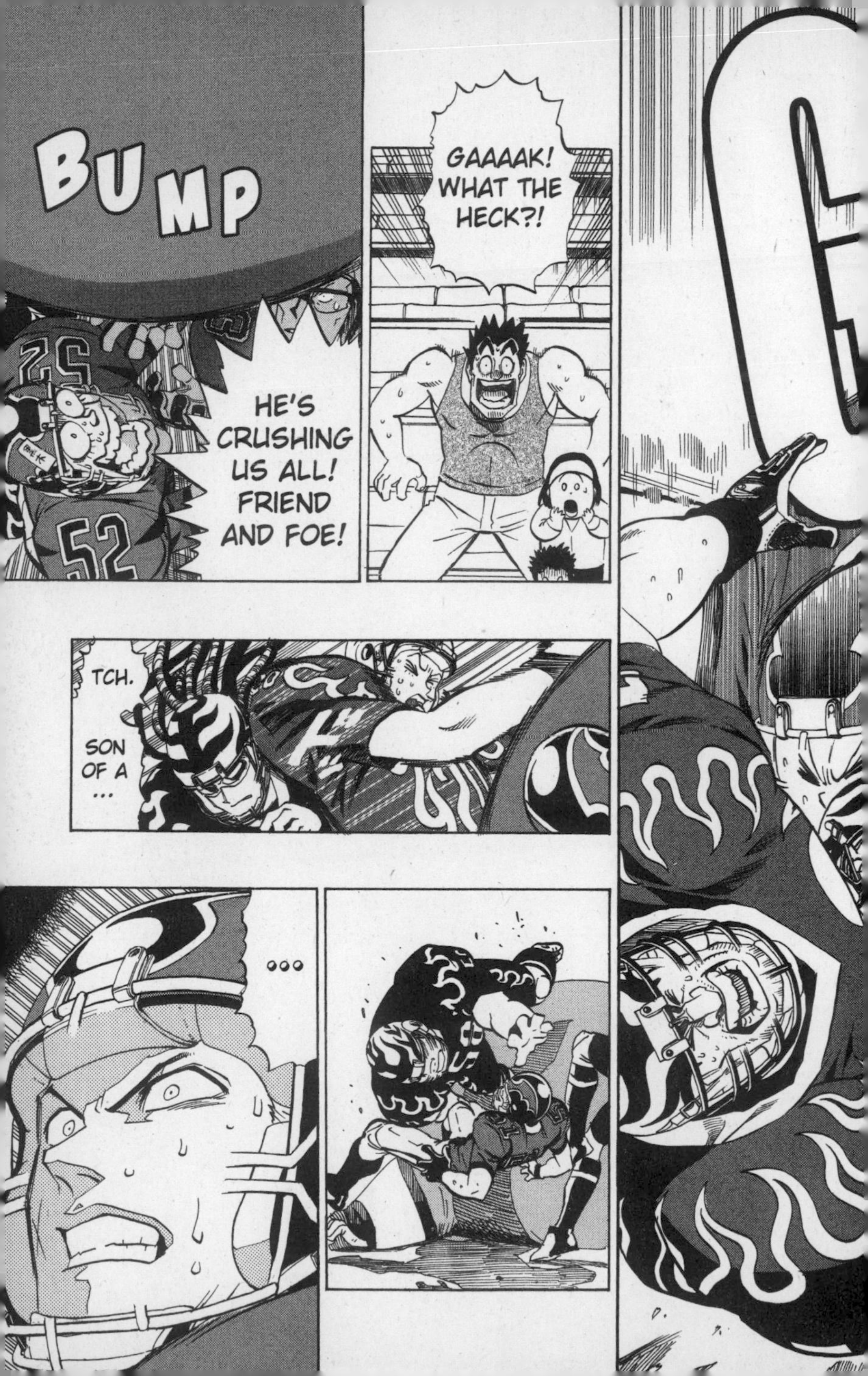
GAAAAK! WHAT THE HECK?!
BUMP
HE'S CRUSHING US ALL! FRIEND AND FOE!
TCH.
SON OF A ...
!
...

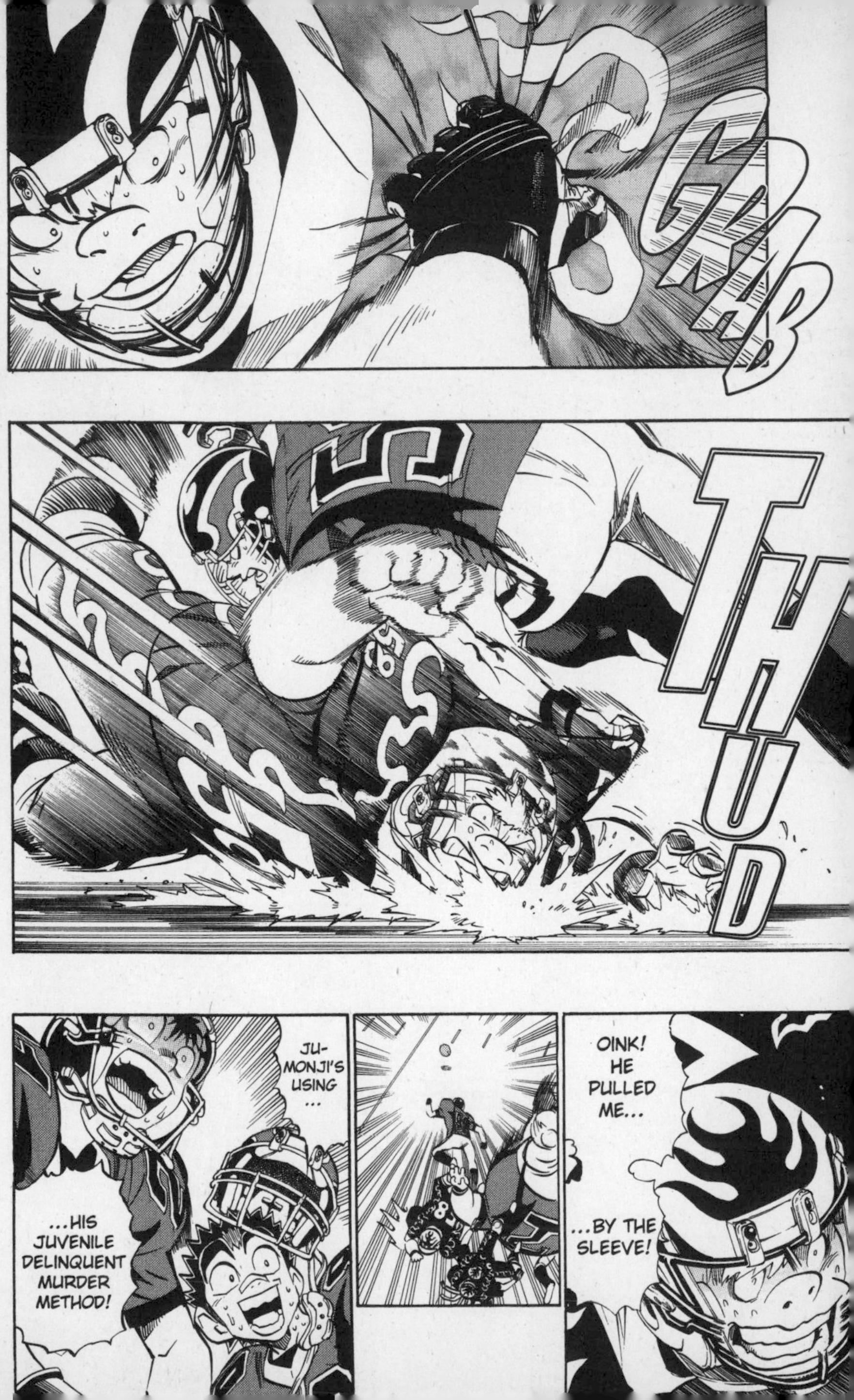
GRAB
THUD
OINK! HE PULLED ME...
...BY THE SLEEVE!
JU-MONJI'S USING ...
...HIS JUVENILE DELINQUENT MURDER METHOD!

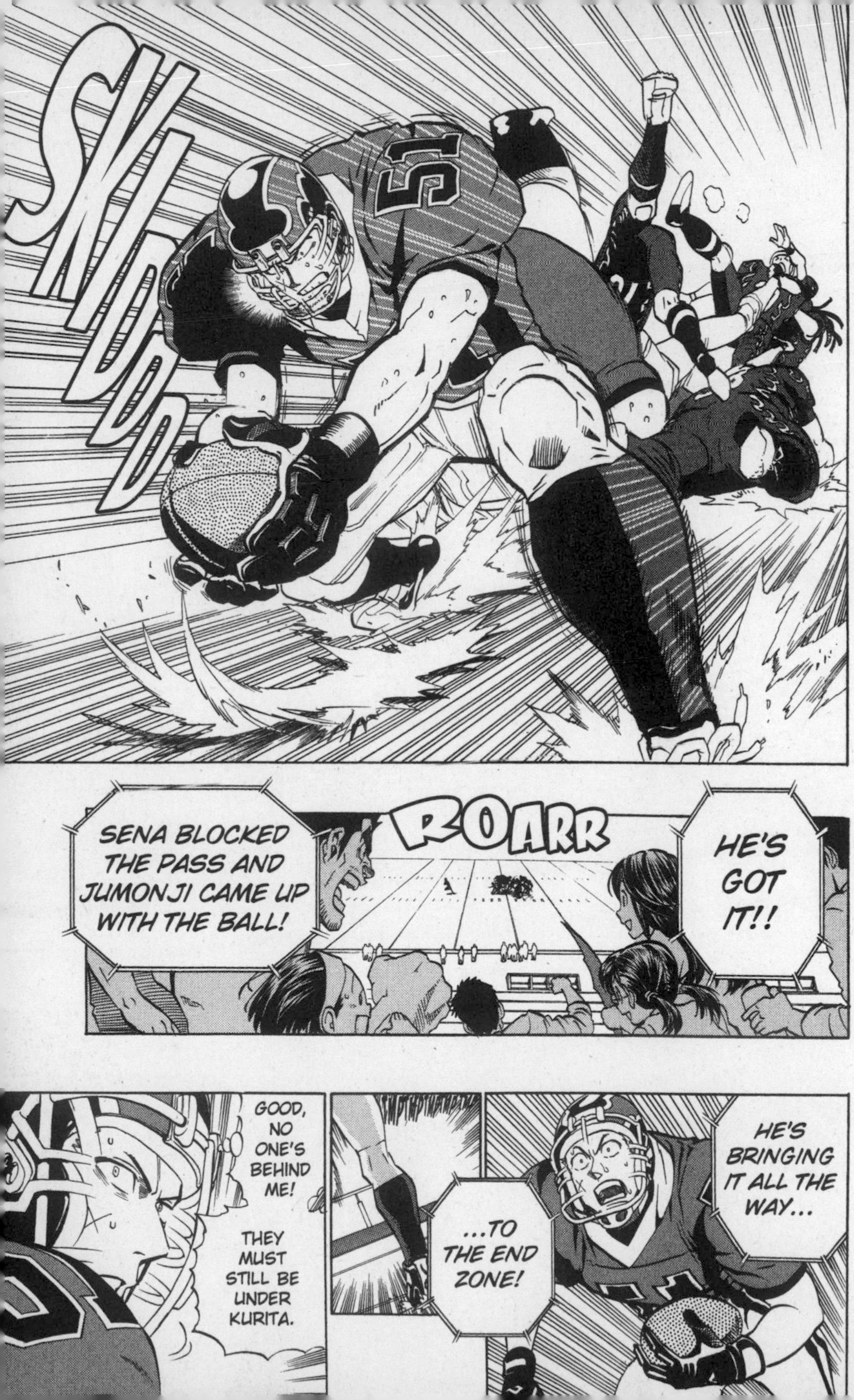
SKIDDDD
HE'S GOT IT!!
ROARR
SENA BLOCKED THE PASS AND JUMONJI CAME UP WITH THE BALL!
HE'S BRINGING IT ALL THE WAY...
...TO THE END ZONE!
GOOD, NO ONE'S BEHIND ME!
THEY MUST STILL BE UNDER KURITA.

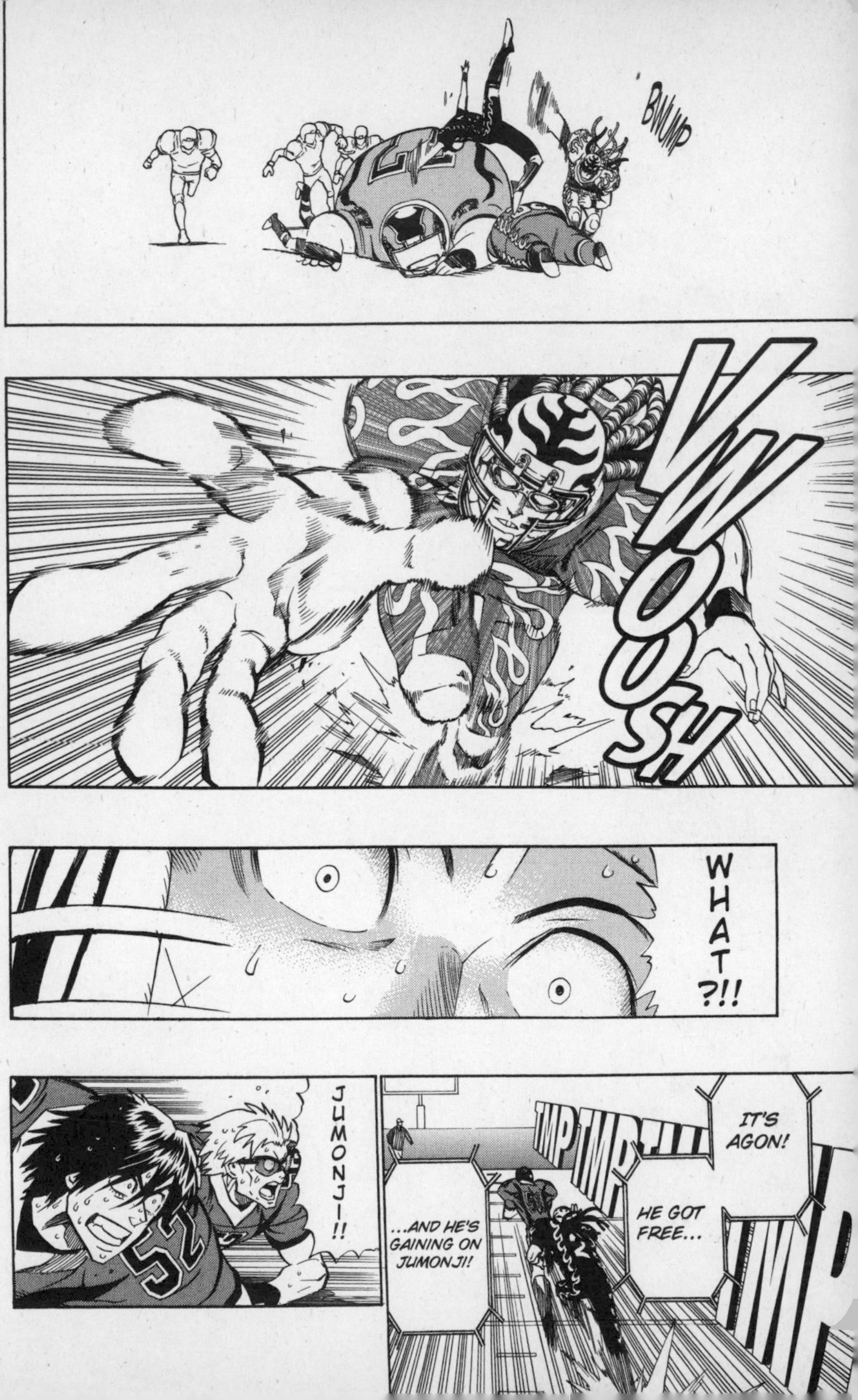
BWUMP
VWOOSH
WHAT?!!
IT'S AGON!
TMP TMP
HE GOT FREE...
...AND HE'S GAINING ON JUMONJI!
JUMONJI!!

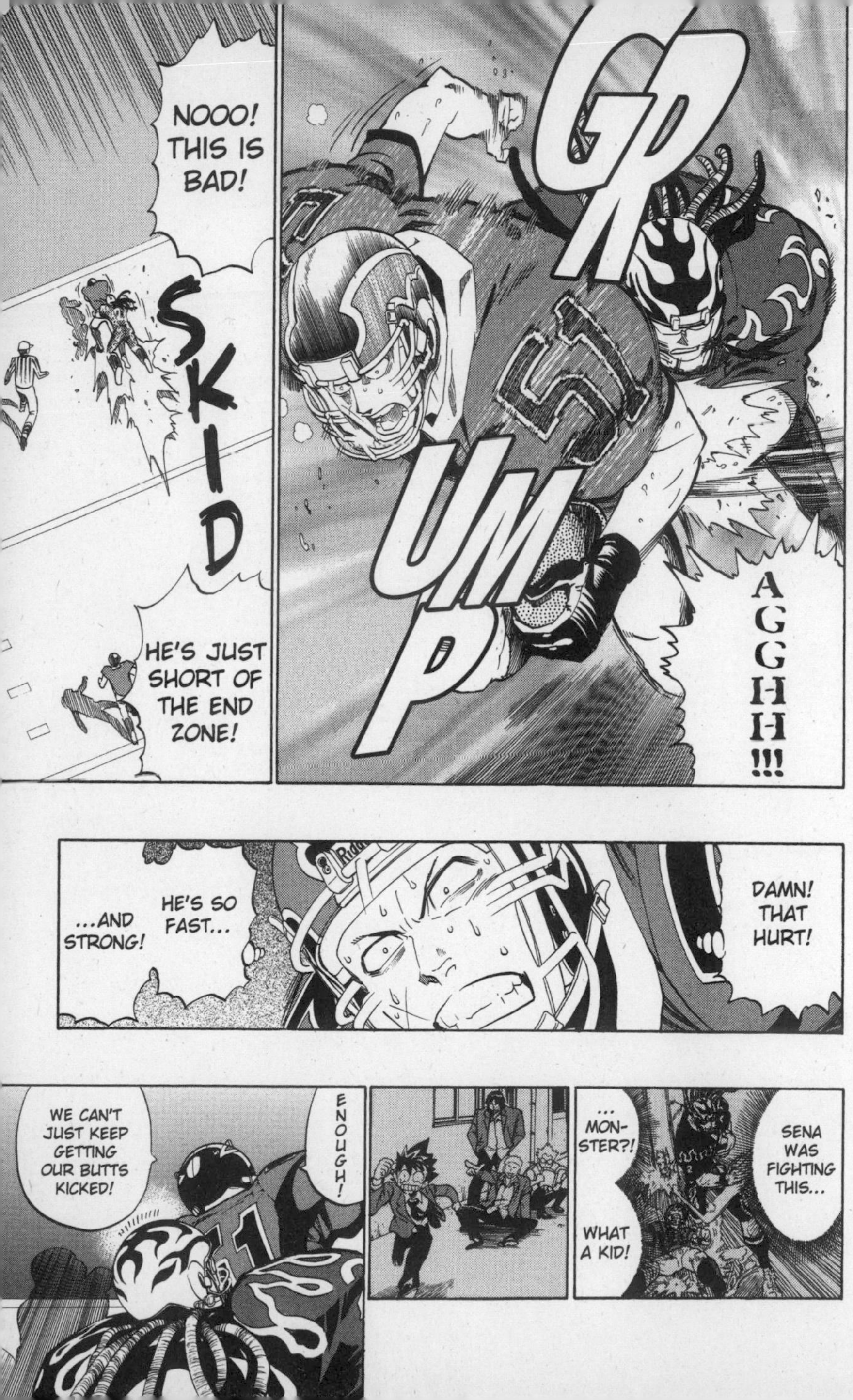
GRUMP
AGGHH!!!
NOOO! THIS IS BAD!
SKID
HE'S JUST SHORT OF THE END ZONE!
DAMN! THAT HURT!
HE'S SO FAST...
...AND STRONG!
SENA WAS FIGHTING THIS...
...MONSTER?!
WHAT A KID!
ENOUGH!
WE CAN'T JUST KEEP GETTING OUR BUTTS KICKED!

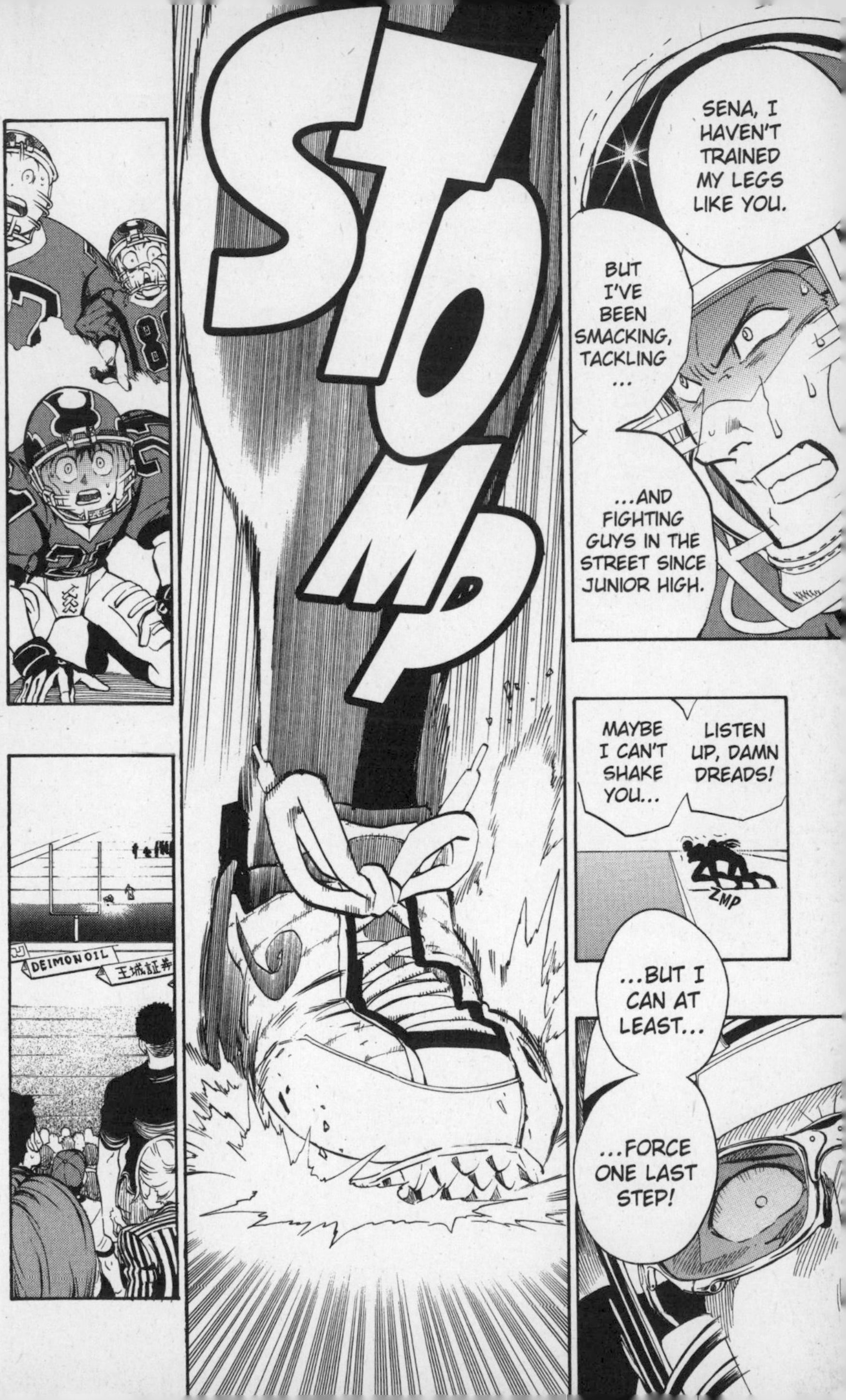
SENA, I HAVEN'T TRAINED MY LEGS LIKE YOU.
BUT I'VE BEEN SMACKING, TACKLING ...
...AND FIGHTING GUYS IN THE STREET SINCE JUNIOR HIGH.
LISTEN UP, DAMN DREADS!
MAYBE I CAN'T SHAKE YOU...
ZMP
...BUT I CAN AT LEAST...
...FORCE ONE LAST STEP!
STOMP
DEIMON OIL
王城証券

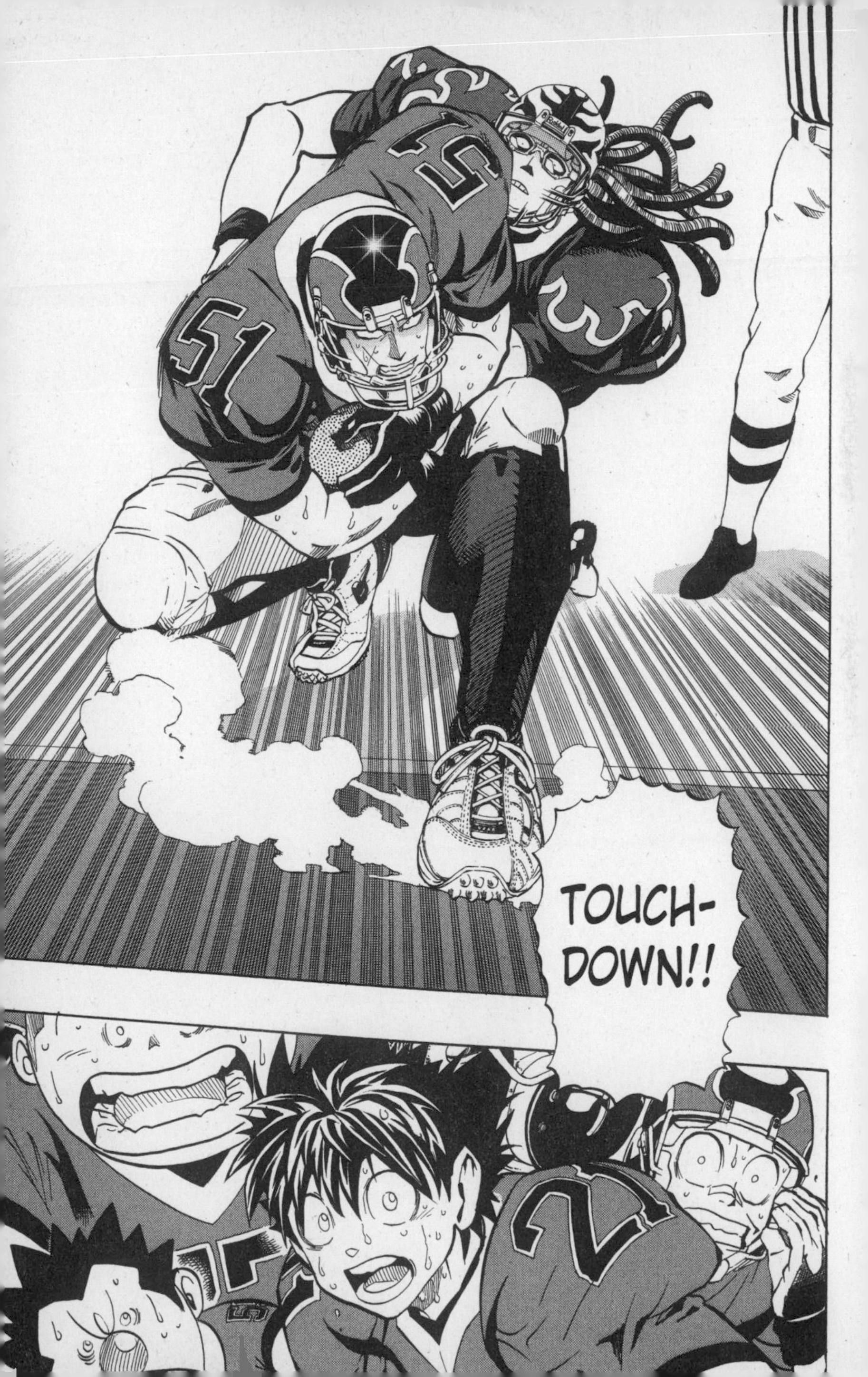
TOUCH-
DOWN!!

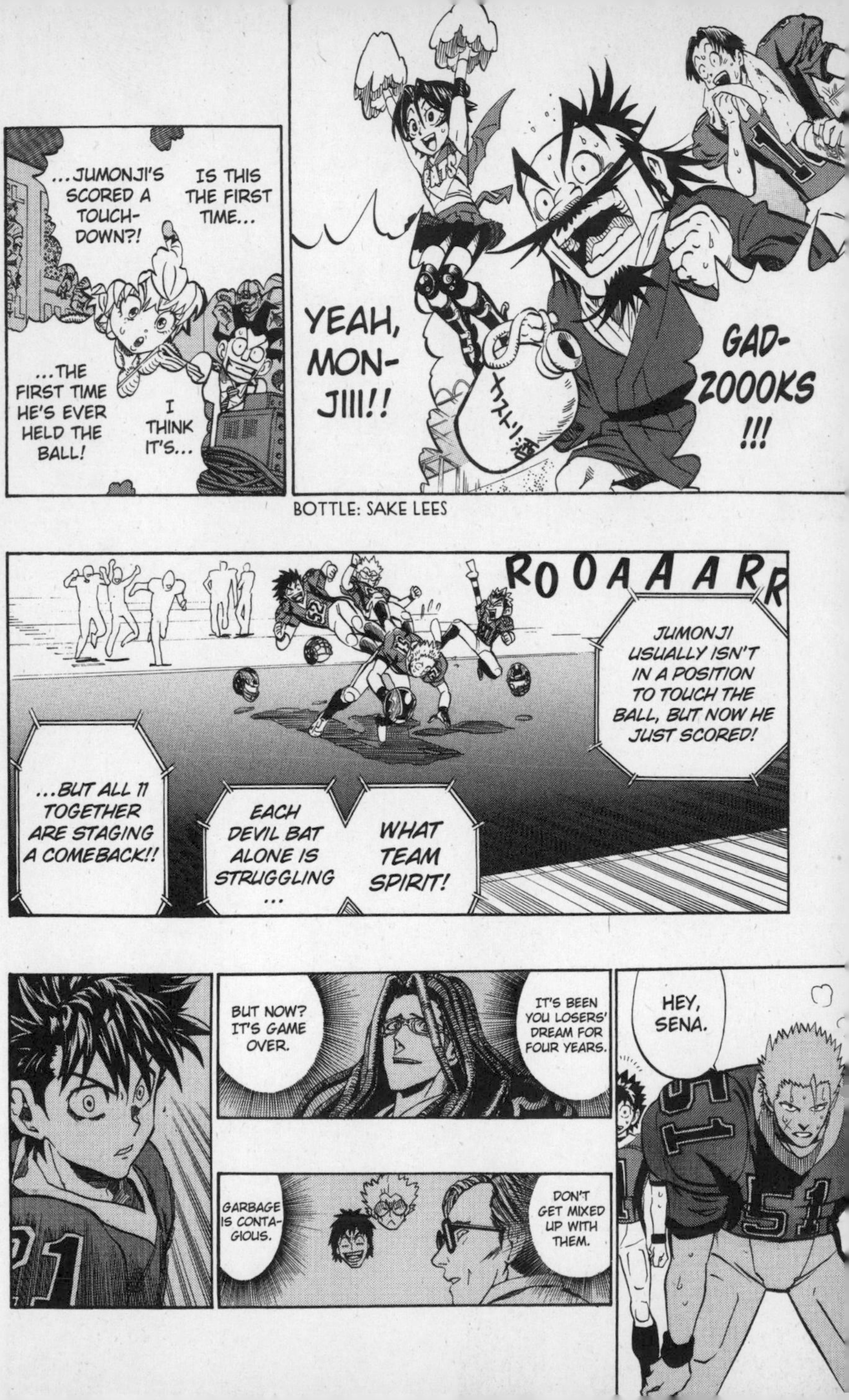
GAD-ZOOOKS!!!
YEAH, MON-JIIII!!
IS THIS THE FIRST TIME...
...JUMONJI'S SCORED A TOUCH-DOWN?!
I THINK IT'S...
...THE FIRST TIME HE'S EVER HELD THE BALL!
ROOAAAARR
JUMONJI USUALLY ISN'T IN A POSITION TO TOUCH THE BALL, BUT NOW HE JUST SCORED!
WHAT TEAM SPIRIT!
EACH DEVIL BAT ALONE IS STRUGGLING...
...BUT ALL 11 TOGETHER ARE STAGING A COMEBACK!!
HEY, SENA.
IT'S BEEN YOU LOSERS' DREAM FOR FOUR YEARS.
BUT NOW? IT'S GAME OVER.
DON'T GET MIXED UP WITH THEM.
GARBAGE IS CONTAGIOUS.
BOTTLE: SAKE LEES

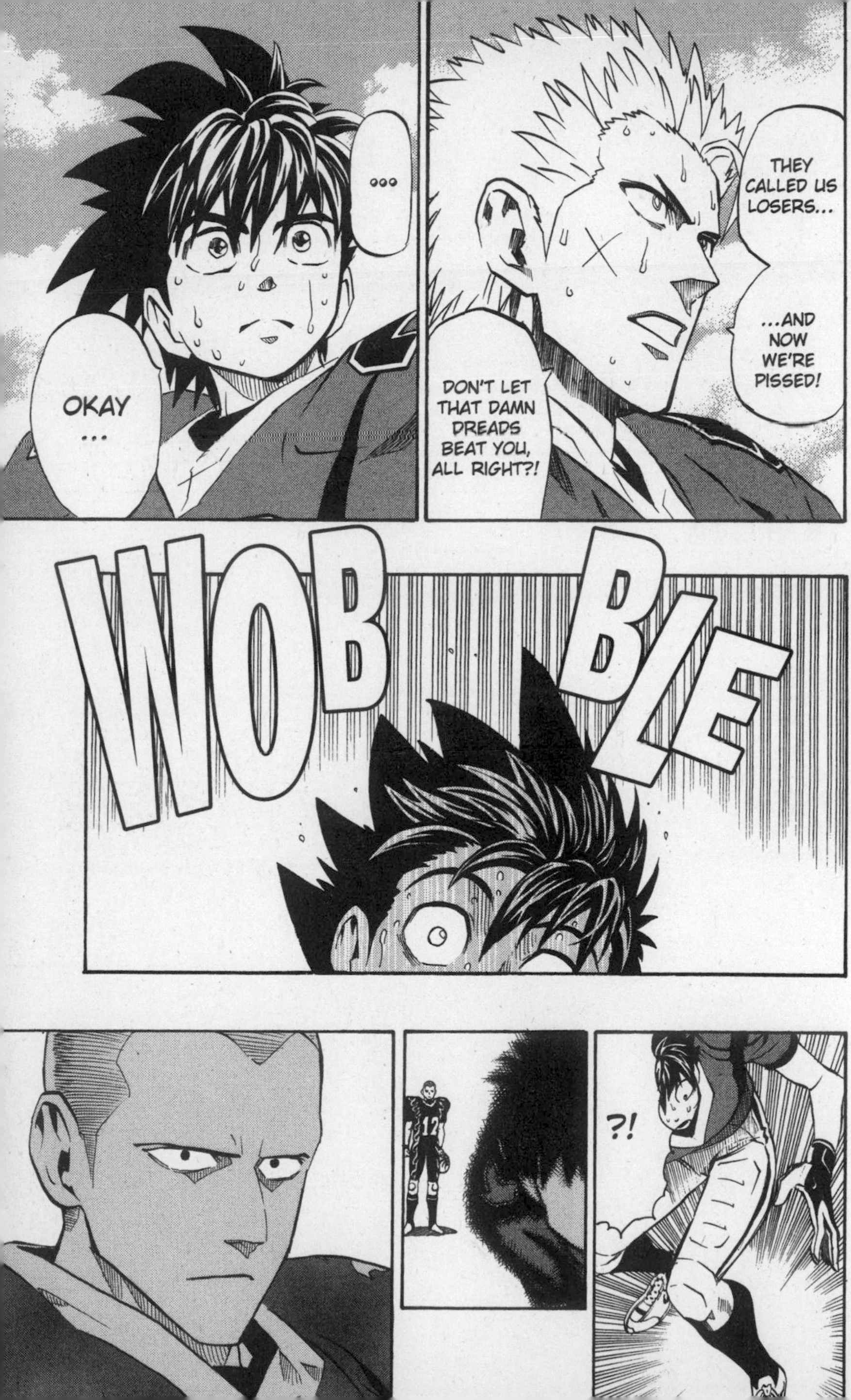
THEY CALLED US LOSERS...
...AND NOW WE'RE PISSED!
DON'T LET THAT DAMN DREADS BEAT YOU, ALL RIGHT?!
...
OKAY ...
WOBBLE
?!

Eyeshield 21 Survey Corner **Devil Bat 021**

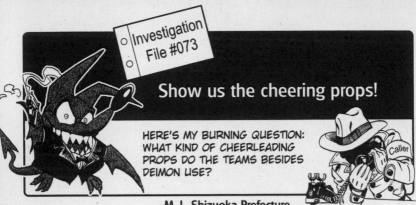

Investigation File #073

Show us the cheering props!

HERE'S MY BURNING QUESTION: WHAT KIND OF CHEERLEADING PROPS DO THE TEAMS BESIDES DEIMON USE?

Caller

M. I., Shizuoka Prefecture

- Ojo White Knights

Excaliballoon

white Knights

GUNMEN

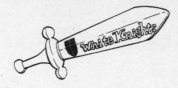

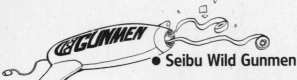

- Seibu Wild Gunmen

Party-popper Pistol

- Taiyo Sphinx

Great Pyramid Megaphone

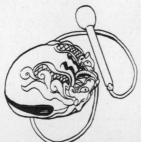

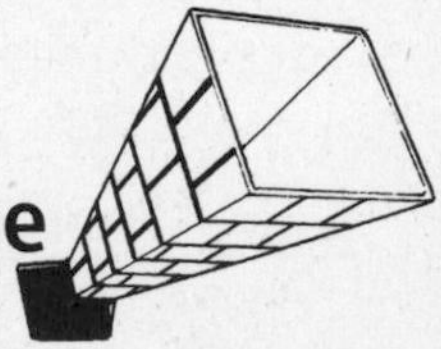

- Shinryuji Nagas

Chinese Temple Block Balloon

It's stupid, so no one uses it.

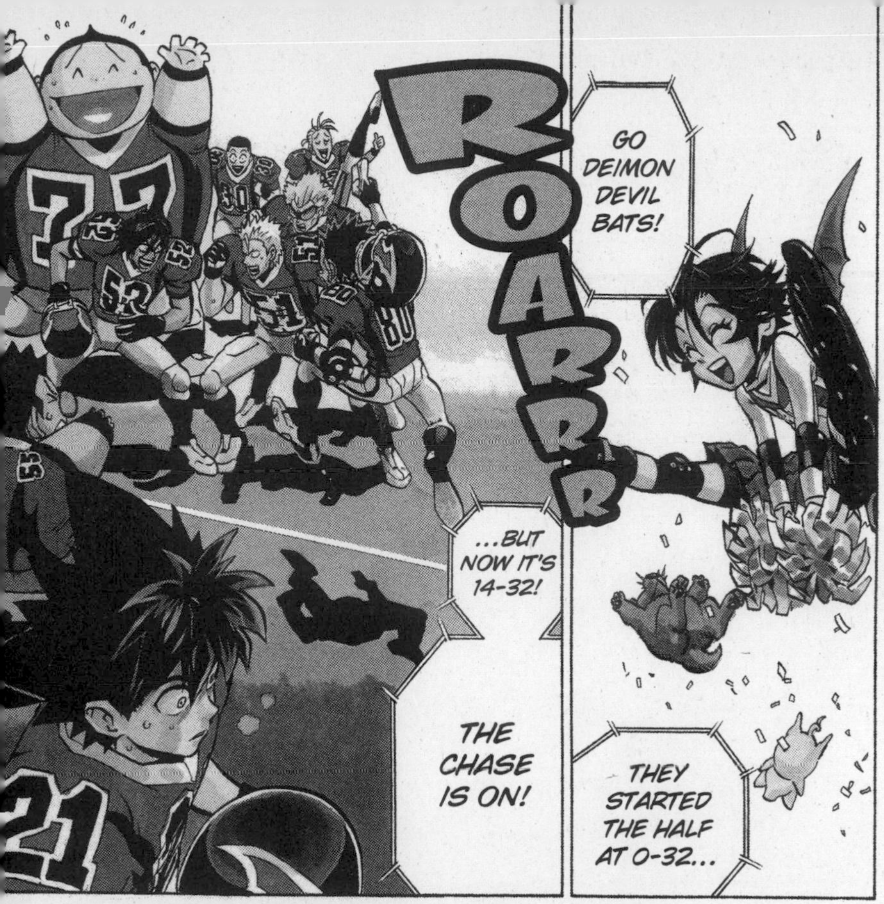
GO DEIMON DEVIL BATS!
ROARRR
THEY STARTED THE HALF AT 0-32...
...BUT NOW IT'S 14-32!
THE CHASE IS ON!

Chapter 185 Agon and Unsui

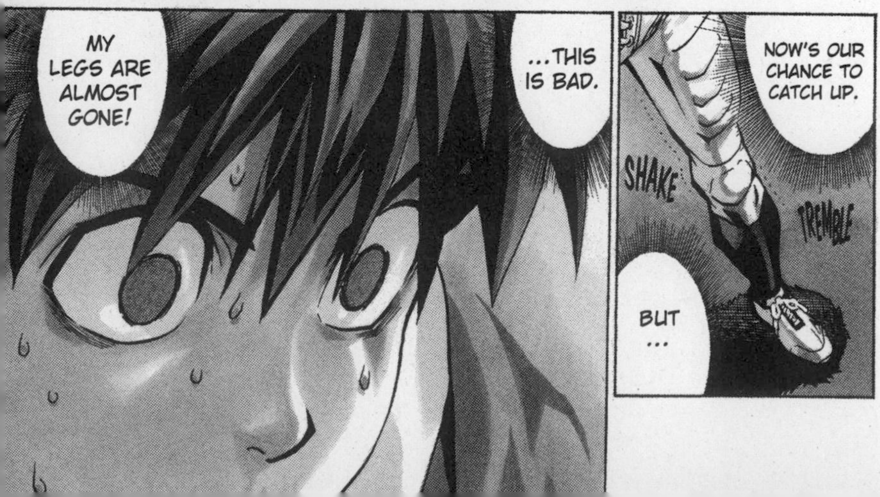
NOW'S OUR CHANCE TO CATCH UP.
SHAKE
TREMBLE
BUT ...
...THIS IS BAD.
MY LEGS ARE ALMOST GONE!

Agon and Unsui

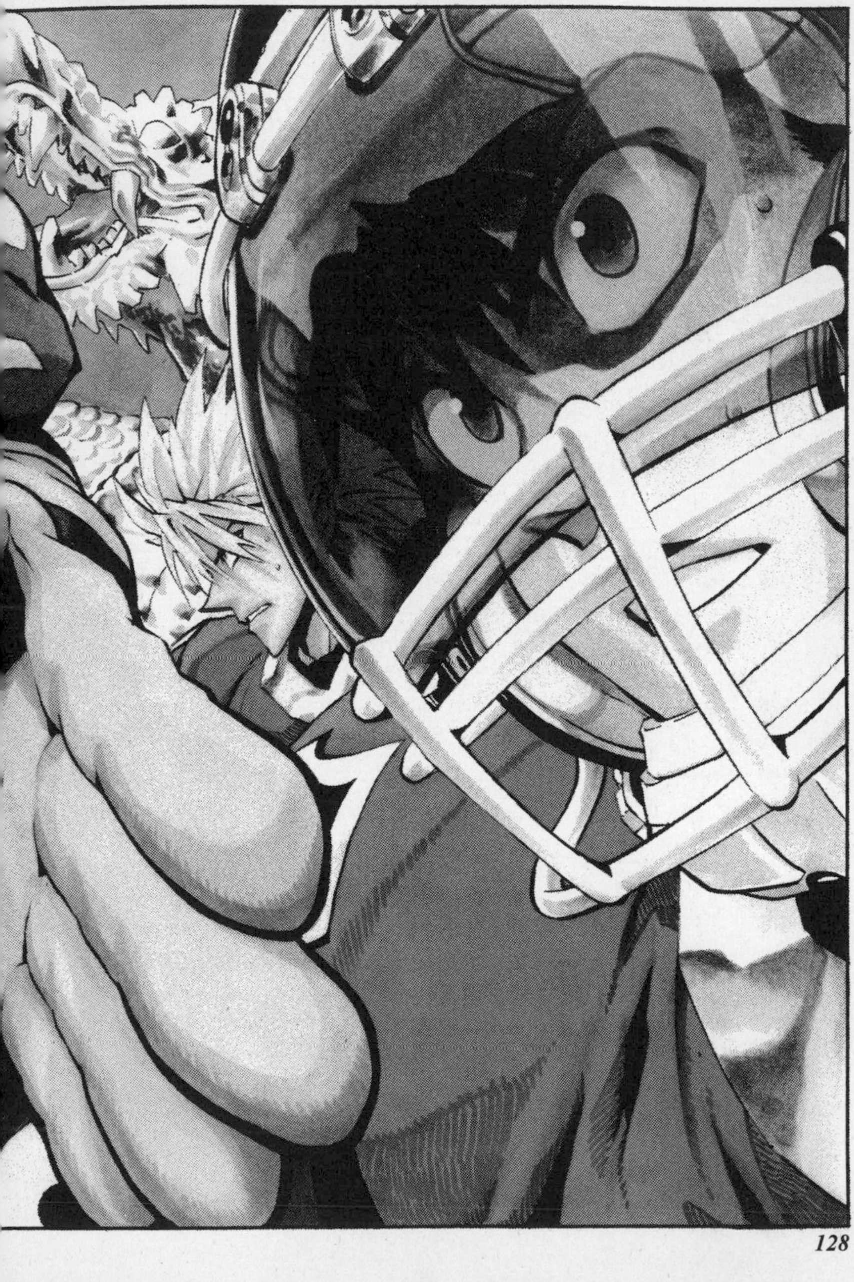

Chapter 185

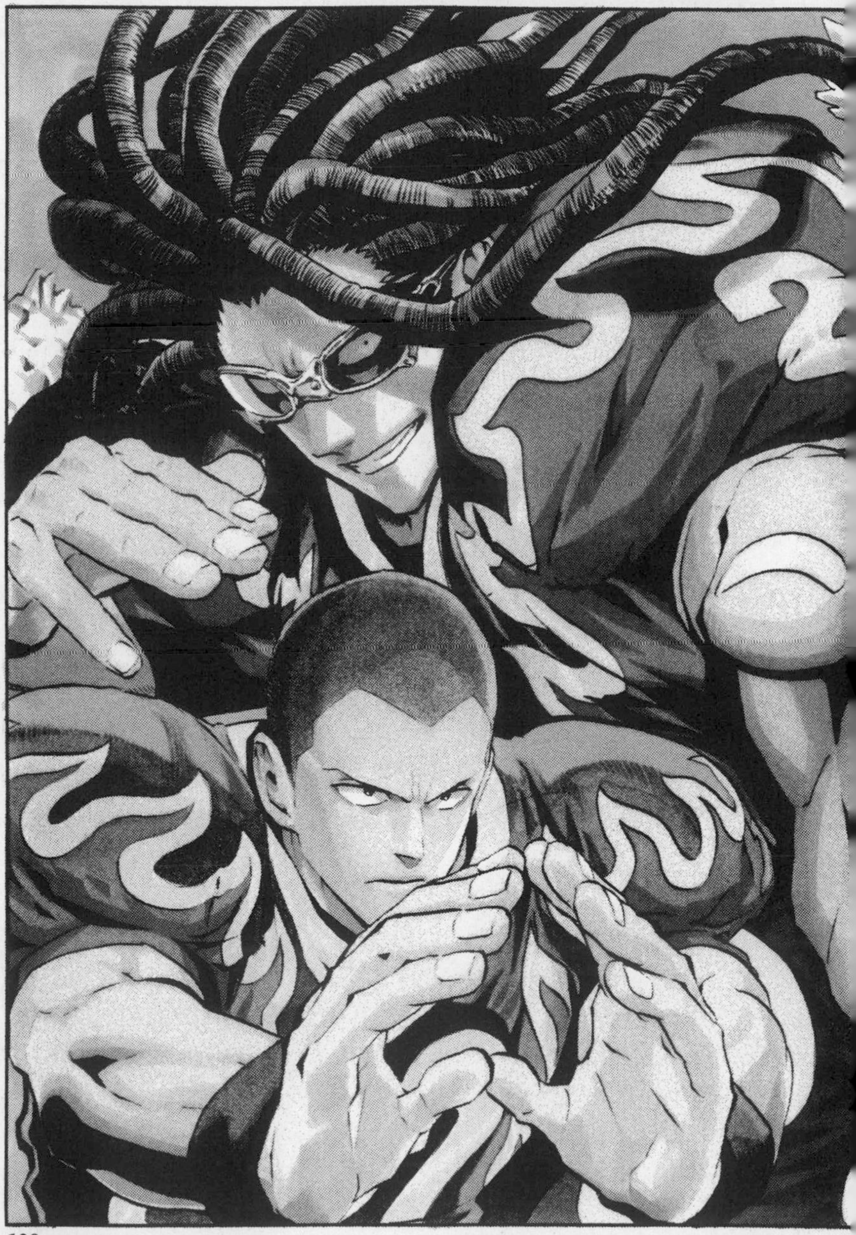

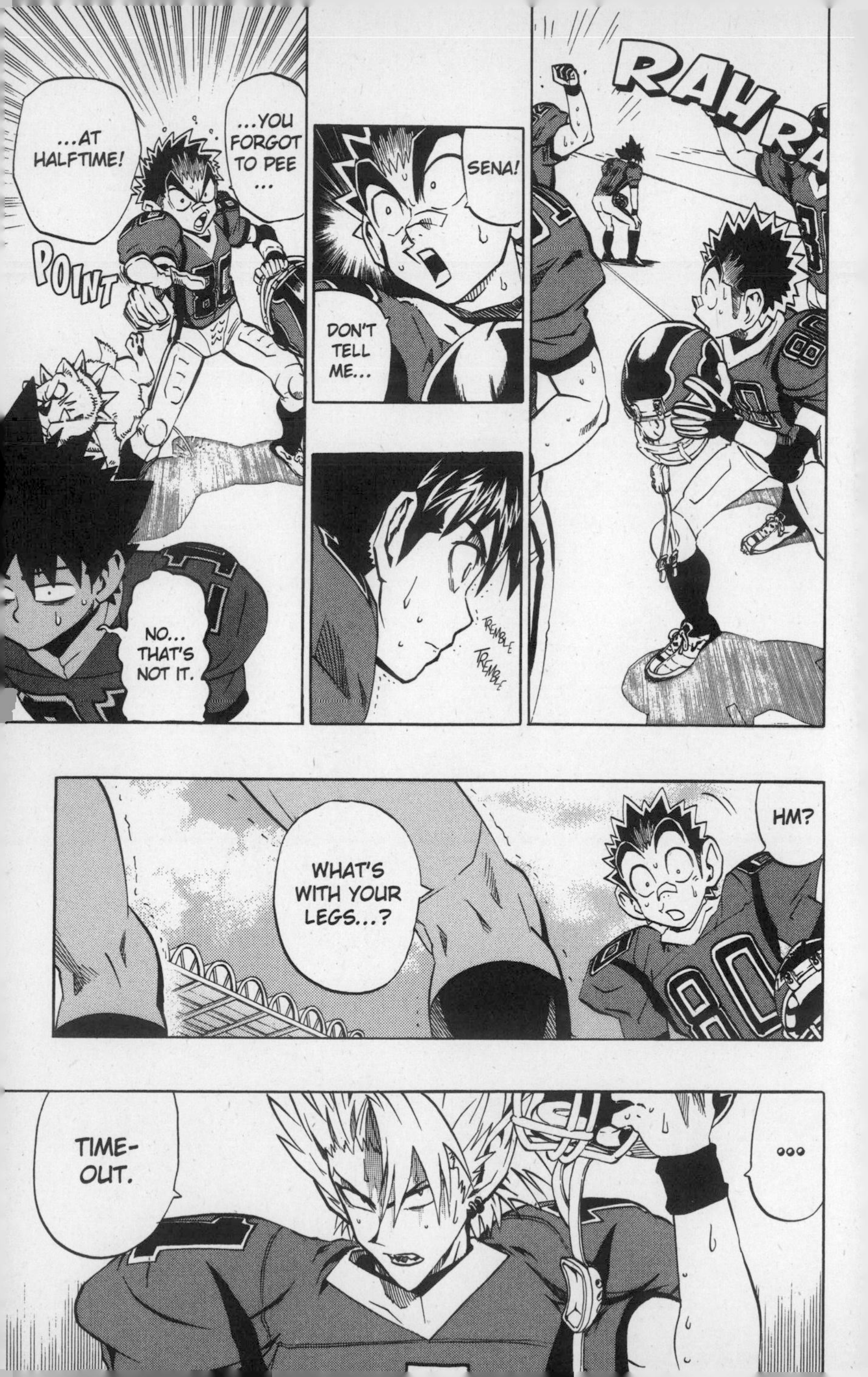
RAHRA
SENA!
DON'T TELL ME...
TREMBLE TREMBLE
...YOU FORGOT TO PEE ...
...AT HALFTIME!
POINT
NO... THAT'S NOT IT.
HM?
WHAT'S WITH YOUR LEGS...?
...
TIME-OUT.

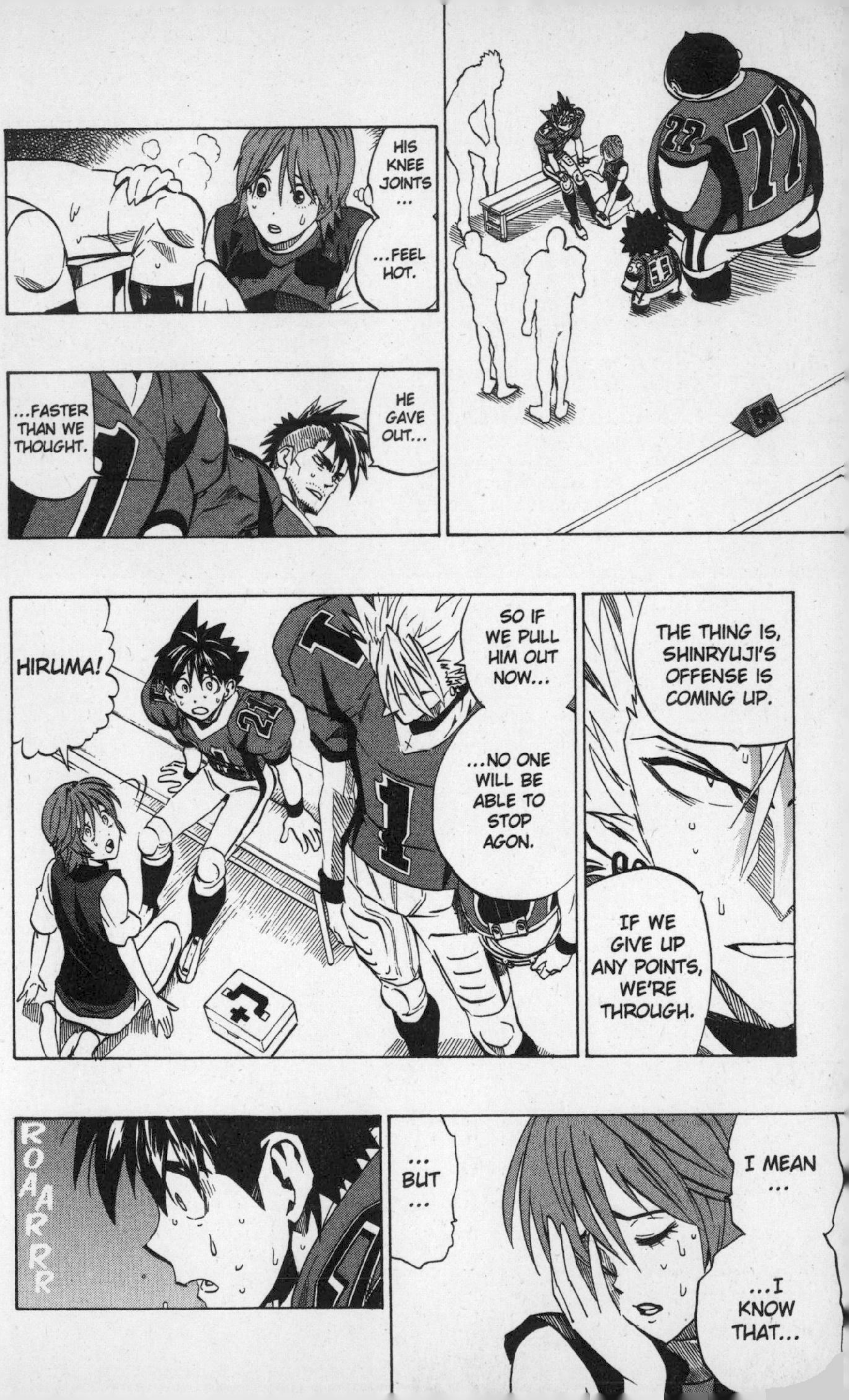
HIS KNEE JOINTS...
...FEEL HOT.
HE GAVE OUT...
...FASTER THAN WE THOUGHT.
THE THING IS, SHINRYUJI'S OFFENSE IS COMING UP.
IF WE GIVE UP ANY POINTS, WE'RE THROUGH.
SO IF WE PULL HIM OUT NOW...
...NO ONE WILL BE ABLE TO STOP AGON.
HIRUMA!
I MEAN...
...I KNOW THAT...
...BUT...
ROAARRR

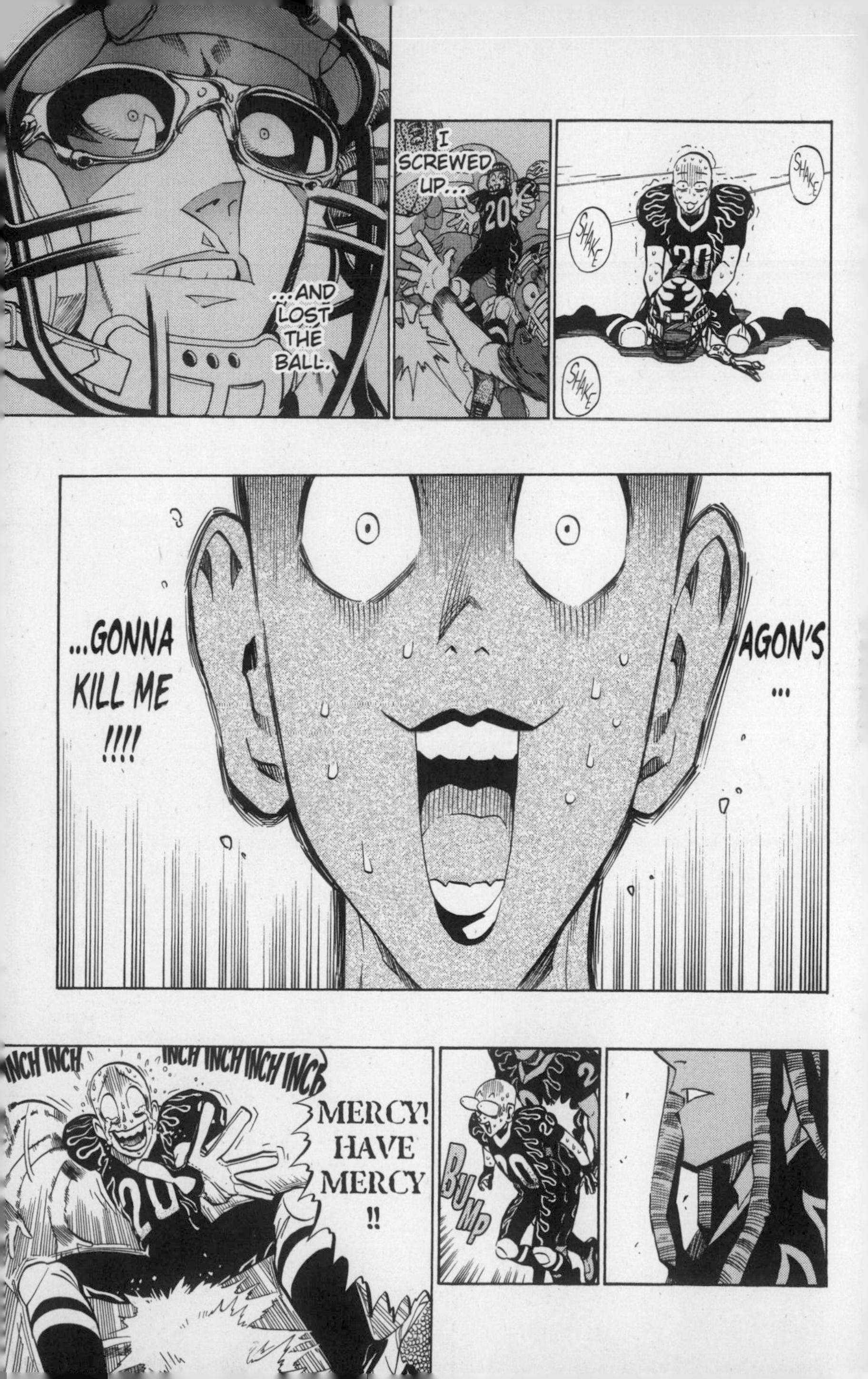
SHAKE
SHAKE
SHAKE
I SCREWED UP...
...AND LOST THE BALL.
AGON'S ...
...GONNA KILL ME !!!!
BUMP
INCH INCH INCH INCH INCH INCH
MERCY! HAVE MERCY !!

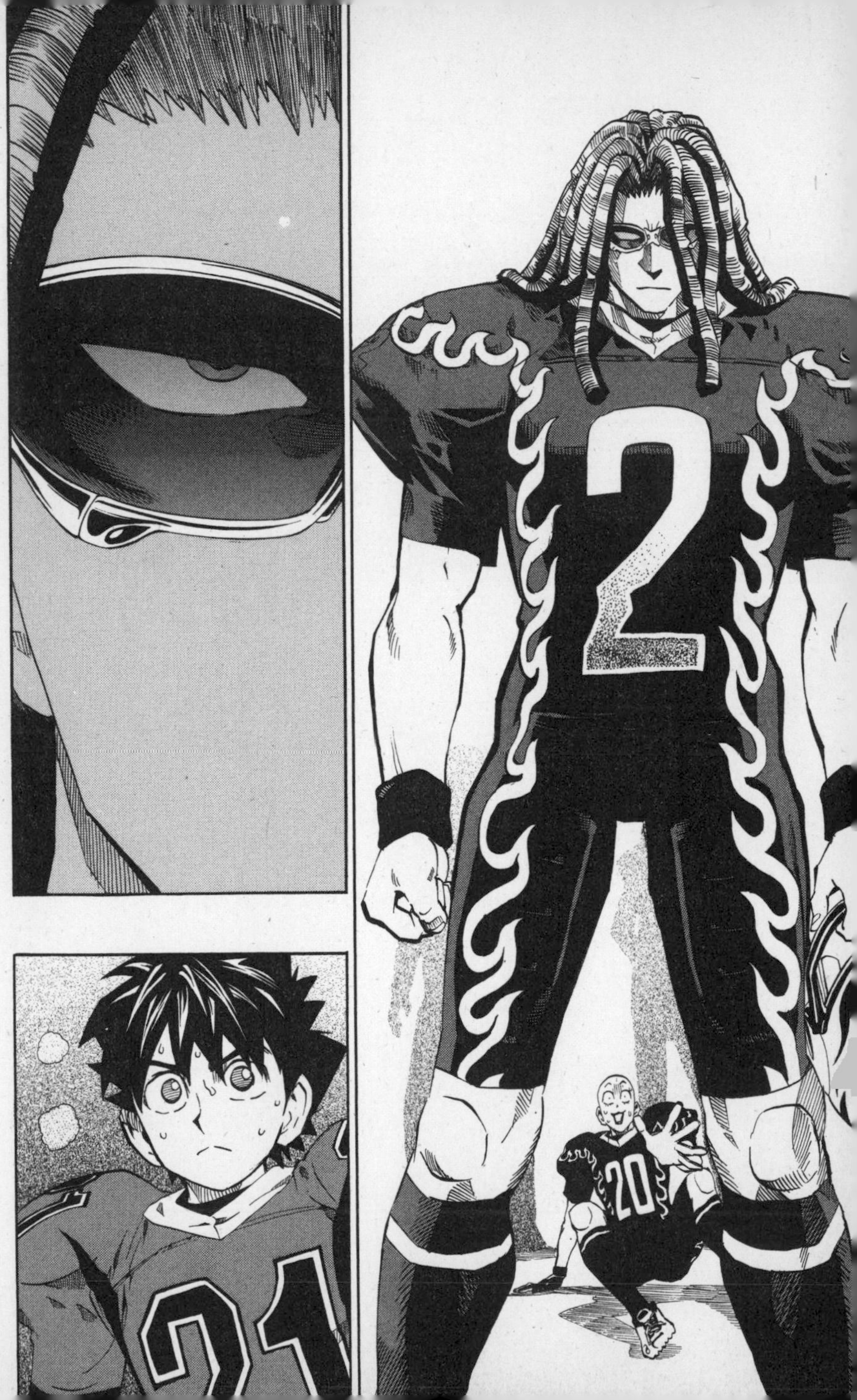

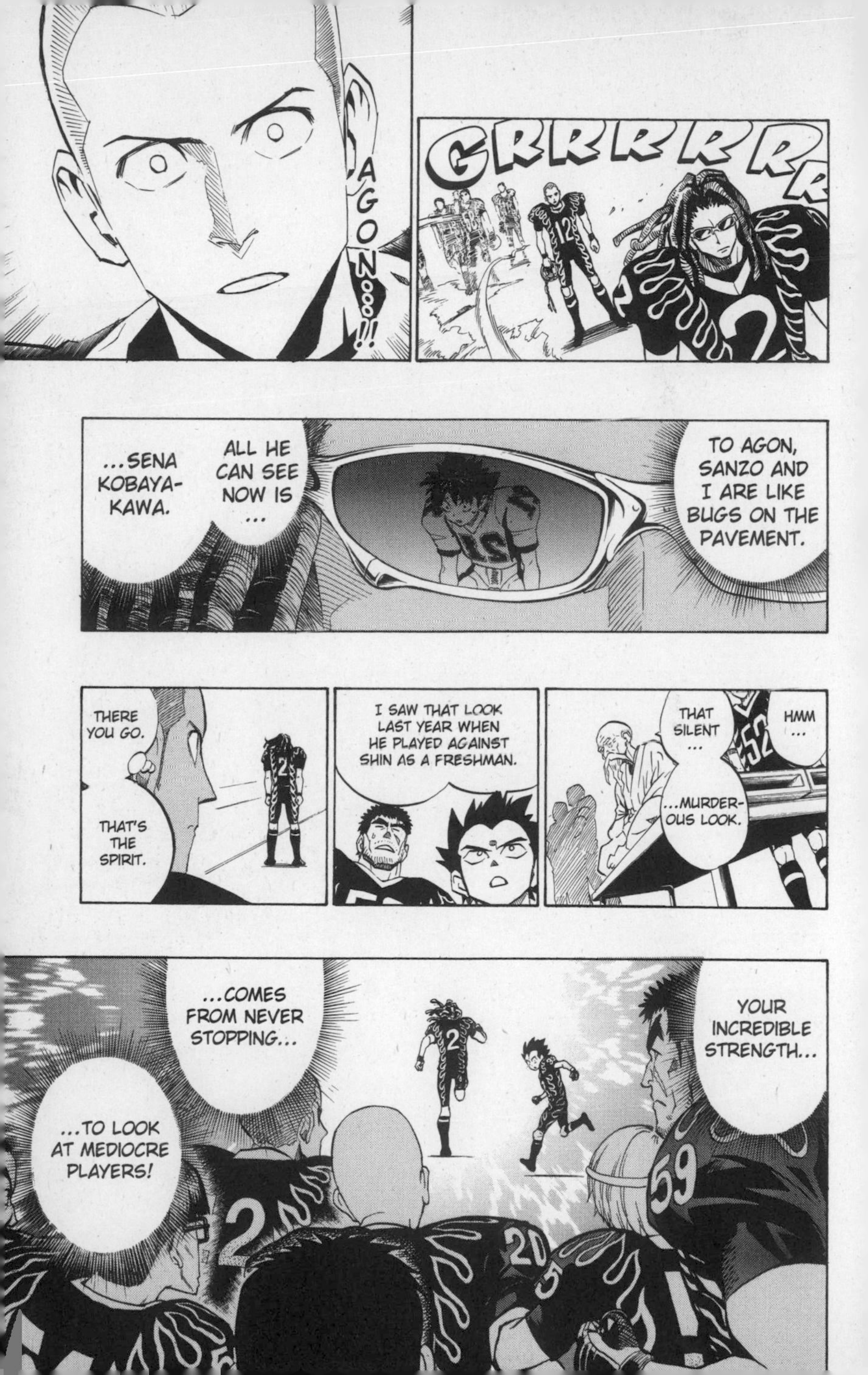
GRRRRRRR
AGONOOO!!
TO AGON, SANZO AND I ARE LIKE BUGS ON THE PAVEMENT.
ALL HE CAN SEE NOW IS ...
...SENA KOBAYA-KAWA.
HMM ...
THAT SILENT ...
...MURDER-OUS LOOK.
I SAW THAT LOOK LAST YEAR WHEN HE PLAYED AGAINST SHIN AS A FRESHMAN.
THERE YOU GO.
THAT'S THE SPIRIT.
YOUR INCREDIBLE STRENGTH...
...COMES FROM NEVER STOPPING...
...TO LOOK AT MEDIOCRE PLAYERS!

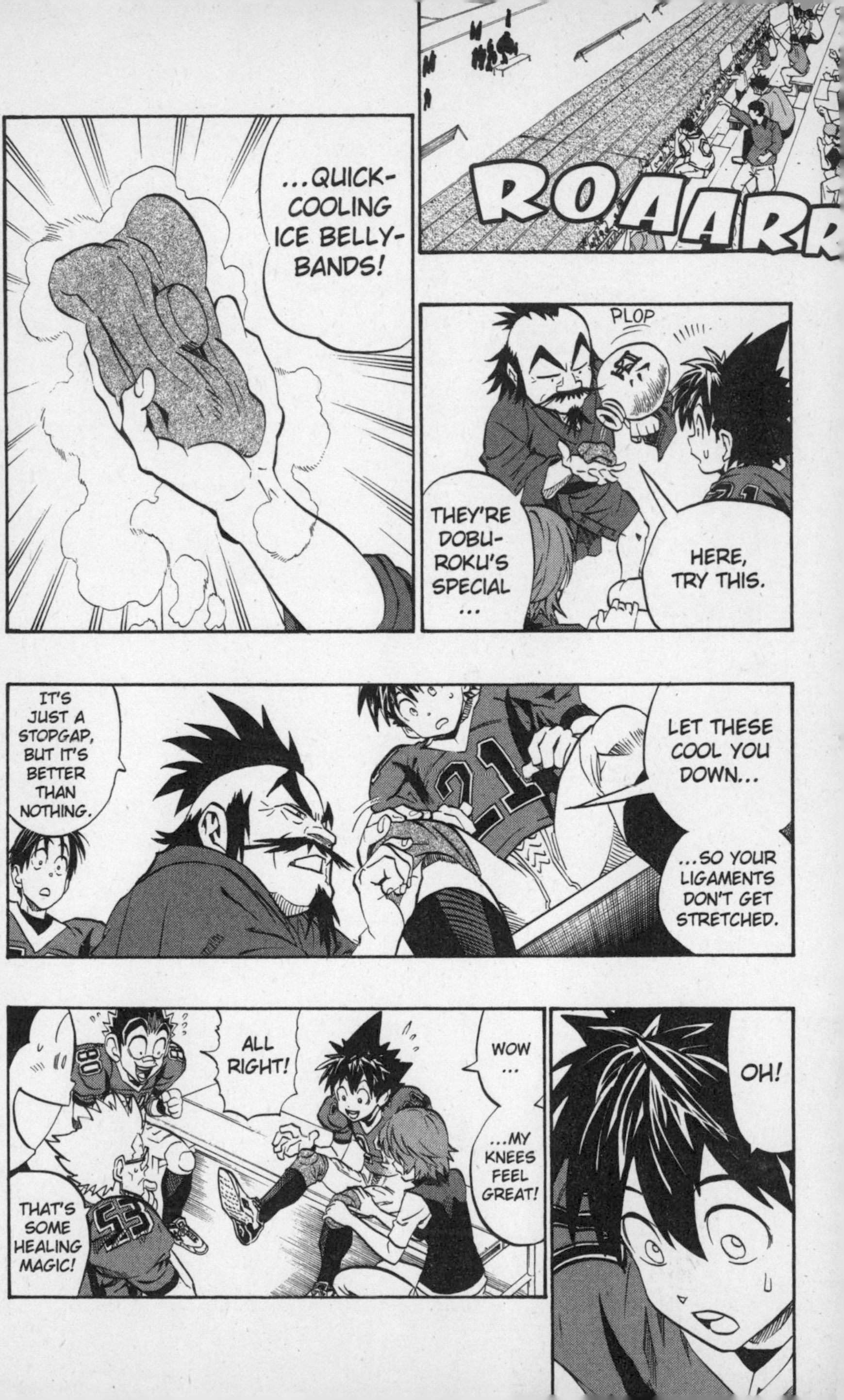
ROAARR
PLOP
HERE, TRY THIS.
THEY'RE DOBUROKU'S SPECIAL...
...QUICK-COOLING ICE BELLY-BANDS!
LET THESE COOL YOU DOWN...
...SO YOUR LIGAMENTS DON'T GET STRETCHED.
IT'S JUST A STOPGAP, BUT IT'S BETTER THAN NOTHING.
OH!
WOW...
...MY KNEES FEEL GREAT!
ALL RIGHT!
THAT'S SOME HEALING MAGIC!

READ THIS WAY

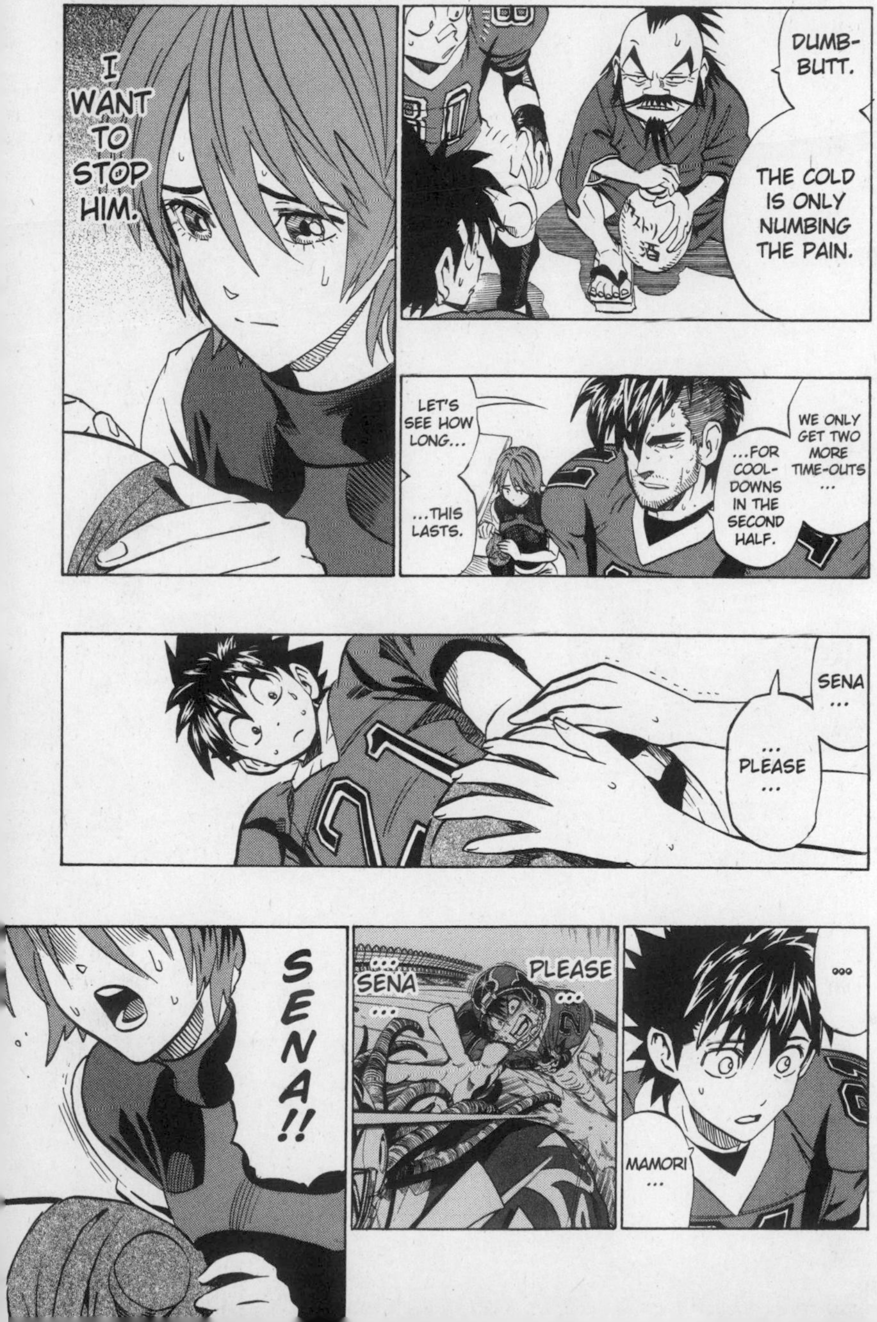
DUMB-BUTT.
THE COLD IS ONLY NUMBING THE PAIN.
WE ONLY GET TWO MORE TIME-OUTS ...
...FOR COOL-DOWNS IN THE SECOND HALF.
LET'S SEE HOW LONG...
...THIS LASTS.
I WANT TO STOP HIM.
SENA ...
... PLEASE ...
...
MAMORI ...
PLEASE ...
... SENA ...
SENA!!

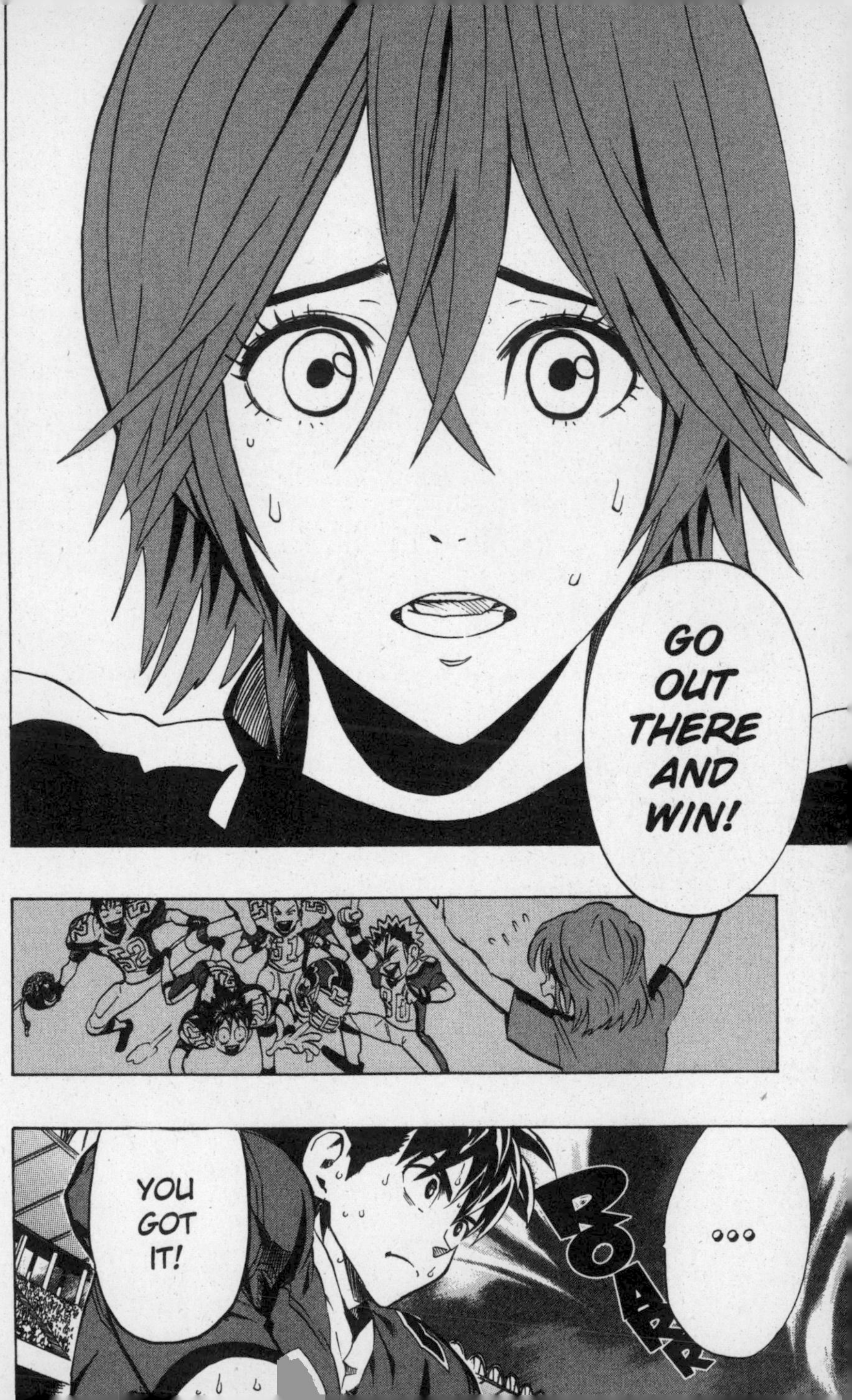
GO OUT THERE AND WIN!
...
BOOAAR
YOU GOT IT!

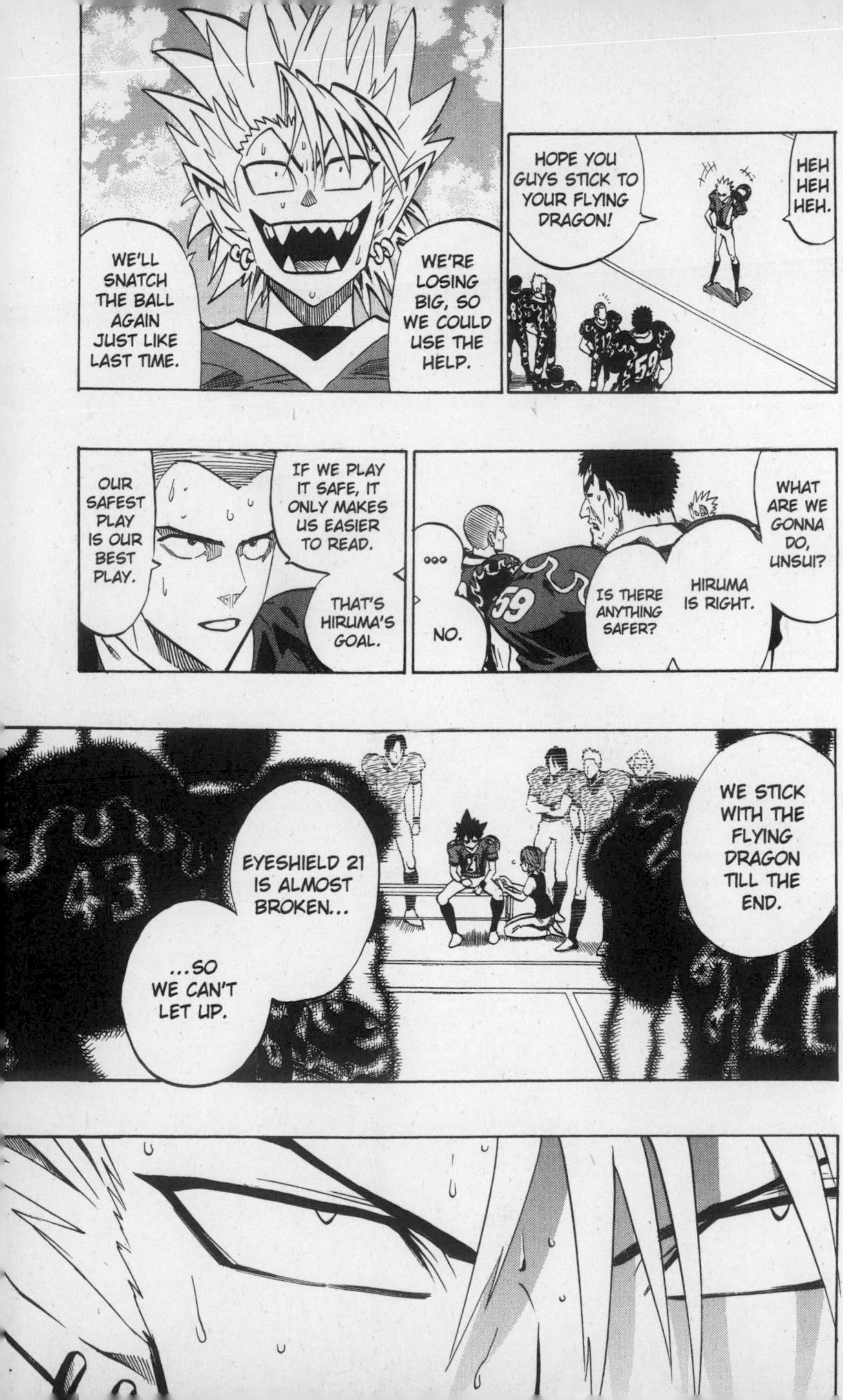
HEH HEH HEH.
HOPE YOU GUYS STICK TO YOUR FLYING DRAGON!
WE'RE LOSING BIG, SO WE COULD USE THE HELP.
WE'LL SNATCH THE BALL AGAIN JUST LIKE LAST TIME.
WHAT ARE WE GONNA DO, UNSUI?
HIRUMA IS RIGHT.
IS THERE ANYTHING SAFER?
...
NO.
IF WE PLAY IT SAFE, IT ONLY MAKES US EASIER TO READ.
THAT'S HIRUMA'S GOAL.
OUR SAFEST PLAY IS OUR BEST PLAY.
WE STICK WITH THE FLYING DRAGON TILL THE END.
EYESHIELD 21 IS ALMOST BROKEN...
...SO WE CAN'T LET UP.

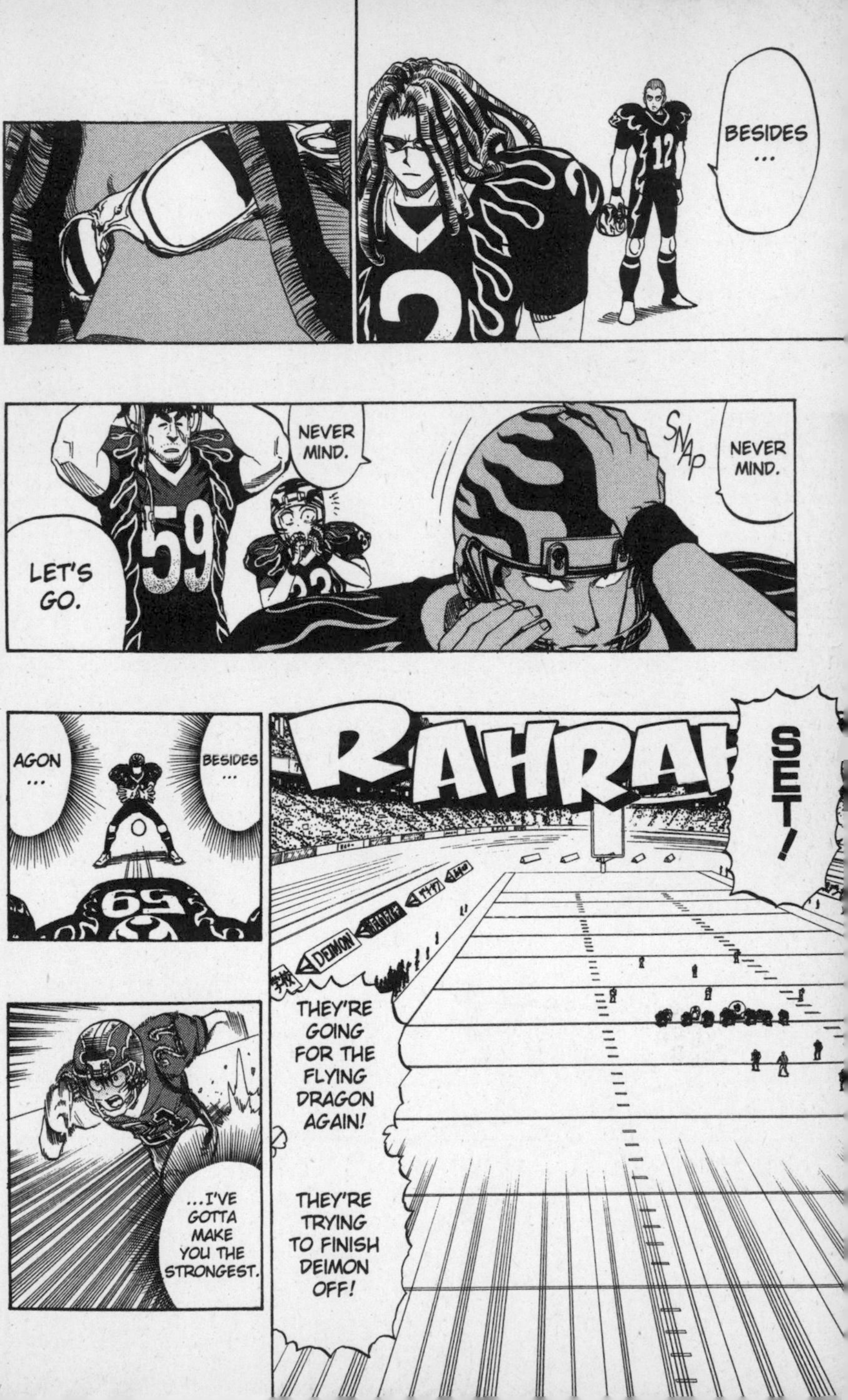
BESIDES ...
SNAP
NEVER MIND.
NEVER MIND.
LET'S GO.
SET!
RAHRAH
DEIMON
THEY'RE GOING FOR THE FLYING DRAGON AGAIN!
THEY'RE TRYING TO FINISH DEIMON OFF!
BESIDES ...
AGON ...
...I'VE GOTTA MAKE YOU THE STRONGEST.

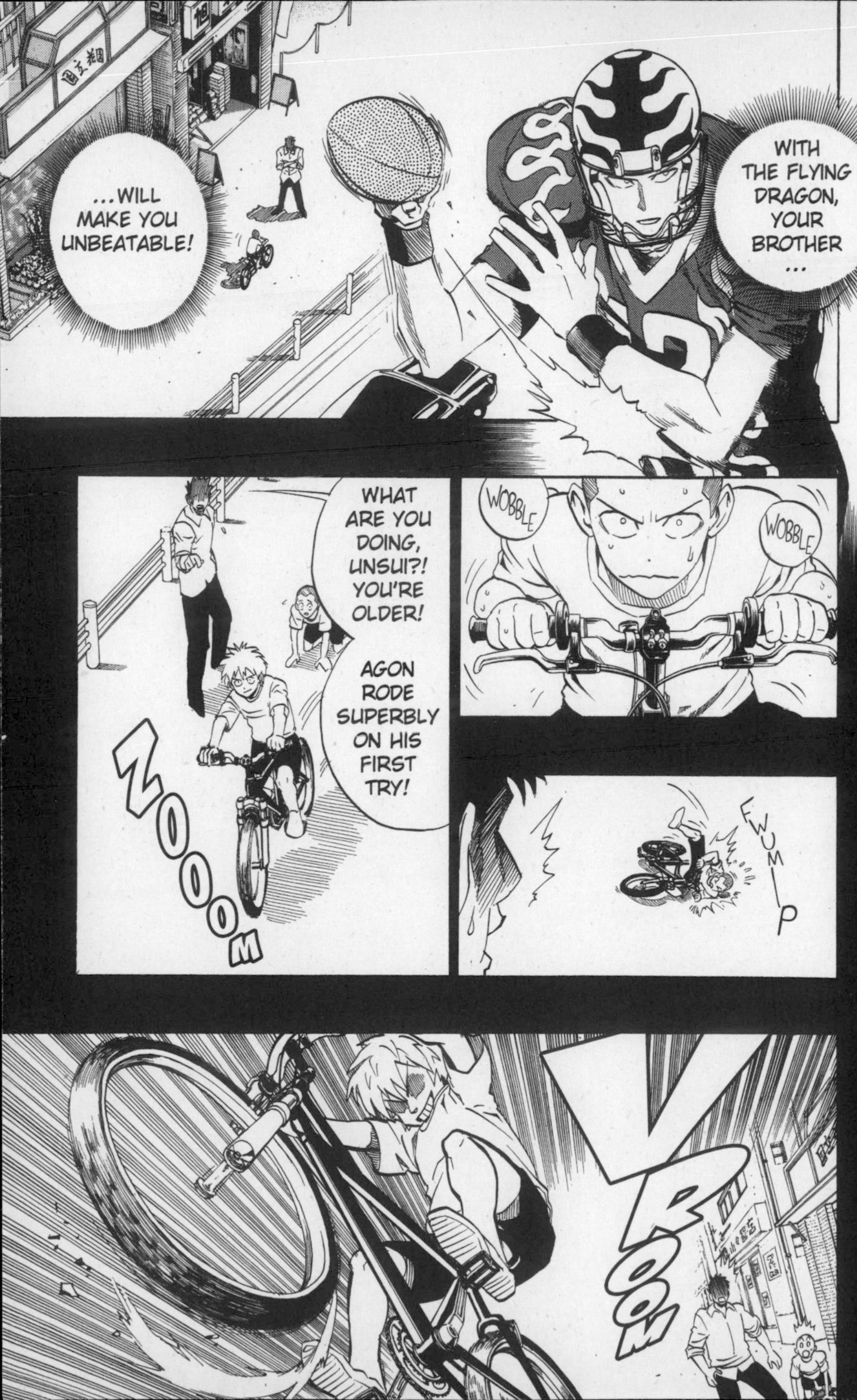
WITH THE FLYING DRAGON, YOUR BROTHER...
...WILL MAKE YOU UNBEATABLE!
WOBBLE
WOBBLE
FWUMP
WHAT ARE YOU DOING, UNSUI?! YOU'RE OLDER!
AGON RODE SUPERBLY ON HIS FIRST TRY!
ZOOOOM
VROOOM

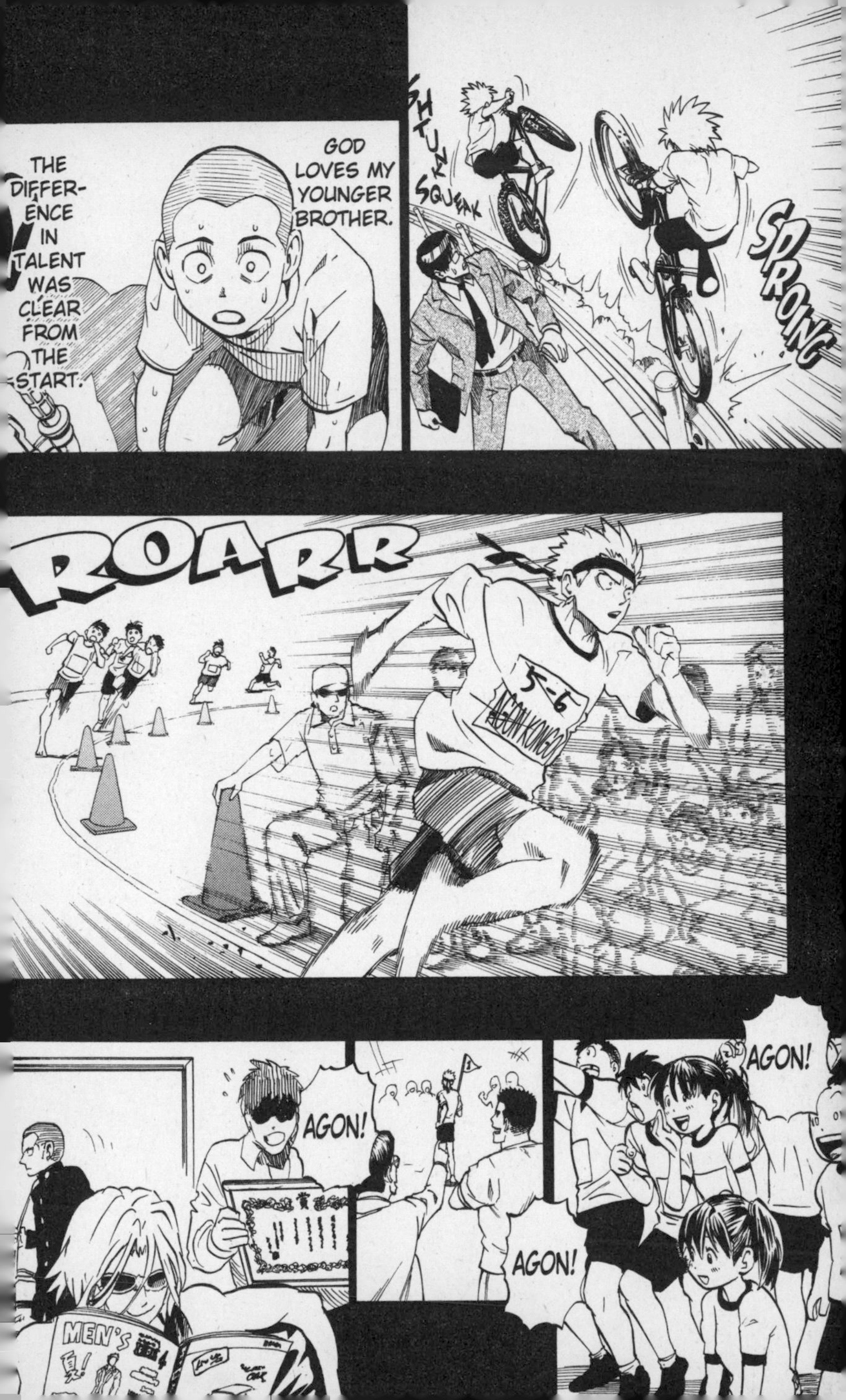
SHTUNK
SQUEAK
SPROING
GOD LOVES MY YOUNGER BROTHER.
THE DIFFERENCE IN TALENT WAS CLEAR FROM THE START.
ROARR
5-6
AGON KONGO
AGON!
AGON!
AGON!
MEN'S

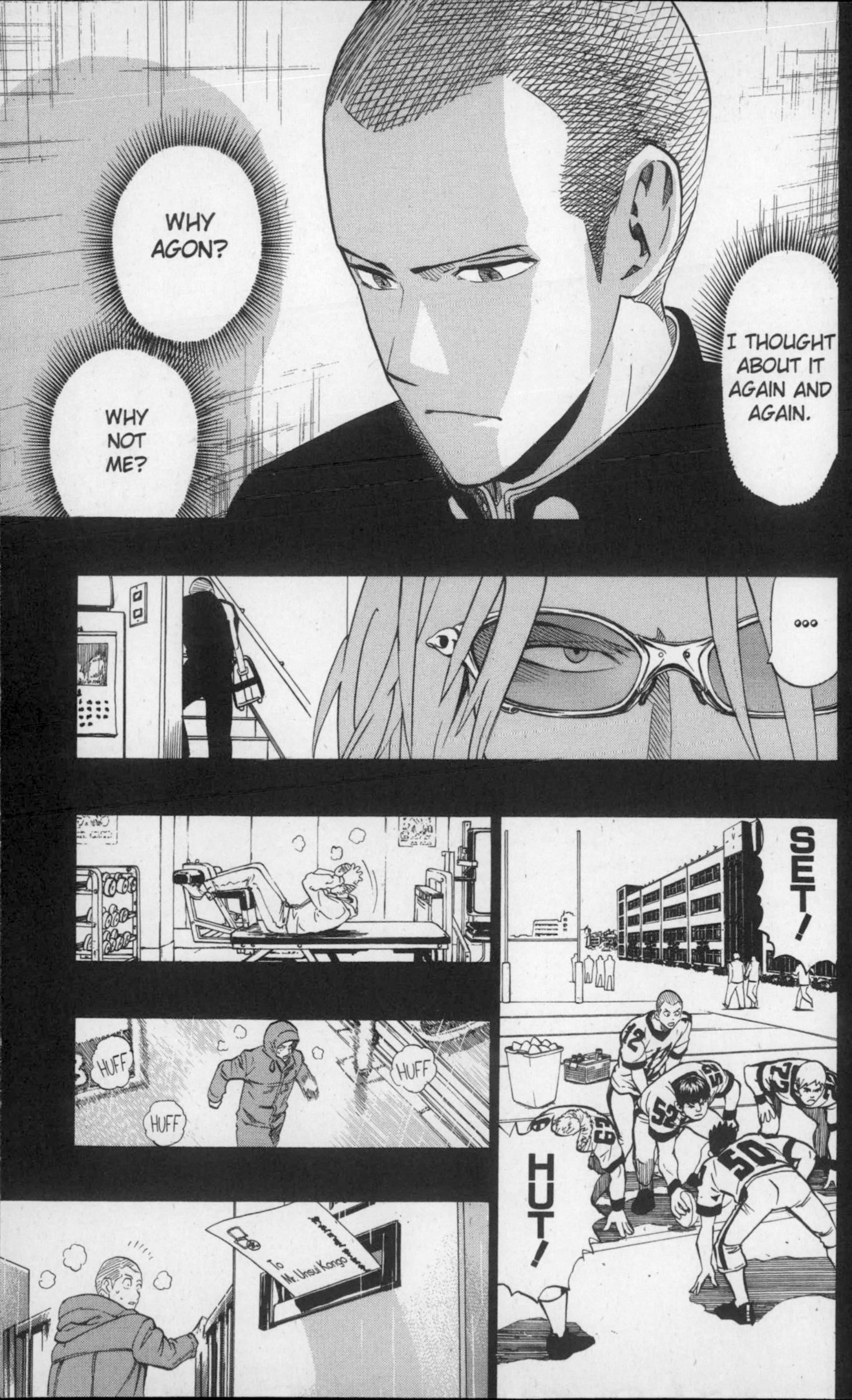
I THOUGHT ABOUT IT AGAIN AND AGAIN.
WHY AGON?
WHY NOT ME?
...
SET!
HUT!
HUFF
HUFF
HUFF
To Mr. Unsui Kongo

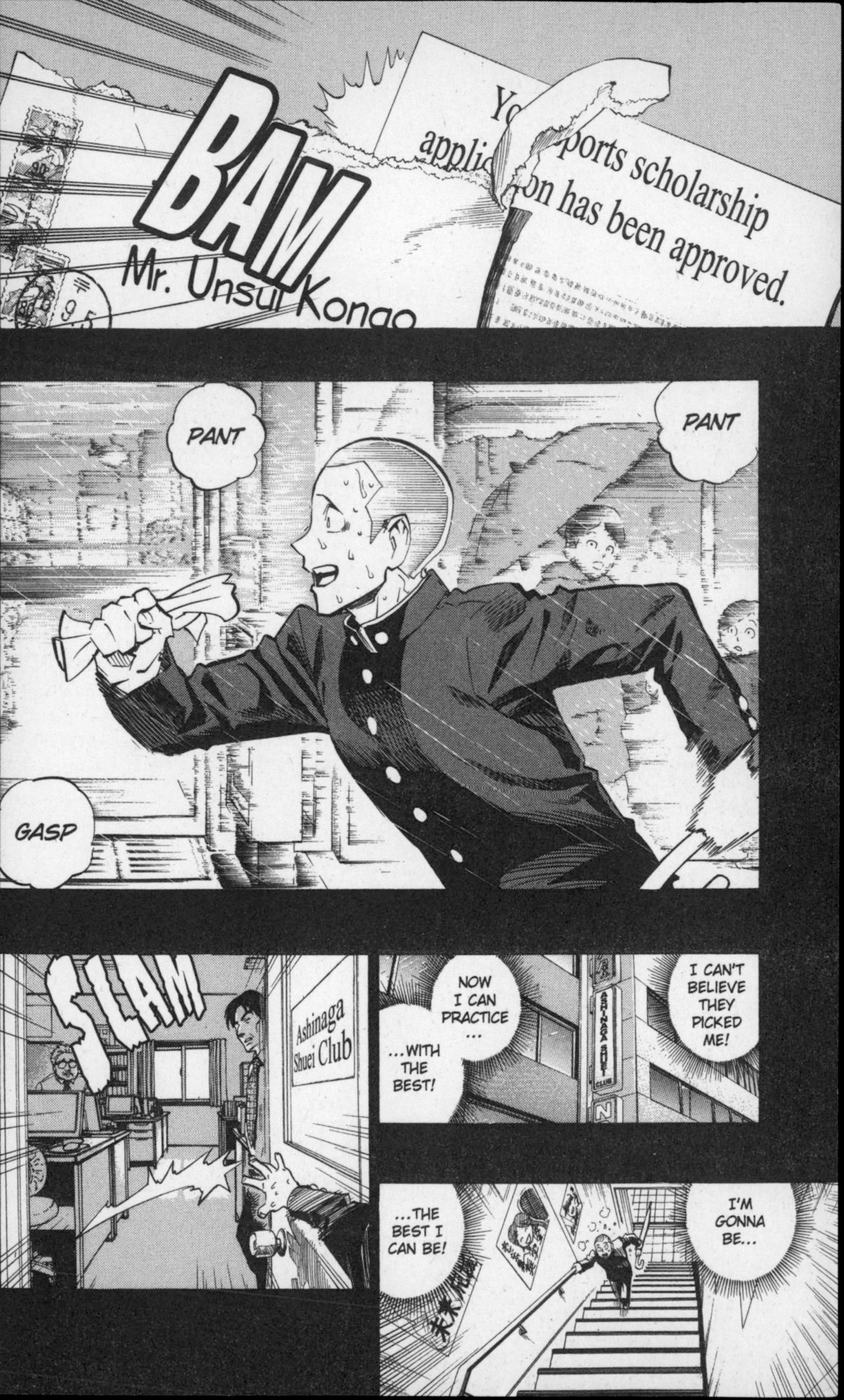
Yo
ports scholarship
applic
on has been approved.
BAM
Mr. Unsui Kongo
PANT
PANT
GASP
I CAN'T BELIEVE THEY PICKED ME!
NOW I CAN PRACTICE ...
...WITH THE BEST!
ASHINAGA SHUEI CLUB
SLAM
Ashinaga Shuei Club
I'M GONNA BE...
...THE BEST I CAN BE!

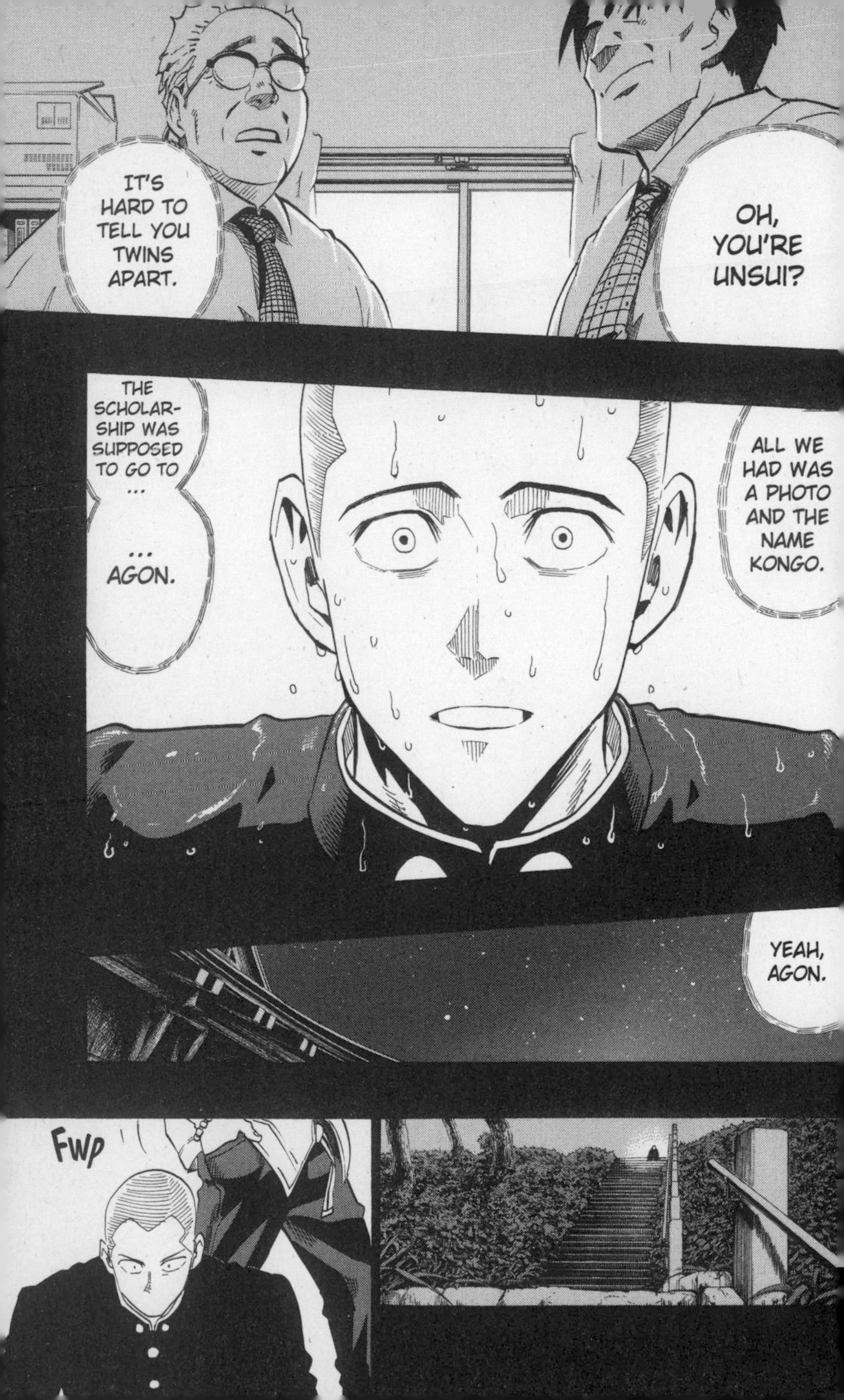
OH, YOU'RE UNSUI?
IT'S HARD TO TELL YOU TWINS APART.
ALL WE HAD WAS A PHOTO AND THE NAME KONGO.
THE SCHOLAR-SHIP WAS SUPPOSED TO GO TO ...
... AGON.
YEAH, AGON.
FWP

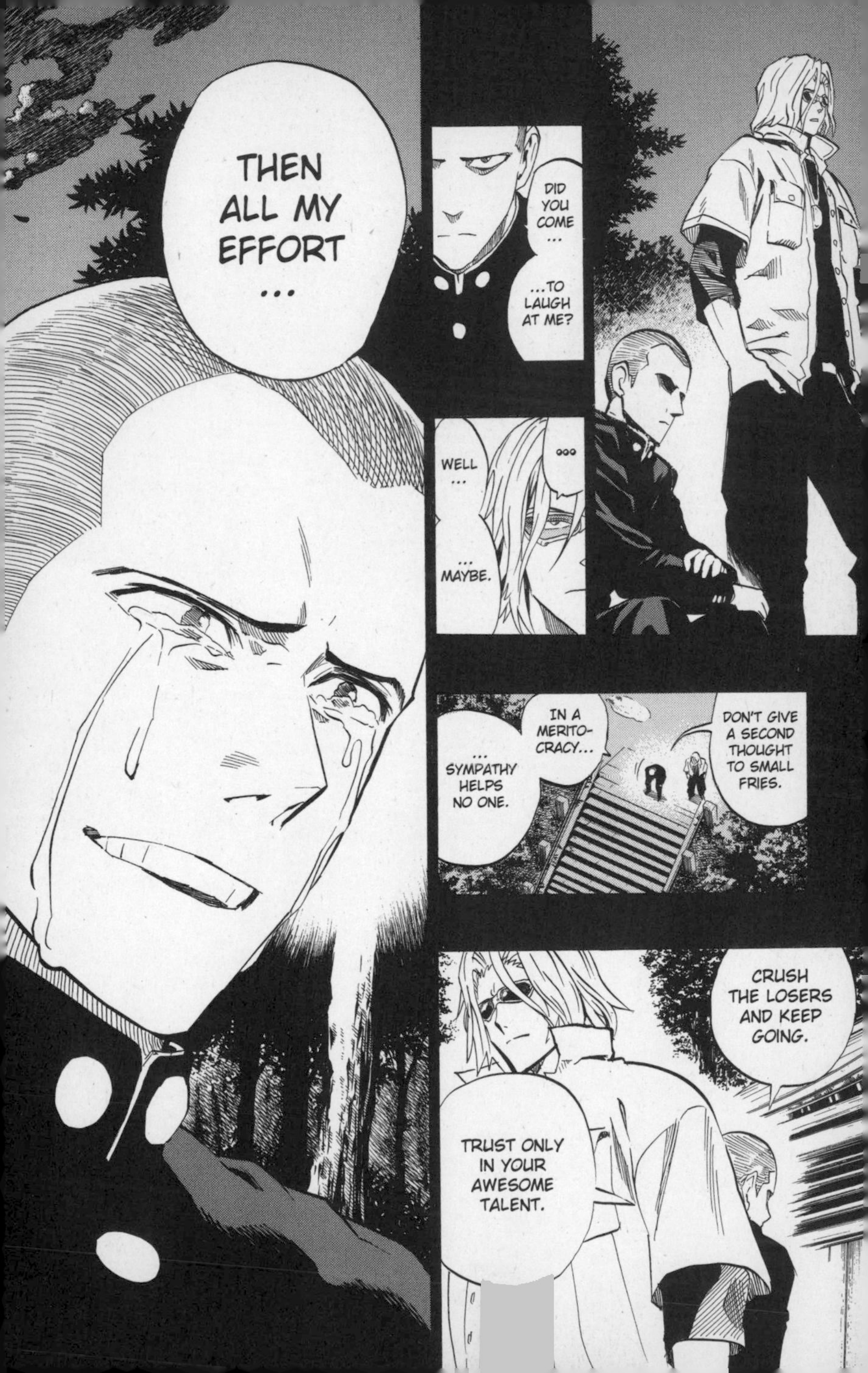
DID YOU COME ...
...TO LAUGH AT ME?
...
WELL ...
... MAYBE.
DON'T GIVE A SECOND THOUGHT TO SMALL FRIES.
IN A MERITO-CRACY...
... SYMPATHY HELPS NO ONE.
CRUSH THE LOSERS AND KEEP GOING.
TRUST ONLY IN YOUR AWESOME TALENT.
THEN ALL MY EFFORT ...

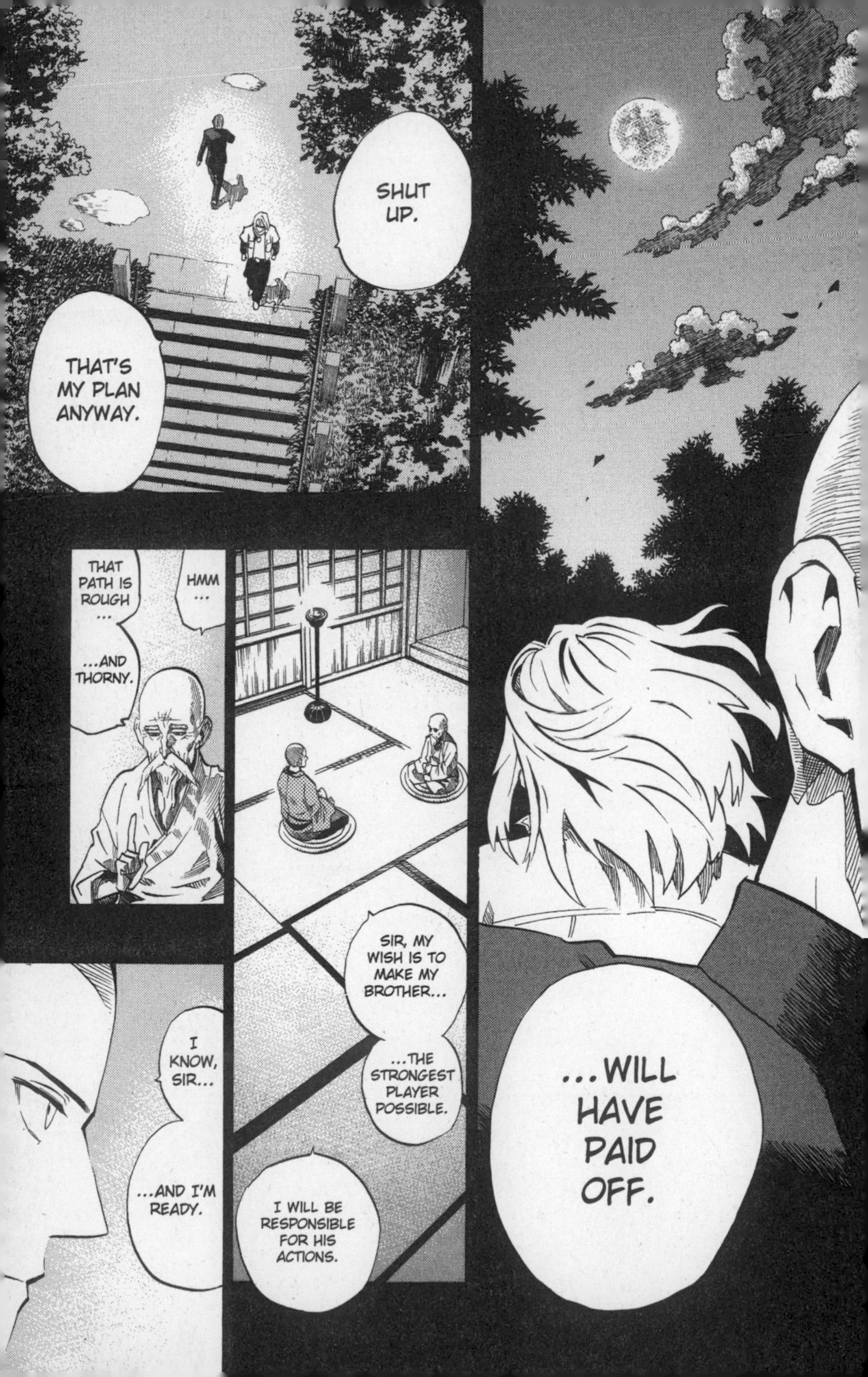
...WILL HAVE PAID OFF.
SHUT UP.
THAT'S MY PLAN ANYWAY.
HMM...
THAT PATH IS ROUGH...
...AND THORNY.
SIR, MY WISH IS TO MAKE MY BROTHER...
...THE STRONGEST PLAYER POSSIBLE.
I WILL BE RESPONSIBLE FOR HIS ACTIONS.
I KNOW, SIR...
...AND I'M READY.

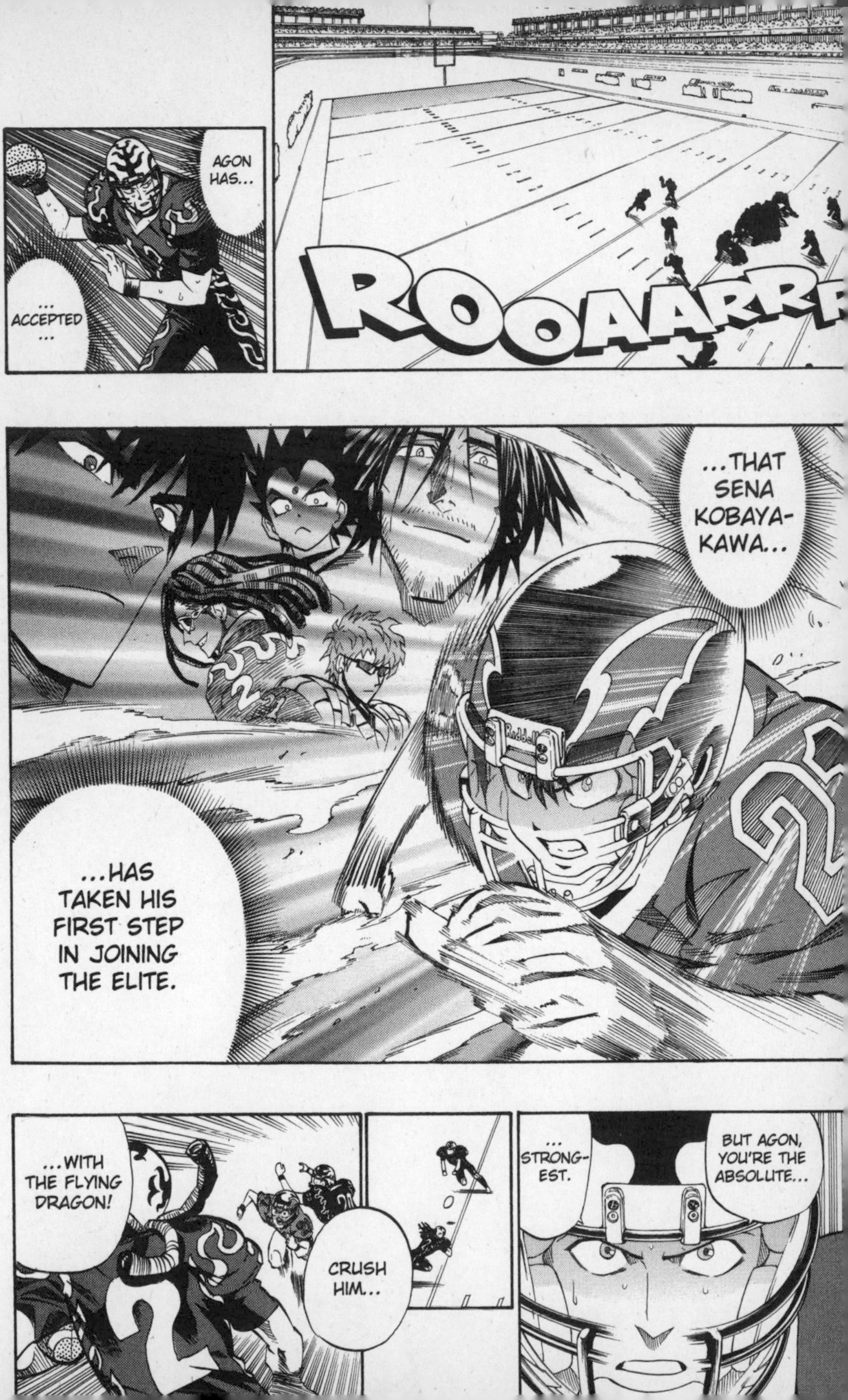
ROOAARRR
AGON HAS...
...ACCEPTED...
...THAT SENA KOBAYAKAWA...
...HAS TAKEN HIS FIRST STEP IN JOINING THE ELITE.
BUT AGON, YOU'RE THE ABSOLUTE...
...STRONGEST.
CRUSH HIM...
...WITH THE FLYING DRAGON!

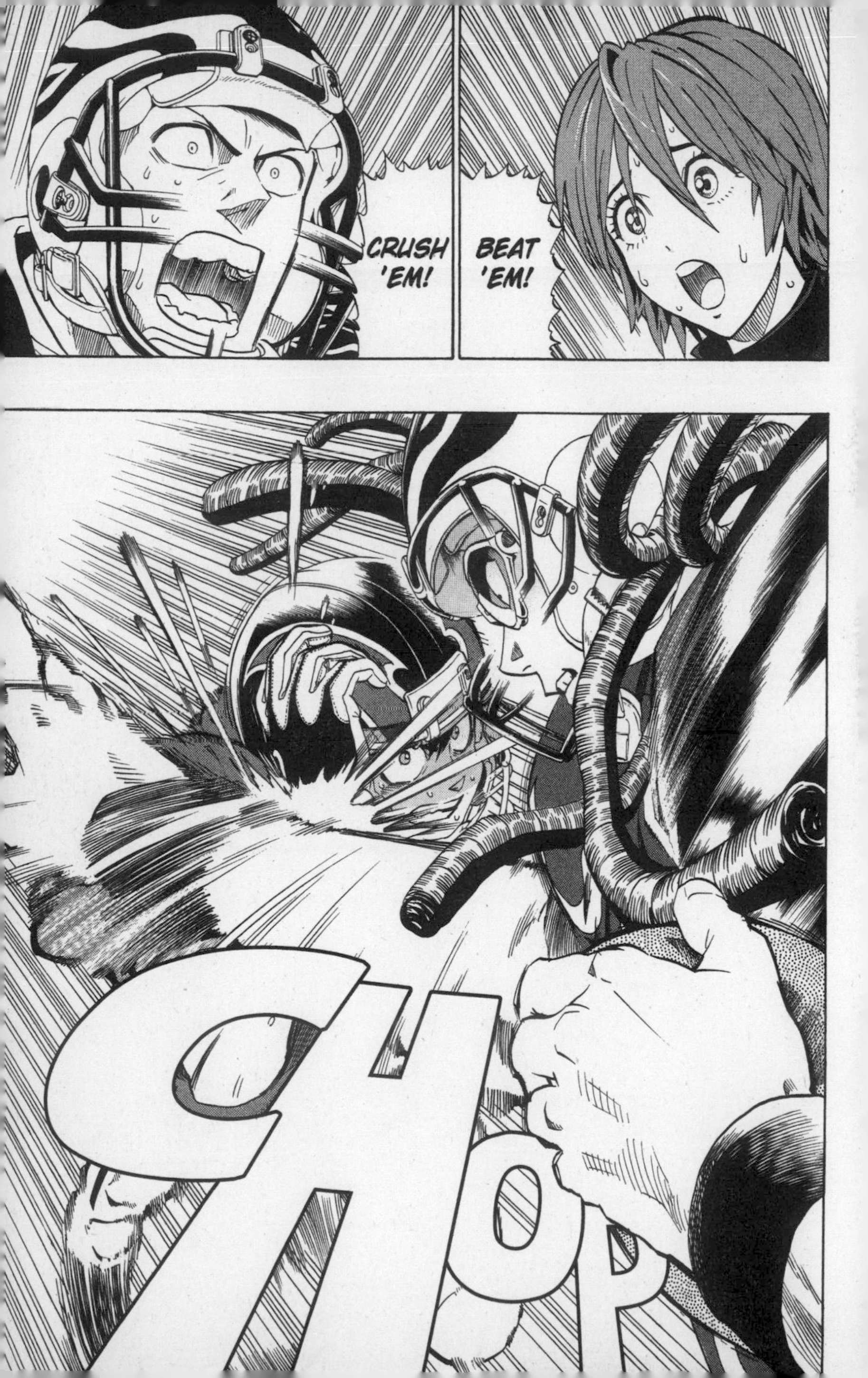
BEAT 'EM!
CRUSH 'EM!
CHOP

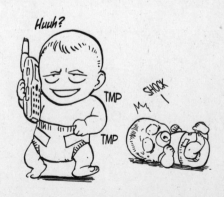

AGON AND UNSUI: 5 MONTHS OLD

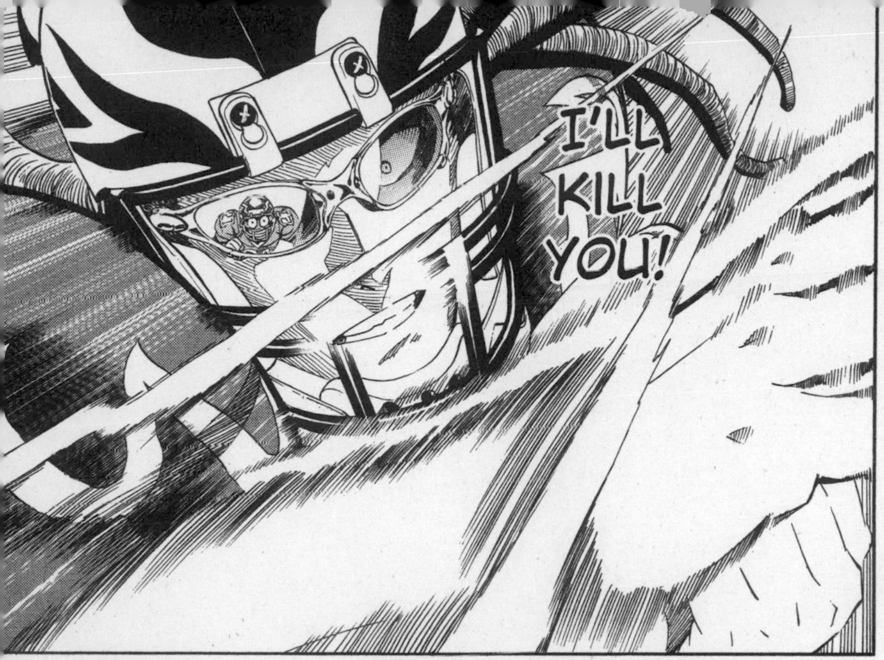
I'LL KILL YOU!

Chapter 186 Twenty-one Is Game Point

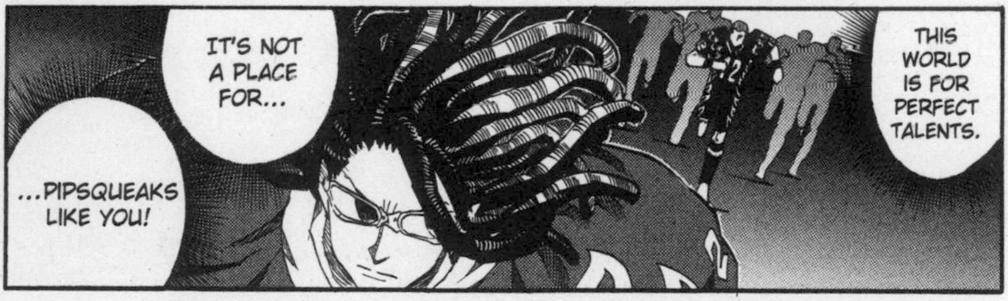
THIS WORLD IS FOR PERFECT TALENTS.
IT'S NOT A PLACE FOR...
...PIPSQUEAKS LIKE YOU!

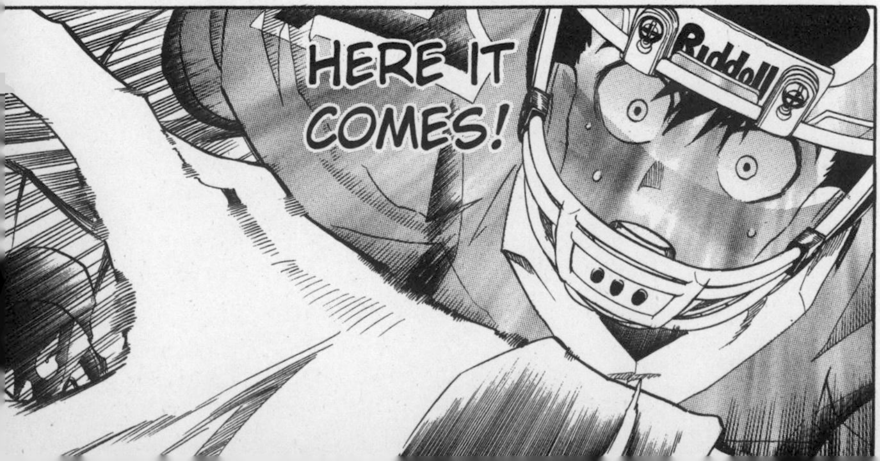
HERE IT COMES!
Riddell

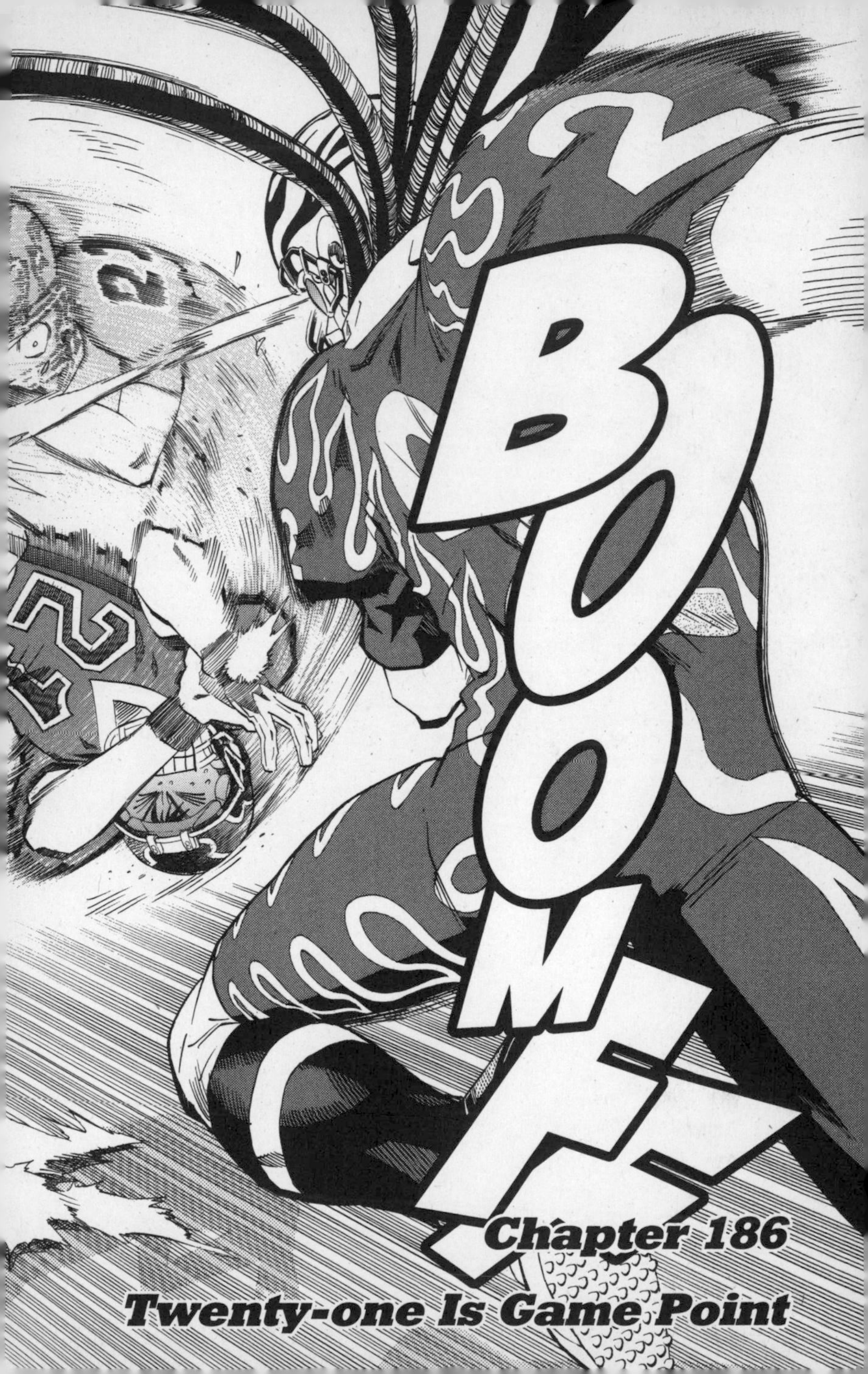
BOOMFF

Chapter 186
Twenty-one Is Game Point

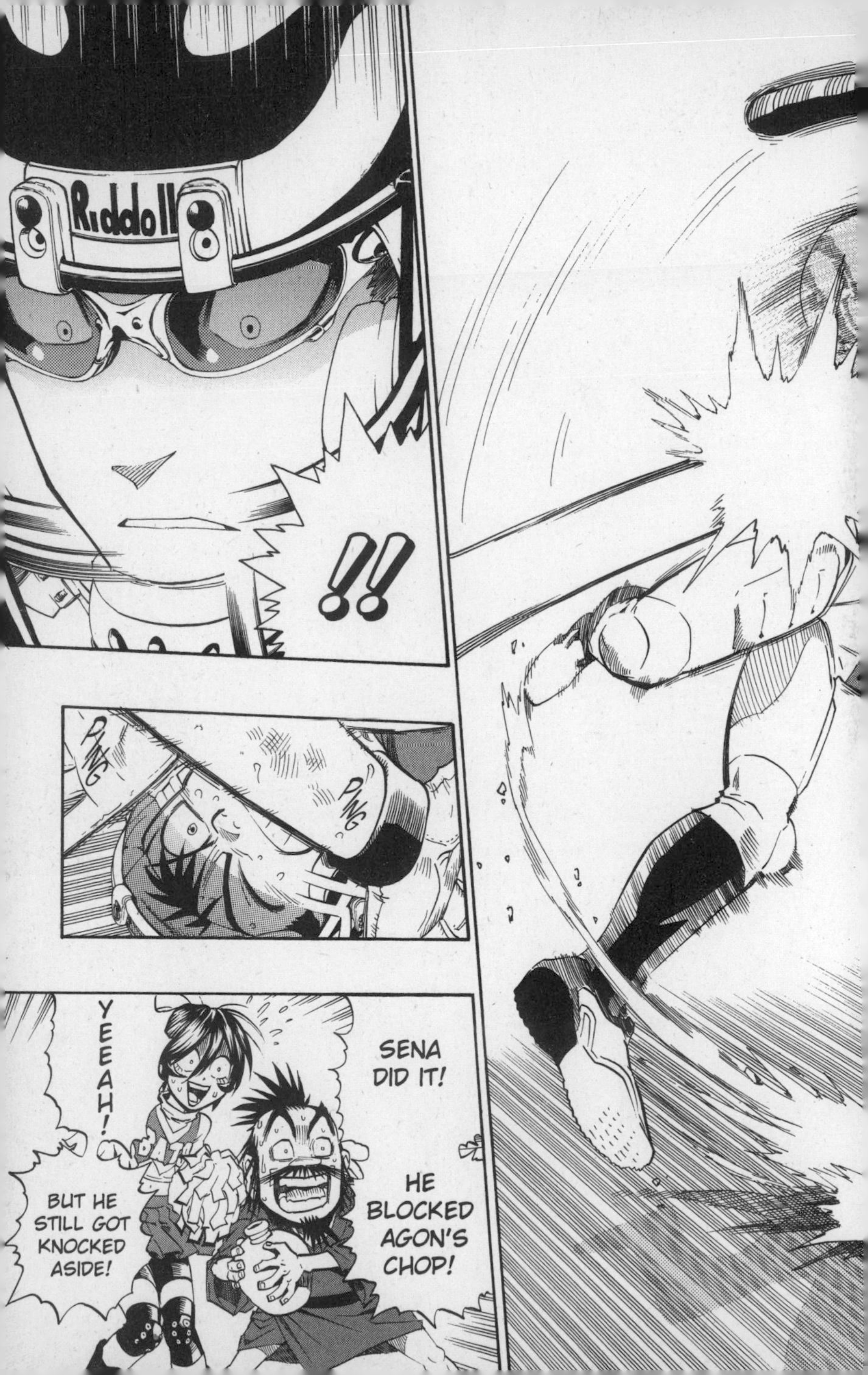
!!
PING
PING
SENA DID IT!
HE BLOCKED AGON'S CHOP!
YEEAH!
BUT HE STILL GOT KNOCKED ASIDE!

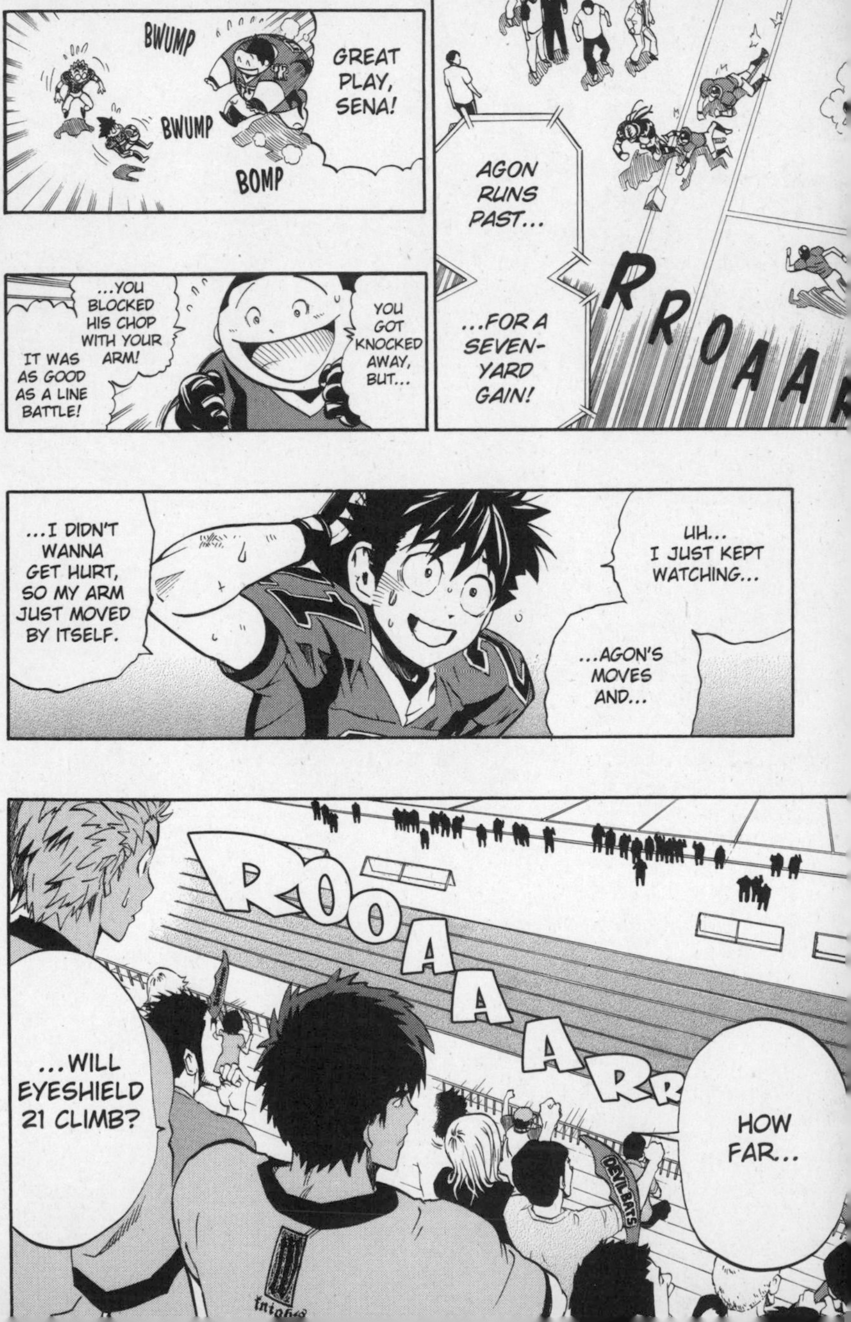
AGON RUNS PAST...
...FOR A SEVEN-YARD GAIN!
RROAAR
BWUMP
GREAT PLAY, SENA!
BWUMP
BOMP
YOU GOT KNOCKED AWAY, BUT...
...YOU BLOCKED HIS CHOP WITH YOUR ARM!
IT WAS AS GOOD AS A LINE BATTLE!
UH... I JUST KEPT WATCHING...
...AGON'S MOVES AND...
...I DIDN'T WANNA GET HURT, SO MY ARM JUST MOVED BY ITSELF.
HOW FAR...
ROOAAAARR
DEVILBATS
...WILL EYESHIELD 21 CLIMB?

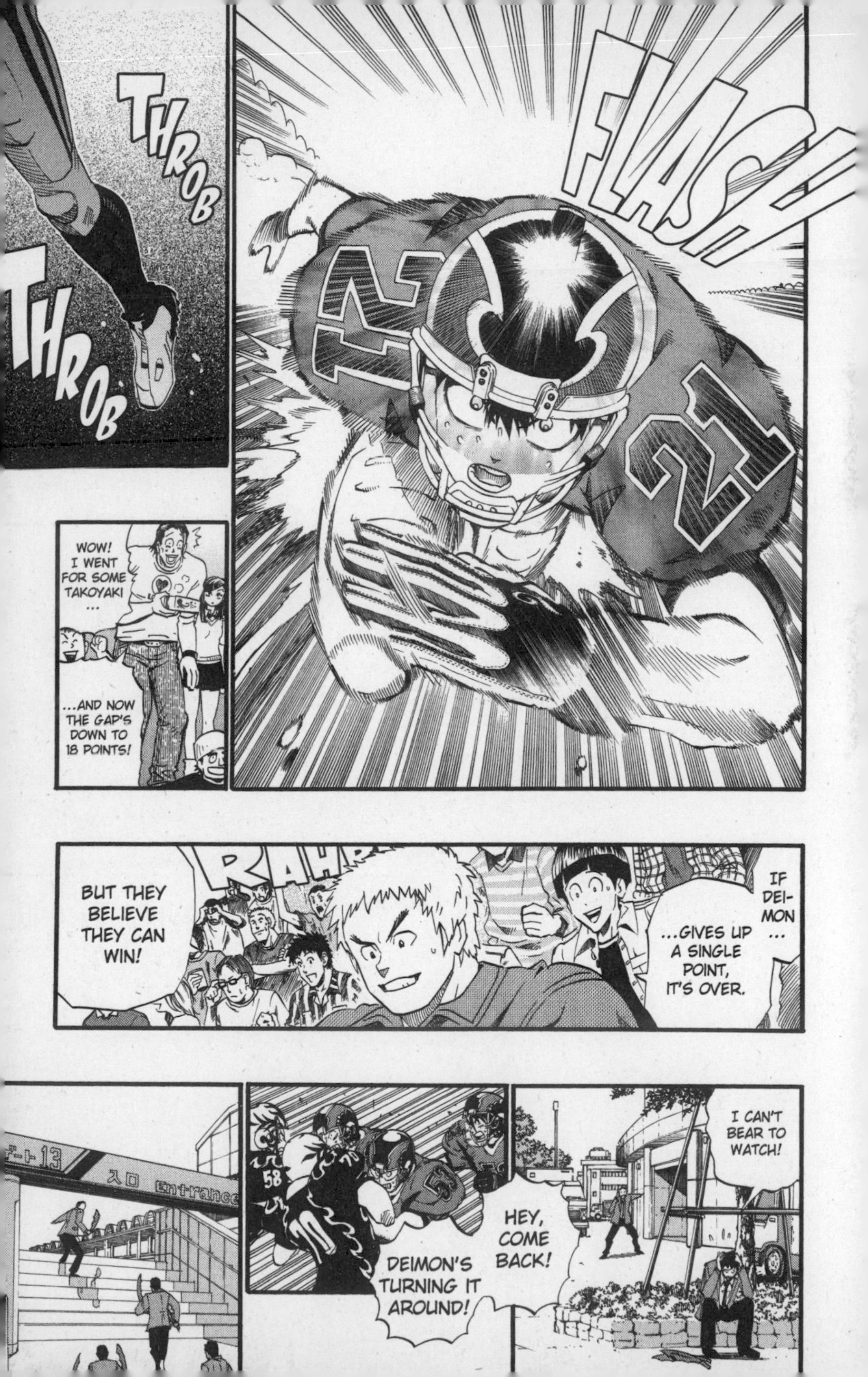
FLASH
THROB
THROB
WOW! I WENT FOR SOME TAKOYAKI ...
...AND NOW THE GAP'S DOWN TO 18 POINTS!
IF DEI-MON ...
...GIVES UP A SINGLE POINT, IT'S OVER.
BUT THEY BELIEVE THEY CAN WIN!
I CAN'T BEAR TO WATCH!
HEY, COME BACK!
DEIMON'S TURNING IT AROUND!
入口 Entrance

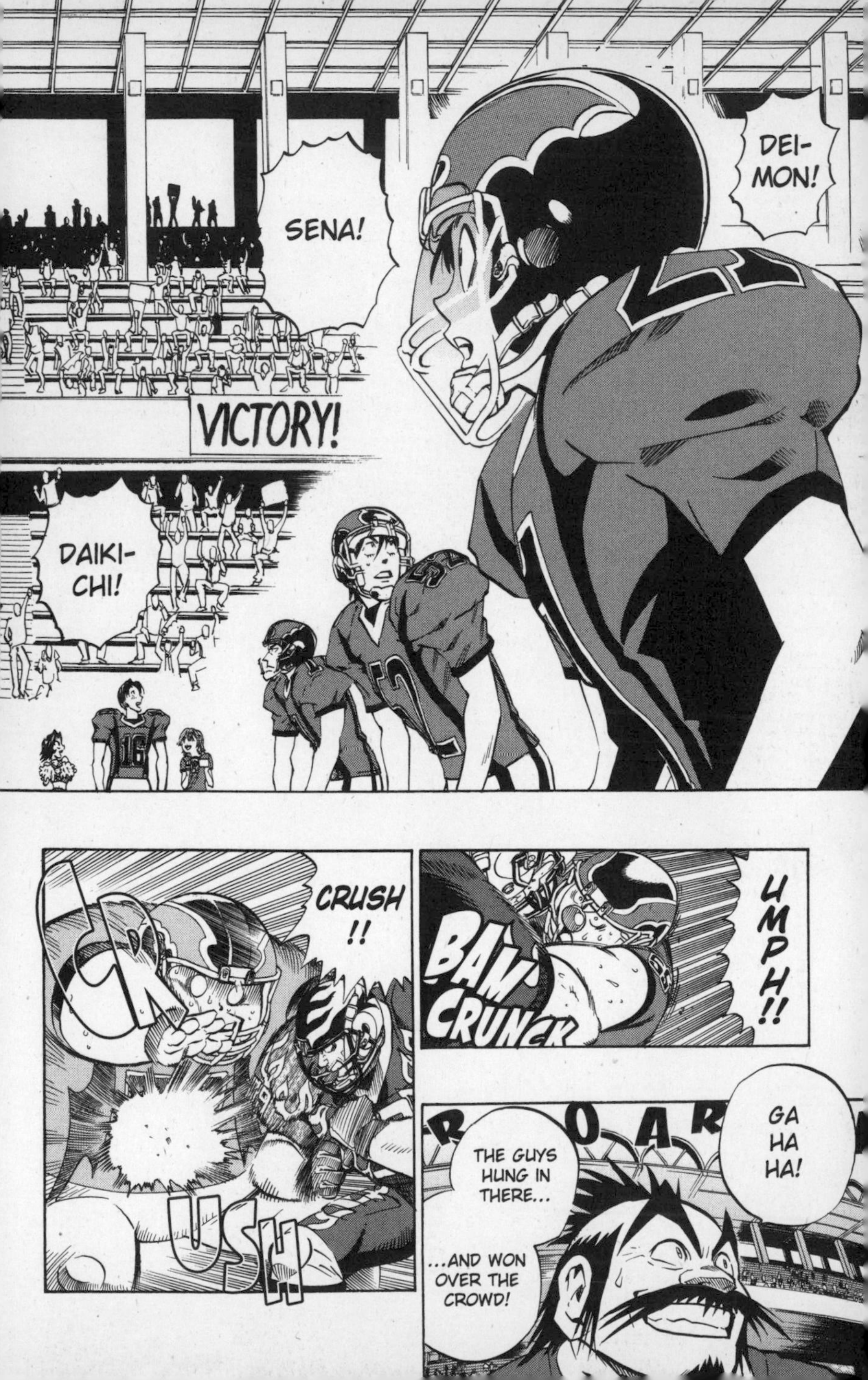
DEI-MON!
SENA!
VICTORY!
DAIKI-CHI!
UMPH!!
BAM
CRUNCK
ROAR
GA HA HA!
THE GUYS HUNG IN THERE...
...AND WON OVER THE CROWD!
CRUSH !!

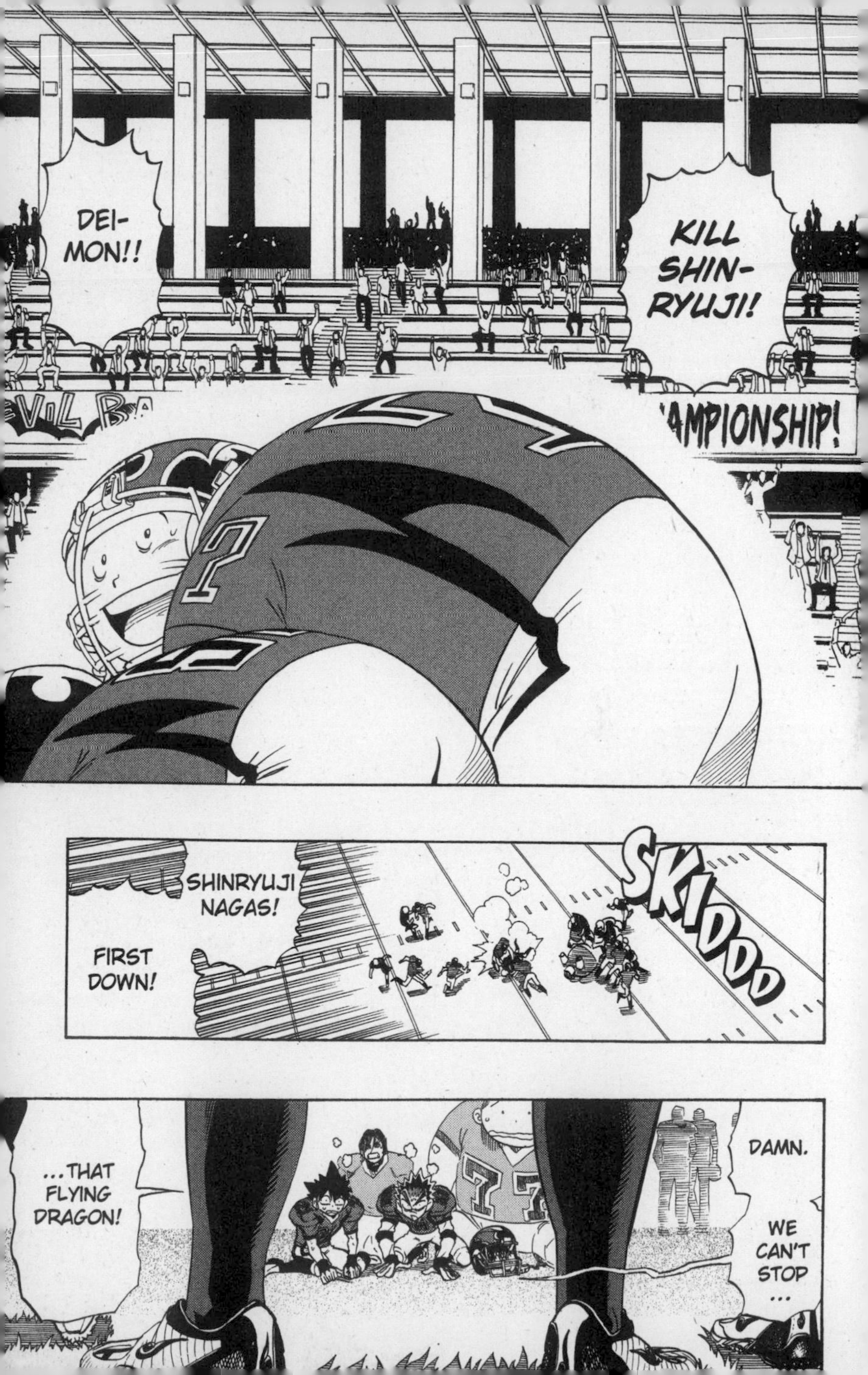
KILL SHIN-RYUJI!
DEI-MON!!
SKIDDD
SHINRYUJI NAGAS!
FIRST DOWN!
DAMN.
WE CAN'T STOP ...
...THAT FLYING DRAGON!

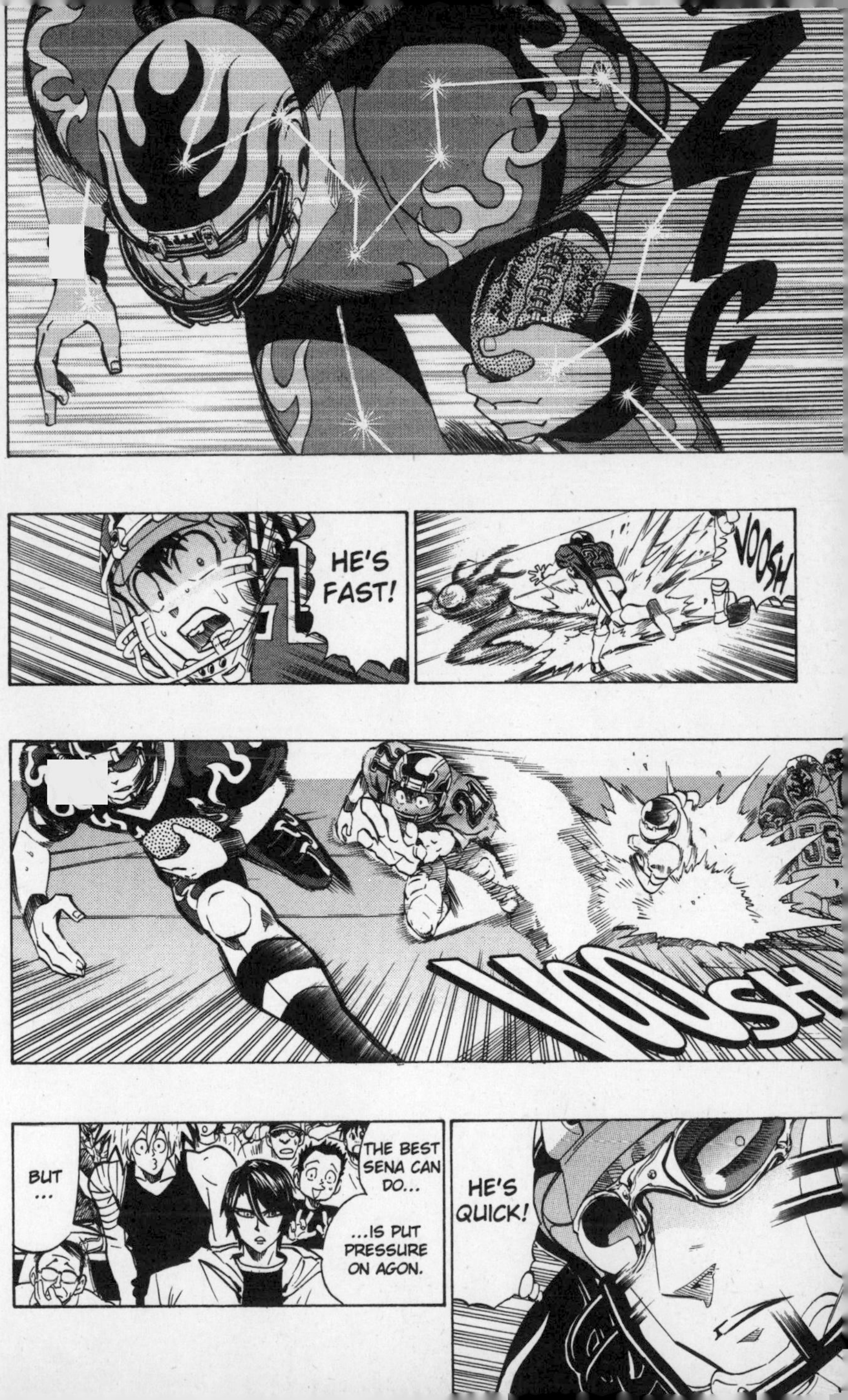
ZIG
VOOSH
HE'S FAST!
VOOSH
HE'S QUICK!
THE BEST SENA CAN DO...
...IS PUT PRESSURE ON AGON.
BUT...

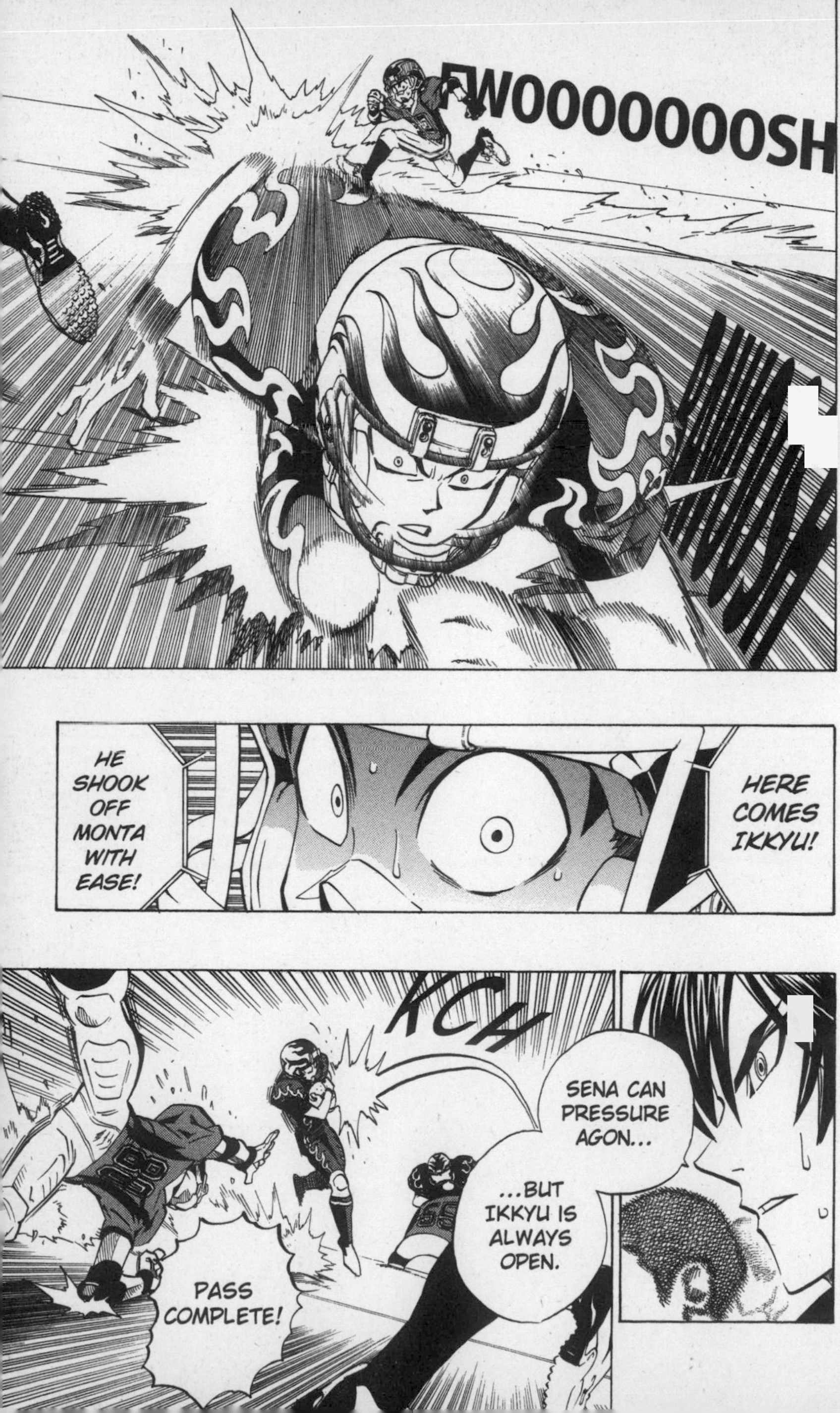
FWOOOOOOOSH
HERE COMES IKKYU!
HE SHOOK OFF MONTA WITH EASE!
SENA CAN PRESSURE AGON...
...BUT IKKYU IS ALWAYS OPEN.
KCH
PASS COMPLETE!

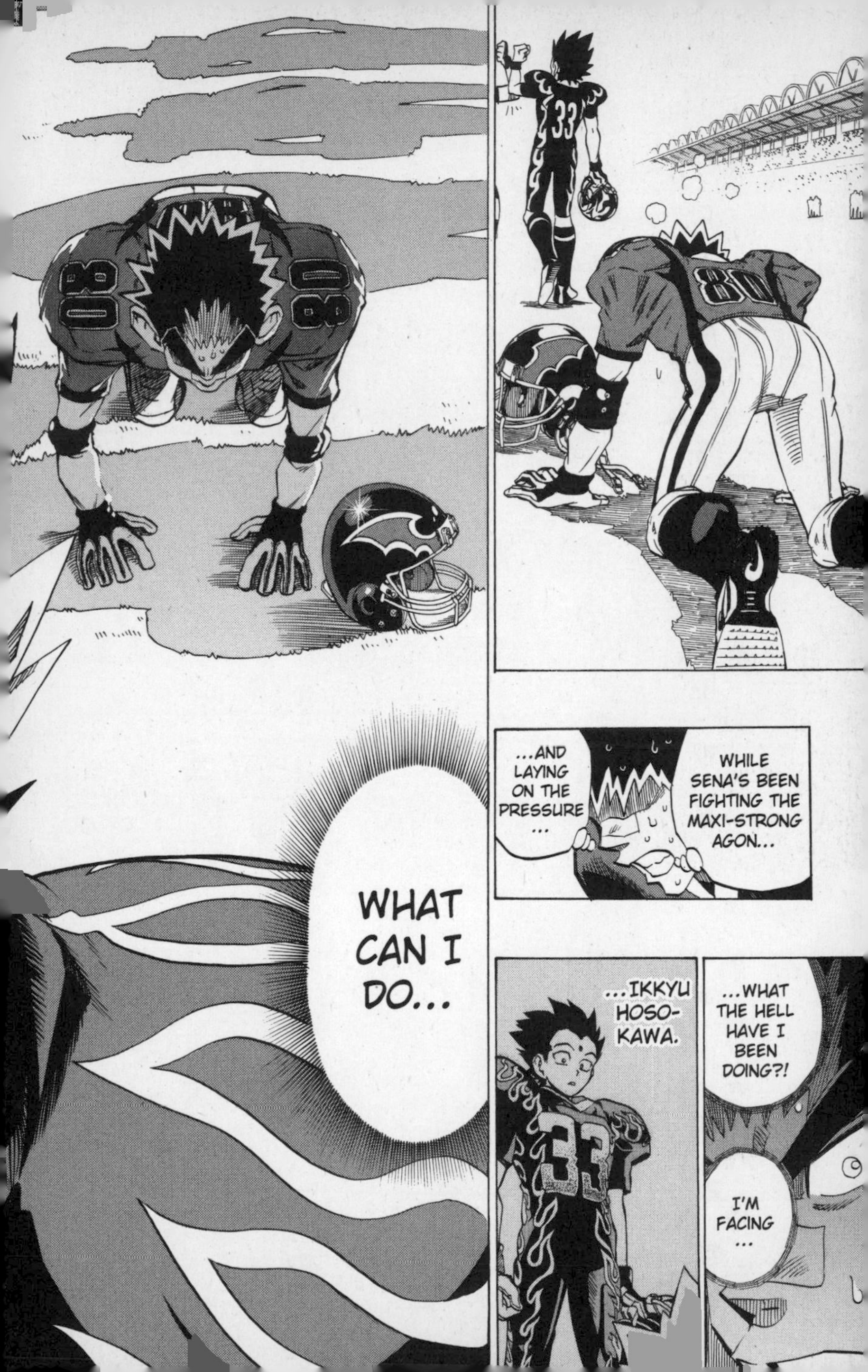
WHILE SENA'S BEEN FIGHTING THE MAXI-STRONG AGON...
...AND LAYING ON THE PRESSURE...
...WHAT THE HELL HAVE I BEEN DOING?!
I'M FACING...
...IKKYU HOSO-KAWA.
WHAT CAN I DO...

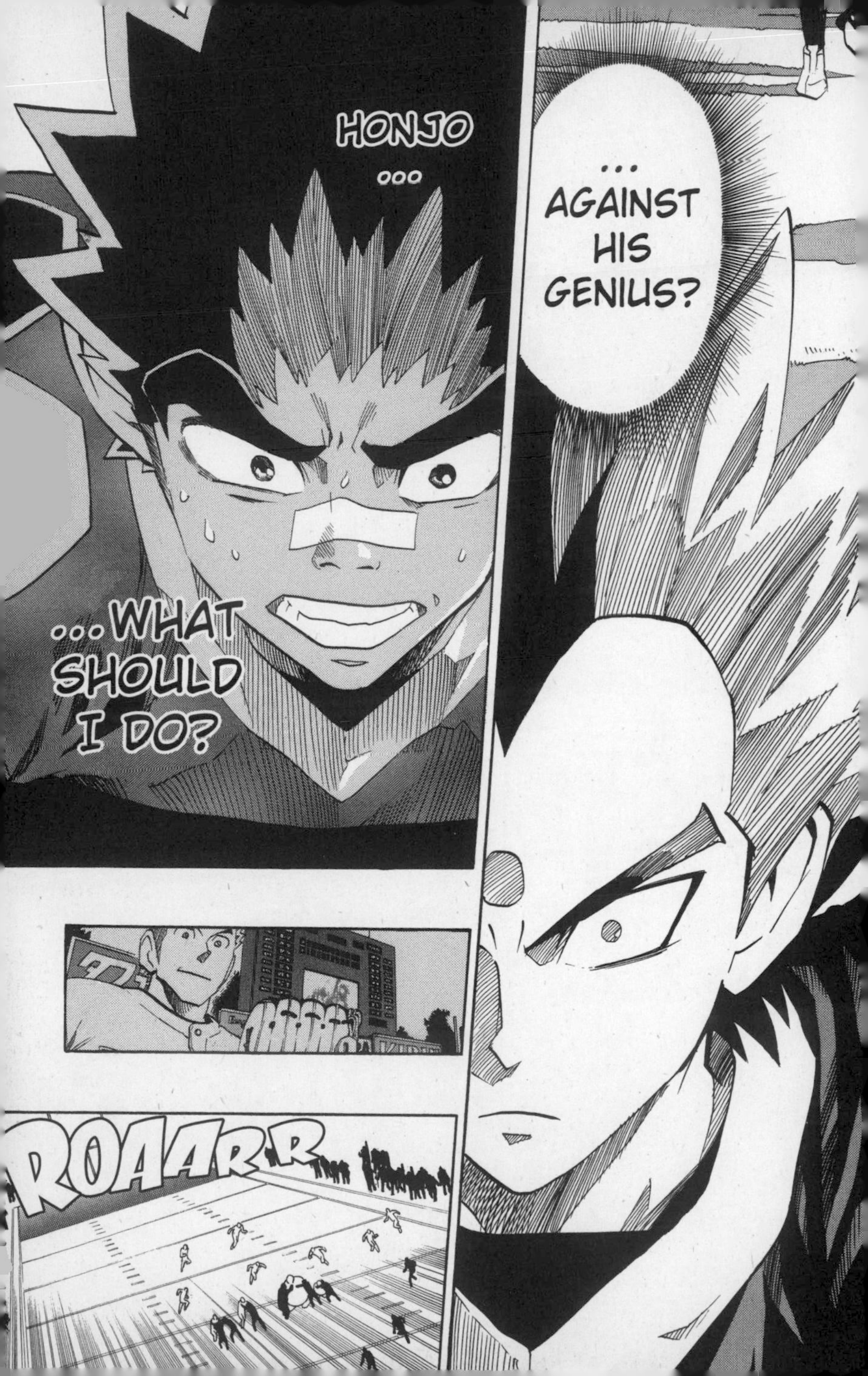
... AGAINST HIS GENIUS?
HONJO ...
...WHAT SHOULD I DO?
ROAARR

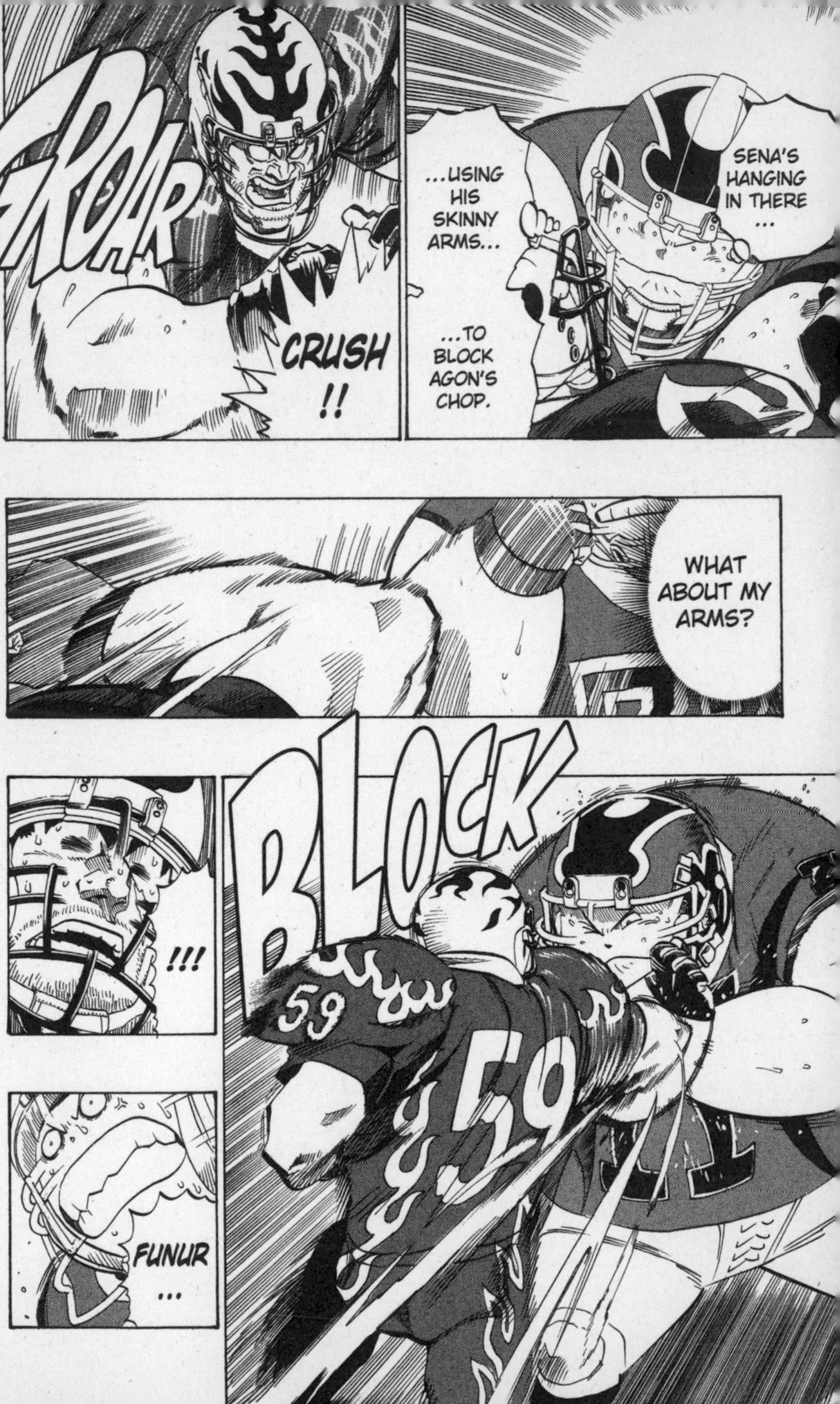
SENA'S HANGING IN THERE ...
...USING HIS SKINNY ARMS...
...TO BLOCK AGON'S CHOP.
GROAR
CRUSH !!
WHAT ABOUT MY ARMS?
BLOCK
!!!
FUNUR ...

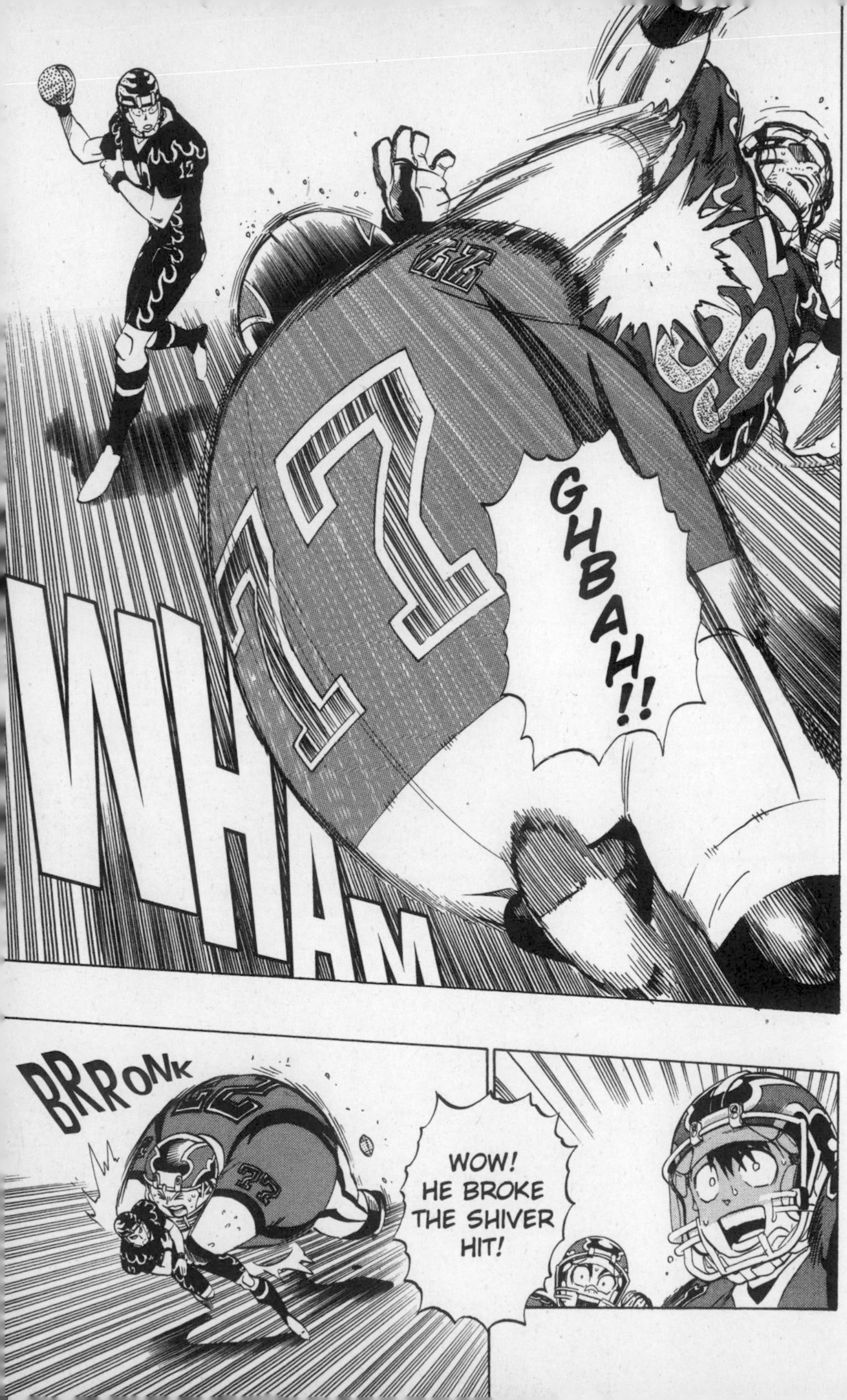
WHAM
GHBAH!!
WOW! HE BROKE THE SHIVER HIT!
BRRONK

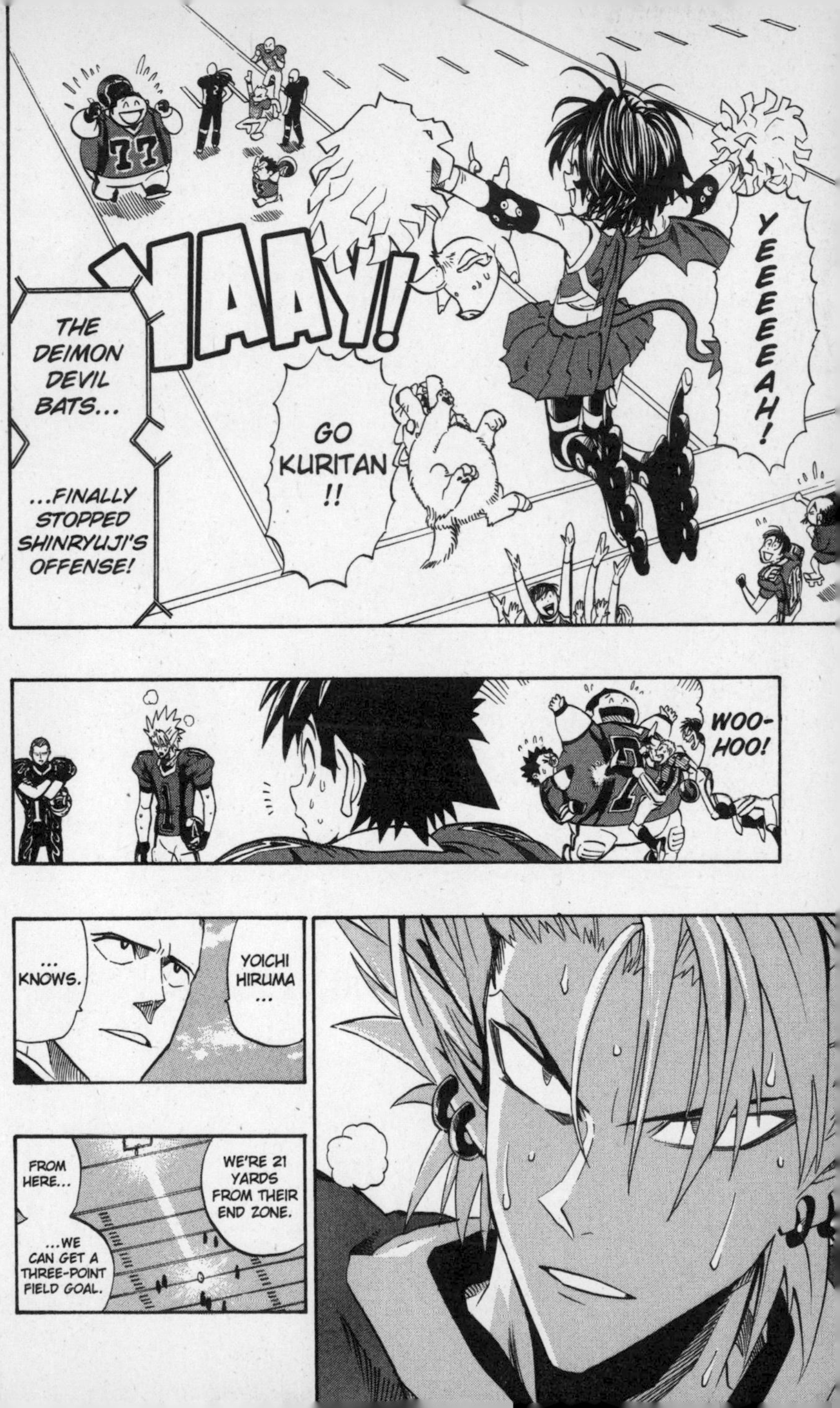
YEEEEEAH!
YAAY!
THE DEIMON DEVIL BATS...
GO KURITAN!!
...FINALLY STOPPED SHINRYUJI'S OFFENSE!
WOO-HOO!
YOICHI HIRUMA ...
... KNOWS.
WE'RE 21 YARDS FROM THEIR END ZONE.
FROM HERE...
...WE CAN GET A THREE-POINT FIELD GOAL.

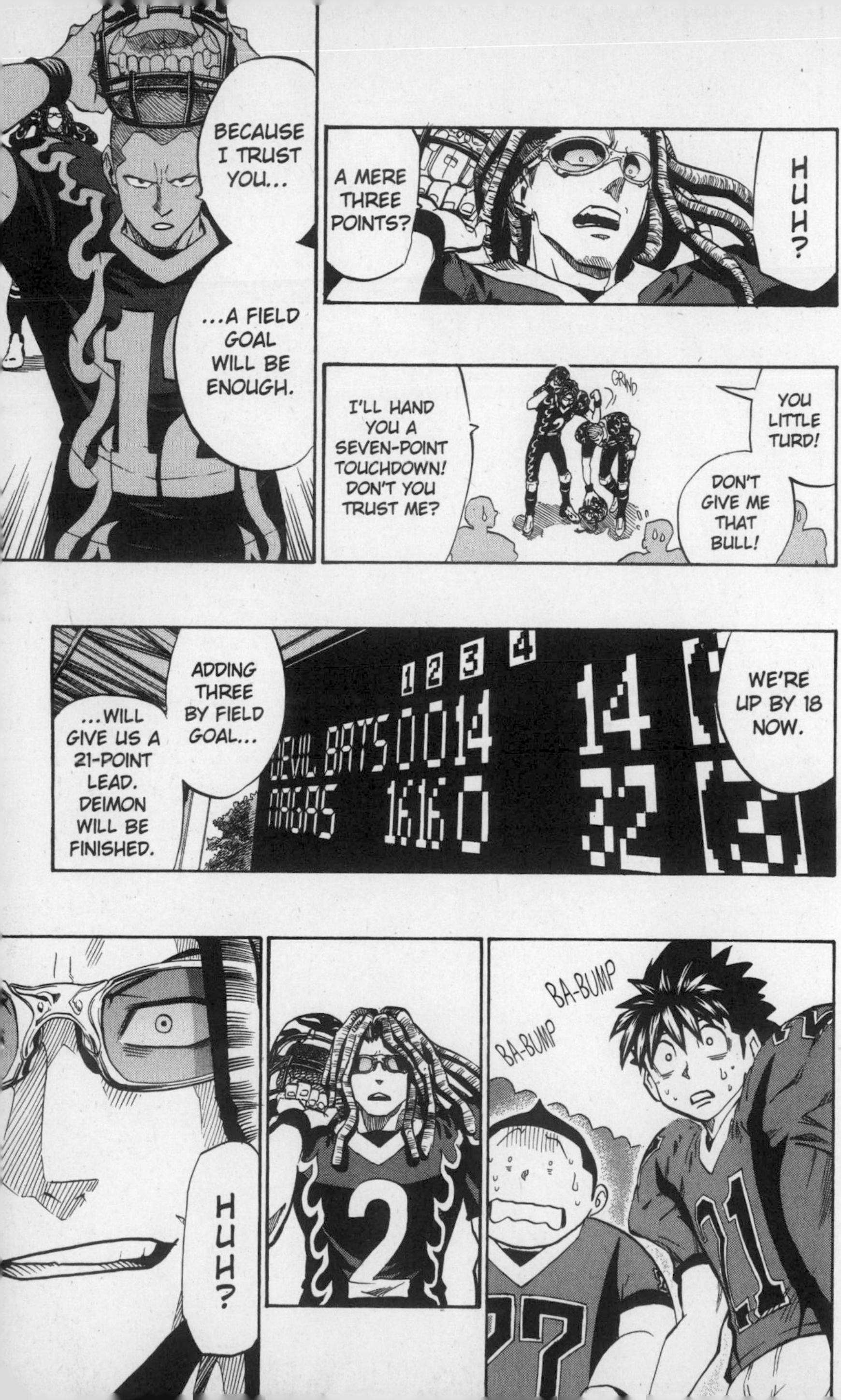
HUH?
A MERE THREE POINTS?
YOU LITTLE TURD!
DON'T GIVE ME THAT BULL!
GRIND
I'LL HAND YOU A SEVEN-POINT TOUCHDOWN! DON'T YOU TRUST ME?
BECAUSE I TRUST YOU...
...A FIELD GOAL WILL BE ENOUGH.
WE'RE UP BY 18 NOW.
ADDING THREE BY FIELD GOAL...
...WILL GIVE US A 21-POINT LEAD. DEIMON WILL BE FINISHED.
BA-BUMP
BA-BUMP
HUH?

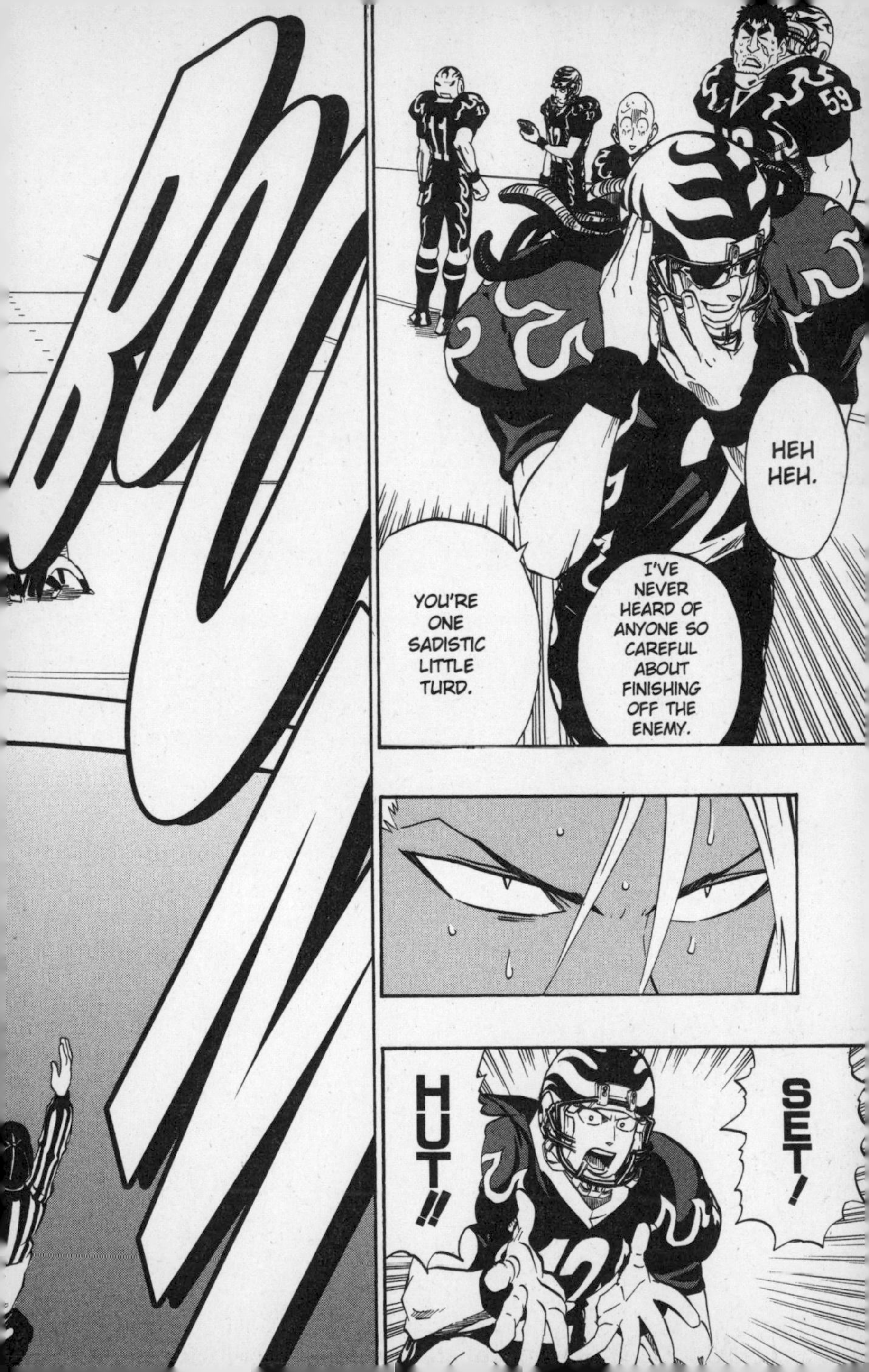
HEH HEH.
I'VE NEVER HEARD OF ANYONE SO CAREFUL ABOUT FINISHING OFF THE ENEMY.
YOU'RE ONE SADISTIC LITTLE TURD.
SET!
HUT!!

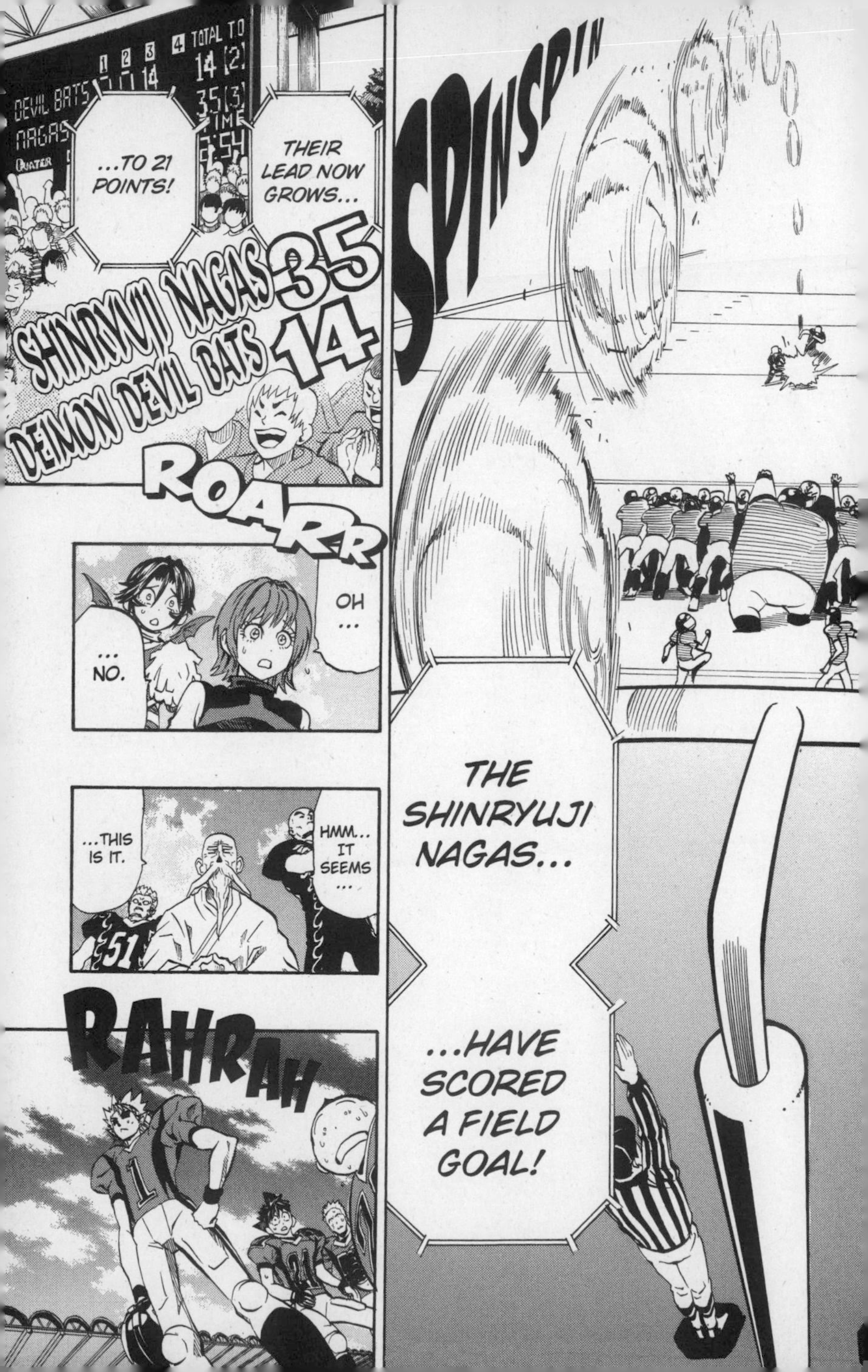
SPIN SPIN
THE SHINRYUJI NAGAS...
...HAVE SCORED A FIELD GOAL!
THEIR LEAD NOW GROWS...
...TO 21 POINTS!
SHINRYUJI NAGAS 35
DEIMON DEVIL BATS 14
ROARR
OH...
...NO.
HMM... IT SEEMS...
...THIS IS IT.
RAHRAH

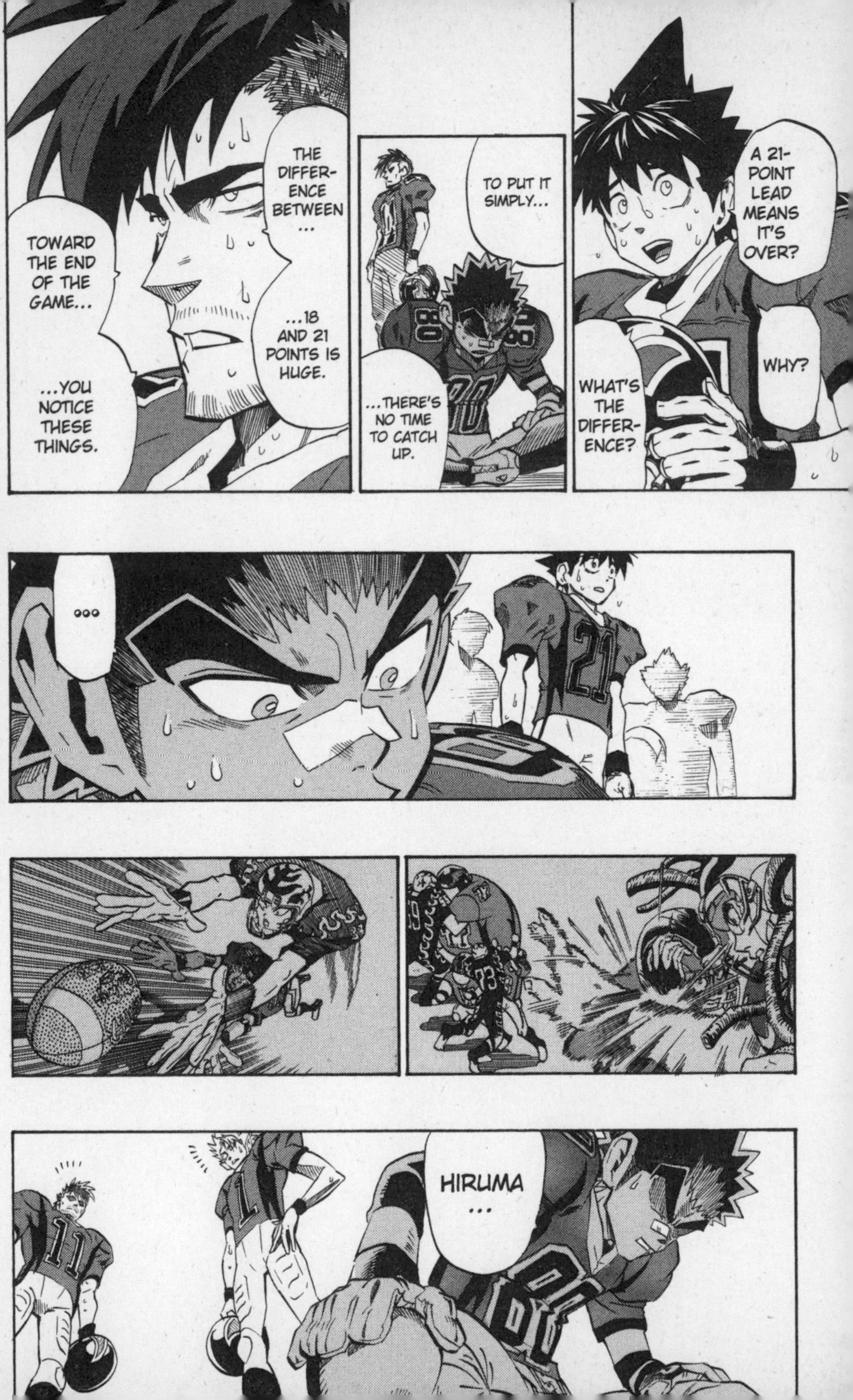
A 21-POINT LEAD MEANS IT'S OVER?
WHY?
WHAT'S THE DIFFERENCE?
TO PUT IT SIMPLY...
...THERE'S NO TIME TO CATCH UP.
THE DIFFERENCE BETWEEN...
...18 AND 21 POINTS IS HUGE.
TOWARD THE END OF THE GAME...
...YOU NOTICE THESE THINGS.
...
HIRUMA...

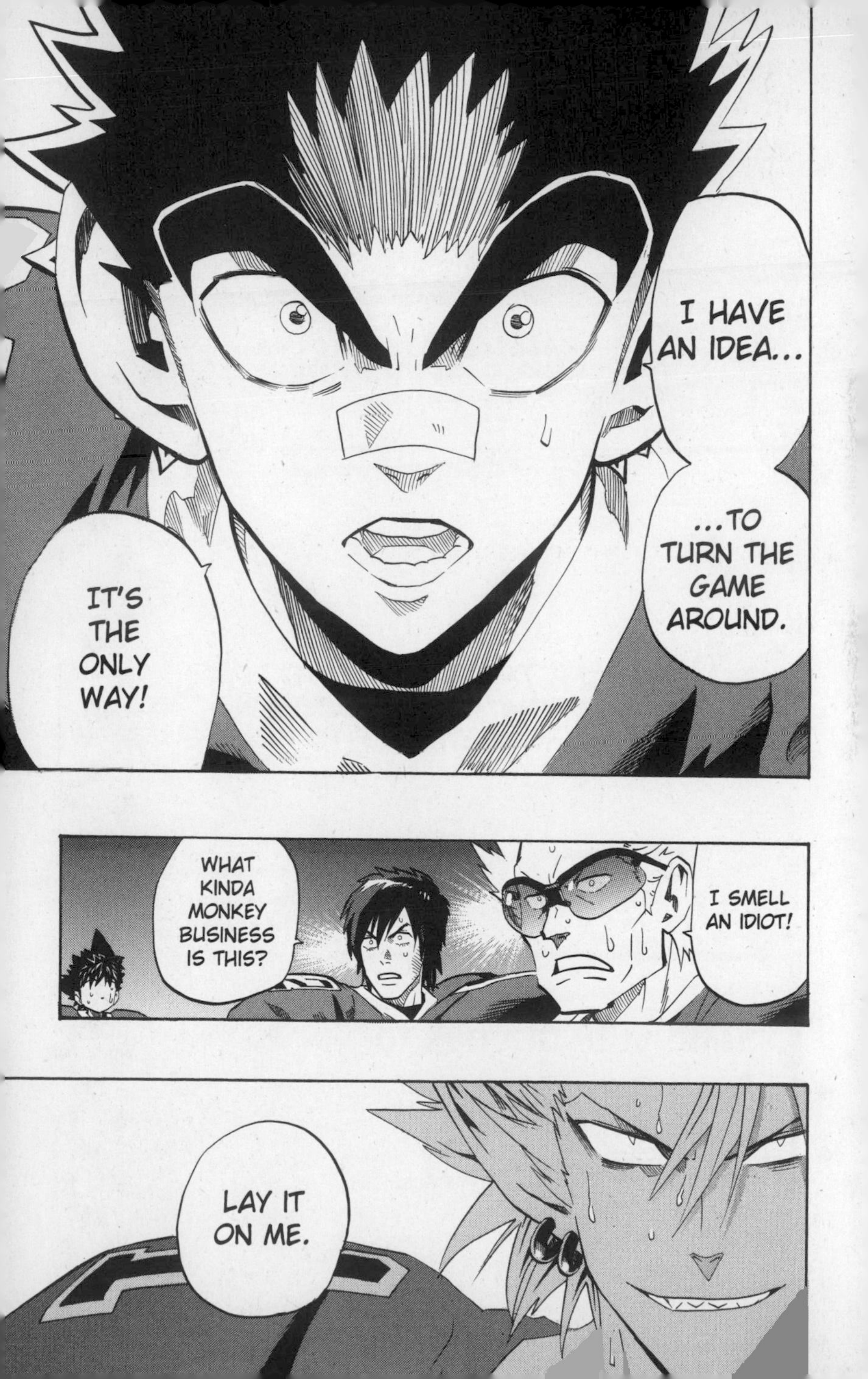
I HAVE AN IDEA...
...TO TURN THE GAME AROUND.
IT'S THE ONLY WAY!
I SMELL AN IDIOT!
WHAT KINDA MONKEY BUSINESS IS THIS?
LAY IT ON ME.

Devil Bat 021

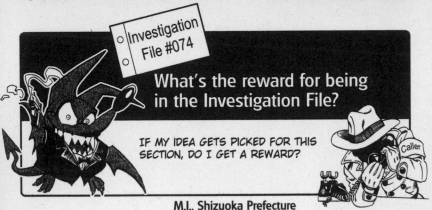

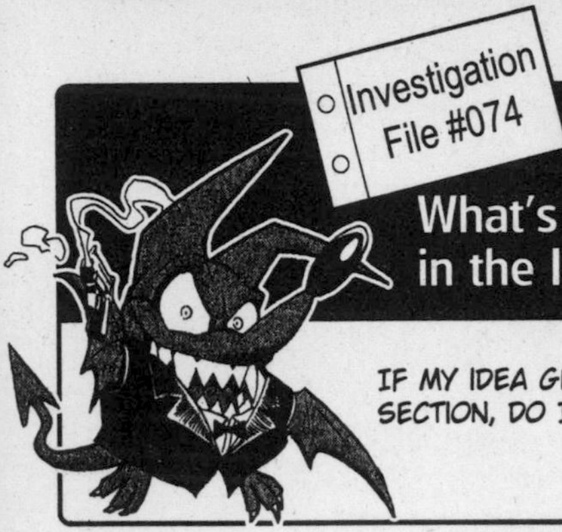
Investigation
File #074

What's the reward for being in the Investigation File?

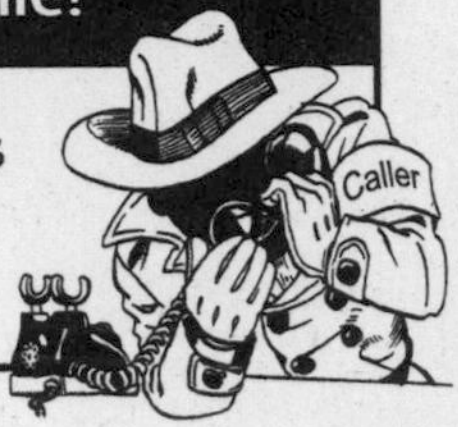
Caller

IF MY IDEA GETS PICKED FOR THIS SECTION, DO I GET A REWARD?

M.I., Shizuoka Prefecture

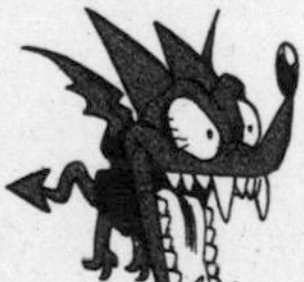

YOU GET ***THE RESULTS TO YOUR INVESTIGATION REQUEST*** AND ***THE RIGHT TO SHOW OFF TO YOUR FRIENDS!!***

Send your queries for Devil Bat 021 here!!

Devil Bat 021
Shonen Jump Advanced/Eyeshield 21
c/o VIZ Media, LLC
P.O. Box 77010
San Francisco, CA 94107

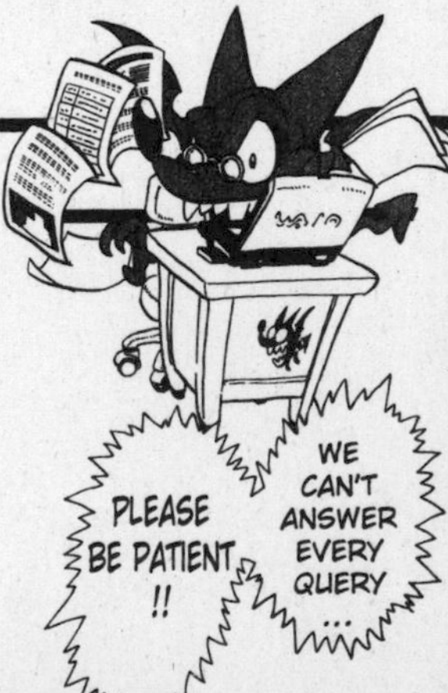
PLEASE BE PATIENT!!
WE CAN'T ANSWER EVERY QUERY...

Chapter 187
Ave Maria

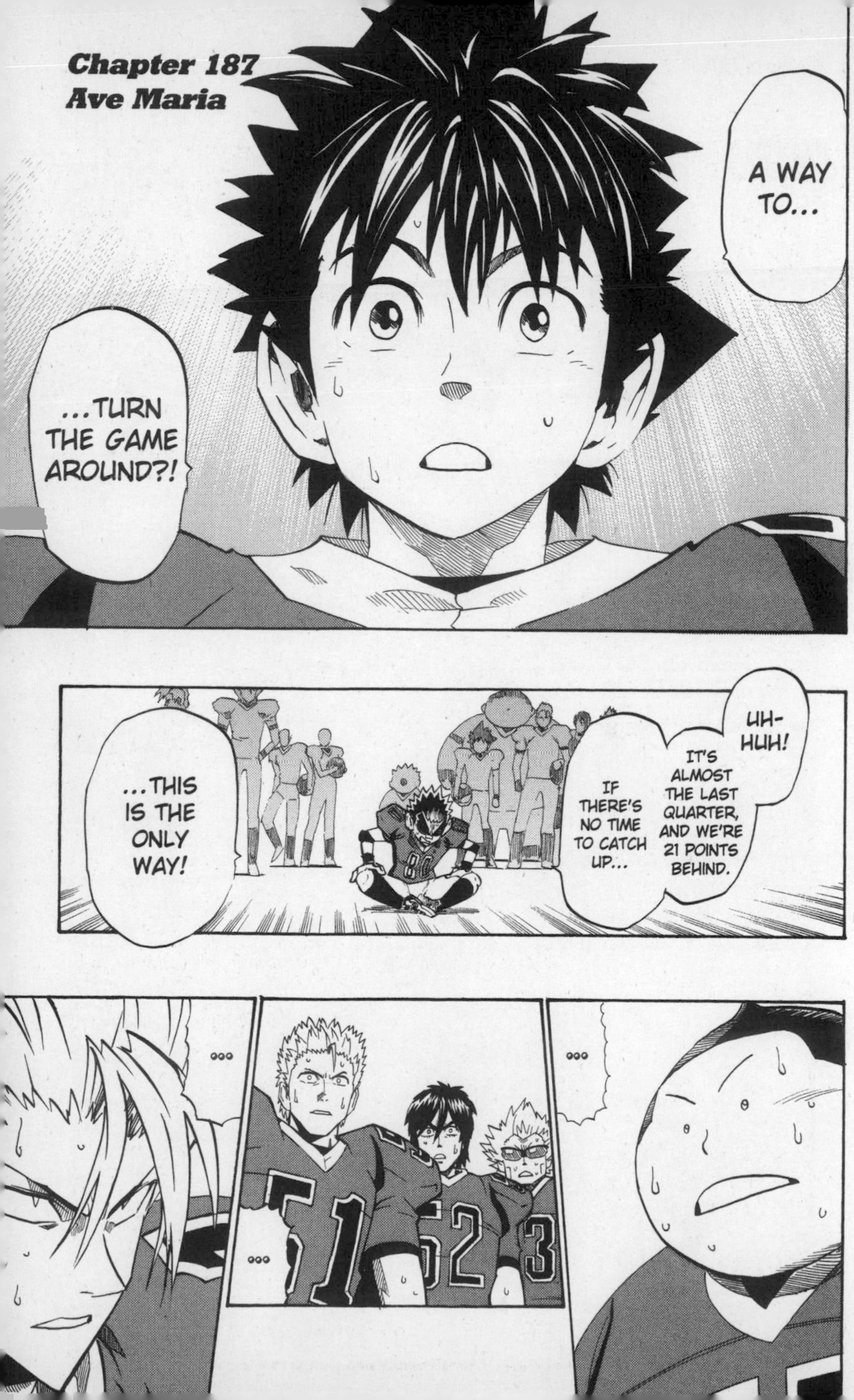

A WAY TO...
...TURN THE GAME AROUND?!
UH-HUH!
IT'S ALMOST THE LAST QUARTER, AND WE'RE 21 POINTS BEHIND.
IF THERE'S NO TIME TO CATCH UP...
...THIS IS THE ONLY WAY!
...
...
...
...

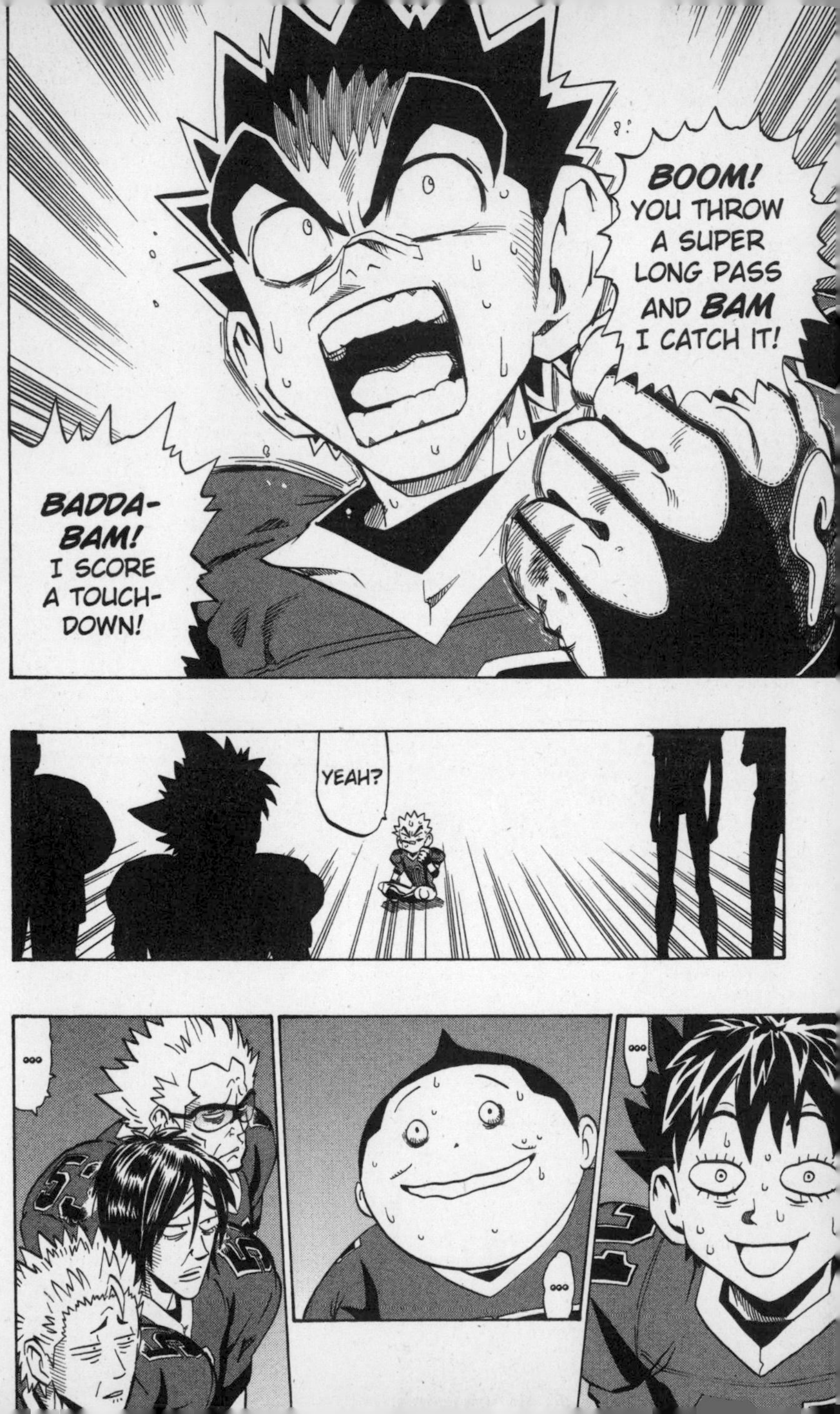
BOOM! YOU THROW A SUPER LONG PASS AND BAM I CATCH IT!
BADDA-BAM! I SCORE A TOUCH-DOWN!
YEAH?
...
...
...

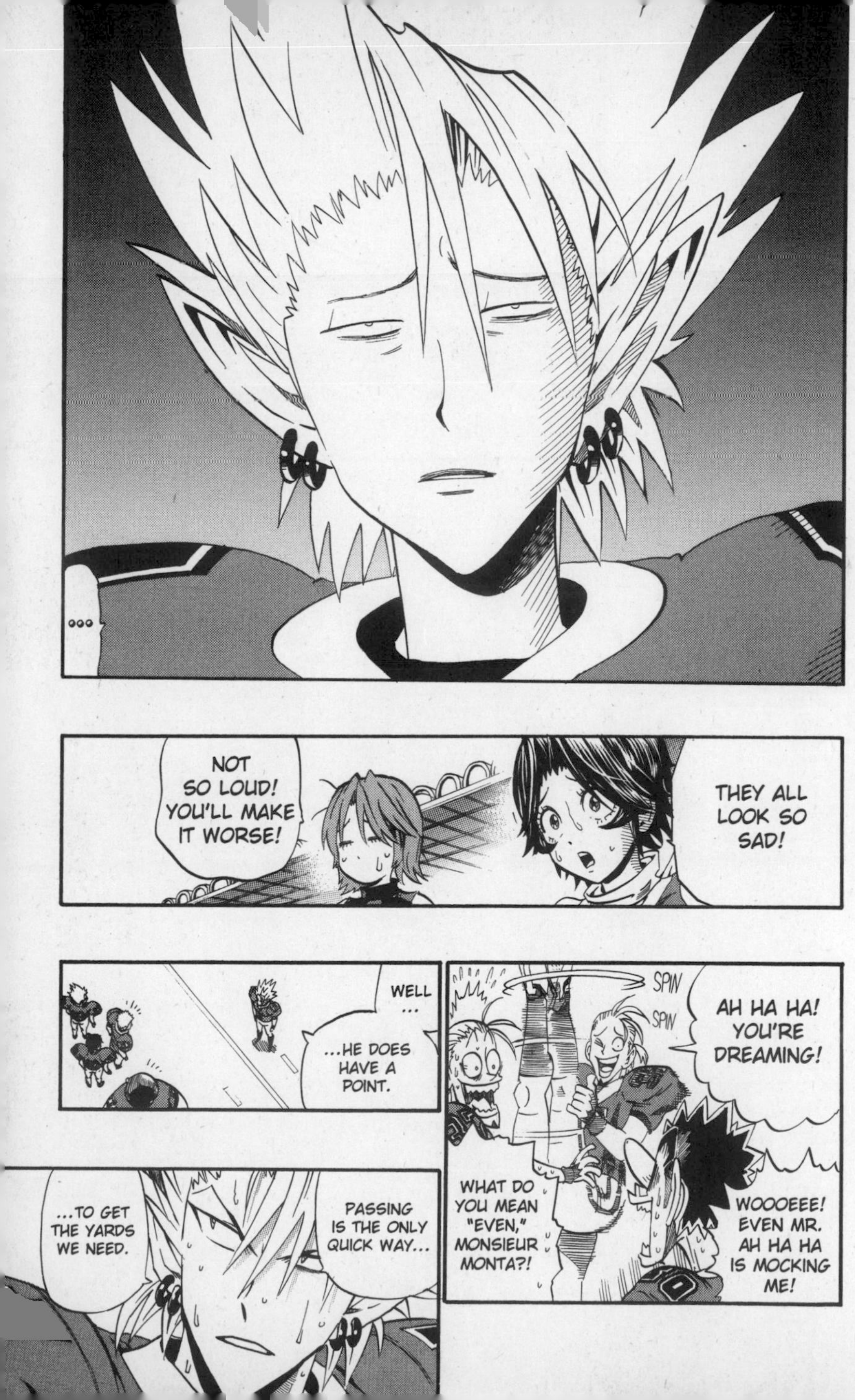
...
THEY ALL LOOK SO SAD!
NOT SO LOUD! YOU'LL MAKE IT WORSE!
SPIN
SPIN
AH HA HA! YOU'RE DREAMING!
WOOOEEE! EVEN MR. AH HA HA IS MOCKING ME!
WHAT DO YOU MEAN "EVEN," MONSIEUR MONTA?!
WELL...
...HE DOES HAVE A POINT.
PASSING IS THE ONLY QUICK WAY...
...TO GET THE YARDS WE NEED.

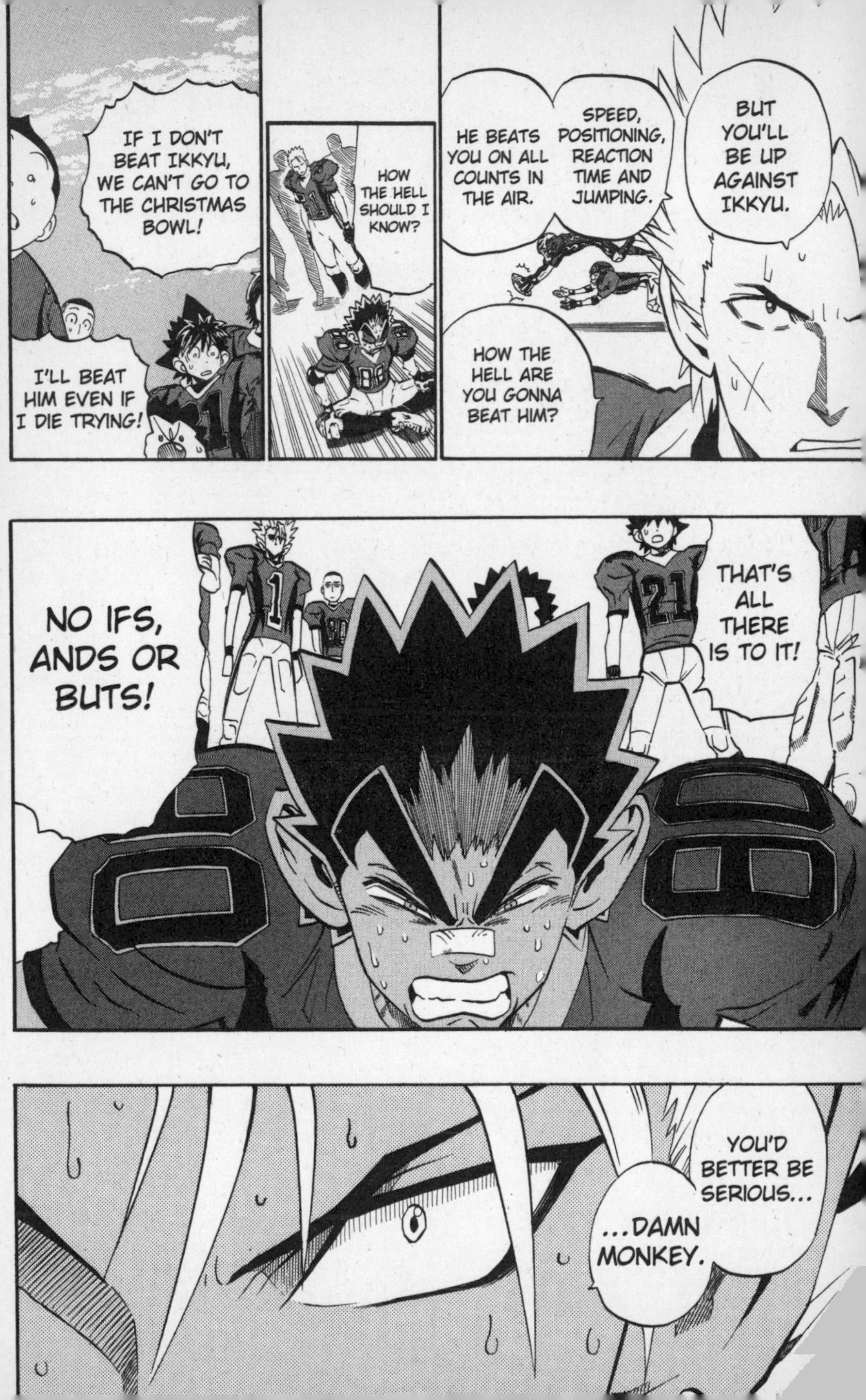
BUT YOU'LL BE UP AGAINST IKKYU.
SPEED, POSITIONING, REACTION TIME AND JUMPING.
HE BEATS YOU ON ALL COUNTS IN THE AIR.
HOW THE HELL ARE YOU GONNA BEAT HIM?
HOW THE HELL SHOULD I KNOW?
IF I DON'T BEAT IKKYU, WE CAN'T GO TO THE CHRISTMAS BOWL!
I'LL BEAT HIM EVEN IF I DIE TRYING!
THAT'S ALL THERE IS TO IT!
NO IFS, ANDS OR BUTS!
YOU'D BETTER BE SERIOUS...
...DAMN MONKEY.

Chapter 187 Ave Maria

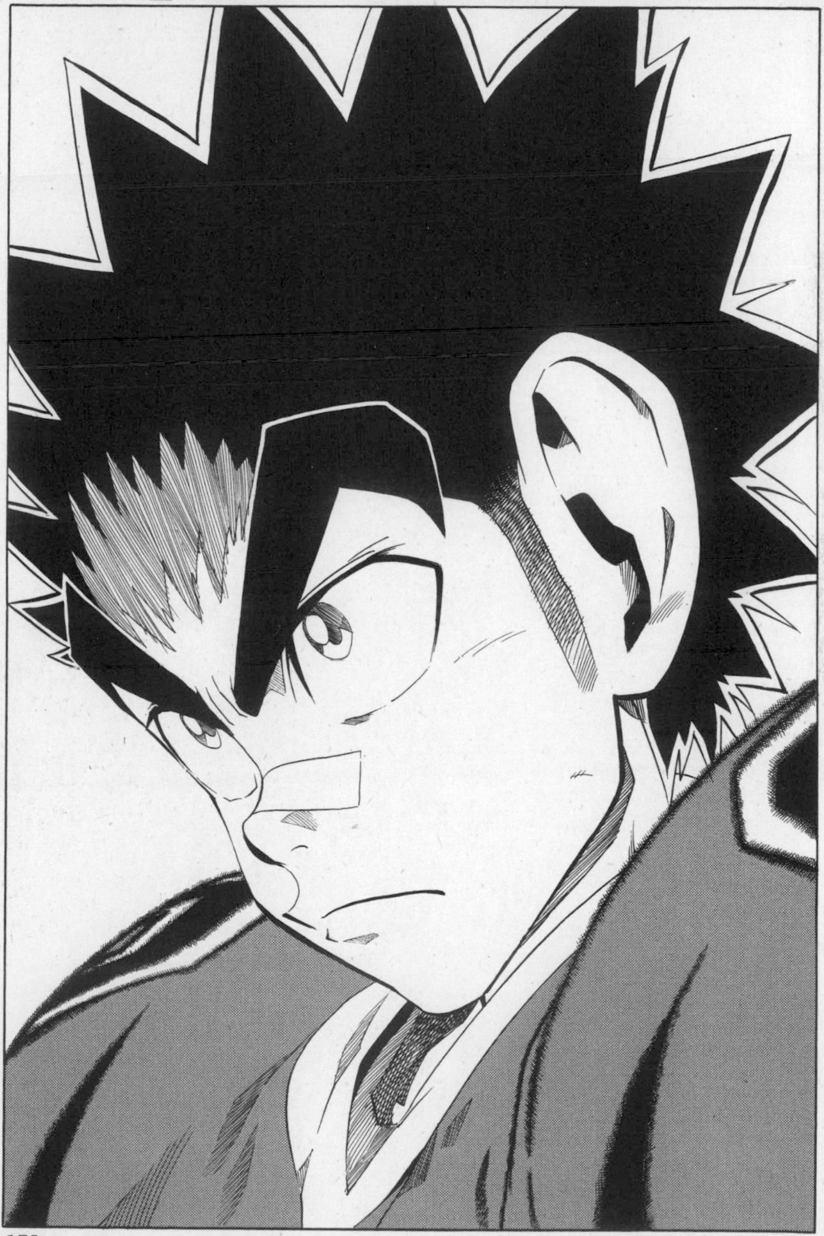

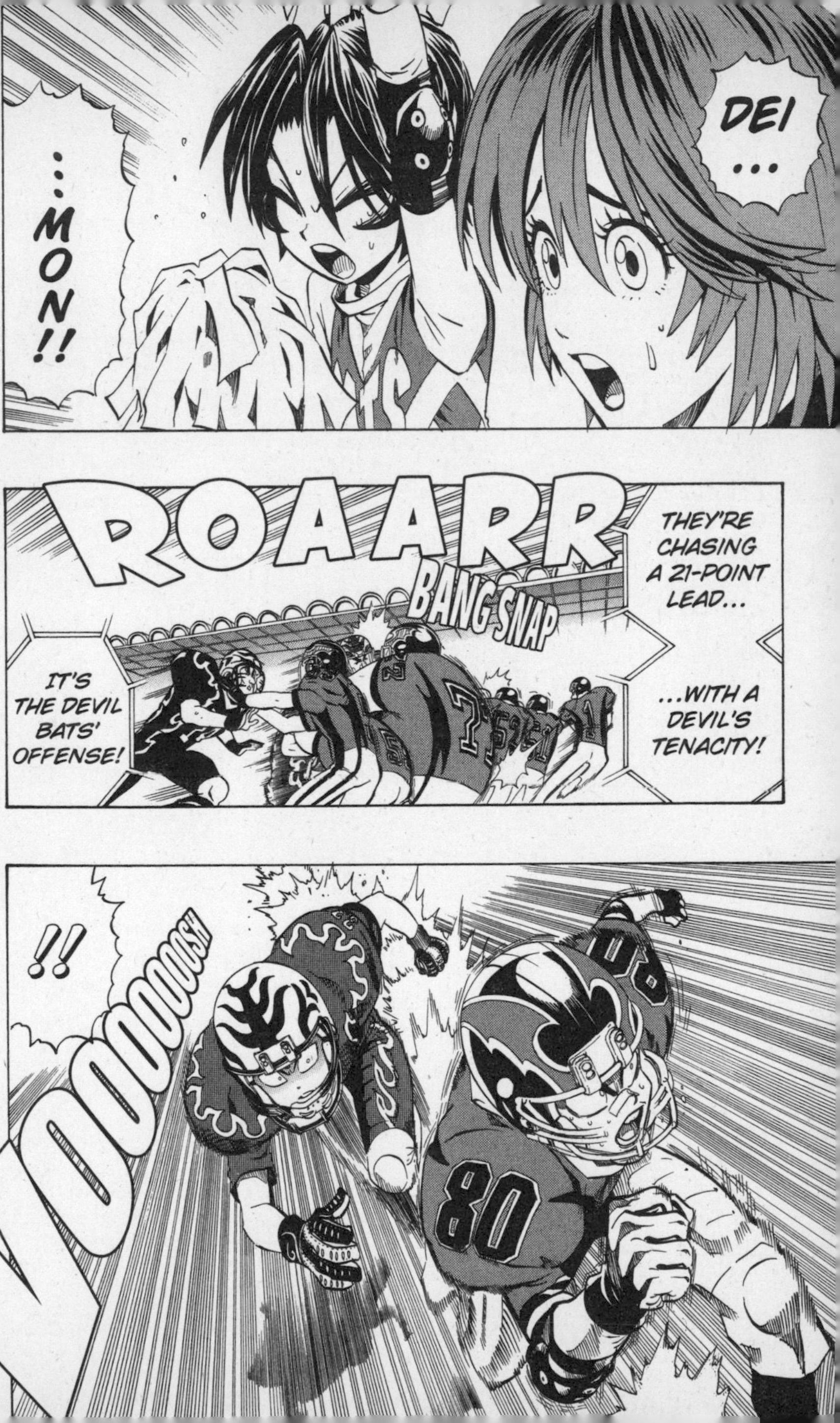
DEI...
...MON!!
ROAARR
THEY'RE CHASING A 21-POINT LEAD...
BANG SNAP
...WITH A DEVIL'S TENACITY!
IT'S THE DEVIL BATS' OFFENSE!
!!
VOOOOOOOSH

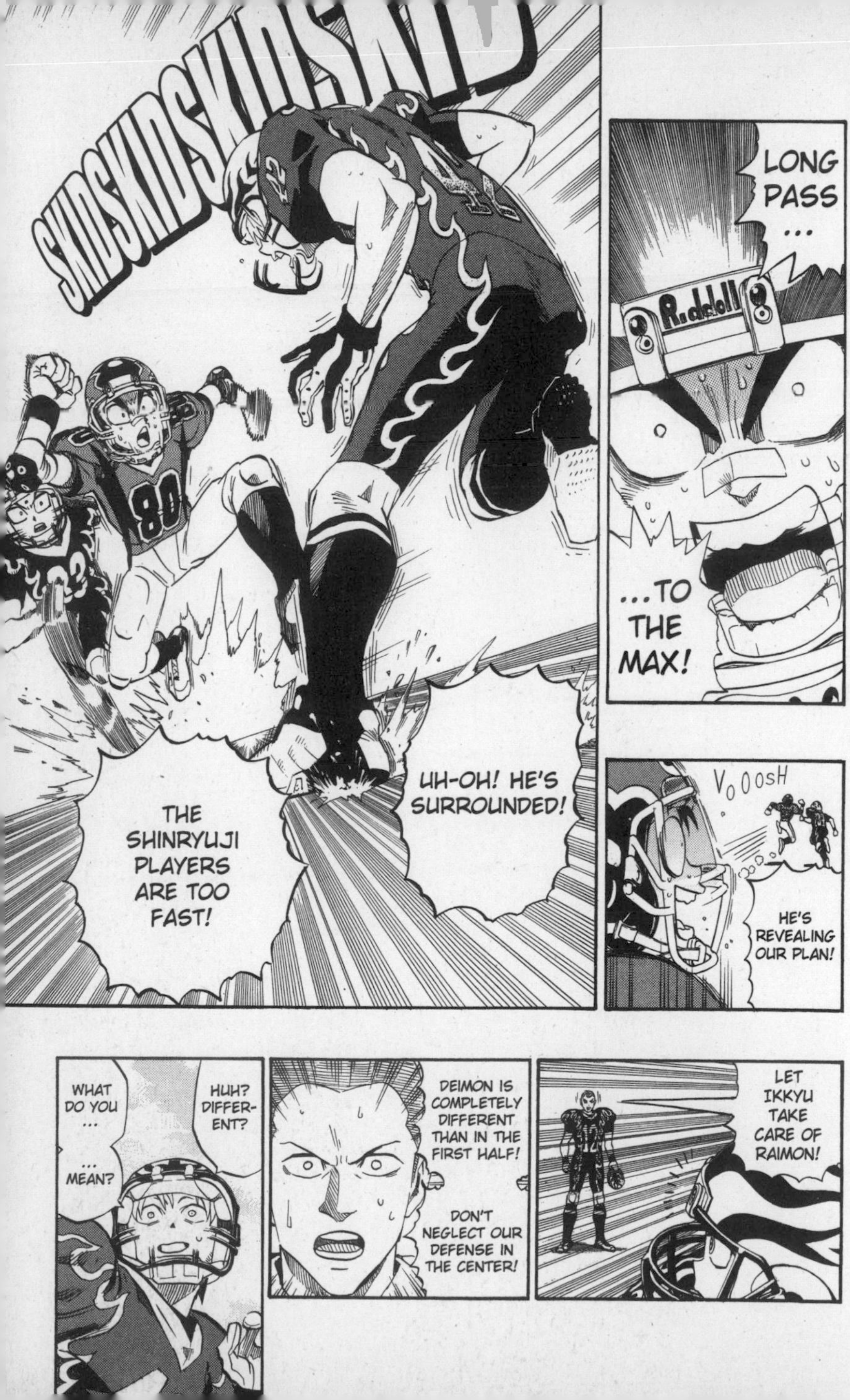
LONG PASS ...
...TO THE MAX!
VOOOSH
HE'S REVEALING OUR PLAN!
SKIDSKIDSKIDSKID
UH-OH! HE'S SURROUNDED!
THE SHINRYUJI PLAYERS ARE TOO FAST!
LET IKKYU TAKE CARE OF RAIMON!
DEIMON IS COMPLETELY DIFFERENT THAN IN THE FIRST HALF!
DON'T NEGLECT OUR DEFENSE IN THE CENTER!
HUH? DIFFERENT?
WHAT DO YOU ...
... MEAN?

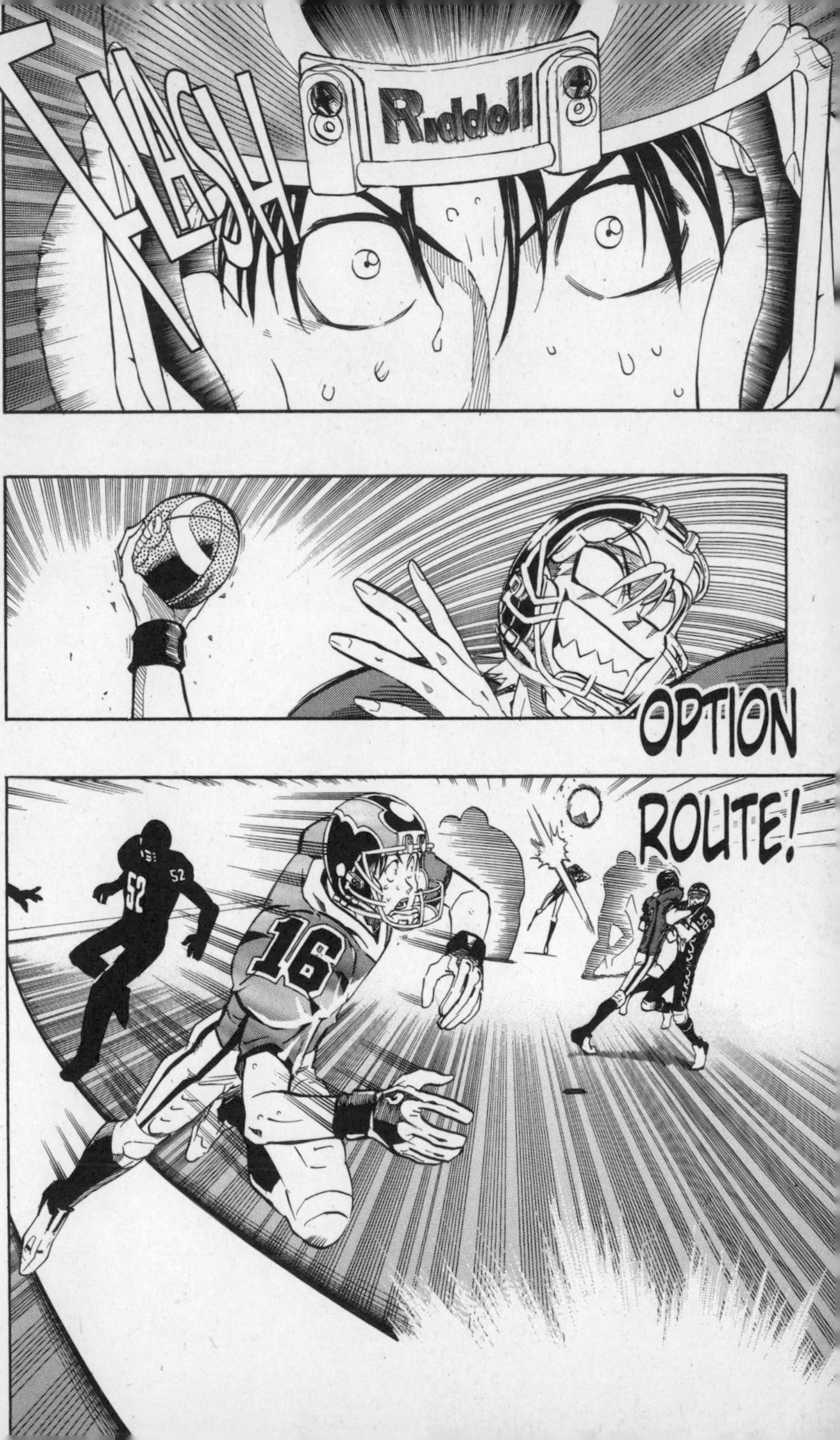
FLASH
OPTION ROUTE!

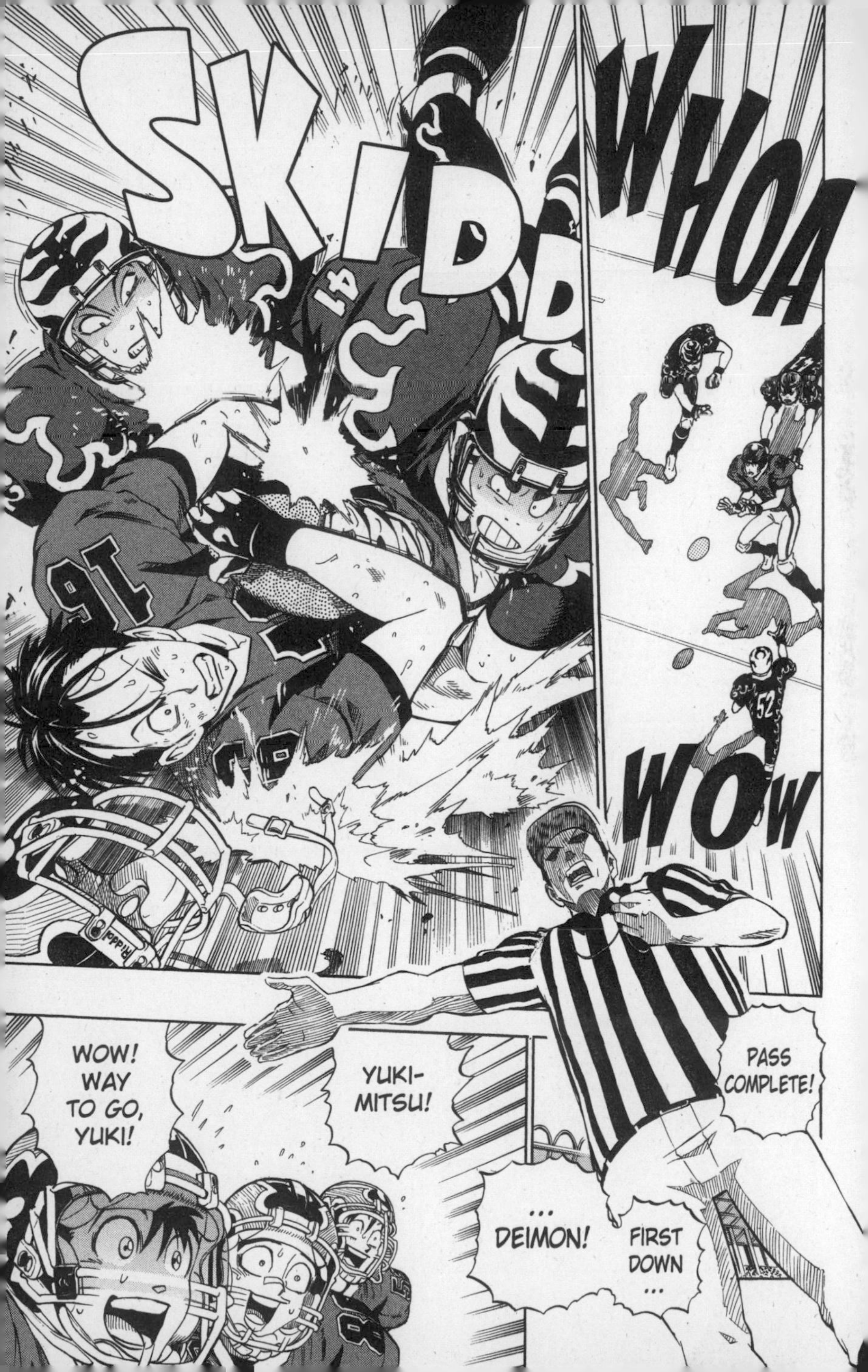
WHOA
WOW
SKIDD
PASS COMPLETE!
FIRST DOWN ...
... DEIMON!
YUKI-MITSU!
WOW! WAY TO GO, YUKI!

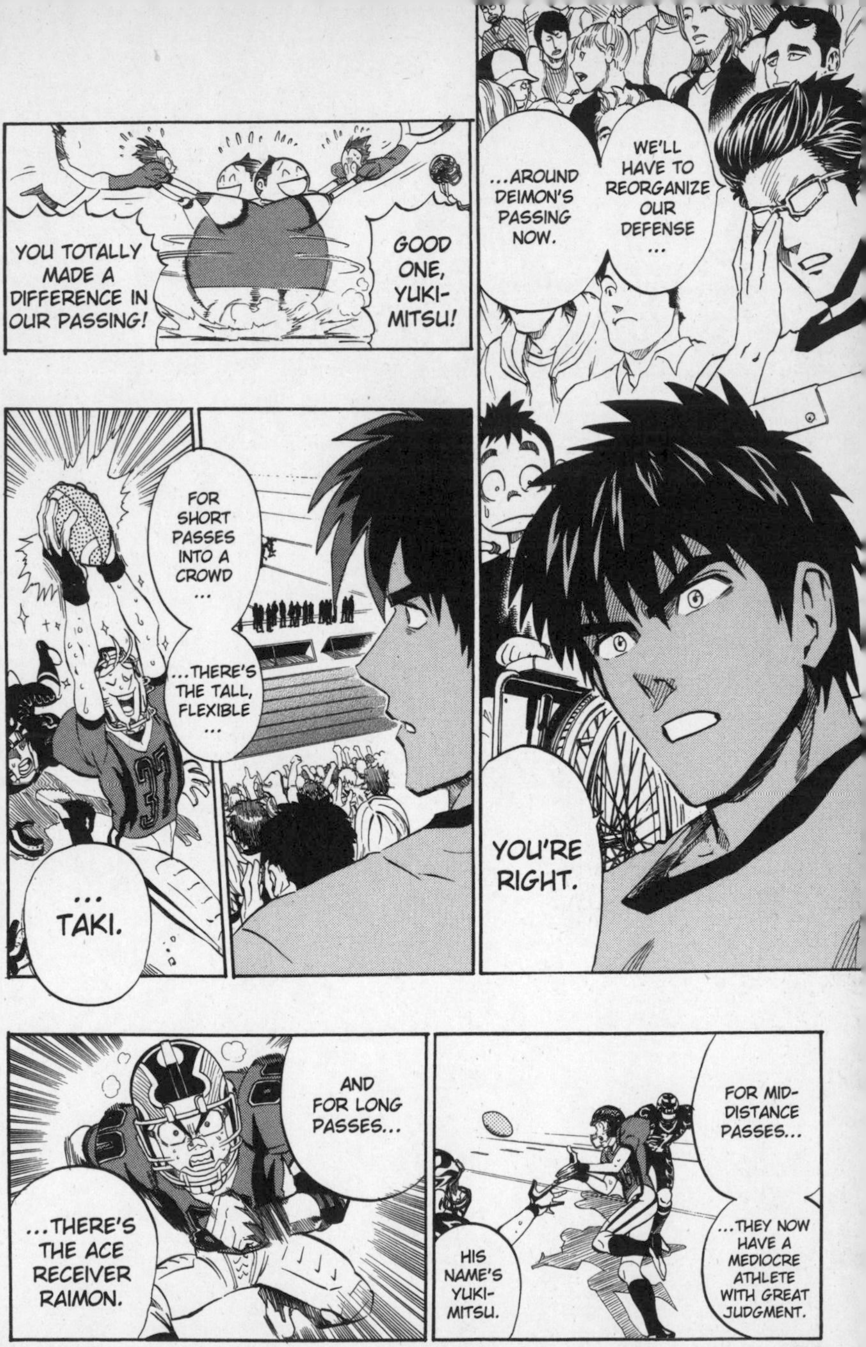
WE'LL HAVE TO REORGANIZE OUR DEFENSE ...
...AROUND DEIMON'S PASSING NOW.
GOOD ONE, YUKIMITSU!
YOU TOTALLY MADE A DIFFERENCE IN OUR PASSING!
YOU'RE RIGHT.
FOR SHORT PASSES INTO A CROWD ...
...THERE'S THE TALL, FLEXIBLE ...
... TAKI.
FOR MID-DISTANCE PASSES...
...THEY NOW HAVE A MEDIOCRE ATHLETE WITH GREAT JUDGMENT.
HIS NAME'S YUKIMITSU.
AND FOR LONG PASSES...
...THERE'S THE ACE RECEIVER RAIMON.

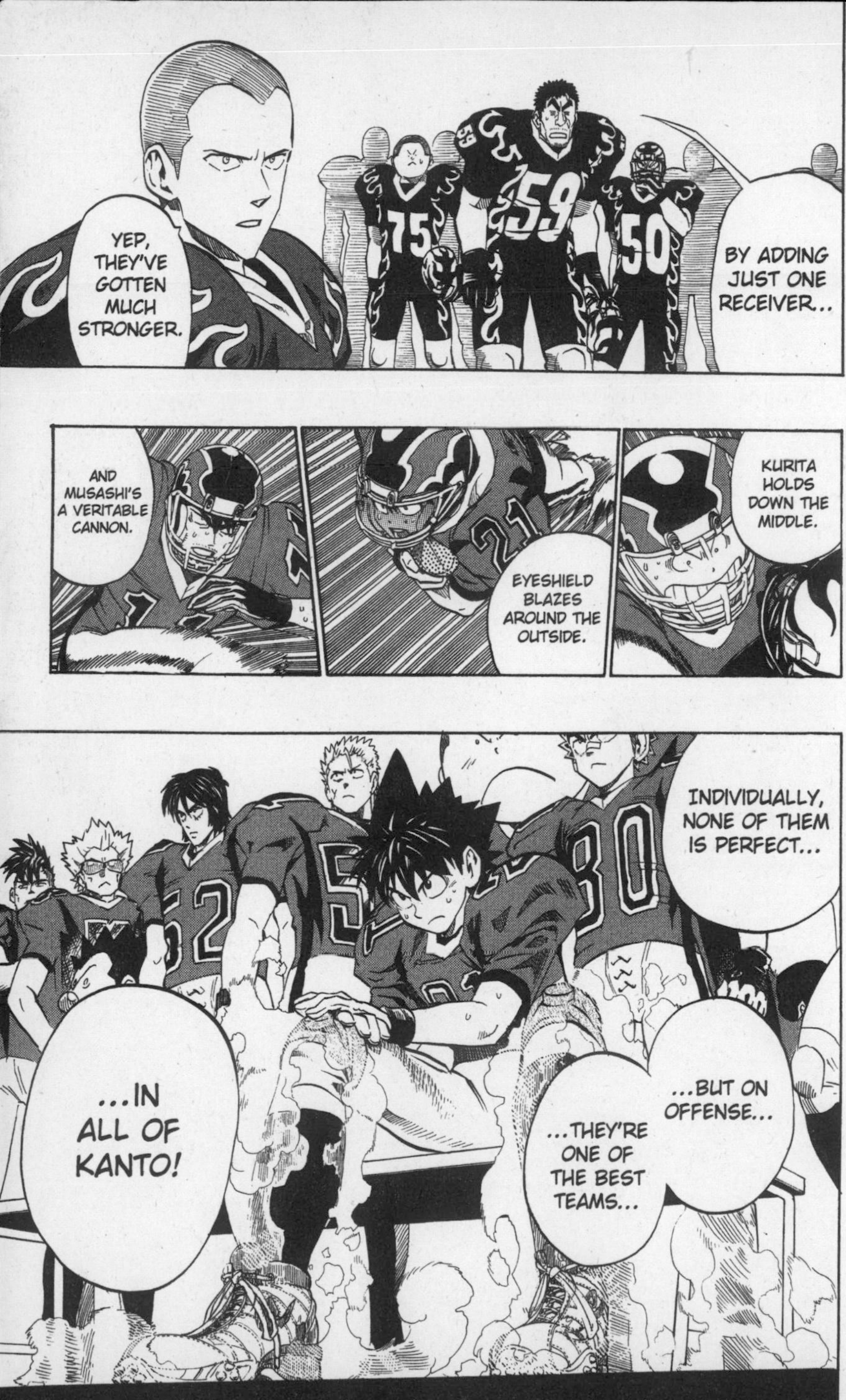
BY ADDING JUST ONE RECEIVER...
YEP, THEY'VE GOTTEN MUCH STRONGER.
KURITA HOLDS DOWN THE MIDDLE.
EYESHIELD BLAZES AROUND THE OUTSIDE.
AND MUSASHI'S A VERITABLE CANNON.
INDIVIDUALLY, NONE OF THEM IS PERFECT...
...BUT ON OFFENSE...
...THEY'RE ONE OF THE BEST TEAMS...
...IN ALL OF KANTO!

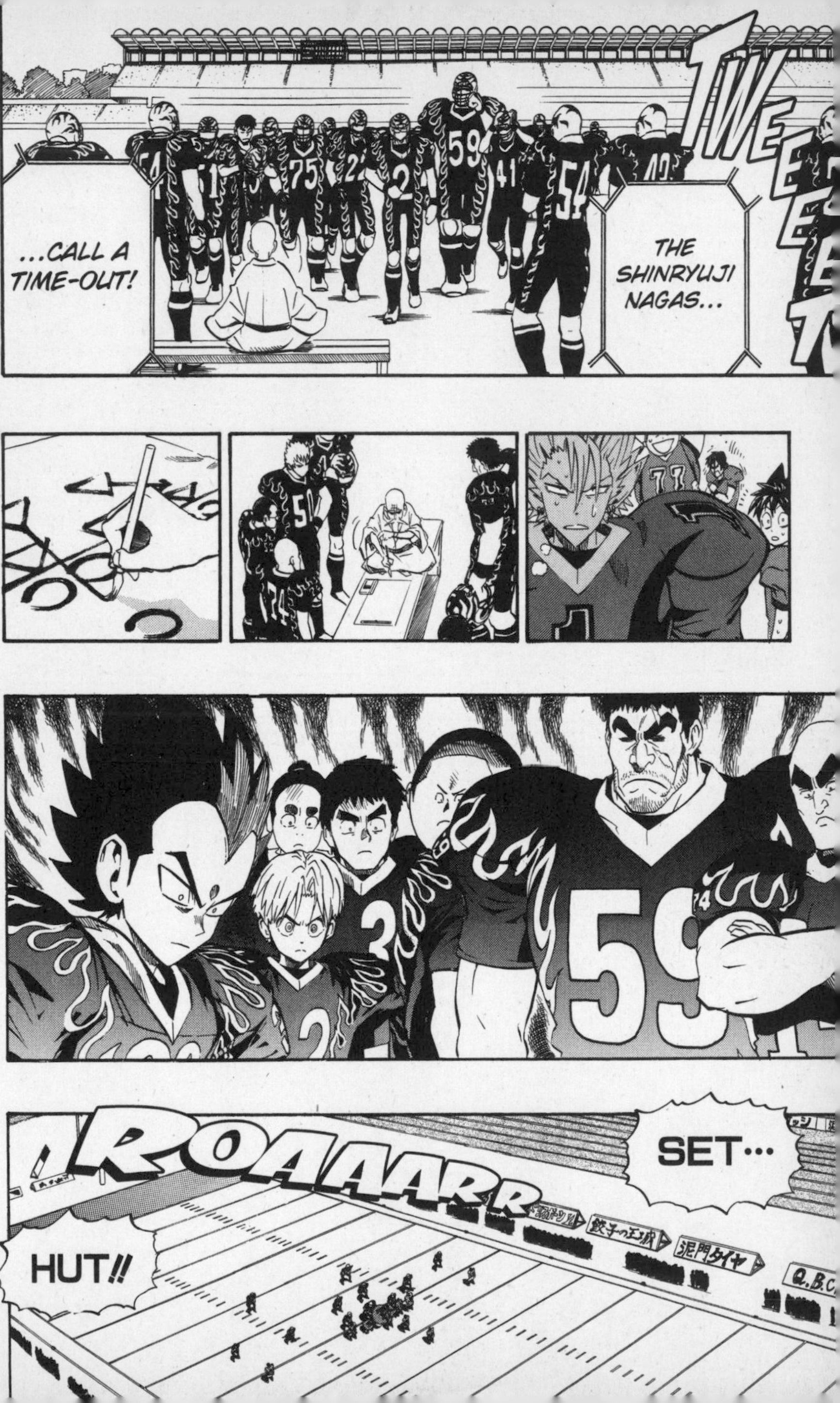
TWEEET
THE SHINRYUJI NAGAS...
...CALL A TIME-OUT!
ROAAAARR
SET...
HUT!!
餃子の王城
泥門タイヤ
Q.B.C.

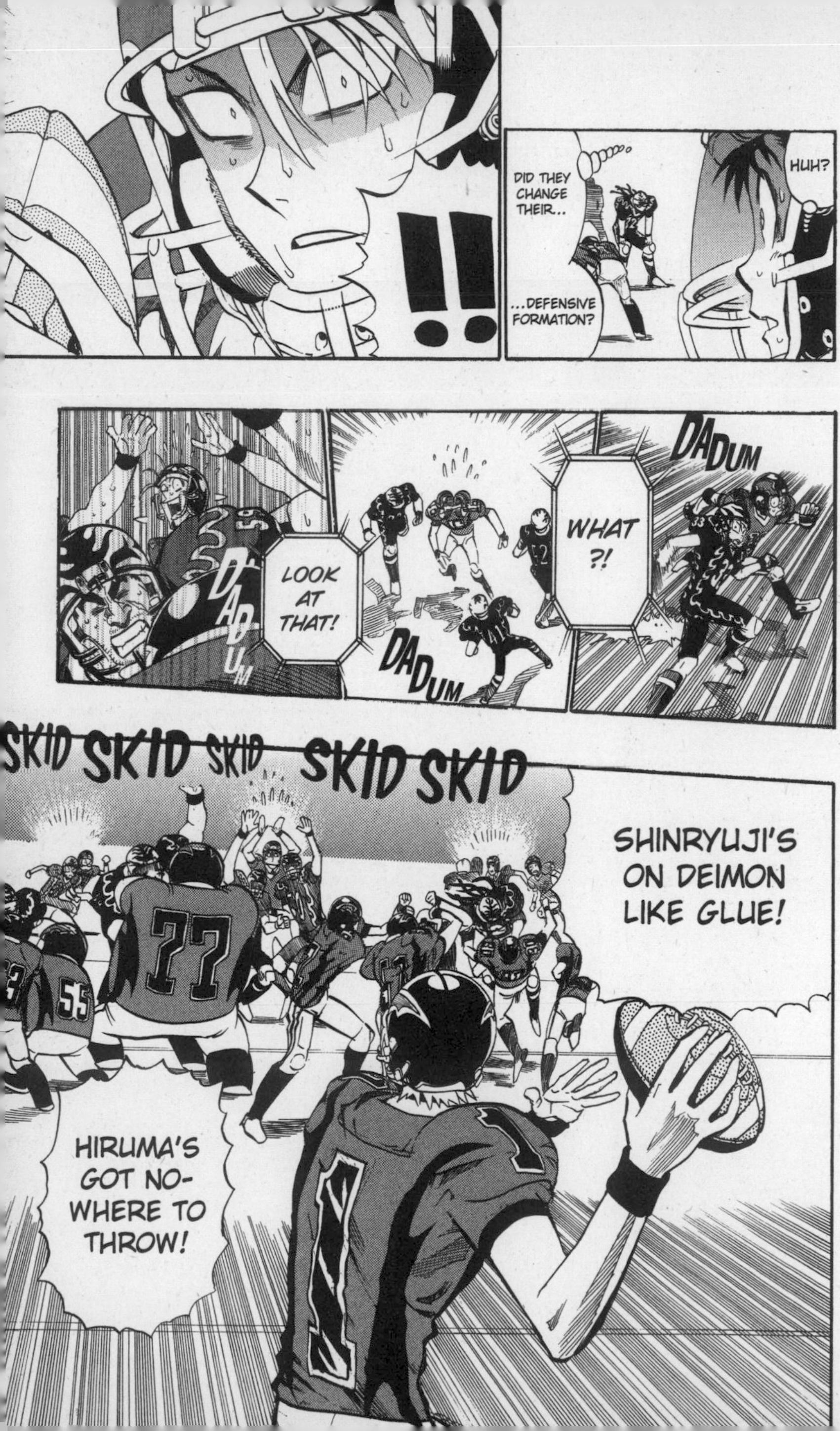
HUH?
DID THEY CHANGE THEIR...
...DEFENSIVE FORMATION?
!!
DADUM
WHAT?!
DADUM
LOOK AT THAT!
DADUM
SKID SKID SKID SKID SKID
SHINRYUJI'S ON DEIMON LIKE GLUE!
HIRUMA'S GOT NO-WHERE TO THROW!

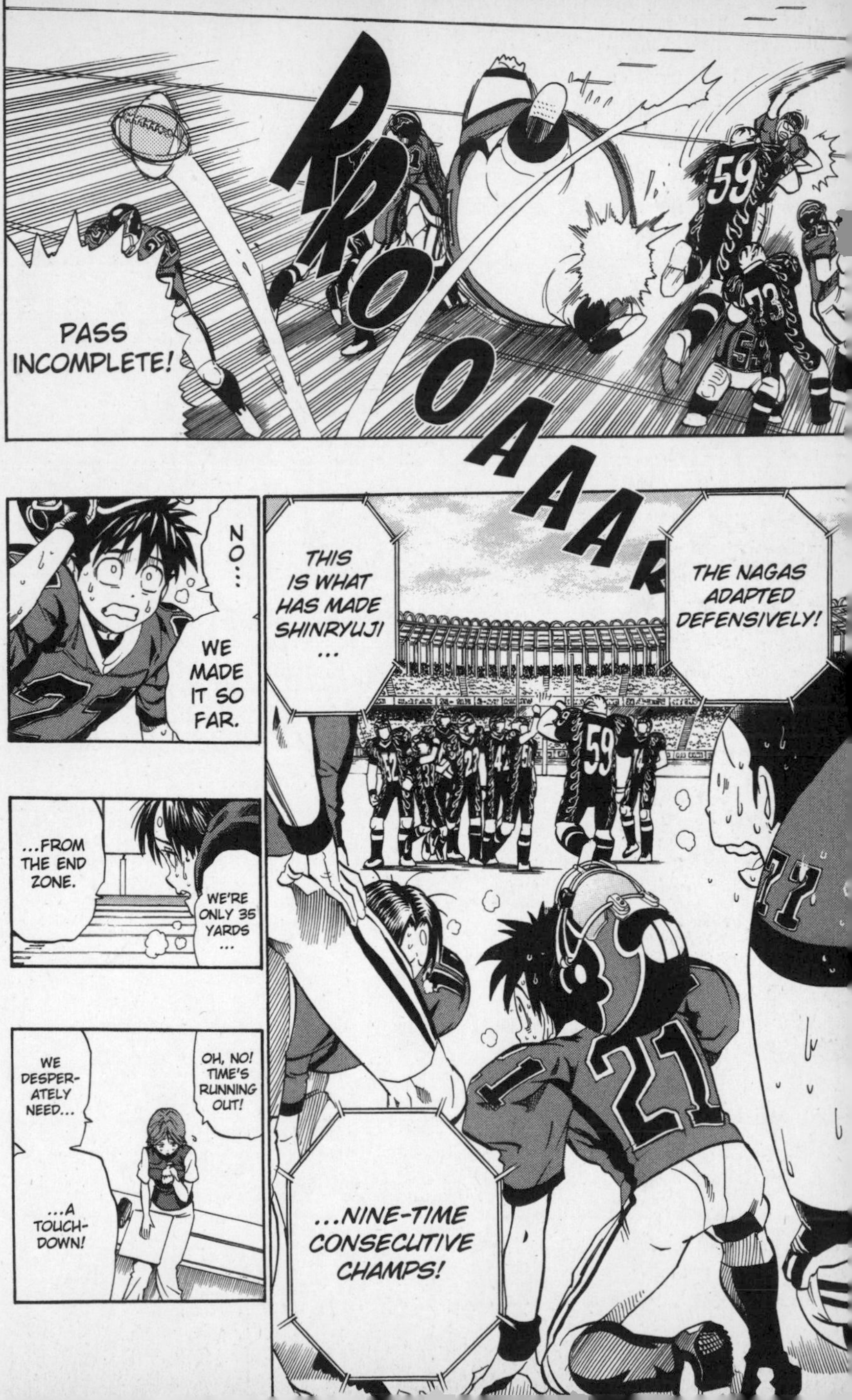
RROOAAAK
PASS INCOMPLETE!
THE NAGAS ADAPTED DEFENSIVELY!
THIS IS WHAT HAS MADE SHINRYUJI ...
...NINE-TIME CONSECUTIVE CHAMPS!
NO...
WE MADE IT SO FAR.
WE'RE ONLY 35 YARDS ...
...FROM THE END ZONE.
OH, NO! TIME'S RUNNING OUT!
WE DESPERATELY NEED...
...A TOUCHDOWN!

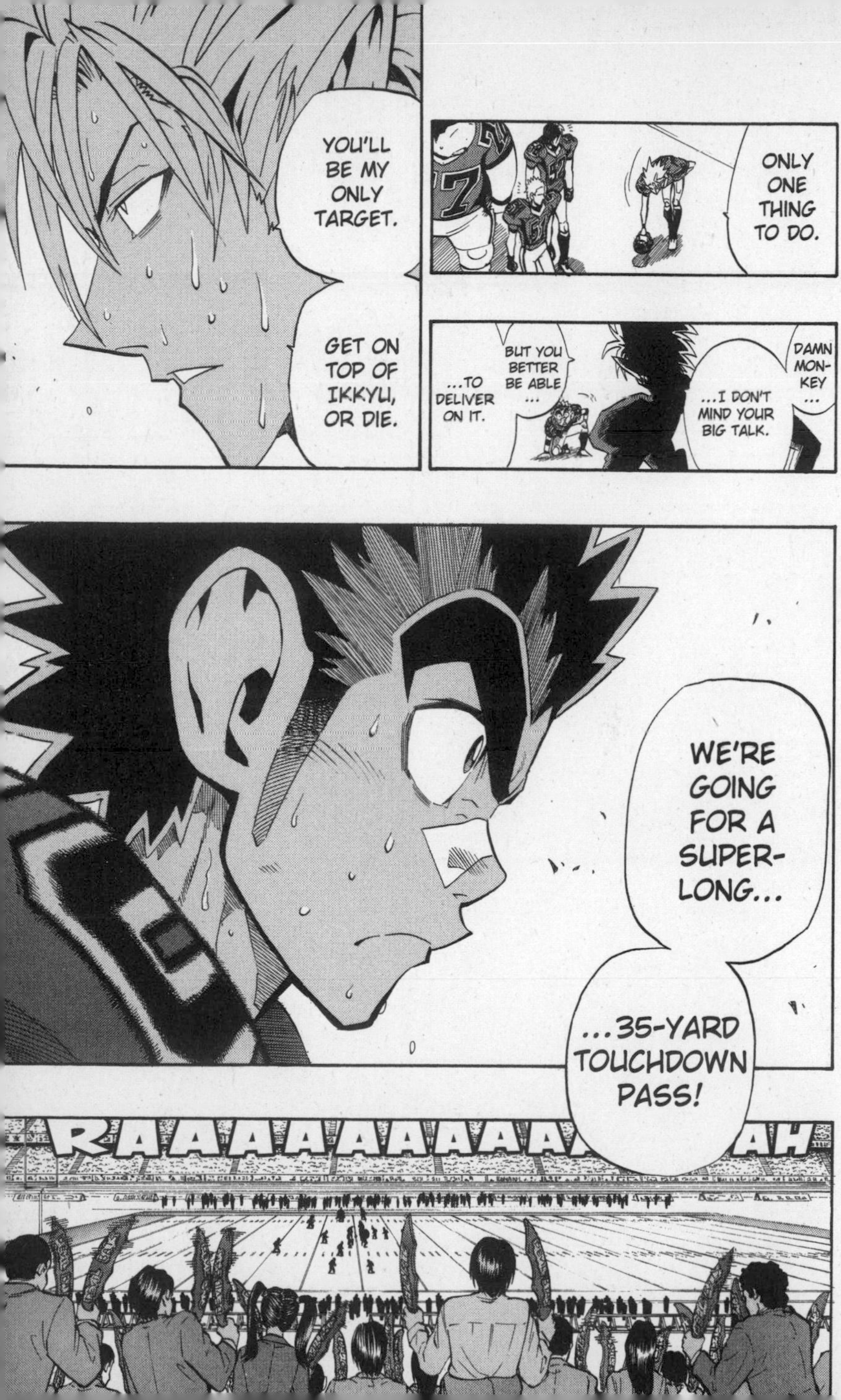
ONLY ONE THING TO DO.
DAMN MON-KEY ...
...I DON'T MIND YOUR BIG TALK.
BUT YOU BETTER BE ABLE ...
...TO DELIVER ON IT.
YOU'LL BE MY ONLY TARGET.
GET ON TOP OF IKKYU, OR DIE.
WE'RE GOING FOR A SUPER-LONG...
...35-YARD TOUCHDOWN PASS!
RAAAAAAAAAAAH

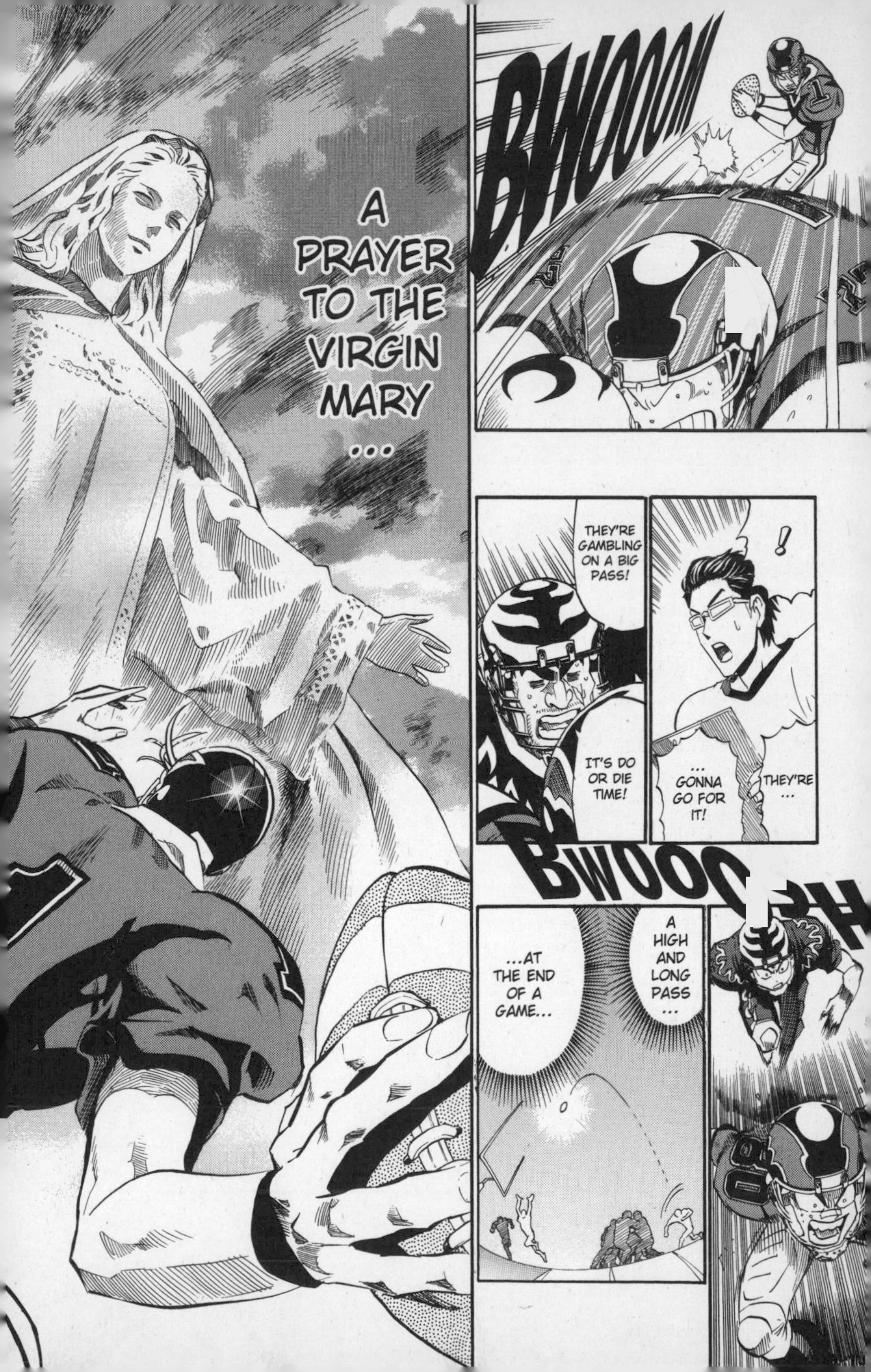
BWOOOM
!
THEY'RE ...
... GONNA GO FOR IT!
THEY'RE GAMBLING ON A BIG PASS!
IT'S DO OR DIE TIME!
BWOOO
A HIGH AND LONG PASS ...
...AT THE END OF A GAME...
A PRAYER TO THE VIRGIN MARY ...

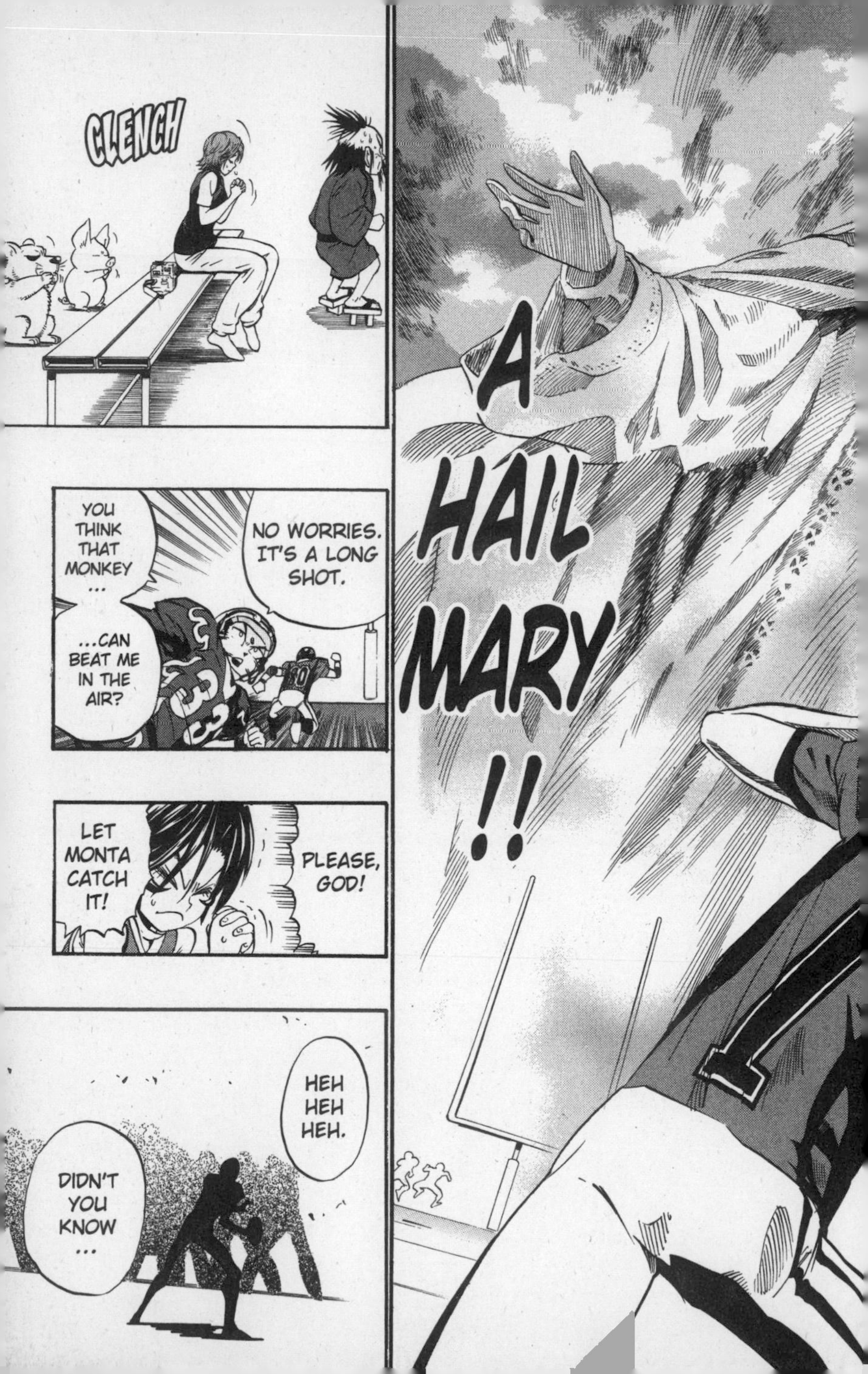
A HAIL MARY !!
CLENCH
NO WORRIES. IT'S A LONG SHOT.
YOU THINK THAT MONKEY ...
...CAN BEAT ME IN THE AIR?
PLEASE, GOD!
LET MONTA CATCH IT!
HEH HEH HEH.
DIDN'T YOU KNOW ...

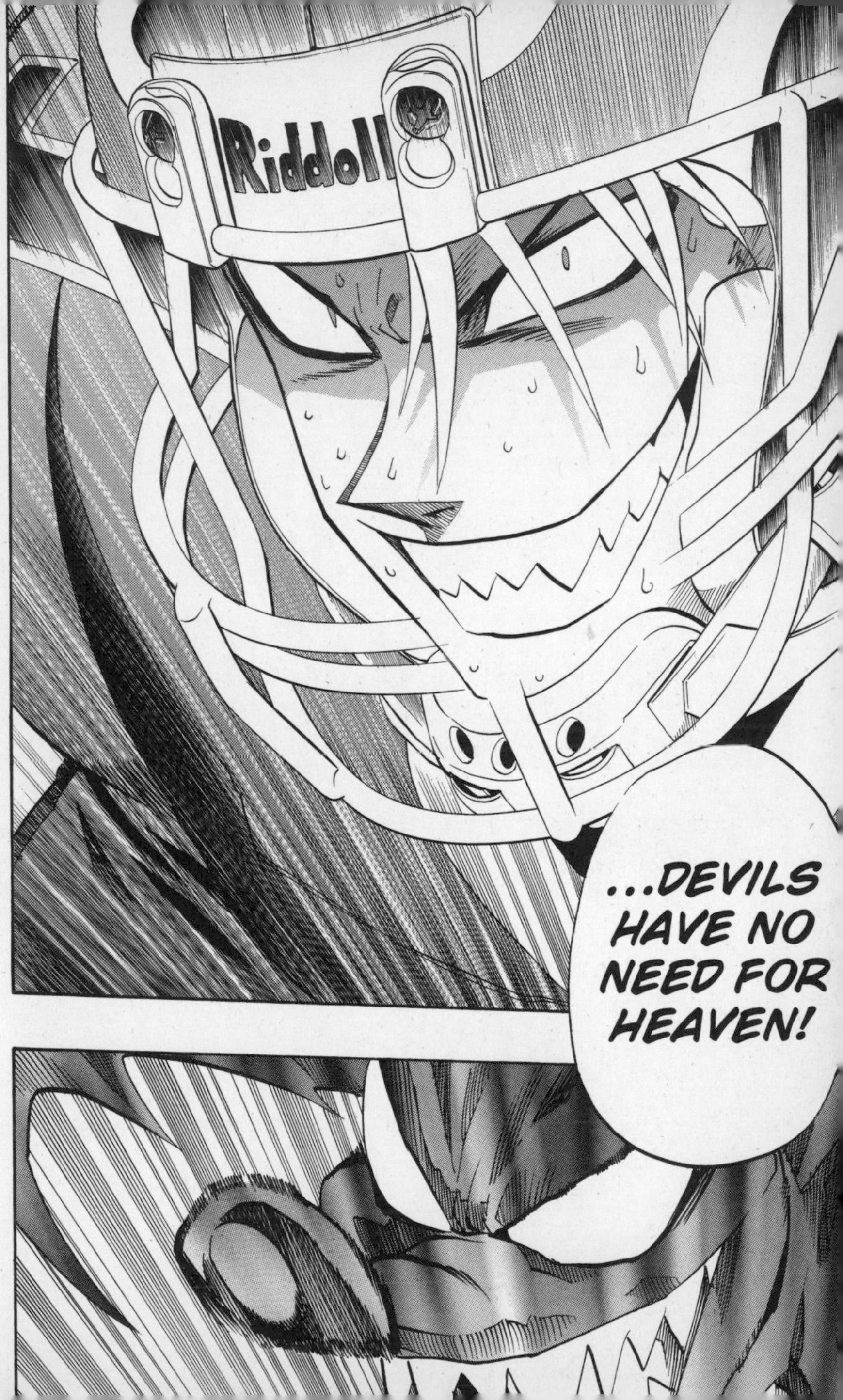
Riddoll
...DEVILS HAVE NO NEED FOR HEAVEN!

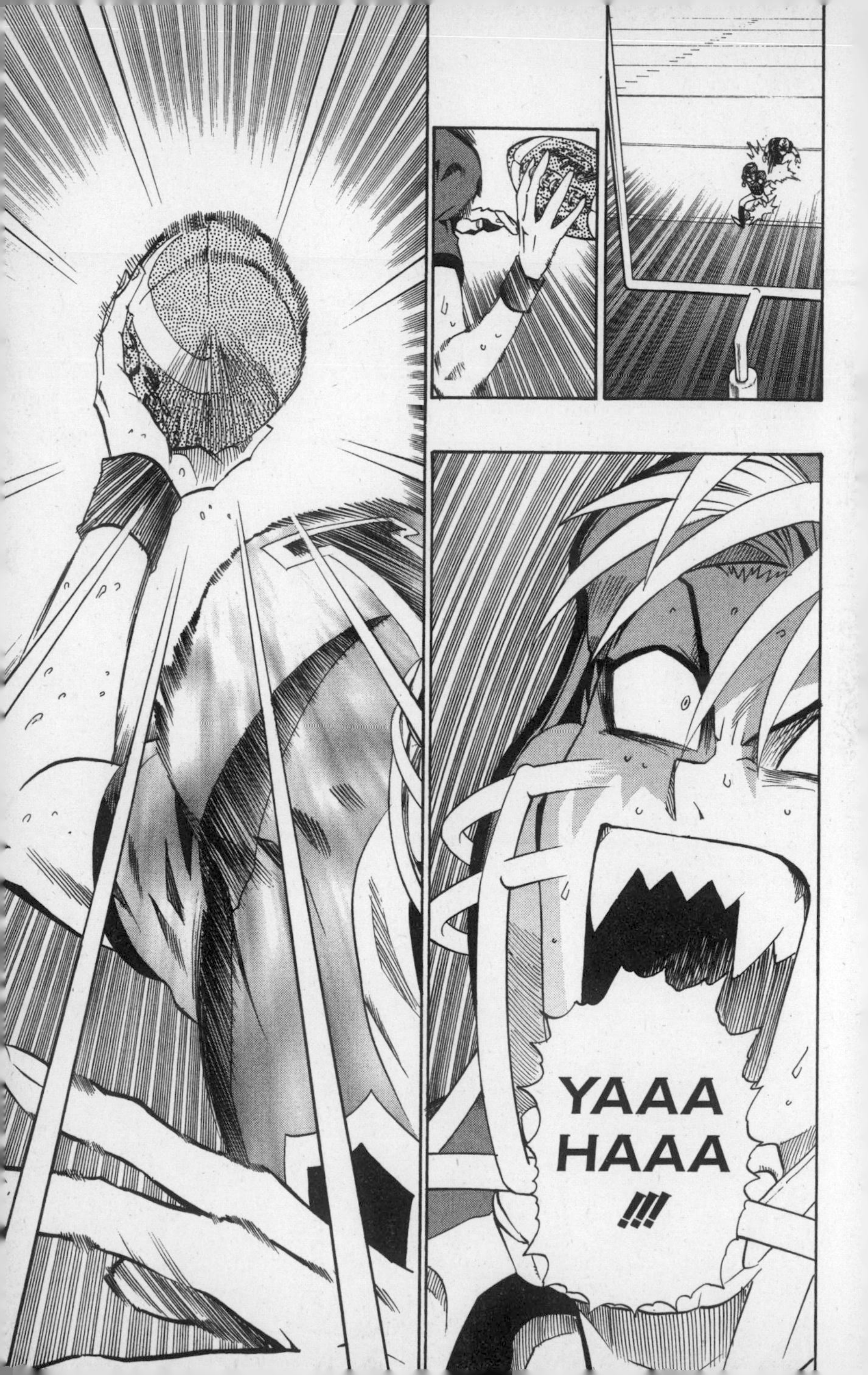
YAAA HAAA !!!

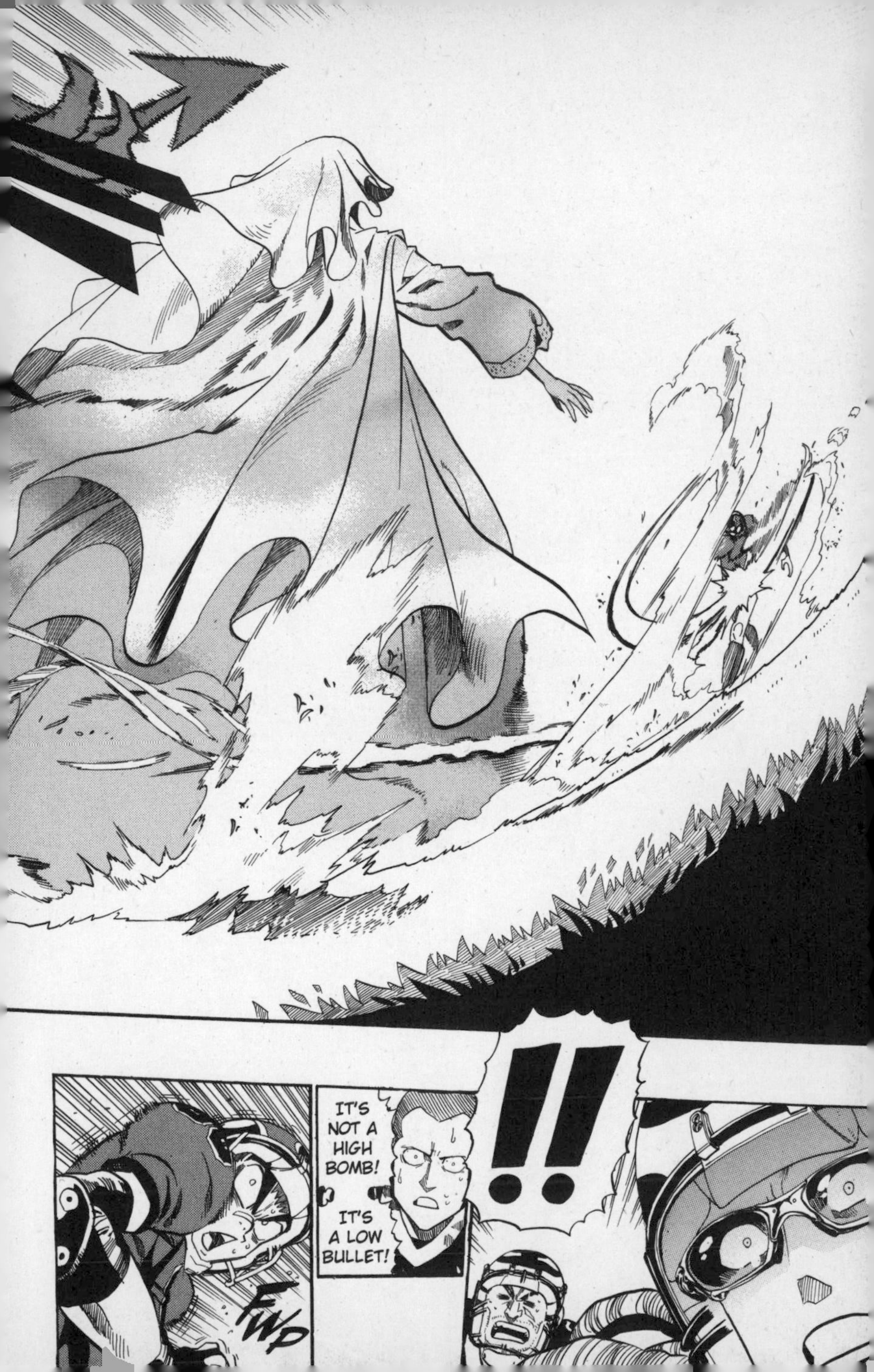
!!
IT'S NOT A HIGH BOMB!
IT'S A LOW BULLET!
FWP

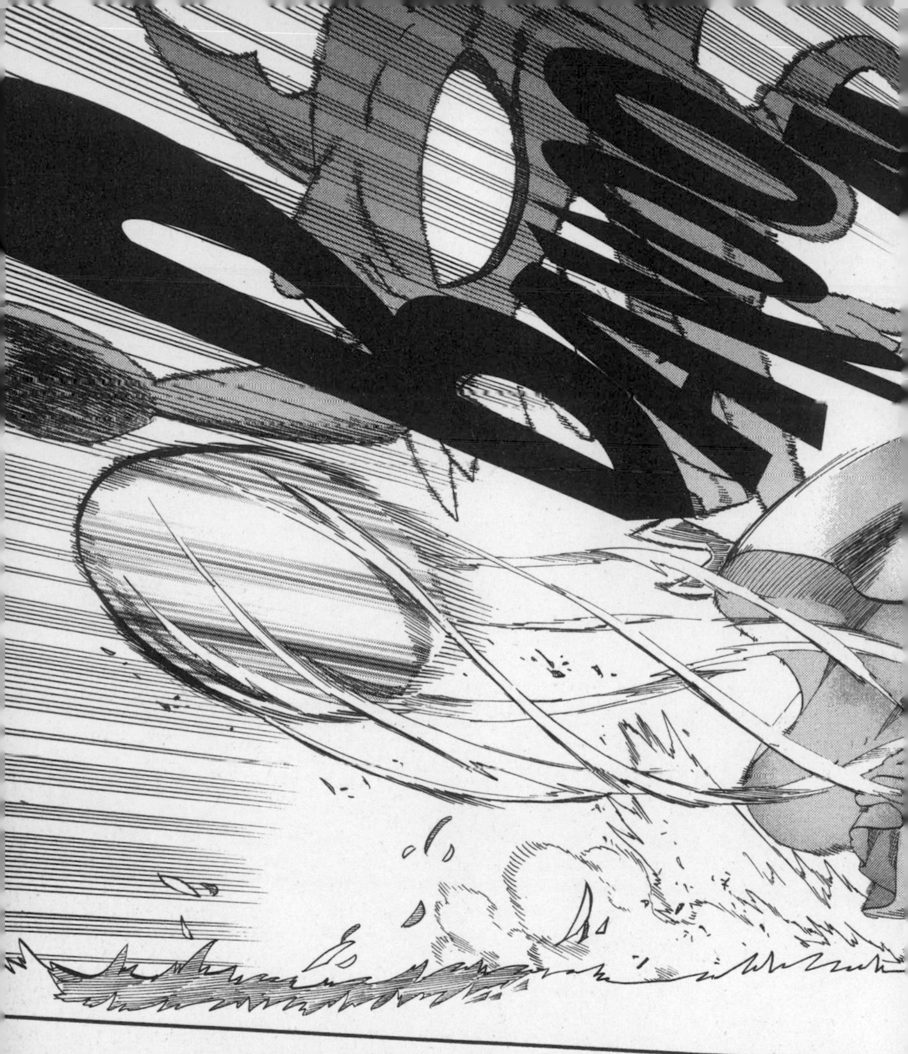

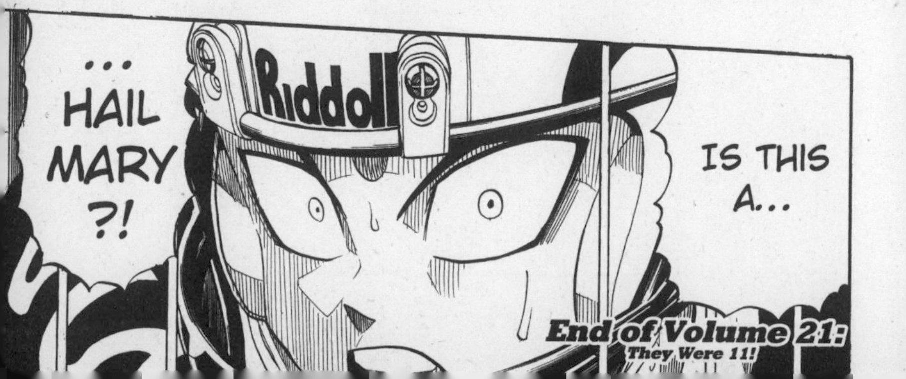
IS THIS A...
... HAIL MARY ?!

End of Volume 21:
They Were 11!

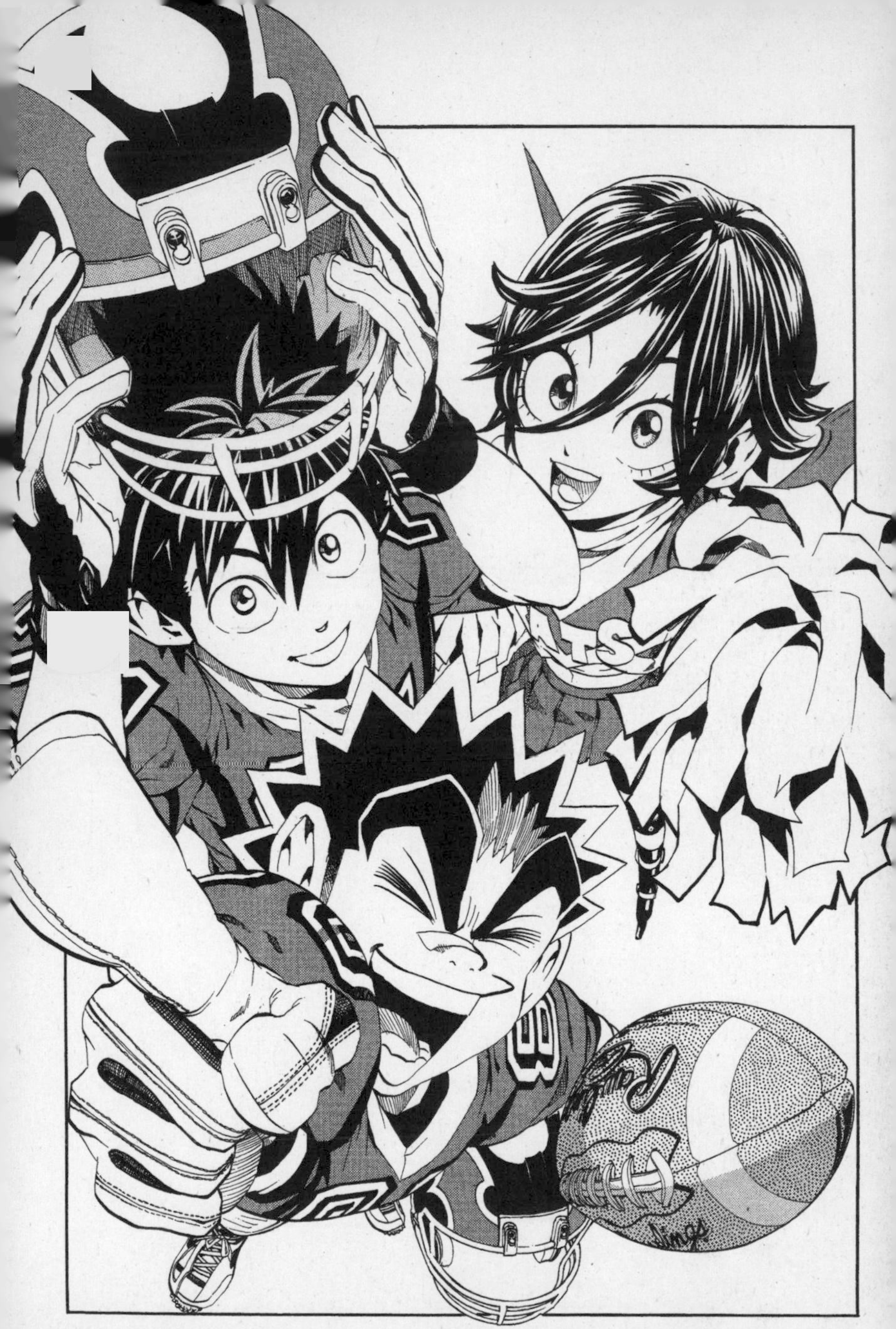

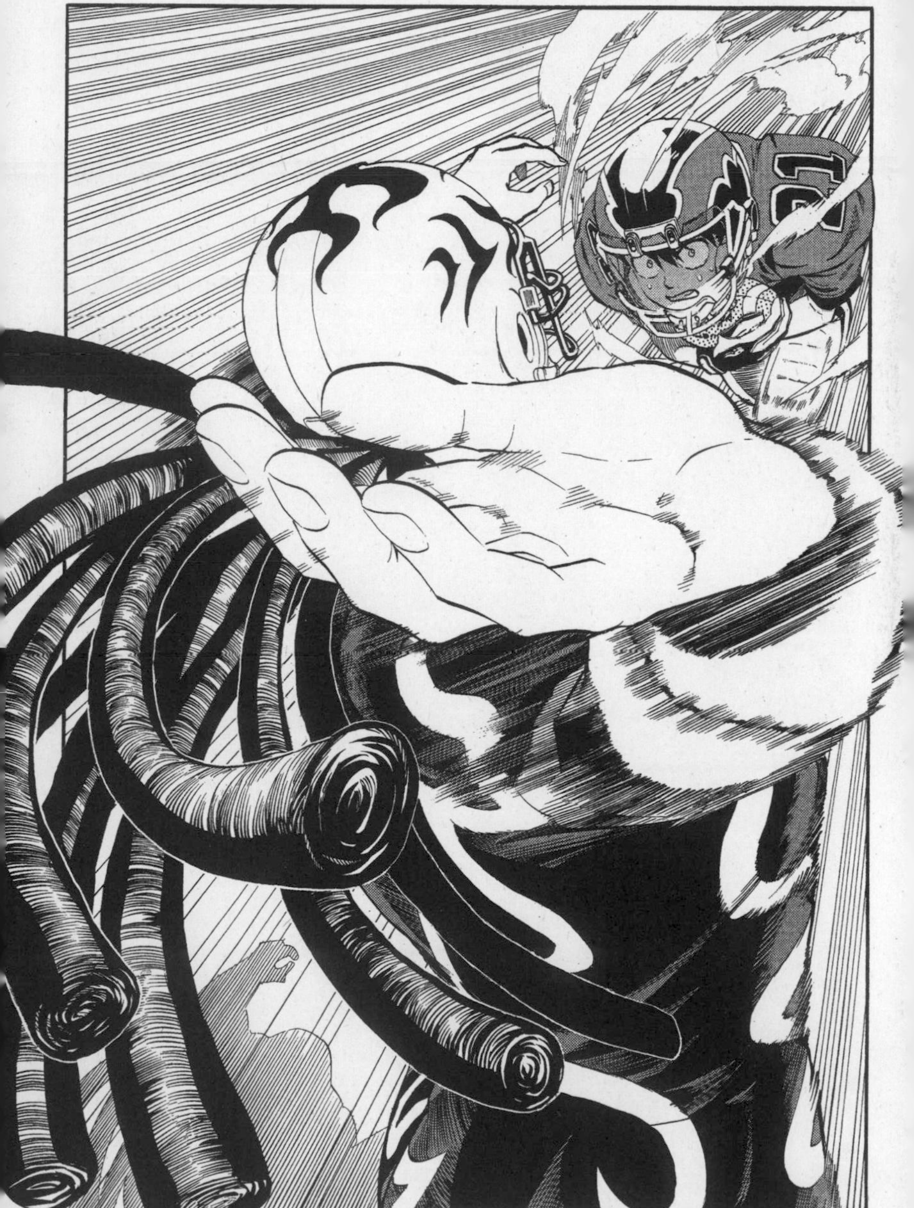

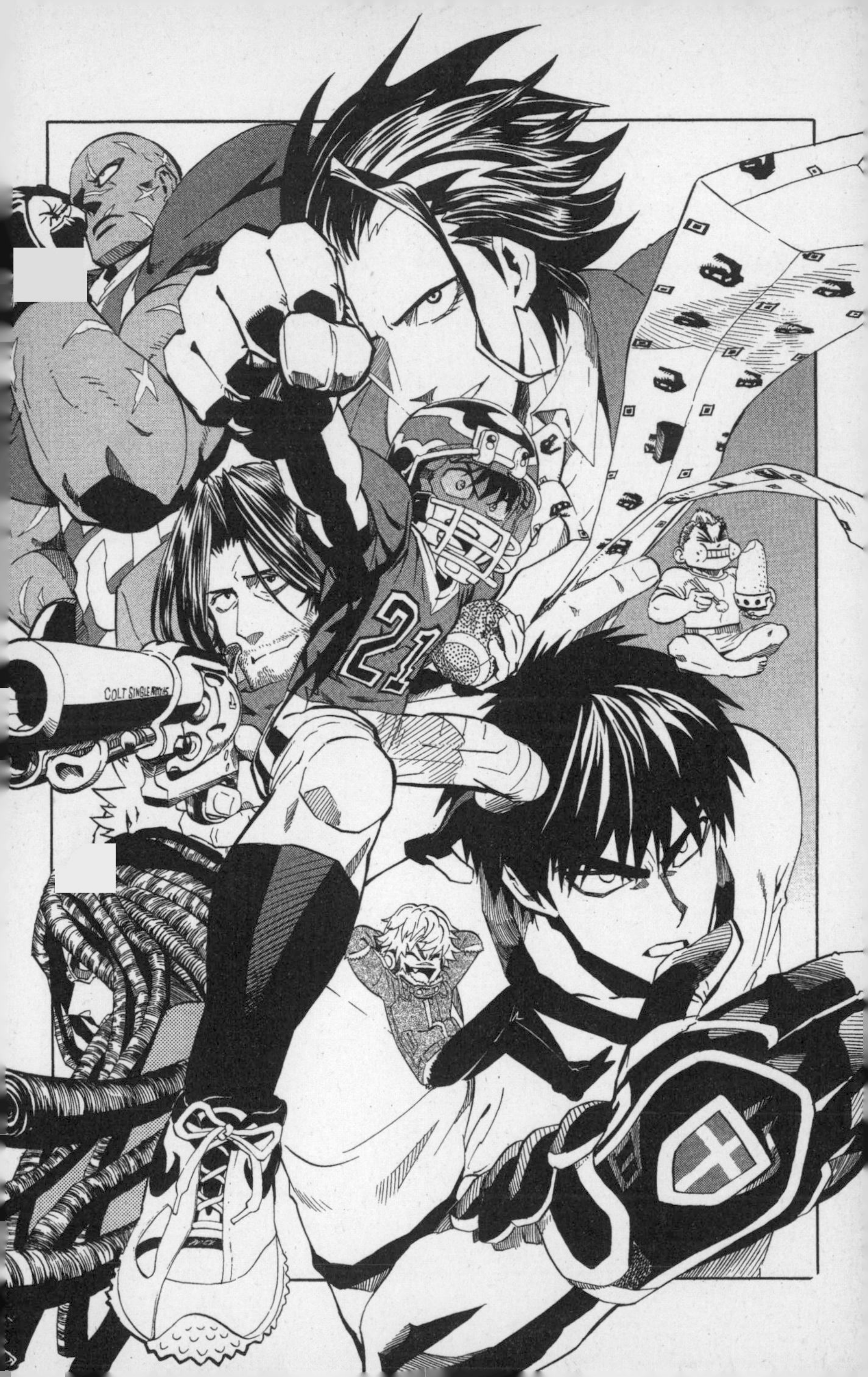
COLT SINGLE

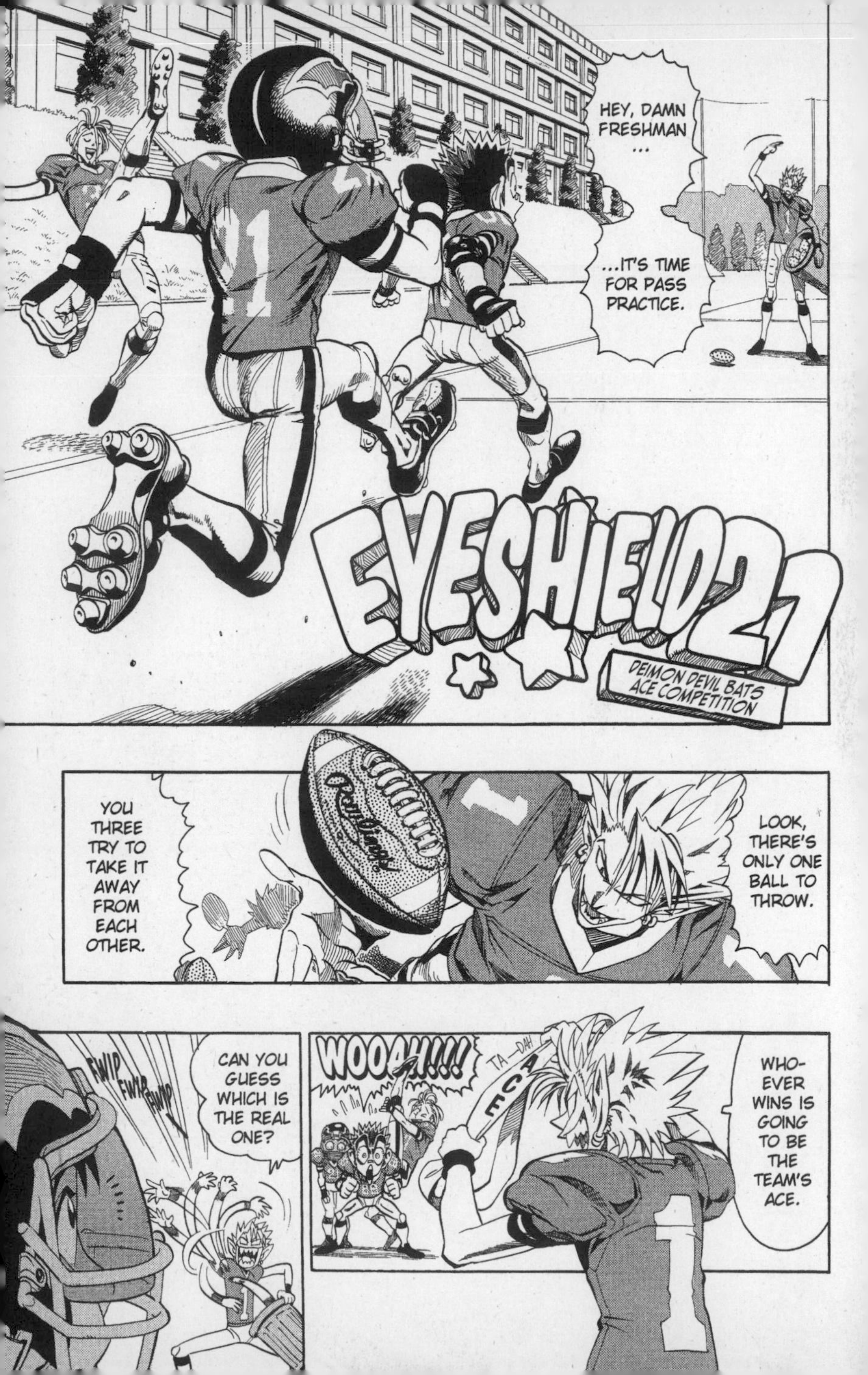
HEY, DAMN FRESHMAN ...
...IT'S TIME FOR PASS PRACTICE.
EYESHIELD 21
DEIMON DEVIL BATS ACE COMPETITION
LOOK, THERE'S ONLY ONE BALL TO THROW.
YOU THREE TRY TO TAKE IT AWAY FROM EACH OTHER.
WHO-EVER WINS IS GOING TO BE THE TEAM'S ACE.
TA-DAH
ACE
WOOAH!!!
CAN YOU GUESS WHICH IS THE REAL ONE?
FWIP FWIP FWIP

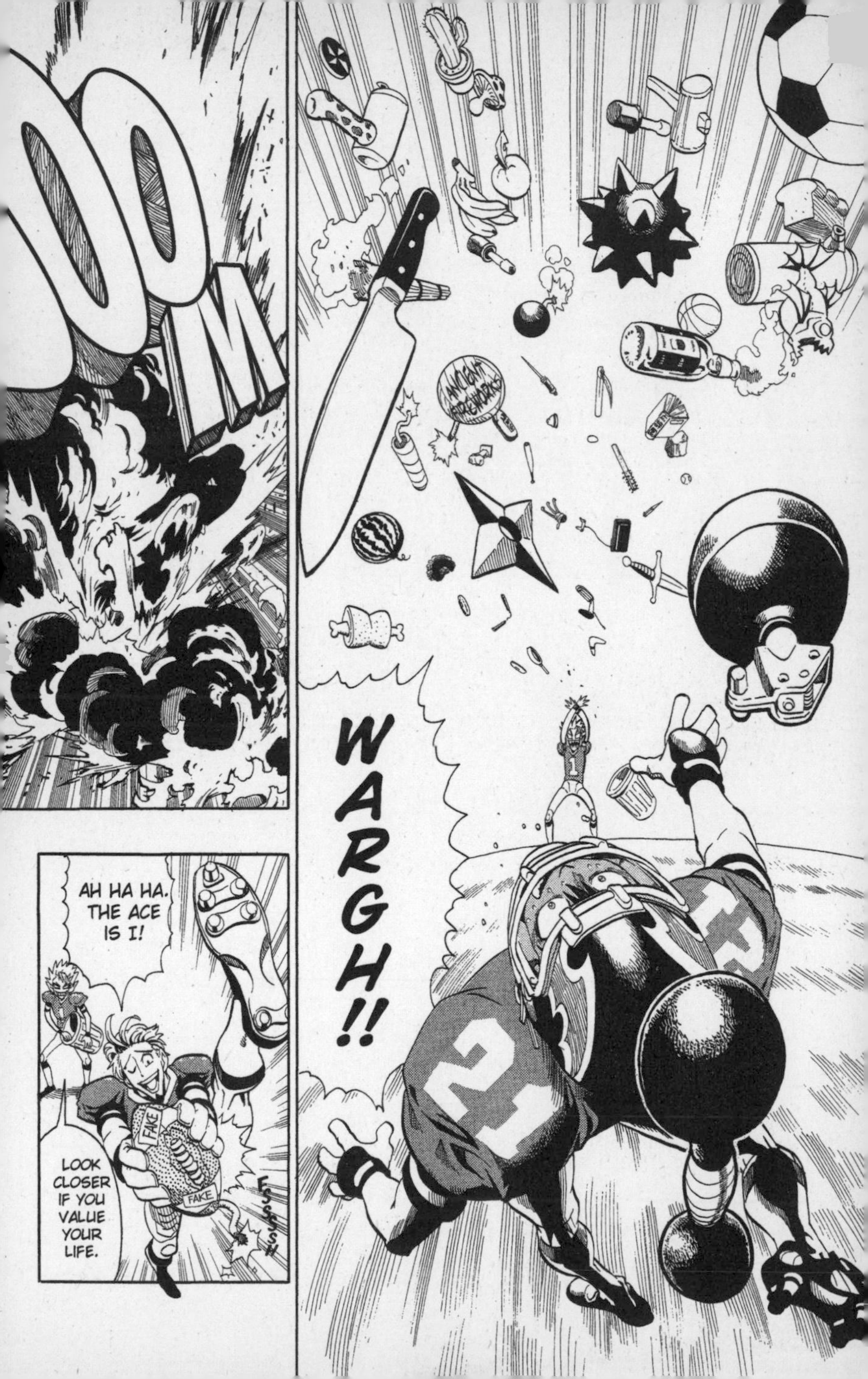
ANCIENT FIREWORKS
WARGH!!
OOM
AH HA HA. THE ACE IS I!
LOOK CLOSER IF YOU VALUE YOUR LIFE.
FAKE
FAKE
FSSSSH

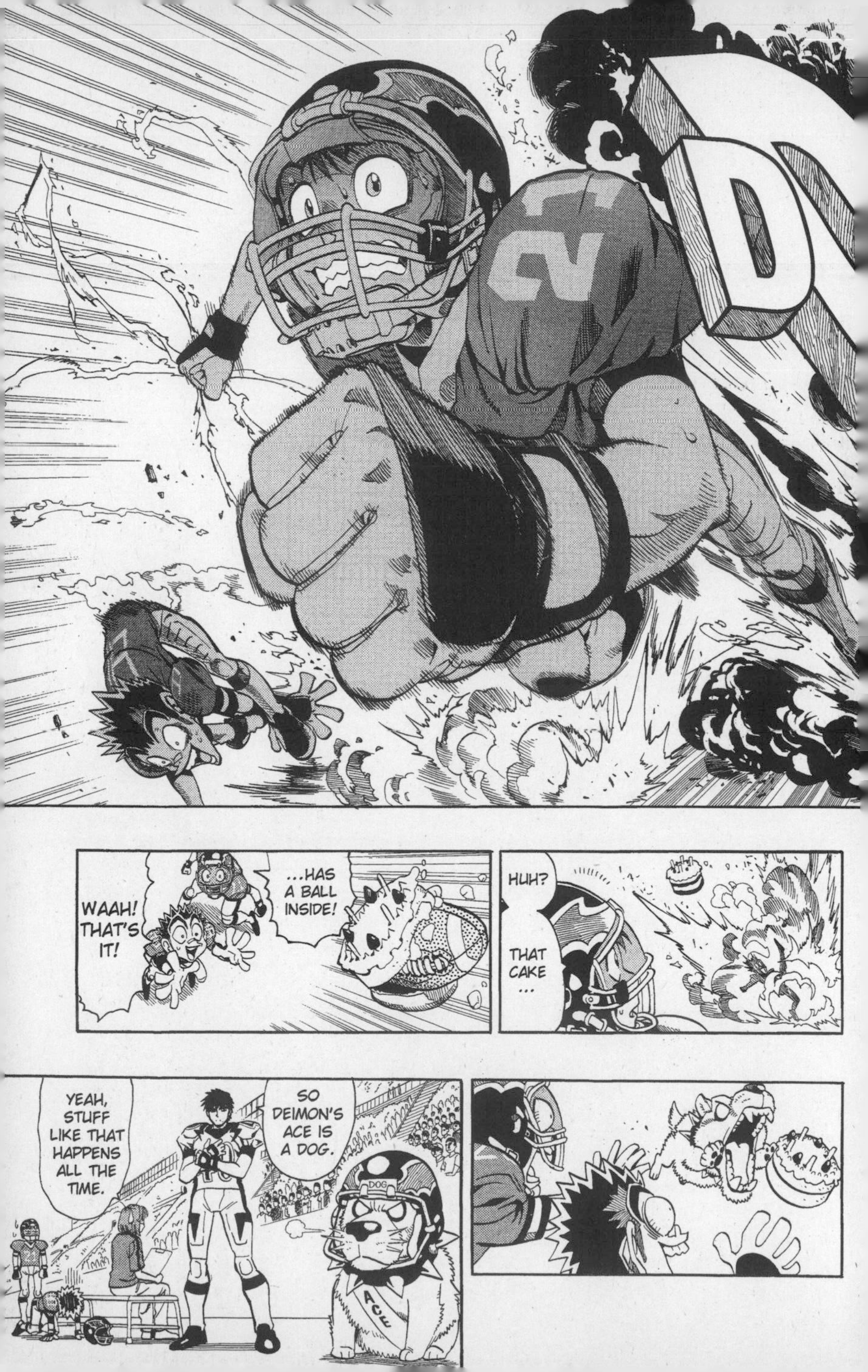
D
HUH?
THAT CAKE ...
...HAS A BALL INSIDE!
WAAH! THAT'S IT!
SO DEIMON'S ACE IS A DOG.
DOG
ACE
YEAH, STUFF LIKE THAT HAPPENS ALL THE TIME.

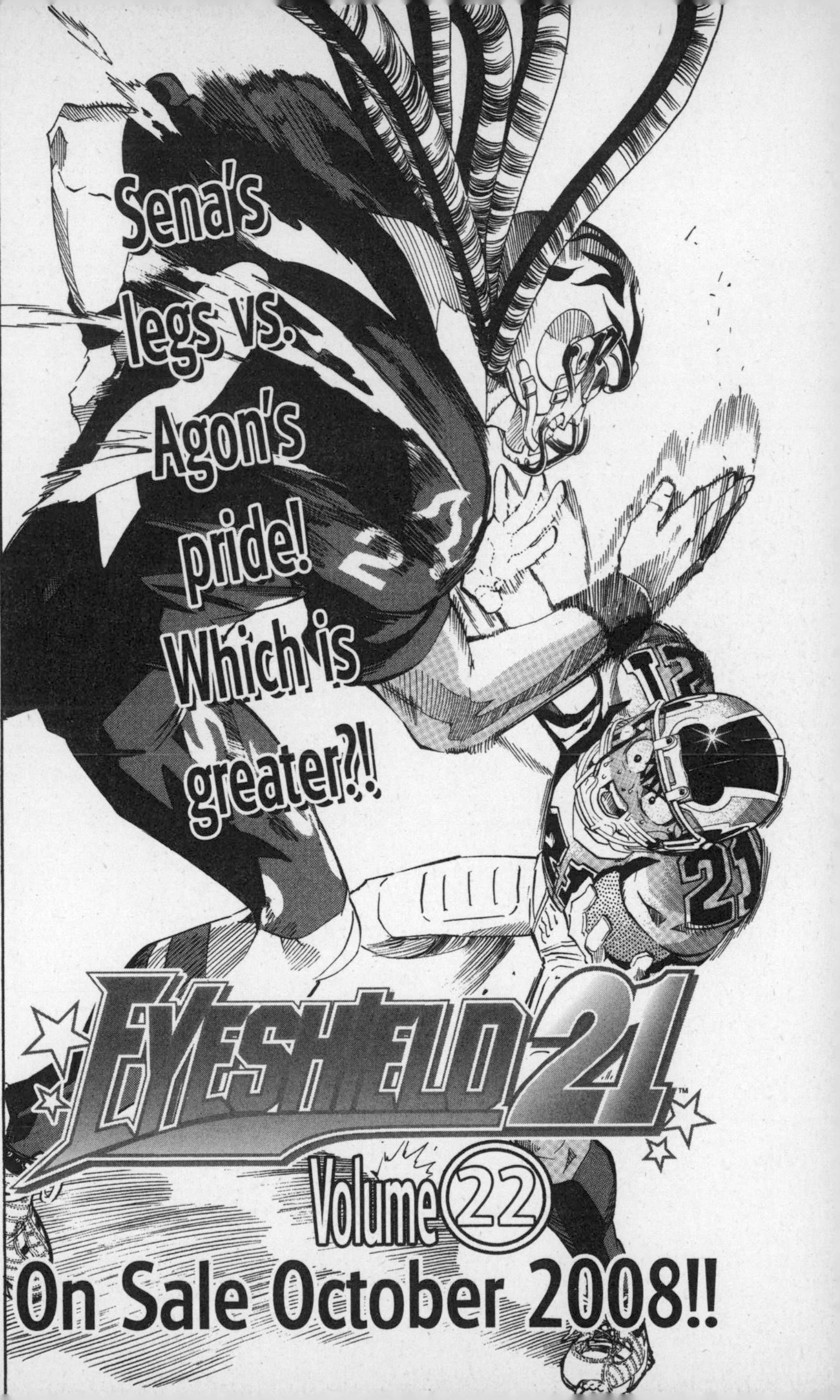
Sena's legs vs. Agon's pride! Which is greater?!
EYESHIELD 21™
Volume 22
On Sale October 2008!!

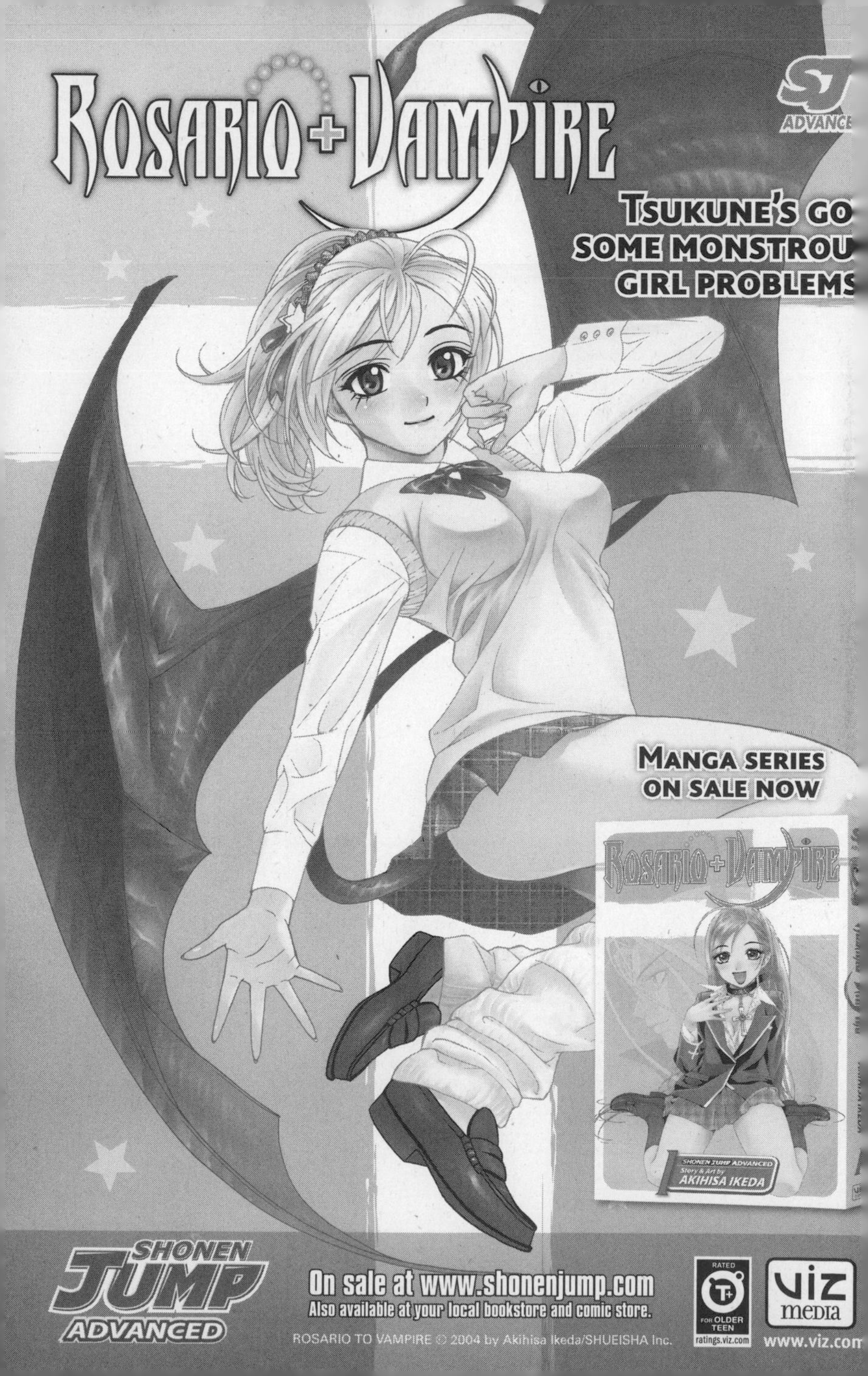
ROSARIO+VAMPIRE
TSUKUNE'S GO
SOME MONSTROU
GIRL PROBLEMS
MANGA SERIES
ON SALE NOW
ROSARIO+VAMPIRE
SHONEN JUMP ADVANCED
Story & Art by
AKIHISA IKEDA
SHONEN JUMP ADVANCED
On sale at www.shonenjump.com
Also available at your local bookstore and comic store.
ROSARIO TO VAMPIRE © 2004 by Akihisa Ikeda/SHUEISHA Inc.
RATED
T+
FOR OLDER TEEN
ratings.viz.com
viz media
www.viz.com

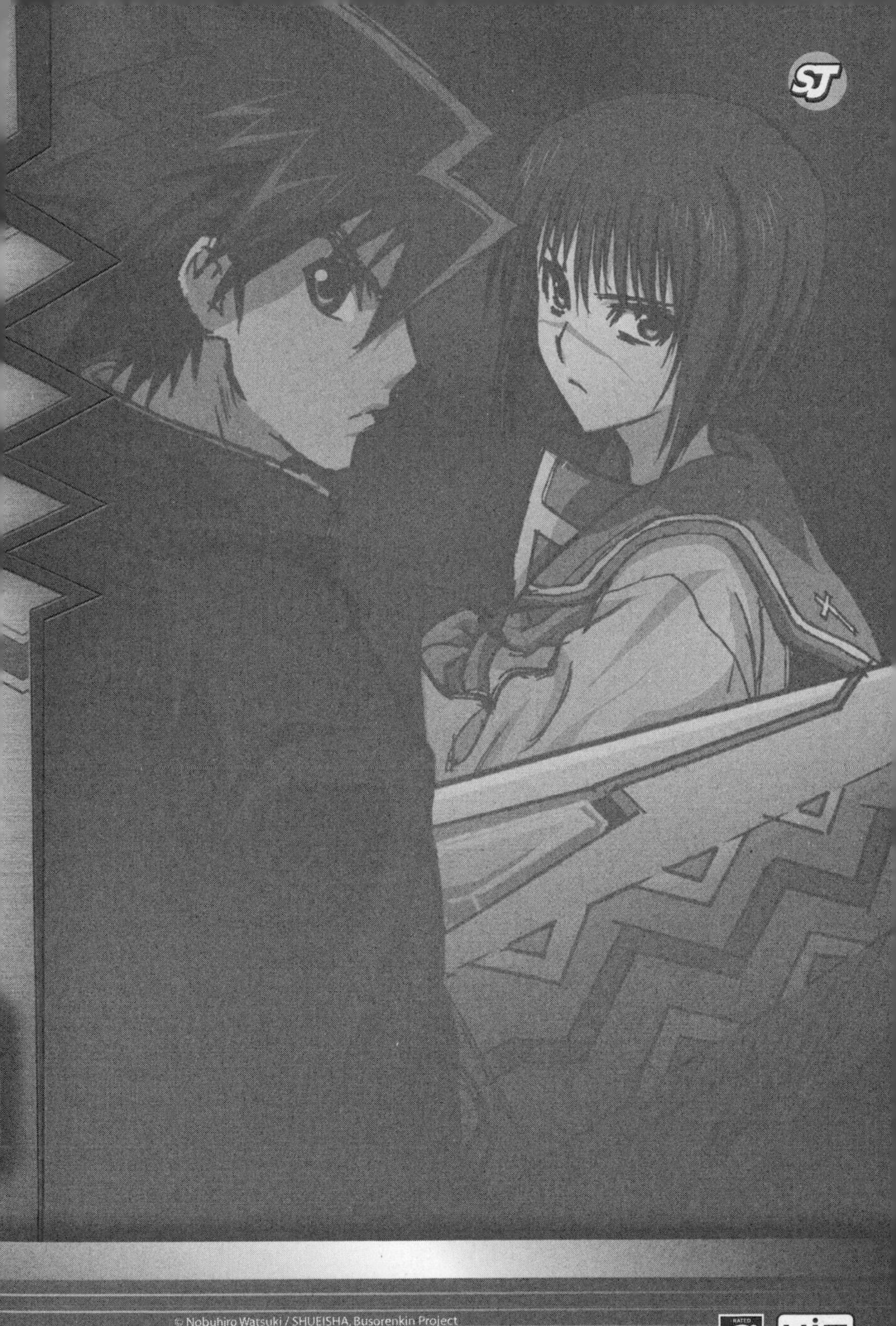

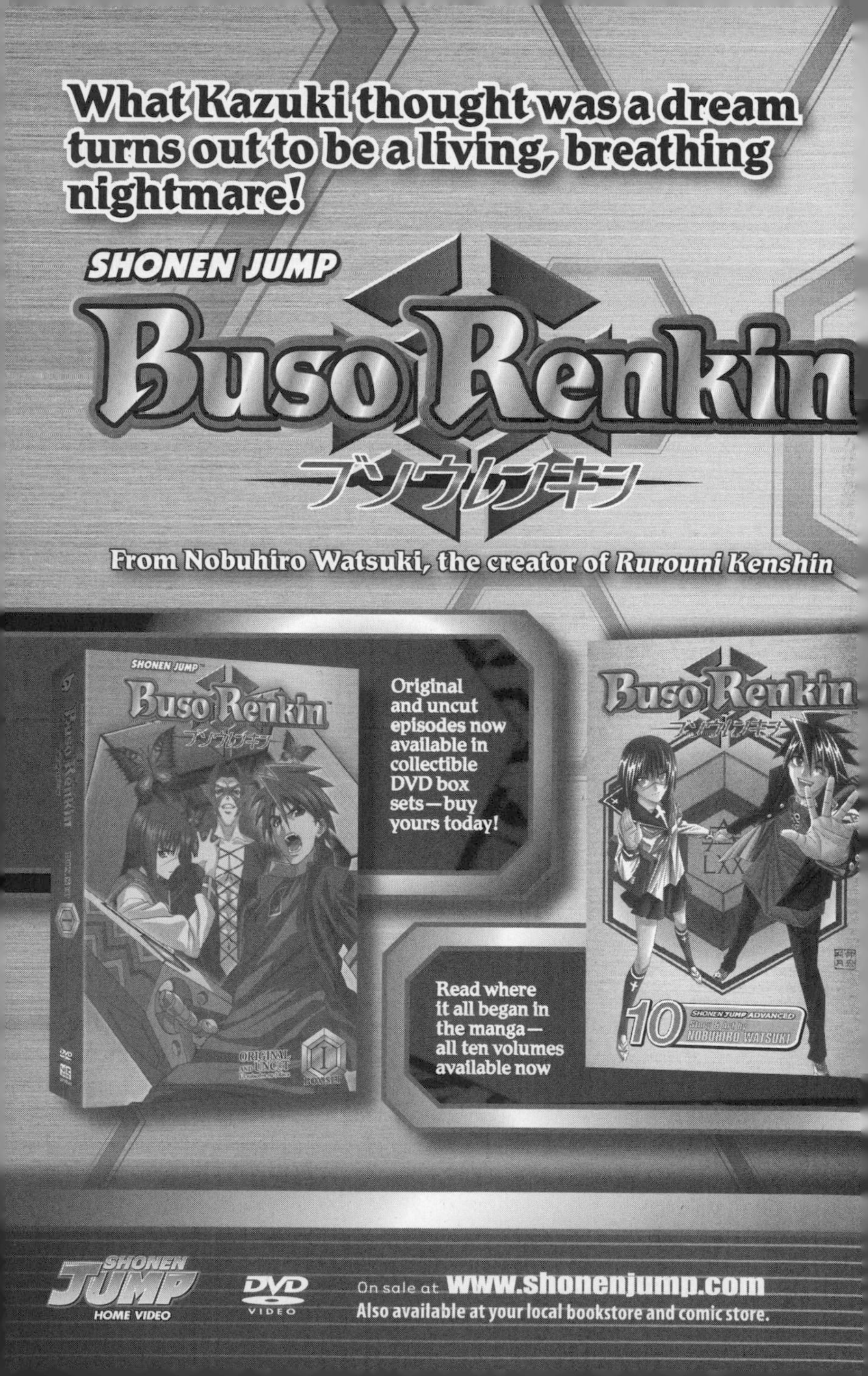

What Kazuki thought was a dream turns out to be a living, breathing nightmare!
SHONEN JUMP
Buso Renkin
ブソウレンキン
From Nobuhiro Watsuki, the creator of Rurouni Kenshin
SHONEN JUMP
Buso Renkin
Original and uncut episodes now available in collectible DVD box sets—buy yours today!
Buso Renkin
10
Read where it all began in the manga—all ten volumes available now
SHONEN JUMP HOME VIDEO
DVD VIDEO
On sale at www.shonenjump.com
Also available at your local bookstore and comic store.

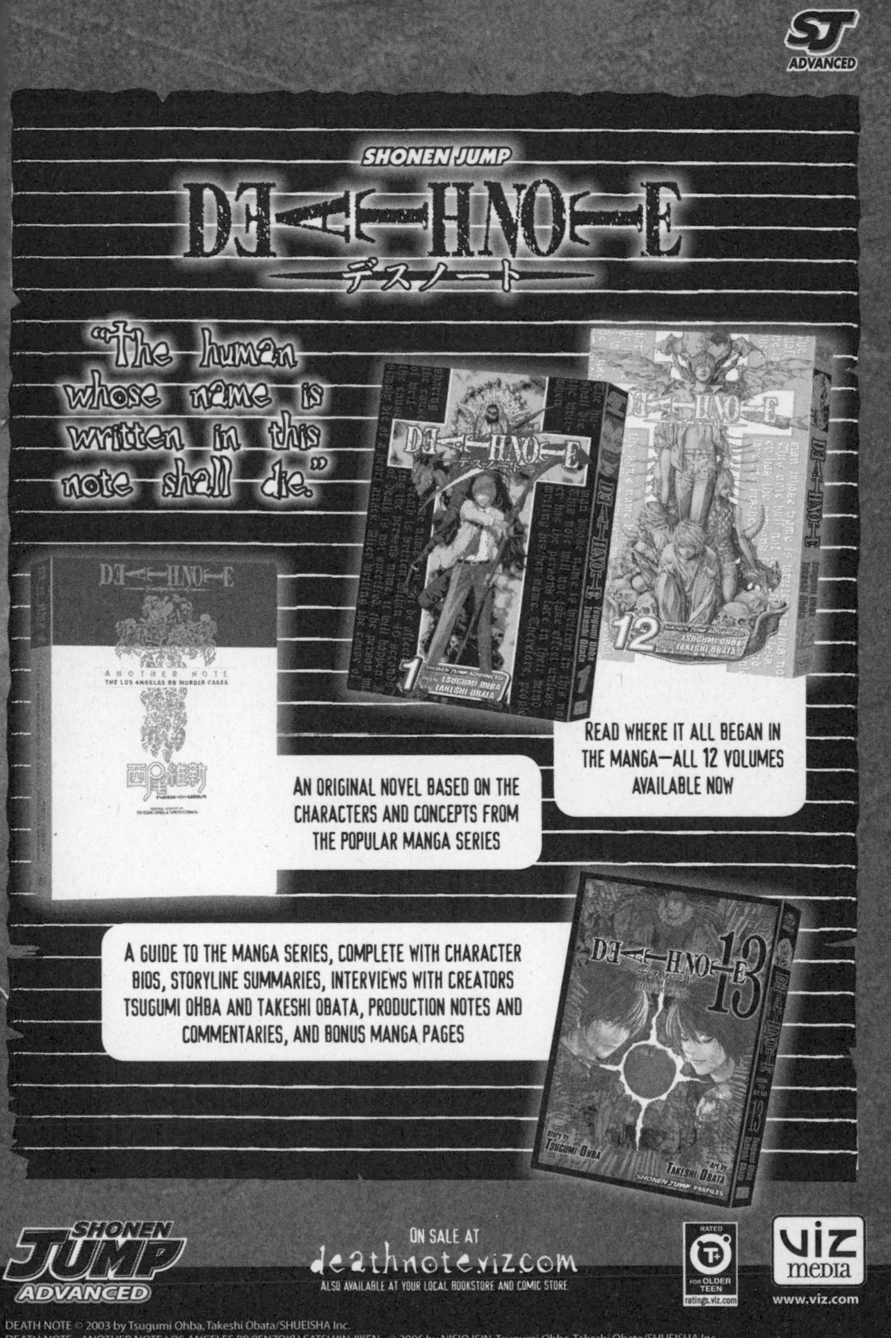
SJ ADVANCED
SHONEN JUMP
DEATH NOTE
デスノート
"The human whose name is written in this note shall die."
AN ORIGINAL NOVEL BASED ON THE CHARACTERS AND CONCEPTS FROM THE POPULAR MANGA SERIES
READ WHERE IT ALL BEGAN IN THE MANGA—ALL 12 VOLUMES AVAILABLE NOW
A GUIDE TO THE MANGA SERIES, COMPLETE WITH CHARACTER BIOS, STORYLINE SUMMARIES, INTERVIEWS WITH CREATORS TSUGUMI OHBA AND TAKESHI OBATA, PRODUCTION NOTES AND COMMENTARIES, AND BONUS MANGA PAGES
SHONEN JUMP ADVANCED
ON SALE AT
deathnote.viz.com
ALSO AVAILABLE AT YOUR LOCAL BOOKSTORE AND COMIC STORE
RATED T+ FOR OLDER TEEN
ratings.viz.com
viz media
www.viz.com

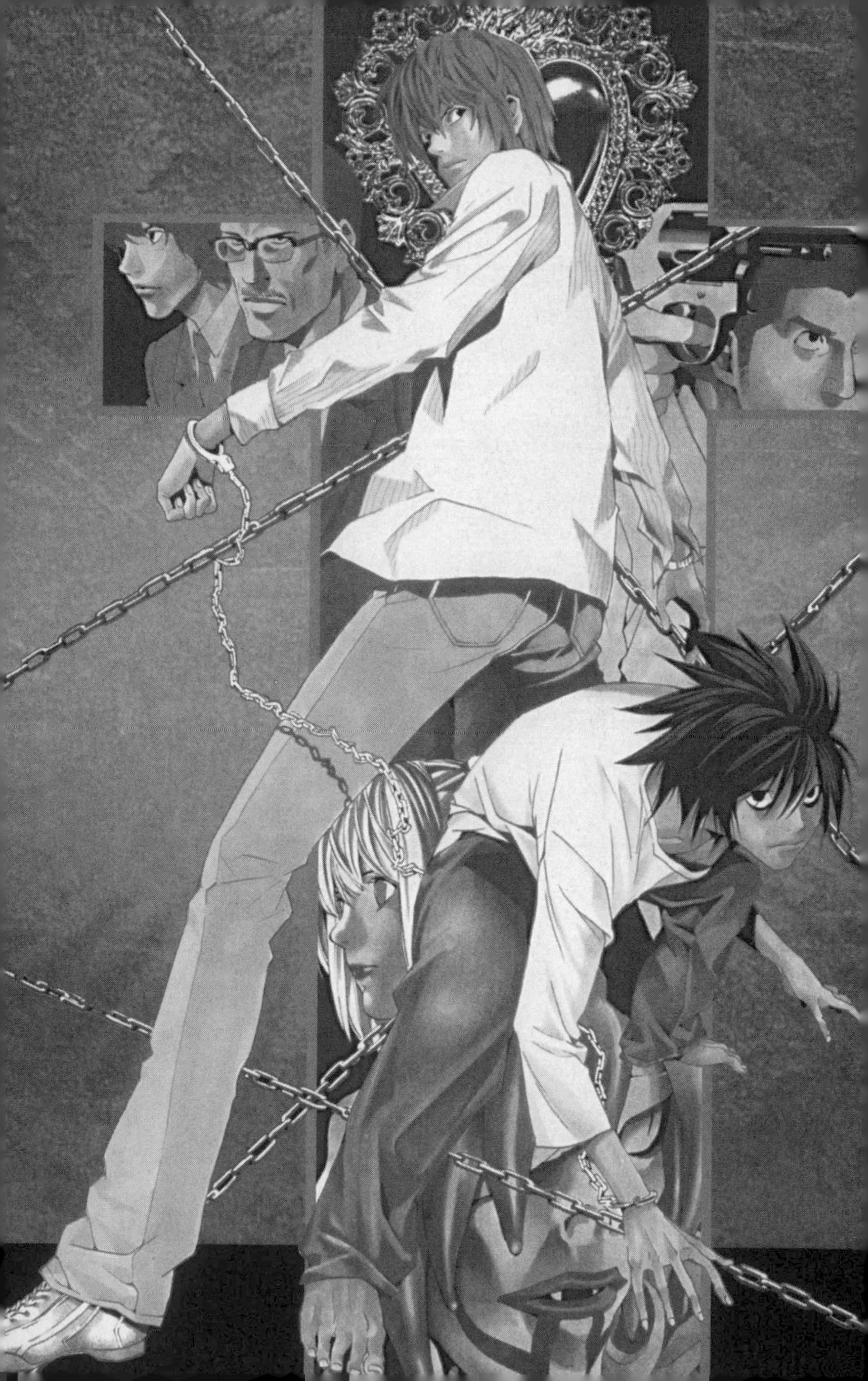

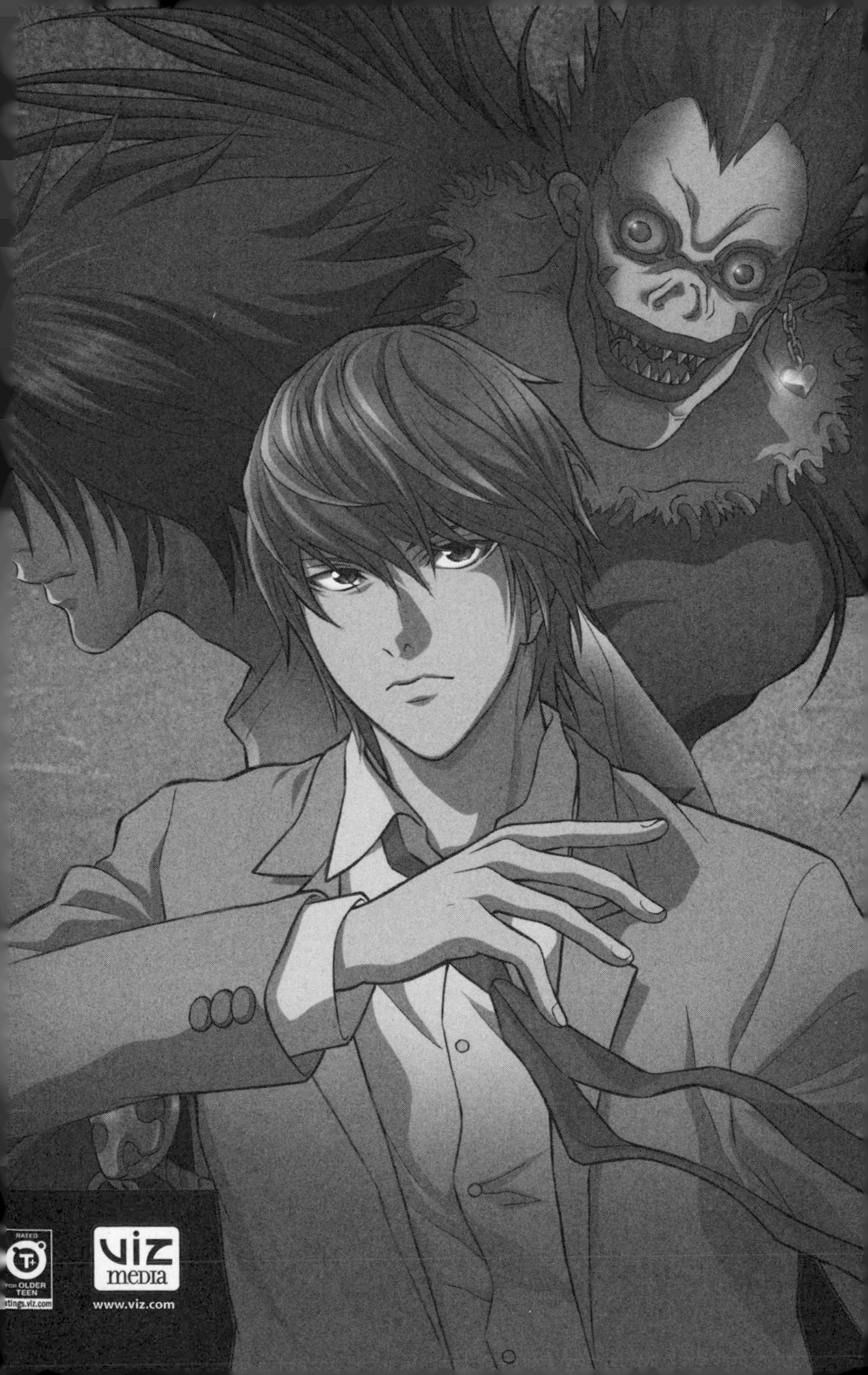

RATED
T+
FOR OLDER TEEN
tings.viz.com
VIZ media
www.viz.com

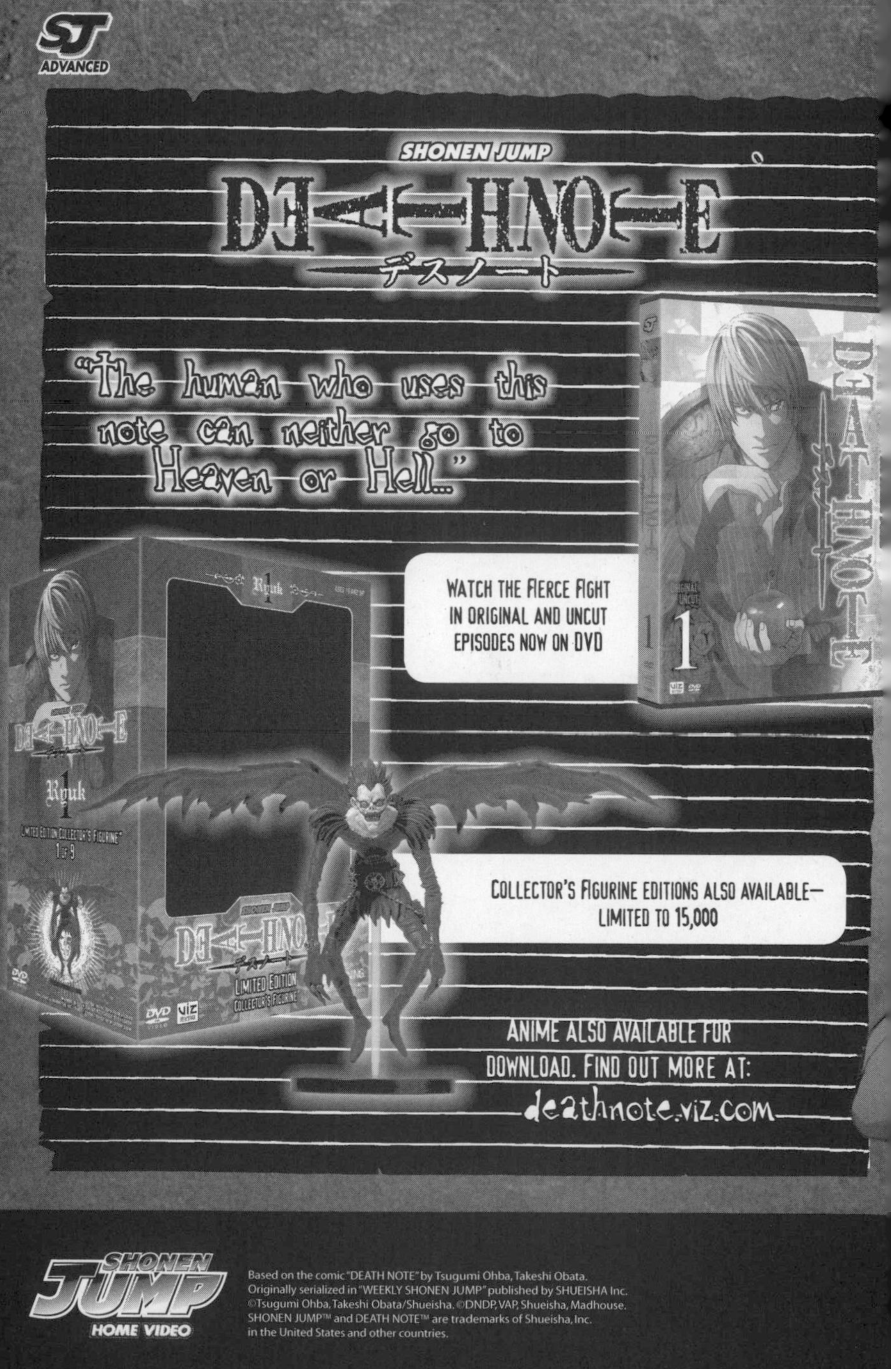
SJ ADVANCED
SHONEN JUMP
DEATH NOTE
デスノート
"The human who uses this note can neither go to Heaven or Hell..."
WATCH THE FIERCE FIGHT IN ORIGINAL AND UNCUT EPISODES NOW ON DVD
COLLECTOR'S FIGURINE EDITIONS ALSO AVAILABLE—LIMITED TO 15,000
ANIME ALSO AVAILABLE FOR DOWNLOAD. FIND OUT MORE AT:
deathnote.viz.com
SHONEN JUMP HOME VIDEO

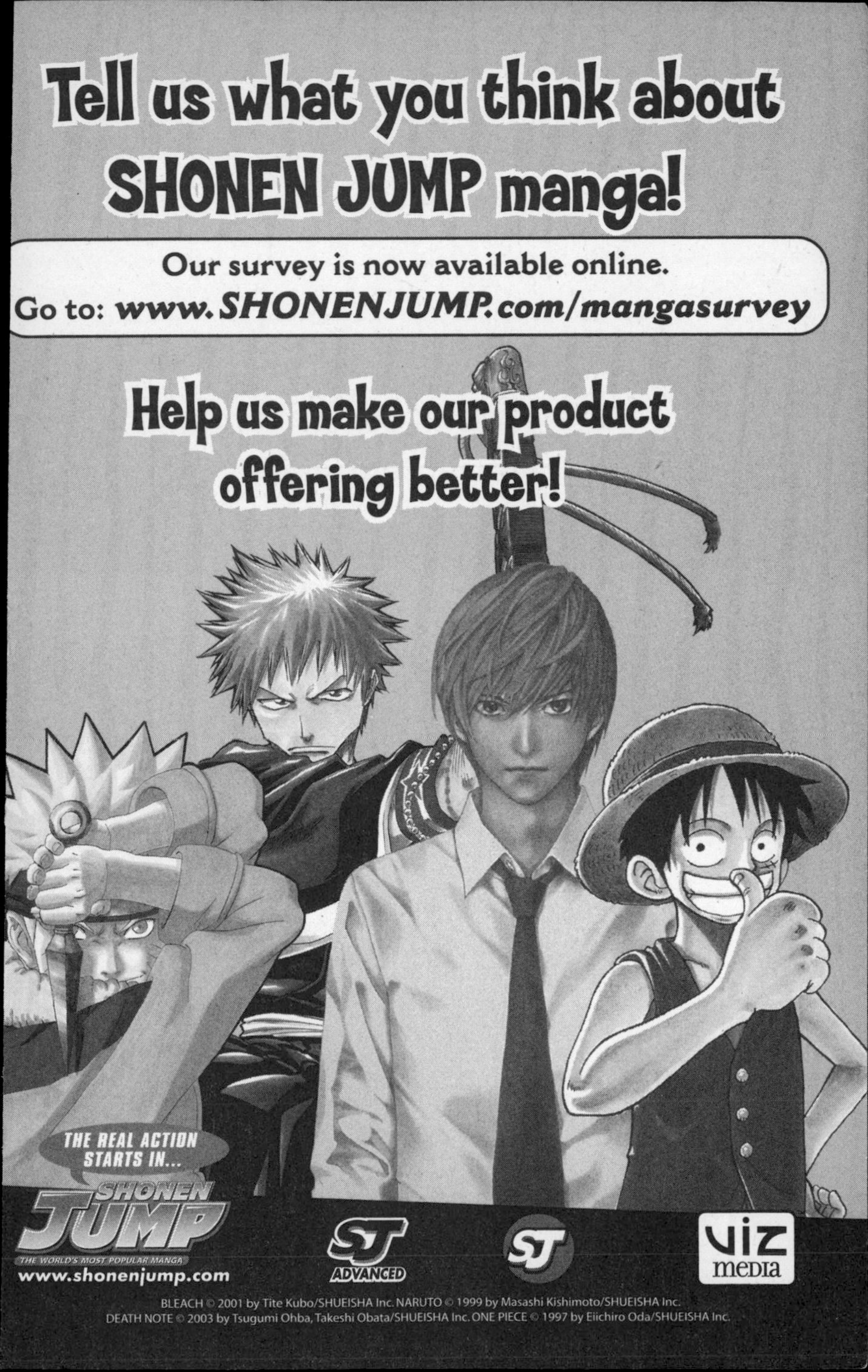
Tell us what you think about
SHONEN JUMP manga!
Our survey is now available online.
Go to: www.SHONENJUMP.com/mangasurvey
Help us make our product
offering better!
THE REAL ACTION
STARTS IN...
SHONEN JUMP
THE WORLD'S MOST POPULAR MANGA
www.shonenjump.com
SJ ADVANCED
SJ
VIZ media
BLEACH © 2001 by Tite Kubo/SHUEISHA Inc. NARUTO © 1999 by Masashi Kishimoto/SHUEISHA Inc.
DEATH NOTE © 2003 by Tsugumi Ohba, Takeshi Obata/SHUEISHA Inc. ONE PIECE © 1997 by Eiichiro Oda/SHUEISHA Inc.

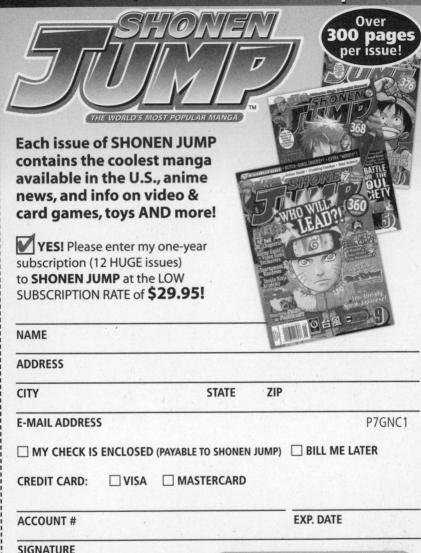

NARUTO

BONUS! Attach this sticker to the back of the entry form that's also in this product.

40th WEEKLY JUMP

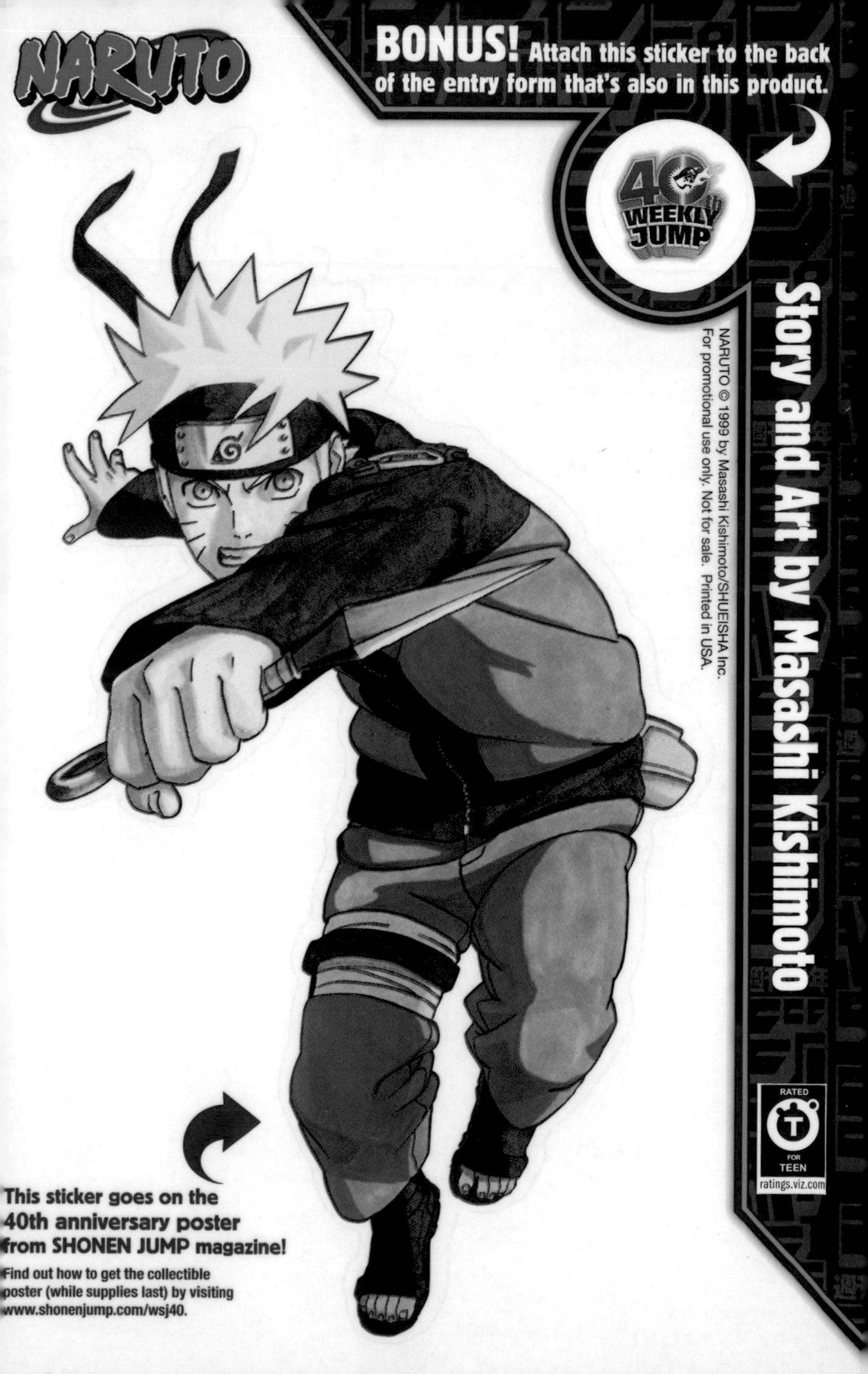

Story and Art by Masashi Kishimoto

RATED T FOR TEEN
ratings.viz.com

This sticker goes on the 40th anniversary poster from SHONEN JUMP magazine!

Find out how to get the collectible poster (while supplies last) by visiting www.shonenjump.com/wsj40.

WIN A TRIP TO JAPAN!

The year 2008 marks the 40th anniversary of *Weekly Shonen Jump*, the biggest manga magazine in Japan and the source for the English-language edition of *SHONEN JUMP*. *Weekly Shonen Jump* is the birthplace of the greatest manga artists and stories, and for 40 years has given the world amazing manga, including *NARUTO*, *BLEACH* and *SLAM DUNK*, to name just a few.

To celebrate this incredible milestone, we are giving away a trip for one winner and a friend to Japan to attend Jump Festa 2009 (Dec. 20-21, 2008), the ULTIMATE convention for everything SHONEN JUMP!

To enter, fill out the entry form that's also in this product and mail it in an envelope for a chance to win:
- A 6 day/5 night trip to Japan for you and a friend in December 2008
- Coach airfare and 5 nights hotel and accommodations
- Two-day passes for two to Jump Festa 2009 (December 20-21, 2008)

Visit www.shonenjump.com/wsj40
for complete sweepstakes rules and details!

www.viz.com

THE WORLD'S MOST POPULAR MANGA

WIN A TRIP TO JAPAN
through the SHONEN JUMP Experience Sweepstakes!

The year 2008 marks the 40th anniversary of *Weekly Shonen Jump*, the biggest manga magazine in Japan and the source for the English-language edition of *SHONEN JUMP*. *Weekly Shonen Jump* is the birthplace of the greatest manga artists and stories, and for 40 years has given the world amazing manga, including *NARUTO*, *BLEACH* and *SLAM DUNK*, to name just a few.

To celebrate this incredible milestone, we are giving away a **trip for one winner and a friend to Japan to attend Jump Festa 2009** (Dec. 20-21, 2008), the ULTIMATE convention for everything SHONEN JUMP!

(Entries must be postmarked by October 15, 2008 in order to qualify.)

(Please print clearly)

Name: _____

Street Address: _____

City: _____ State: _____ Postal Code: _____

Country: _____ Date of Birth (01/01/2000): _____

Phone number: _____

For mailing address information, visit www.shonenjump.com/wsj40.

BONUS!

Whether or not you win the sweepstakes, you can still get a GIFT!

CO[illegible] ...onen Jump
TH[illegible] ...orm, enter
...side, and mail
...00)

PLACE STICKER HERE

40th WEEKLY JUMP

PLACE STICKER HERE

40th WEEKLY JUMP

PLACE STICKER HERE

40th WEEKLY JUMP

* While supplies last. Submissions ... rder to qualify. All three special round stickers must be ma... imit two submissions for surprise gift allowed per house... gift. No mechanical reproduction or copies of form or s... nored. Sponsor is not responsible for lost, late, mutilated ... rohibited.

VIZ media
www.viz.com